The Discipline of Religion

The Discipline of Religion is a lively critical journey through the study of religion as it is practiced today. It looks at recent growth of Religious Studies as an academic discipline and its contemporary effects within and outside the academy. Russell T. McCutcheon argues for a difference between claims of religious belief and academic discourse on such claims. When this distinction is blurred, as it frequently is, Religious Studies has leaped across the divide between religion as a form of historical practice to the pursuit of its actual cosmic and moral meaning. With this leap scholars of religious studies extend their powers far beyond the intellectual domain of universities and into the realm of everyday life with conservative social and political effects.

By marking its discourse with terms such as faith, spirit, conscience, evil, experience, hope, nature and truth, *The Discipline of Religion* endorses regimes of social policing and self-management that are interpreted as the extension of natural urges of interior faith, authentic feelings that originate deep within the confines of the human heart. By perpetuating the useful fiction that human beings naturally enjoy a private, interior life free of political influence and consequence, Religious Studies profoundly legitimates the regulatory forces and institutions of social life. Drawing some inspiration from the work of Michel Foucault and its examples from institutions such as the American Academy of Religion, from the crises of academic labour, and the use of evil as a rhetorical device, *The Discipline of Religion* investigates how the academy's classification and ranking of the world supports the creation of specific senses of freedom and zones of conduct, thereby managing and curtailing specific types of speech and dissent.

Russell T. McCutcheon is Chair of the Department of Religious Studies at the University of Alabama. He is author of *Manufacturing Religion* (1997) and *Critics Not Caretakers: Redescribing the Public Study of Religion* (2001), editor of *The Insider/Outsider Problem in the Study of Religion* (1999), and co-editor with Willi Braun of *Guide to the Study of Religion* (2000).

The Discipline of Religion

Structure, meaning, rhetoric

Russell T. McCutcheon

Routledge
Taylor & Francis Group

LONDON AND NEW YORK

First published 2003
by Routledge
11 New Fetter Lane, London EC4P 4EE

Simultaneously published in the USA and Canada
by Routledge
29 West 35th Street, New York, NY 10001

Routledge is an imprint of the Taylor & Francis Group

©2003 Russell T. McCutcheon

Typeset in Goudy by Taylor & Francis Books Ltd
Printed and bound in Great Britain by MPG Books Ltd, Bodmin

British Library Cataloguing in Publication Data
A catalogue record for this book is available from the British
Library

Library of Congress Cataloging in Publication Data
McCutcheon, Russell T., 1961–
The discipline of religion: structure, meaning, rhetoric / Russell T.
McCutcheon.
Includes bibliographical references and index.
1. Religion – Study and teaching. I. Title.
BL41 .M349 2003
200'.71–dc21   2002036925

ISBN 0–415–27489–3 (hbk)
ISBN 0–415–27490–7 (pbk)

For all those who permitted this uninvited, intellectual squatter to eavesdrop on their thoughts and learn from watching them tend to our collective garden.

The beauty of our society is: it isolates everybody. Each person is sitting alone in front of the tube. And it's very hard to have ideas or thoughts under those circumstances.

Noam Chomsky (1994: 195)

Criticism is a matter of flushing out ... thought and trying to change it: to show that things are not as self-evident as one believed, to see that which is accepted as self-evident will no longer be seen as such. Practicing criticism is a matter of making facile gestures difficult. ... As soon as one can no longer think things as one formerly thought them, transformation becomes both very urgent, very difficult, and quite possible.

Michel Foucault (1988a: 155)

Contents

PART III
Reworking the residue from our imperfect past   **189**

Preface: a dispatch from the provinces

Several years ago, I had the good fortune to be invited to visit an undergraduate class of religious studies majors at another university that was using a book of mine. The professor had designed their course to use the book as a springboard into a variety of theoretical issues in the contemporary field. The students tackled one chapter each week and, each week, the professor invited different department colleagues to attend their class, to provide their own input and take the discussion wherever they wished. The professor then arranged for me to arrive near the conclusion of the course; his students had a number of questions, comments, and insightful criticisms, and so I was suitably – and quite enjoyably – grilled by his sharp students.

What stands out most in my mind from that wonderful visit was the professor's aside that a number of colleagues found the critique of what I then termed the discourse on *sui generis* religion, or what I have since then also termed the private affair tradition in the study of religion, to be a straw man. In other words, during their visits to the class many of them informed the students that, although scholars such as Mircea Eliade (d. 1986), along with his many University of Chicago graduates, did indeed have an impact on the field in the 1960s and 1970s, few people read his work anymore or studied religion in that manner. Simply put, they informed the students that my critique of the politics of the so-called "Chicago school" and its presumption that religion, religious impulses, and religious experiences were free of the kinds of social pressures that condition all other historical moments was a rather misguided witch hunt that misportrayed the discipline into which they were being initiated.

Taking seriously this criticism – a criticism that went to the very heart of my book, and one which some of the students repeated to me in person – I replied by asking my friend how many of these colleagues would, then, agree that those practices we generally call religious are utterly ordinary human events explicable by appeal to any one of the epistemological tools used throughout such human sciences as sociology or psychology or anthropology. The answer: few, if any. For the majority of them, I learned, "things religious" were somehow distinct and set apart (literally the meaning of the Latin root from which we derive our field's most prominent but elusive adjective and noun, "sacred") from the hurly-burly world of mundane human comings and goings – an apartness they signaled (and I would say, established) by appeals to various rhetorics, e.g., deep meaning, origins, authenticity, uniquely personal experiences, and aesthetic sensibilities.

Hearing this answer to my question, I realized I had a paradox on my hands: on the one hand my critique was said to be a straw man, yet on the other, the people maintaining this position held – to my way of thinking, at least – the very views I thought I was critiquing. I found it fascinating that, for some reason, my friend's colleagues were not able to see themselves in the mirror I thought I was holding up to them. Perhaps they misread my critique as being concerned only with Eliade's work, I thought, rather than being a critique of the tactics in use throughout an entire academic discipline – a critique that just happened to use Eliade's work (along with the work of such influential scholars as the late Wilfred Cantwell Smith, Huston Smith, and many others of the current generation of scholars) merely as a convenient entry point, treating him as one scholar among others who happened to represent trends far larger than himself. Although they may not have been ardent readers of, say, Eliade's work, they nonetheless appeared to me to share a viewpoint basic to his work. But attributing a misreading to my friend's colleagues struck me as hardly fair; after all, they are intelligent people and astute readers skilled in the nuances of searching for the deep meaning of a text. What's more, attributing a misreading would rest on a troublesome notion, my supposedly privileged authorial intention, thus lodging the matter within problems of hermeneutics. Since I place myself within a tradition of scholarship that problematizes the field's enduring preoccupation with issues of interpretation and meaning, it seemed hardly fair to invoke the privilege of "right meaning" in my own defense. Surely there had to be something more to it than this.

Because there may be nothing worse than for a young scholar to be told his work is *passé*, this memory stuck with me, and so I continued to mull over how academic disciplines develop, how scholars develop a sense of themselves as inhabiting these disciplines, how they rise to dominance, how they are interconnected to larger economic and political forces, how those who oppose such developments can effectively make tactical interventions that have some consequence, and what all this had to do with that slippery collection of things that some of us call religion. During the coming years I explored these topics in discrete essays, each of which was prompted by some specific question or, more than likely, some irritation. Now, in hindsight, some of these essays strike me as all exploring a common issue: applying a theory of social formation to an academic discipline in order to understand the role played by various rhetorics in creating and sustaining seemingly coherent social identities. These identities, like all social identities, come with issues of turf and privilege and the never-ending threat of fracture and dissolution. What's more, just as formerly unrelated and historically discrete essays can be revised and reworked based on concerns not apparent to the author at the time of their writing, so as to reappear as ordered chapters in a book, the apparent homogeneity of these social identities is a continual, hindsight concoction.

In first writing, and then later rewriting, the essays that comprise the chapters of this book, I kept coming back to an aside made by Gary Lease concerning the need to write a "natural history" of institutions, such as the institutions made possible by using "religion" to name and thereby privilege part of the otherwise contingent, social world. As I have quoted him before, writing such a history would require assembling a "catalog of strategies for *maintaining* paradoxes, *fighting* over dissonances, and *surviving* breakdowns" (Lease 1994: 475). As I went on to say elsewhere, "[s]uch a catalog would amount to a map of the many social sites where myths and rituals are developed and deployed for one of the primary ways in which social formations are constructed, maintained, contested, and rebuilt is through the active process of mythmaking" (2001b: 31). In assembling the chapters to that previous book, I became convinced more than ever that, as with all social formations, this mythmaking activity takes place within academic disciplines by means of certain rhetorical techniques that comprise "the play of forces at work in a field of power and knowledge" (Ransom 1997: 24), forces that can be tracked across the various stages in the discipline's natural history.

Now, by "natural history" I mean something significantly less than our overly ambitious predecessors once did; I mean simply that it is a history which, to borrow from the late British Marxist literary critic Raymond Williams (1990: 121–127), goes through at least three stages that are analytically distinguishable: emergent, dominant, and residual (see also McCutcheon 2001b: ch. 2). In tackling the writing of such a history, several presumptions are key: (i) nothing springs from the ground fully formed; (ii) there exists no narrative necessity to social development (a.k.a. destiny); (iii) all social movements are fractured systems, always in flux, from which (iv) alienated and discarded residue forms the raw materials that, under some new, previously unforseen circumstance, *might* lead to the emergence of new social groups intent on establishing through narrative their own exclusive rights to exist and patrol a specific turf by claims of uniqueness and exceptionality. Or, as James Clifford phrased it: " 'Post-' is always shadowed by 'neo-' " (1997: 277). These presumptions are applicable to all social groups, from the nation-state, ethnic groups, and the family, to collections of scholars we call academic disciplines. For example, the claim to autonomy, turf, and privilege that we commonly refer to as the nationalist doctrine of "American exceptionalism," is a claim that, "in the late nineteenth and early twentieth centuries, [was] especially associated with the newly emergent social sciences" (Smith 2001b: 136; e.g., see Durkheim [1995: 15] for a classic instance of a member of an emergent group of intellectuals claiming that, in this case, society is *sui generis*). The basis of this approach to writing such a natural history of a scholarly pursuit – if we drop the nineteenth-century overtones of "naturalness" and add a heaped tablespoon of irony, we might simply call it a genealogy – can be summed up in two related comments made by

Foucault: "What is found at the historical beginning of things is not the inviolable identity of their origin; it is the dissension of other things. It is disparity";
and "[t]he forces operating in history are not controlled by destiny or regulative
mechanisms, but respond to haphazard conflicts" (1977b: 142, 154). The chapters in this book are an attempt to sketch the outline for just such an inventory
of the ad hoc rhetorical and narrative techniques – what Braun called slippery
abstractions – employed in those onetime chance conflicts and opportunities
that, now in hindsight, we see as comprising one coherent academic discipline.

With all this in mind, I came across an article in one of our field's main
professional, quarterly periodicals, *Religious Studies News*. It was an October
2000 interview with the well-known Princeton scholar, David Carrasco (2000),
an interview I had not read when it first came out but one that my friend, Jack
Llewellyn, later told me that I must read. (As a graduate of the University of
Chicago – though, I should say, not its Divinity School – Jack enables me to say,
with all honesty: "Some of my best friends are Chicago grads.") Because
Carrasco made a point in the interview of championing what he called "real
critical dialogue" among colleagues, rather than a "critical put down of various
positions," I wrote him a letter in late March 2001, pursuing topics that I found
problematic in his interview. In my letter I focused on the fact that the topic of
the "Chicago school" comes up early in the interview, when Carrasco
commented:

> I'm impressed by how often some critics reduce the methods and
> approaches we learned in the '70s and '80s to their own provincial views of
> what Eliade, Long, Smith, Kitagawa, Wheatley and others were and in
> some cases still are doing. The comparative approach, the ensemble of
> texts, the critical respect for various expressions of the sacred continue to
> be valuable tools for me.
>
> (2000: 16)

Later in the interview he elaborated by saying that he therefore maintains in his
work a "respect for religious symbols as religious: vehicles for various modes of
sacrality."

With the paradox presented by my friend's departmental colleagues in my
mind, I was curious about, on the one had, Carrasco's dismissal of so-called
provincial critics of the "Chicago school" and, on the other, with how close his
choice of words was to those themes that critics find all throughout, say, Eliade's
body of work (though not in J. Z. Smith's or Bruce Lincoln's work, of course,
suggesting that we must be careful how we use "the Chicago school"; for this
reason, I prefer talking about the discourse on sui generis religion or the private
affair tradition in our field). For example, we see in both Carrasco and Eliade
references to the "provincial" nature of scholarship with which they disagree,
and they both refer to such things as "expressions of the sacred," "modalities of
the sacred," "religious experience," "religious imagination," "depth of genius,"

etc. Ironically, in criticizing those who have misrepresented the complexity of the Chicago school, Carrasco's brief interview presents a nicely distilled example of the very things that some writers have critiqued for their lack of theoretical specificity and their undisclosed politics. Imperialist rhetorics of center and periphery, home and abroad, *en vogue* and *passé*, domestic and foreign, city and country, relevant and irrelevant coupled with rhetorics of depth and shallowness were used amidst denials of their use.

In fact, it is hard not to hear echoes of previous rhetorics in Carrasco's words; as Johannes Wolfart pointed out to me, we find the technique of provincialization in use at least as far back as Imperial Rome's efforts to manage their conquered areas outside of Italy. For instance, as Peter Brown observes, in documents dating from the late Roman empire,

> [p]easants ... and ... pagans treated as no better than countryfolk, were consistently presented as passive and congenially simple minded, so that they could be expected to follow the gentle, because orderly, lead of their natural superiors into the true faith. Among the upper classes, a combination of browbeating and cajolery was the stuff of late Roman politics.
>
> (1997: 45)

Although the term "provincial" seems to have a delicate, almost cultured ring to it, I hear in it the same "browbeating and cajolery" that, to many contemporary ears, cannot help but be heard in earlier or other groups' efforts to legitimize their own social world by claiming that others were unlearned and thus unenlightened "heathens" (originally referring to those who inhabited the heath, that wide, flat, uncultivated waste area outside the limits of the town), "pagans" (derived from the Latin *paganus* and referring to those who inhabited the *pagus* or the country district), or perhaps "gentiles" (from the pre-pejorative Greek γενος, and then the Latin *genus*, for identity based on birth, kind, or stock, easily then used for defining those of other birthrights). Hearing this rhetoric of centers and peripheries, towns and peasants, cultured and unlettered, proper and improper, meant that, much like my friend's colleagues, Carrasco's interview stuck me as a classic example of "having one's cake and eating it too" – amidst earnest calls for serious exchange we find an unquestioned orthodoxy reproducing its self-declared privilege by means of dismissals and condescension for alternative viewpoints. Amazingly, those who banish competitors to the hinterlands by means of such heavy-handed talk are all too often seen as great liberal pluralists and bold inclusivists forging a new collective will. More recently, Carol Zaleski's "Letter to William James" comes to mind as but another example of this rhetorical technique. "Why does the *Varieties* endure when other academic studies of religion become so quickly dated?" she asks. "[Y]our work endures while others lose currency as soon as they wear thin enough to reveal their ideological slant" (2002: 32). Apparently those with whose work we agree are free of ideology, influence, and point of view; the merely fashionable, those whose stitching fails to win a place among the items of *haute couture*, are of obviously lesser quality.

Despite the widespread presence of this rhetoric, and in the spirit of real, critical dialogue, my letter's question to Carrasco was twofold. First, given the quintessential "Chicago" manner in which he spoke of the field, its data, the scholar of religion's respectful task, etc., precisely how have critics misread Eliade and others? After all, his interview struck me as a case in point for the Chicago school's shortcomings, for when I finished reading it I was no clearer on precisely what the scholar of religion actually studies. And this led to my second question: to what, I asked, in the observable world of human practices does the taxon "the sacred" actually refer? Surely, *its* supposed expressions are observable (hence scholars' enduring preoccupation with the categories of myth, ritual, and symbol), but what is the antecedent to the possessive pronoun "its"? Is it merely a necessary theoretical/disciplinary postulate, as Dan Pals maintained more than a decade ago in a spirited exchange with Robert Segal and Donald Wiebe? Is it an intentional being, as in when Eliade talks about "the sacred manifesting itself"? Or, still further, is it an irreducible component of human consciousness, much as Rudolf Otto asserted and, more recently, as Bryan Rennie believes Eliade actually meant? In other words, apart from rhetorics of genius, so-called depth experiences, and the circular and terribly uninformative claim of needing to treat "religious symbols as religious," Carrasco's interview left me unilluminated as to what it is that we as scholars of religion are actually doing when we say we are studying religion. But what was most fascinating was that such circular and, to my way of thinking at least, unilluminating comments have taken on the role of truisms – they routinely appear in the literature in our field and seem to be persuasive to most (or at least many) of the field's practitioners and certainly to many, if not most, of its students. Because "treating religious symbols as religion" is utterly meaningless to me, I became curious as to how it could be meaningful to someone else.

Now, of course the people whom we study employ such rhetorics all the time; given the sort of social theory with which some critics work, such rhetorics are thought to play an important role in reproducing various groups' social identities, authorities, etc. Insomuch as our students are largely drawn from these very communities, it should come as no surprise that, when used in our classes, these rhetorics strike them as very comfortable and familiar. In fact, strong teaching evaluations in our field may be more an indication of the instructor's ability to placate his or her students by parading out a few therapeutically useful rhetorical phrases than of their ability to provoke people to have a novel thought. But the hope for strong teaching evaluations cannot fully explain the continued use of these rhetorics in our classrooms. So just why is it that we continue to find so many scholars of religion reproducing these very rhetorics in their purely descriptivist scholarship, rather than, as Emile Durkheim did a hundred years ago, redescribing them in a new, explanatory vocabulary? "If one isn't content with description," Foucault wrote, "if one wants to try and explain a victory or a defeat, then one does have to pose the problems in terms of strategies and ask, 'Why did that work? How did that hold up?'" (1980: 209). This book, then, is an effort to document further, and attempt to account for, the victory of a certain sort of institution by means of its specific, strategic rhetoric.

To be sure, the North American study of religion as practiced over the past forty years has gained considerable institutional turf by reproducing these rhetorical techniques – attesting to the social impact of these devices. However, as observed by Jonathan Z. Smith some time ago, coming out of our mouths and our pens, these rhetorics are a rather unoriginal and unimaginative repetition of what the people under study (at least those on the politically liberal end of things) are already saying about themselves, prompting me to wonder what scholarship-as-repetition has to gain? As should be clear, I tend to think that we're in the business of doing something other than simply rewording indigenous reports; the scholar of religion is not a prophet (lit. a mouth-piece). Now, "the sacred" is, of course, part of a second-order, reductive language, making it more than a mere paraphrase – after all, I'm not sure anyone thinks they are experiencing "the sacred" when they, say, eat a wafer and drink wine while hearing the words, "Take, eat, in remembrance of me." "The sacred" reduces and thus productively homogenizes various potentially competing local taxonomies into one grand discourse, thus allowing comparison and juxtaposition to take place. (Question: without "the sacred" as an organizing concept, how would Eliade have written his *Patterns in Comparative Religion?*) Should one already believe that there is something enduring and deeply human(e) that escapes the grasp of observation, then I suppose talk of "the sacred," "creativity," and "depth," and "genius" passes unnoticed. But, as I have argued elsewhere, such a study is more akin to a liberal practice of religious pluralism than a species of the human sciences as practiced in the public university. For those of us who study religion as a fascinating yet all-too-human socio-cognitive activity, a means whereby historical agents accomplish this or that practical activity – one of which is social formation – utilizing the language of "the sacred," and the motives that drive such utilization, are insufficient for attaining our goals.

It is precisely this hope to do something other than merely paraphrase the participant taxonomies under study that drives what Carrasco and many others deride as the provincial critiques of the Chicago school. Given that Foucault understood the role of critique to be "the art of not being governed so much" (1996: 384), this book, then, is a collection of dispatches from those unruly provinces. Its rhetorical setting is thus very different from, say, Eliade's own early series of Romanian articles entitled "Letters to a Provincial" in which he addressed what he took to be the so-called young generation of interwar Romanians. In this series of articles he wrote to a constructed

> "provincial" or parochial type. ... To this "provincial" I gave lessons in manliness and heroism, I summoned him to shake off clichés, indolence, and mediocrity. ... I was obsessed by the fear that our generation, the only

free generation in the history of the Romanian people, would not have time
to accomplish its "mission."

(Eliade 1990a: 135)

Rather than offering such wise counsel to those on the margins of the self-
appointed center, this book revels in its edginess and is a reaction against the
pomposity of the center. This book is therefore an extended letter *from* a
provincial to his peers who are, inevitably, but other provincials – because, at
the end of the day, all we've got is a "dispersion of centers" (Foucault 1990: 34)
where members of differing groups work tirelessly to authorize their specific
local as the universal.

So as to avoid the impression that I think the representatives of the Chicago
school, the discourse on sui generis religion, the private affair tradition, the
humanistic study of religion, whatever name it goes by, are merely "putting
down" competing viewpoints and the competing institutions in which these
viewpoints have developed, I therefore offer the following chapters for their
consideration, taking my colleagues up on their offer of a real, critical dialogue.
However, I'm not naive about a serious reply; practical interests are threatened
by the sort of retooling the following chapters recommend. Despite the fact that
hope springs eternal, "here, on the outskirts of life, dreams seldom come true,"
as the Canadian band, Blue Rodeo, once sang. My ideal reader, then, might be
something like my friend's young son, mentioned in the acknowledgments:
someone who, after taking a deep breath, is up to the task of sorting through the
slippery jargon of a discipline and then game to make up something new.

The chapters that follow attempt to chart some features of this jargon, and
some of their consequences, across various discrete moments during the establishment, rise, and enviable success of an academic pursuit. As already observed,
they are the very rhetorics employed by "the religious" themselves, despite the
fact that the scholars of religion whose work I examine have usually, and vehemently, disowned the label "religious" in their attempts to construct a so-called
objective history of religions. This could also be seen as a paradox, if it were not
for the insight made possible by a social-rhetorical approach. Such an approach
enables us to theorize that the rise and maintenance of an academic discipline
can be studied in precisely the same fashion as any other social group – those we
sometimes call religions included. This means that so-called religious rhetorics
are hardly religious at all. Instead, they can easily be redescribed as social engineering techniques or, to borrow Foucault's phrasing, *disciplinary techniques for
helping to make subjects and the settings in which they interact* – both the intellectual and political senses of "discipline" and "subject" are fully intended here (as
in Foucault 1990: 60). Perhaps this is why I have come to think that the study
of nation-building overlaps so easily with the study of discipline-building; for, in
both cases, specific rhetorics of unity and homogeneity are used to control and
re-present back to potentially distinct and unmanageable human beings their
own necessary and inevitable groupness and utility – not only to one another,

but also to "the State" or "the profession." The following chapters are thus concerned with examining discrete and seemingly mundane socio-rhetorical moments in an academic discipline's emergent and dominant phases, looking for what helps to make them tick, for what provides this discourse with its conditions of possibility, as Bernard Faure and others, phrase it (1993); my hope is that the very existence of the theoretical work on which I draw in making this critique signals that the dominant phase has already begun its slow but inevitable move into a residual phase, ripe with possibility. After all, Carrasco's use of "provincial" has little in common with Eliade's, since the latter was attempting to forge an institutional identity by wrestling "the sacred" from the anthropologists, the psychologists, and the sociologists. Having won that victory decades ago, we must inquire why a scholar of religion would still resort to the same rhetoric of center/periphery. If critics were so sadly off the target, why not just ignore them? My conjecture is that a loosely knit group of critics, writing over the past twenty years, has had far more impact than some scholars are willing to acknowledge, an impact that threatens the study of religion as it has been constructed these past few decades. These gains have prompted the field's gatekeepers to fall back on tired and worn assertions concerning irreducible sacredness, all in an effort to recreate what some of us believe to be a bankrupt exercise. Nothing lasts forever; who knows what the future holds ...

I do admit, however, to having an interest in what one possible future might hold; my work is therefore not innocent navel-gazing. This book is motivated by an interest to help to establish an alternative object of study, constitutive of an alternative "we." Although I develop this argument gradually throughout the book and then in greater detail in the final chapters, for the time being I can say that this "we" I have in mind is a group interested in examining those devices whereby our colleagues establish what Peter Brown, in his studies of early Christianity, has nicely termed an "imaginative room for manœuvre" (1997: 14). By this I mean the techniques and devices whereby colleagues understand themselves self-evidently *as* colleagues – or maybe I should say think and act themselves *into* colleagues, *into* scholars, *into* members of a guild, *into* sharing common values, *into* pursuing common disciplinary goals, and, in fact, *into* individuals with stable subjectivities and even *into* citizens possessing such intangible things as "inalienable rights." The following chapters, then, attempt to begin answering a question posed by Foucault: "Which kind of political techniques, which technology of government, has been put into work and used and developed in the general framework of the reason of state in order to make of the individual a significant element for the state?" (1988b: 153). My answer to his question is that such concepts as "religion," "faith," "spirit," "experience," "authenticity," etc. – and the organized domains of human practice entailed and curtailed by such concepts – are just such techniques. The future of this one academic field, then, may have more to do with studying the production of subjectivities, privacies, and the sorts of self/State complexes that they make possible than it does with having "respect for religious symbols as religious," whatever that may mean. The future, then, may lie more with historicizing "religion," "spirit," and "faith," etc., as "the new techniques by which the individual could be integrated into the social entity" (Foucault 1988b: 153), than simply using such tools to study the history and meaning of religions, spiritualities, and faiths. This future field is thus occupied with the conceptual and practical techniques of political marginalism" (Foucault 1988b: 152).

The critique offered in the following chapters therefore focuses on a rhetorical "play of forces" that helps to provide the conceptual and practical context for disparate people to experience themselves *as* private selves, related in this or that manner to other selves. Without intending to be any sort of orthodox or definitive (whatever *that* may be) application of Foucault's work, it aims to investigate "the way by which, through some political technology of individuals, we have been led to recognize ourselves as a society, as a part of a social entity, as part of a nation or of a state" (1988b: 146). In attempting to study what Foucault termed "political technology of individuals" (146), there can be little hope that the alien image that appears to some of my readers will be easily recognizable. Although I have no interest in exploring his developmental psychoanalytic theory, it is nonetheless somewhat as Jacques Lacan argued in a 1949 conference paper, later published as, "The Mirror-stage as Formative of the Function of the I" (1982); the image will more than likely appear to many as a lie, as a silly, maybe even offensive, caricature that dances briefly on the outskirts of town in a fun house mirror, distorting beyond all recognition that which they see when, in the safety of their mind's eye, they experience themselves *as* selves integrated into various groups. Shifting attention from enjoying such self-perceptions to problematizing how they are possible is therefore a tough sell. Recalling the two epigraphs that open the book (and despite the obvious differences between Foucault's and Chomsky's work), I take it to be the role of the critic "to disturb people's mental habits," all in an effort to help change the circumstances in which we have ideas and build groups.

Take, for example, at the 2001 national meeting of the American Academy of Religion and the Society for Biblical Literature held in Denver, Colorado, at which some of us attempted to critique the self-important ribbons that hang from some attendees' name badges. Instead of saying "Author," "Exhibitor," "Program Unit Chair," or "Donor," a small number of us proudly displayed colorful ribbons proclaiming "I can count to ten," "I like myself," "I try my best," "I'm a winner," and "Old Fart." I elected to wear a bright yellow one with cute little red and blue stars on it, saying in gold print, "4th Place." Although some people immediately "got" it – since not many people draw attention to themselves by displaying a ribbon that basically says they lost so badly that they didn't even mount the podium – a surprising number of well-meaning people congratulated me and then asked what I had done to win it (i.e., to lose so badly). The expectant looks on their faces, while they waited for my answer, were like little exclamation marks, highlighting their inability to see the structure of self-importance that we employ to make sense of ourselves at such mass meetings – techniques that enable a supposedly seamless "us" (after all, we are all simply "members of the academy," something communicated by the fact of our name badges and institutional affiliations) to rank and distinguish amongst ourselves, thus making the academy a meaningful, discursive space where difference and similarity can co-mingle. Instead, they could only put these rules into practice and use them to understand my – and, in relation to me, now their own – apparently newfound status. That something is lost in explaining parody – saying, "Well, you see, as with all signifiers, in itself the ribbon is meaningless and empty, and is thus a lampoon of the supposedly stable meaning and self-identity that we all seem to derive from those other ribbons some of us get to wear ..." – goes without saying. Looking into their faces, I felt like I was trying to explain why the campfire scene in Mel Brooks's "Blazing Saddles" was funny or how a "Knock-Knock" joke is supposed to work. Such moments are awkward because they make clear that both you and your well-meaning interlocutor are part of the discourse, are implicated, and thus the joke is on – in fact, *is* – us. Sometimes I simply answered by saying, "Ah, don't ask" – which, at the time, I thought was quite funny, but which I now see to have been a way of side-stepping the entire issue, making it akin to what Roland Barthes once called a faint at the right moment or what Donald Wiebe aptly termed a failure of nerve. Having now had a little more time to think about my answer and to work up my nerve, I offer the following chapters as my attempt to explain the joke more fully.

Of course, there is a risk that attends trying to explain such jokes. Magicians who share secrets do not win friends. Jonathan Smith has written on the manner in which keeping the joke's principles close to home actually allows us to pull the wool over our students' eyes.

> In the case of the introductory courses, we produce incredibly mysterious objects because the students have not seen the legerdemain by which the object has appeared. The students sense that they are not in on the joke, that there is something that they don't get, so they reduce the experience to "Well, it's his or her opinion."

While calling on scholars to show their students what is up their sleeves, he identifies another sort of what he calls disciplinary lies, lies necessary for any productive scholarship to take place.

> On the other hand, disciplinary lying – the conventions within a discipline – enables me to get moving. You have to allow me some measure of mono-mania if I am to get anywhere. I can't do my work when I have to stop and entertain every other opinion under the sun. This is why such work must always be done in a corporate setting, so that the monomanias mutually abrade against, so that they relativize each other; so that the students, the initiates, are let in on the joke.
>
> (Smith n.d.)

Identifying the rhetorics and recipes and "lies" that circulate and make possible these things we call religion and the study of religion is thus not meant as a criticism of either – as if we could get on with the business of studying religion or human behavior free of such devices. Extrapolating from Smith's comments we can say that such rhetorical devices are necessary for any sense of a group to exist and, subsequently, for any sense to be made of the group's existence. Identifying these rhetorics is simply an attempt to deflate the monomania that exists when one set of local interests are so dominant as to be effectively represented as the only interests worth pursuing, as the only game in town, and thus portraying them as altogether free of the competitive marketplace of ideas and interests.

As should by now be clear, this attempt to trace the rhetorical structure of the discourse on religion is generally, though not exclusively, informed by the work of Foucault and it continues to develop a form of analysis found in some of my previous work (e.g., 1997b, 2001b). I therefore see the following chapters as being simply the most recent installment in an effort "to learn to what extent the effort to think one's own history can free thought from what it silently thinks, and so enable it to think differently" (Foucault 1985: 9). Such a different thinking requires not only that scholars come to see that their own textual productions are just as deserving of study as are the aged parchments and scrolls that were produced by previous generations' scribal elites, it also requires a change in the practical conditions that make this thinking possible, a change that is accomplished and reflected – at least in part – by a change in rhetorical style. Although not necessarily intended when earlier versions of some of these chapters were first written, in hindsight I now think that the style of the following chapters helps to accomplish such a change – a style dismissed by an anonymous referee for a previous book as mere "journalism," and what one anonymous referee for this volume likened to "literary pieces" rather than "scholarship" or "science." I happen to agree with Routledge's referee, for I do indeed write with what this person called a "colloquial and familiar style." In fact, my grade twelve English teacher – a certain Ms. McKinnon – once tossed me a sly, back-handed compliment by saying that I had the greatest grasp of the vernacular that she had ever seen. So feel free to call it the vernacular, the colloquial, or read this book as something other than scholarship – whatever that is or ought to be. I freely admit that there are times when, as the protagonist of Walter Kirn's recent novel commented about his own writing, "I fear … that the book is just the overflow of a brain so overstuffed with jargon that it's spontaneously sloughing off the excess" (2001: 66).

Whether or not the following chapters – first written in such cities as Toronto, ON, Knoxville, TN, Springfield, MO, Iowa City, IA, and Tuscaloosa, AL – are op-ed pieces, travelogues, rants, or, like this preface, a dispatch smuggled in from somewhere out near the edge of town, I think that the Routledge referee was onto something in commenting that "[t]his use of the literary essay in order to undermine the more traditional way of looking at matters of

Religious Studies may very well be the only form in which an effective criticism of Religious Studies as an element of modern culture can exist." So I hold out the hope that this shift in style can somehow help, to whatever degree, to move some of us toward an effective critique of both the colorful ribbons we proudly wear on our chests and the overstuffed jargon that fills the pages of scholarly periodicals. In the process, perhaps they will help to recreate a new sense of "us" – complete with alternative name badges and ribbons – along with a new sense of our object of study – complete with alternative ways of conceptualizing and studying the activity of naming parts of the human world of historic practices as religion.

Acknowledgments

Apart from thanking the various publishers, journals, and book editors for granting their permission to revise and collect together those portions of this book that originally appeared separately elsewhere, I would like to thank all of those people whose critical insight and friendship have assisted me in tackling the topics addressed in the following pages. If, as the sociologist, Randall Collins, argues "[t]hinking is a fantasy play of membership inside one's own mind" (1998: 49), then the group of which I have imagined myself to be a member needs to be acknowledged as having done the hard labor of carving out an intellectual and social space into which people like me – people who study "religion" rather than religions – could move their things and set up house. It is a group that includes people whom I have never met but whose work I have read, people who are now dead but whose writings live on, people I have known as close friends and many others I have met only on email or in passing at conferences, and people who were patient enough to have sat through classes with me and who asked questions I'd not anticipated, prompting me to think a new thought. Some of their names appear in the chapters that follow and in the reference section but that's just the tip of the iceberg. Because my debt to all of these people is far greater than I will ever be able to document fully or repay, this book is dedicated to you.

My thanks also go to the colleagues with whom I now work, and students I now have the privilege to teach, at the University of Alabama. There is a very real challenge to practicing the academic study of religion far from the more widely recognized centers of the discipline; Alabama, after all, is a state where it is not hard to find an active and ongoing debate concerning the need to display the Ten Commandments in court rooms and, along with the Declaration of Independence and the Magna Carta, as part of displays of so-called historical documents in public school classrooms. Working as a scholar of religion in such a context brings with it a very real sense of challenge and accomplishment; because we are hardly preaching to the choir, we must continually reinvent ways of persuading students and the public that the study of religion practiced as part of the historically grounded human sciences has some utility. My gratitude also goes out to the people at Routledge who have toiled over and produced this book and to their anonymous referees for their helpful comments on a much earlier draft of the entire manuscript. My thanks also goes to Kim Davis who assisted with proofing the final text and to the College of Arts and Sciences of The University of Alabama for helping to make her assitance possible by means of a grant.

And, as always, I wish to mention my tremendous debt to my wife, Marcia, who is currently working on her own Ph.D. – in audiology, sensibly far away from the study of religion. The strength of our relationship is, in part, built on her complete lack of interest in what I write, keeping ever-present in my mind the fact that studying religion is not some deeply important activity whereby one peers into the dark night of the human soul. No; it's just something some of us happen to do.

I must also mention a young friend in Canada, Michael Hamel. Late one winter evening a couple of years ago, while spending a few days with friends just north of Toronto, Michael and I had one of the most earnest and illuminating conversations that I have ever had concerning such imponderable topics as God, the Bible, and Jesus. Lying on the floor, cozy in the sofa cushion "tent" that his dad had just helped him to make, 5-year-old Michael patiently answered all of my naive questions. Beginning with a long sigh at my profound ignorance, then followed by a pause and a deep breath to gather his energy and his thoughts, he taught me all that he knew about these and other such topics. And the amount that he knew about the gods was surpassed only by his quick-witted ability to work out – or just make up – those parts he did not know. With his big sister long since upstairs asleep and his mother, father, and my wife all seated silently in the room, each drifting off to sleep just a little, Michael gained speed with every question and went on to tell me the high points of the Bible story. When he finished, he nodded and told me that, if I ever read the Bible, "You can skip that part coz now you already know it."

Michael's sincerity and commitment to converse with those who did not share his knowledge are enviable traits. Making his contribution to what Emile Durkheim referred to as "la vie sérieuse," this little boy propped up on his elbows late one night, making it up as he went, reminded me just why I find the study of human behavior so fascinating – our own included, and not just those so-called exotic behaviors down the block and around the corner. My hope is that scholars of religion, like Michael, are able to take themselves seriously enough so as to become interested in their own behaviors.

I would like to think that this book provides something new to readers who may already be familiar with earlier versions of some of the following chapters. For those who see something familiar in the following pages, I offer the following advice, which is itself a repetition: as young Michael said, skip that part coz you already know it. With this warning in mind, I wish to thank the following list of editors and publishers for kindly allowing me to repeat myself by granting their permission to draw on these previously published works:

Chapter 1 is based on "Theorizing at the Margin: Religion as Something Ordinary," ARC (Journal of the Faculty of Religious Studies, McGill University,

Montreal) 28 (2000): 143–157. My thanks to the editor of ARC for permission to use this material.

Chapter 2 is based on a review essay in *Method & Theory in the Study of Religion* 5/2 (1993): 198–207. My thanks to Brill Academic Publishers for permission to use this material.

Chapter 4 is based on "Classification and the Shapeless Beast: A Critical Look at the AAR Research Interest Survey," *Religious Studies News* 12/3 (1997): 7, 9. My thanks to the American Academy of Religion for permission to use this material.

Chapter 5 is based on an editorial published in *Bulletin of the Council of Societies for the Study of Religion* 26/2 (1997): 26–28. My thanks to the Council of Societies for the Study of Religion for permission to use this material.

Chapter 6 is based on "The Crisis of Academic Labour and the Myth of Autonomy: Dispatch from the Job Wars," *Studies in Religion/Sciences Religieuses* 27/4 (1998): 387–405. My thanks to Wilfrid Laurier University Press for permission to use this material.

Chapter 7 is based on "The Study of Religion as an Anthropology of the Credible" in *Religious Studies, Theology, and the University*, Delwin Brown and Linell Cady (eds). Albany, NY: State University of New York Press, 2002. My thanks to SUNY Press for permission to use this material.

Chapter 8 is based on "The Jargon of Authenticity and the Study of Religion," *Religion & Theology* 8/3 (2002): 17–40. My thanks to Brill Academic Press for permission to use this material.

Chapter 9 is based on "Methods, Theories, and the Terrors of History: Closing the Eliadean Era With Some Dignity." *Reconsidering Eliade*, 11–23. Bryan Rennie (ed.). Albany, NY: State University of New York Press, 2000. My thanks to SUNY Press for permission to use this material.

Chapter 10 is based on "Bruce Lincoln's *Theorizing Myth*: The Perfect Past and the Jargon of Authenticity," *Studies in Religion/Sciences Religieuses* 30/1 (2001): 79–90. My thanks to Wilfrid Laurier University Press for permission to use this material.

For granting permission to quote Malvina Reynolds' "Little Boxes" (words and music by Malvina Reynolds, © 1962, renewed 1990, all rights reserved), I would like to thank Schroder Music Co., of Berkeley CA. The lyrics from "Born in the U.S.A." by Bruce Springsteen (© 1984 Bruce Springsteen [ASCAP]), have been reprinted with permission.

Introduction

> These remarks about simple vocabulary have in reality important political implications.
>
> Michel Foucault (1979: 8)

In my memory, two ordinary and solitary moments stand out from many others as prompting me to ask some of the questions pursued in the chapters that follow. Both occurred while I was "sitting alone in front of the tube," as Chomsky might say.

First: it is 1988 and I'm at home, living just outside Toronto, watching a television special on the Olympic torch relay across Canada to Calgary, the host of that year's winter Olympic Games. I recall seeing a young boy, lucky enough to be selected to carry the torch for his designated distance, running through the crowded street with the torch held out over his head, obviously excited. His father runs alongside with his video camera, matching his son's pace, documenting the event for posterity. The boy looks at his father, and into the camera, and says, "I can't wait to get home and see this on TV." I recall thinking to myself, "You're living it now, kid, so why do you have to get home to see it on television?"

Second: it is only a couple of years ago and I am living in Springfield, MO. I am working at my laptop in the living room with – you guessed it – the television on once again, listening in the background to the onetime member of the Monty Python troupe, Terry Jones, host a three-part television series on the U.S. Discovery Channel entitled, "Ancient Inventions" (Seventh Art Productions, 1997/1998). I heard him say in passing that the invention of the corridor in elite, European homes could be dated to sometime around the late seventeenth to early eighteenth century. Prior to that, medieval domestic space was generally limited mainly to a building which contained a multi-purpose great hall, where the lord of the house's bed – the most private zone within the dwelling – was in close proximity to the lesser beds (more than likely straw mats) of others in his household. With the development of multi-room dwellings during the period known as the Renaissance – for those wealthy enough to live in a space separate from their work and, in addition, for those who could afford multiple private spaces within one dwelling – each room opened directly into the next. In fact, "architects prided themselves," in seventeenth-century France, "on aligning all the doors *enfilade* [from the French, *enfiler*, meaning "to thread,"], so that there was an unobstructed view from one end of the house to the other. ... [A]ll traffic, servants as well as guests, passed through every room to get to the next" (Rybczynski 1988: 41). These newly minted private spaces were therefore public thoroughfares. Until, that is, the internal hallway or corridor was invented.

Unlike the moment from watching the Olympic torch relay, which obviously registered somewhere in my mind but pretty much just stayed put for the time being, this time my curiosity had got me off the couch. After digging through some dusty books on the history of furniture and the fascinating history of the home (quoted just above) written by the architectural historian, Witold Rybczynski (1988; esp. ch. 2, "Intimacy and Privacy"), I learned that beds in these semi-private rooms could occupy a curtained-off niche or alcove, built into one wall, making for a private (and warmer) zone within the semi-privacy of the (drafty) room. Over time, as the great hall receded into an atrium, and as additional rooms were added by the wealthy, the hallway was invented – a public passageway within the private home – making possible new private domestic spaces, and new forms of private selves in opposition to one's presentation of one's various public selves. Thus, we are able to link changes in social practices and home architecture to changes in their inhabitants' senses of family, domesticity, privacy, and even their interior selves (Rybczynski 1988: 36). No longer did the four-poster bed, complete with curtains and canopy, stand as the sole means of avoiding the scrutiny of one's domestic peers. In fact, somewhat like modern-day teenagers hanging a "Do Not Disturb" sign on their bedroom door, I found a painting by Memmo di Filippucio, *Couple Preparing for Bed* (ca. 1320; see Duby *et al.* 1988: 215) depicting a maid about to let the curtain fall on the bed of a naked couple (possibly newlyweds?).

Although the internal corridor is hardly a European invention – I have since learned that the Romans had them long before, in their multi-unit dwellings – this seemingly benign point in the history of European domestic architecture caught my attention. I quickly came to realize that, although I took hallways and private rooms to be an obvious architectural feature, they were in fact an artful technique that made it possible for some group members occasionally to be exempt from the gaze of their peers. Unexpectedly, moving to a new job at the University of Alabama helped me along in my thinking since the Department in which I now work is housed in a late-nineteenth century, L-shaped building (re)built shortly after the U.S. civil war. (Much of the campus – then, a military training facility – was destroyed by Union troops as they triumphantly marched through Tuscaloosa.) The three-story, red brick building, completed in 1888, has no hallways, just a wide public veranda complete with black rod iron railings on each floor, onto which each private office or classroom opens. With no hallways within which to congregate, have coffee and gossip with colleagues and students, or just idly pass the time, I have found the social dynamic to be rather different from some previous universities where I have worked. We are either in our office, in someone else's office, or outside and thus away from work entirely. Although the pleasant southern U.S. spring and autumn weather permits office doors to be propped wide open, the cool winters and humid summers ensure that, when we are not teaching in the classroom, we are often huddled in our offices in front of our computers writing books such as these, loudly yelling "Come in!" when we hear a knock on our thick office doors. I now realize more than ever that such structural circumstances as weather and architecture play an unseen but crucial role in our developing social senses of selves. But what is more fascinating than this realization is that it took so long for me to figure this out. That such seemingly invisible structures control not only *how* we label and experience ourselves as selves but, more importantly, *who* gets to have a self, has often been painfully obvious to some people, making my late-in-life realization evidence of my own membership in a privileged caste. For example, a visit to my own campus's old Foster Auditorium makes this more than apparent, for there one can read a plaque commemorating the federalization of the Alabama National Guard, a technique that the Kennedy administration employed on June 11, 1963 to ensure that the University's first African-American students were able to enroll successfully. So, outside my office door is not only a veranda but a tangible history of overt dissent and civil rights marches, all aimed at persuading the state and federal governments to grant legal selfhood to a group of people who previously were forced to be all but invisible.

At the time when all this was first dawning on me, several of the following chapters were as yet unwritten and others were in need of a good rewrite. In the light of Terry Jones's aside, I began to see that a theme was emerging in some of my work on the modern problem of religion. Long before, a friend in Toronto had suggested that I read E. P. Thompson's classic study of religion and the British Industrial Revolution, *The Making of the English Working Class*. I now recalled his thoughts on the "psychic masturbation" of Methodist frenzies. Of course, there was also the work of Jonathan Z. Smith, who first started me thinking about what it meant to study the very classification term "religion"; influenced by Bruce Lincoln's and Roland Barthes's work I had focused on what the latter called the decorative displays of language and rhetoric and their relationship to bourgeois and liberal ideologies, a point brought home powerfully in the post-September 11, 2001, rhetorics of "terrorist," "freedom," "freedom fighter," "infidel," etc. (see Lincoln 2002a). Although I do not share his presumption of a universal, Cartesian common sense, as he has phrased it, Noam Chomsky's thoughts on the manner in which large sectors of the public are effectively separated from one another and thereby managed also played a role in my thinking. Add to all this Terry Jones's aside, which got me mulling over physical, architectural features and their relationship to privacy and one's sense of self, and the image of that excited, little boy with the torch and his dad with the ever-present video camera, both of whom seemed only to understand their present, varied sensations to count as meaningful experiences in light of their anticipation of a future ordering and containment on a television screen. We thus seem to make sense in the moment by anticipating a future when we have the luxury of hindsight. Or, as my colleague, Kurtis Schaeffer, aptly phrased this technique for creating significance by means of a remembered past in an anticipated future: "Just wait until I tell somebody about this!" And now, seated in my hallway-less office in Alabama, I am no longer able to routinely keep the door open and casually interact with passing colleagues and students. With all this in my mind, I found myself revisiting several of Michel Foucault's works, to help me order – and thus make sense of – some of these impressions and new ideas and, in the process, to help me rethink some writing I hoped to assemble into a book.

As a result of this rethinking it became clear that the tension between private and public, internal and external, was a two-way street, ensuring a site in which one could escape an otherwise constrained life (e.g., the modern, angst-ridden teenager retreating to his bedroom or someone entering the darkened theater to vicariously enter the fantasy of the movie) while simultaneously acting as but an additional site of constraint (e.g., the prison cell, the limited visual frame of the television or movie screen, or, better yet, the medieval woman's bedroom which, serving as a site of pious devotion and spiritual exercises, also functioned to ensure her political set-apartness [Duby *et al.* 1988: 307–308]). Privacy, made possible by busy hallways and solid doors, and experience made possible by various framing devices, were simultaneously both a valued refuge and an impenetrable prison. But I was interested in not only the physical means of accomplishing this tidy bit of social engineering, but also the rhetorical means – wondering if our very effort to link the practice of cloistering to such interior, privatized things as piety, spiritual exercises, emotions, beliefs, and devotion – rather than, say, detention – might itself be yet another technique for accomplishing the venting/constraint technique of refuge/imprisonment. After all, a contemporary feminist historian would find it very difficult to think of such things as the Counter-Reformation slogan, "*Aut murus aut maritus*" ("Either a [cloister] wall or a husband" [see Tracy 1999: 315, n. 9]) without immediately posing questions about the ways in which power was once exercised on certain human bodies by means of rhetoric and architecture. So why is it that many scholars of religion still seem persuaded that privatization is essentially about matters of the spirit, somehow exempt from the tug-and-pull of historical existence? Why is it that, one hundred years after William James delivered his Gifford Lectures, later published as *The Varieties of Religious Experience* (1902), a scholar of religion could celebrate its enduring quality in the following fashion:

> *Varieties* should have been the death knell of reductionism for all time. You demonstrated beyond reasonable doubt that there is "a wider self through which saving experiences come" and that "where God is, tragedy is only

provisional and partial, and shipwreck and dissolution are not the absolutely final things." Yet in every generation the battle must be fought anew, for the spirit of reductionism is always with us, altering its face only enough to fool the unaware. No longer does one hear faith reduced to disorders of the liver or spleen: the new reductionism claims that we can explain all of our spiritual longings, our idols and fears, our sexual identity, our image of God, as cultural constructions. You are still needed to knock over needless obstacles and clear the path to faith, a path you discerned even when you could not follow it.

(Zaleski 2002: 32)

Instead of seeing James as an artful political actor, an effective rhetorician working to authorize a certain way of organizing conducive at least to her own group's interests, historically embedded writers such as Zaleski paint a pleasing picture of the pious, empathetic explorer making land in some uncharted inner cove of the human soul, and returning from his journey with a precious discovery: the enduring self. That she does so in explicitly combative language – "in every generation the battle must be fought anew" – with an ever so mild hint of elitism – the unaware can be fooled easily, it seems – is no doubt lost on those readers eager to share in James's discoveries (and the social benefits that come with them).

So, I began wondering if, like the invention of the now taken-for-granted hallway, and the sorts of selves/groups it helped to make possible, certain seemingly self-evident rhetorical tools and common classifications could also be understood to be responsible for wider senses of an enduring self and group, private and public, allowable and disallowable that is somehow thought to ride the waves of historical change. What follows is the book that resulted from putting these puzzle pieces together. It concerns certain common rhetorical techniques used in other books and in classrooms, techniques that make possible particular ways of organizing perceptions of the world, thinking about the world, talking about the world, acting in the world, and organizing individuals as members of groups with a very particular sense of their relations to others. It is thus concerned with some of the techniques whereby an "everyday bit of theater" (i.e., certain parts of routine human behavior) becomes knowable as an item of "solemn discourse" (to borrow some words from Foucault [1990: 32]).

The specific group that produces and is dependent upon this solemn discourse, and thus the one that occupies most of the study, is a collection of people known as scholars who now routinely inhabit university corridors – and verandas – although such other groups as the nation-state are of interest as well. The book is therefore concerned with the relationship between various sorts of group identities and how they co-exist by means of such intertwined pairs of concepts as subject/object, private/public, emotion/rationality, belief/practice, sacred/secular, spirit/body, church/state, and, most generally and importantly, religion/politics. Like European hallways a millennium and a half after their Roman predecessor, or an instant replay of the torch relay, my thesis is hardly original: in the discursive space created by means of these sets of abstract ideals worlds of meaning and action are created and negotiated.

Therefore, despite what is written in the books of many scholars of religion, what follows is neither about that thing some people call "the sacred" or "the holy" nor does it take a normative stance on such matters as how the so-called private zone of the church ought to interact with the public zone of politics (a concern of great significance to many writers in the U.S.). It is thus not a description or interpretation of any particular religious thing, and it is not an attempt at building an explanatory theory of religion. Instead, it examines how it is that we as students, scholars, and even citizens come to form ourselves into just these specific selves by means of certain rhetorical styles and conventions. It argues that self-perception and self-understanding – the manner in which we daily are staked out as bounded entities – are the result of wider structural circumstances that, much like a language's grammar or house's frame, operate almost invisibly in the background, thus making a very specific meaning and experience possible.

As already suggested, the classification of religion itself is the specific mapping device of most interest in the following chapters. As such, the book is an attempt to write a political theory of "religion." Presuming this thing we call reality to be what the U.S. essayist, Joan Didion (whom I cite later in the book) terms a phantasmagoria of disparate sensory stimuli, or what I am simply calling the unruly past, the book is thus about the ordinary conventions – but what I could just as easily term a formidable and repressive institutional system (Barthes 1988: 14) – that are routinely employed to tame this raucous collection of sensations, judgments, events, behaviors, coincidences, plans, accidents, values, and people, along with the ways in which knowledge, those who possess knowledge, and the things that are knowable by means of this knowledge, are organized, regularized, disciplined, and governed.

If the object of study is the slippery point at which the discursive moments of subject/object and private/public intersect, then it is my hope that readers will flatter me by keeping in mind that the "I" and the "group," the "us" and the "them," the "dilettante" and the "expert" are inextricably related points of reference along a continuum of scarce and thus contested resources – none of which exists in the raw or independent of the other, but only as abstract ideals against which historically embedded actors in the everyday theater, along with their competing viewpoints and practical interests, are plotted and ranked and thus experienced as something distinguishable from the unruly phantasmagoria. I say all this from the outset of the book to problematize in advance one possible reading of all that follows. Although the autobiographical voice appears here and there throughout the following pages – my opening anecdotes are an instance of this – it would be a disservice to the thesis being argued to hear this voice as self-authorizing or as speaking some sort of pristine truth or authenticity that resides deep within "me," the privileged author. Nothing could be further from the point being argued. Because the book argues that scholars ought to shift their attention from adjudicating truth, authenticity, experience, content, and meaning, to the wider structures that make such things as truth, authenticity, experience, content, and meaning possible – what Barthes called "the body of rules and recipes" (1988: 13) – the use of the self-disclosure, the anecdote, the first-person singular pronoun "I," is always an entry point into examining a considerably wider and generally undisclosed grammar and economy of identity concoction. The former is not understood as an end unto itself or something that requires our vigilant protection but, rather, as a cue or a prompt to the practical, historical conditions that make just this, historic "I" a possible item of discourse. After all, "[t]o talk about oneself, to throw personal testimony into the balance, to profess that personal conviction must be taken into account provided only that it is sincere is a Christian, indeed an eminently Protestant idea that the ancients never dared to profess" (Veyne 1987: 232). So, please think of the "I," perhaps, as a shoe-horn or a can opener, a necessary and practical instrument that, once used, makes it possible to enter a tight place and scrutinize the conditions of this seemingly mundane subjectivity. For, to examine the intentional self it is necessary to examine the non-intentional contexts in which selves come to exist and interact; in this regard all that follows is rather different from, say, Ann Taves's recent book on religious experience (1999). Although she is well aware of the long history of attempts to account for such reported experiences and their associated behaviors, in the end she proposes a safe, middle path between self-reports and scholarly study, one that does not "distort" the reported experience of the people whom we study and one that therefore locates agency firmly within the individual subject (1999: 8, 363, n. 1). I fear something is lost if we do not take seriously that subjectivity is an historical event – not that we must assume "history" has agency, as Taves fears, but that the thing we come to call the self or Human Nature is the product of countless prior events, some planned, some complementary, some contradictory, and many completely unforeseen and the result of sheer, blind happenstance. To examine the "rules and recipes" that govern some of this process is therefore a rather different exercise from Taves's, one that examines the settings in which selves come into existence, the contexts in which they come to write and debate and think and talk and agree and disagree and ignore and invent and persuade, and, at times, coerce and conflict violently. With all these possible outcomes in mind, then, this book asks how it is that seemingly uniform social identities – at virtually any level, from the self to the family, to an academic discipline and even the nation-state – are even possible, given the busy and unruly flood of material and information that comprises the phantasmagoria of historic existence. Swimming against the flood of studies that simply take individual agency as god-given, this book emphasizes some of the rhetorical techniques employed to make selves.

Despite the variety of topics covered in the following chapters, it is the specific role played by a certain historic concept, "religion," in structuring relations between self- and group-consciousness, that is the pre-eminent concern. So, to repeat: the following chapters do not offer a theory of religion but a political theory of "religion." To cite Foucault, we could therefore ask: "Faith, what is that?" and then answer our own question by replying, as he did: "Religion is a political force" (1999: 106). But we may need to tweak his work, just a bit, if it is to assist us in the exercise that follows, for in his work religion is often (and understandably) equated with a specific form of Christianity, as if certain aspects of social life were obviously religions or religious. "Foucault generally uses the term 'religion'," one recent commentator observed, "as a kind of overall phenomenological term to refer to any institutionalized faith tradition" (Carrette 2000: 6). Those who take up Foucault's project and apply it to the study of religion sometimes work as if his critical method allows them to recover a purer, pre-discursive thing – with the above quotation in mind, we can call it the pre-institutionalized faith or prior religious experience – free of the sadly limiting constraints placed on all forms of human expressions. (On different ways in which Foucault has been used by scholars of religion, see Keller 2001: 920.) I find this to be the case in a recent application of Foucault to the study of religion, the above-cited *Foucault and Religion: Spiritual Corporality and Political Spirituality*, by Jeremy Carrette (2000). Arguing that "Foucault's work rejects models of religious transcendence and opens the way for models of religious immanence," Carrette aims to demonstrate that, by means of this shift, "the 'truth' of religious discourse is in effect taken out of the binary opposition between spirit and matter and rewritten in terms of the dynamic of power-knowledge and embodiment" (5, 6). It would appear that Foucault's work can assist in bringing about this recovery of meaning.

What if, instead, we pressed in the direction that, at least in my reading, Foucault blazed in so many of his studies and asked, for example, not what sex means or what is the truth (scare quotes or not) of religion but what prior historical, institutional, and material conditions make it possible to think and enact "sex" or "truth" or "religion" in the first place? Keeping in mind the distinction between the discourse on sexuality, on the one hand, and the classification that this discourse makes possible – i.e., the naming, distinguishing, and (de)valuing of certain generic behaviors as "sex," on the other – what if we asked, "'Faith,' what is that?" Or, subtly rephrasing a point made by Carrette, what if instead of "strategically bringing to light the way religion attempts to create a monopoly on experience through its ordering, categorising [sic], and subjectifying human life" (140), we suspended our apparently commonsense assumption that distinct zones of human praxis ought to be set aside as religion? Then, we could strategically investigate the ways in which those who, like Carrette himself, deploy the category "religion," thus make possible specific sorts of experiences, subjectivities, and political action through their own efforts at ordering and classifying. So, instead of proceeding on the assumption that interior, personal faith or belief was natural or chronologically and logically prior to, and thus separate from and opposed to exterior, public, and derivative practices, institutions, and organizations (i.e., the church, the tradition, or what some call "institutional religion" as opposed to purer "spirituality"), what if we simply stated that "the very discourse 'religion' itself makes 'faith' and 'spirituality' possible and is therefore a political force"?

So, despite any apparent similarities between my own work and Carrette's project, the following chapters have no interest in supporting the claim that:

> Religion needs to be rediscovered outside the superstitions, misconceptions, and illusions through which 'secular' academics have so far dismissed the subject. We need to find religion in the very fabric of the 'secular' – in its absence. … In this 'absence' we are left with questions of how to create new forms of embodied subjectivity through a 'spiritual corporality' and a 'political spirituality'. From this 'absence' a new 'religious space' will emerge in its disappearance.
>
> (152)

If we asked just some rephrased questions we would no longer be concerned with simply describing religions and their effects, searching for a better way of conceptualizing religion, or correcting the lamentable misconceptions of so-called secular people and godless culture. Rather, we would proceed on the assumption that there is no proper conception that is sadly veiled (just what criteria would we ever use to distinguish conception from misconception?). We would begin in earnest the effort at redescribing and thus historicizing the "rules and recipes" that enable certain of us to classify various forms of human praxis *as* religious or spiritual or devotional or authentic, and the practical outcomes of such classifications. This would truly be a history of the subject, of privacy, and interiority.

Take, for example, the image on the cover of this very book as one possible starting point for such a historicization: a fresco from the famous Scrovegni Chapel in Padua, Italy, that depicts the announcement of the angel to St. Anne, foretelling the birth of her daughter, the one who will be known as the Virgin Mary. This painting is but one of over forty celebrated frescoes in this early-fourteenth-century chapel, all of which have an obviously religious theme, some would say. But if my use of this image communicated to some readers that this book was about medieval saints, Italian art, women and religion, or an examination of the rigors of living out a religious vocation, then such readers will by now be sadly disappointed. My interest regards the painting's ability to adopt a god's eye viewpoint to cut across (literally, provides a cross-sectional view of) the worlds of the insider and outsider, private and public, female and male (in the story, husband and wife receive separate visits from angels bearing their good news), servant and master (the woman outside is presumably St. Anne's handmaid, Judith), human and divine. In viewing the painting we could inquire what the subject's experience may have been or what it meant to her, what the artist, Giotto di Bondone (d. 1337), might have intended to convey in his depiction of St. Anne, or what it meant to his contemporaries or modern day pilgrims to enter the chapel and experience its colorful images. Or, we could instead inquire as to how such a site of experience – whether it be the fresco, the chapel as modern, jet-setting tourist destination, the classifications "religious art," "devotional practice," etc. – became possible. In the case of our young Olympic torch bearer, we should not take on the voice of a Romantic and berate him for failing to immerse himself in the moment but, instead, we could take seriously what he said and shift our attention to the necessary frame that organizes the disparate historical moment, thus making such a thing as our experience possible. Context is everything for, as phrased by Rybczynski: "A recreational vehicle in the rain is just a wet metal box; a screened porch with wide, sheltering eaves is a place to *experience* the rain" (1990: 49).

Historicizing or contextualizing the "it" of experience in this manner means pursuing a rather different line of questioning, one that might prompt us to learn that the chapel, built on the site of a Roman arena that once stood in Padua, was once connected to the Scrovegni palace, thus bringing to the forefront the tangled (and, for some at least, the counter-intuitive) relationship between wealth and devotion (i.e, the economics of piety). Given that the chapel appears on many web sites and is regularly open from Monday to Sunday, 9 a.m. to 7 p.m., with an admission of 10,000 lire, this relationship is hardly a thing of the past. From this point we might further inquire as to what is at stake in routinely overlooking the manner in which structural context (e.g., economics) makes the seemingly settled, meaningful content possible. To rephrase, we could examine what is entailed in our *seeing it as* religious art instead of seeing the classification of "religious" (and even "art") as but an extension of wider structures that make a specific experience, and hence subjectivity, possible.

Pursuing these alternative questions sends us to the archives – rather than to record the oral histories of pilgrims – where we soon learn that the owner of the chapel and the onetime occupant of the palace, Enrico Scrovegni (d. 1336), had it built at the turn of the fourteenth century in memory of his father, Reginaldo (d. 1290), both of whom were wealthy bankers – or, what once might have been classified as a money-lender or a usurer. Apparently, both were locally despised as a result of their money-lending practices. For example, in canto XVII, line 64 f., of the *Inferno*, the Scrovegni's contemporary, Dante Alighieri (d. 1321), makes a rather barbed reference to a "Paduan among the Florentine" usurers whom he finds seated in the hot sands on the outer edge of the seventh circle of hell. Although their features are either unfamiliar or indistinguishable to him, Dante recognizes each of them by the various coats of arms stitched to the money pouches hanging around their necks. One such pouch bears the image of "a pregnant blue sow" – a direct reference to the Scrovegni family coat of arms. After speaking briefly with this tormented soul – none other than Reginaldo, we gather – Dante tells his reader that the usurer "twisted his mouth and stuck out his tongue, like an ox that licks its nose" (XVII, line 75). At this, Dante turns his back and "left those weary souls."

Knowing all of this about the context that makes possible the pious display in the chapel, we once again focus on Giotto's narrative cycle, financed by his patron, and based on the Gospel of James and running from Joachim's expulsion from the temple for being childless to Anne's visitation from the angel announcing the birth of their daughter, to Mary's eventual marriage to Joseph, the birth, life, and death of Jesus, culminating in a scene of the Last Judgment. And so we return to the book's cover: the Annunciation to St. Anne. Kneeling alone in her bedroom, as if in prayer, Mary's mother-to-be listens to the angelic messenger who gestures toward her as he squeezes his head and one shoulder through the window. Although this meeting is secluded and in private (remember, the dejected Joachim is out in the fields, soon to receive his own revelatory dream – nicely juxtaposing her secluded indoor from his free roaming outdoor space), only an ornate, cut-away wall separates them from her hand-maid, who patiently waits outside the door. But an even more private place lies in the background, awaiting the angel's departure. With a swift pull of a curtain, Anne could be secluded even more and in the privacy of her bed. But this bed, the most private of places, will soon be site of a wondrous public birth, an event attended by many others and depicted a little later in the fresco cycle.

Private and public mix in and around this painting that decorates a private family's now public chapel, dedicated to the memory of a wealthy father who was likened to "an ox that licks his nose" in one of Italy's most widely read works of literature. The fresco adorns the wall in what some might label a private site of prayer, contemplation, and devotion, but it was made possible by what at least one of Reginaldo's and Enrico's contemporaries thought of as ill-gotten wealth, and it is now visited regularly by international tourists, pious pilgrims, and aspiring connoisseurs of medieval art. It can easily be seen in countless views on the world wide web and rented out for the cover of one's book if one is willing to exchange a small fee.

Only if we succumb to the romance of the chapel's decorative walls and the painting's flimsy curtain will we see this colorful image, or one's status as a pilgrim to Padua, as anything but a commodity traded within a series of busy, public markets where ever changing interests and rates of exchange make and remake selves and groups. Paying attention to the rhetoric allows us to see something else happening in the colors and composition. This may be no more apparent than in the final scene of Giotto's narrative where we find what art historians term the dedicatory scene, in which Enrico himself appears, painted above the chapel's entrance (bearing a youthful likeness, the web site tells us, to the aged depiction of him found on his marble tomb elsewhere in the chapel). There he kneels, at the foot of the cross, presenting to the Virgin Mary herself a scale model of the chapel, being carried on the shoulder of a cleric. Enrico the usurer as pious gift-giver, in intimate cooperation with a monk, an artist, and a viewer.

Asking different questions therefore makes this moment in the history of European art a useful example of the wider structural circumstances and conflicting interests that delimit and set the stage for the public creation of memorable and thus manageable experiences, selves, and groups. Framing it as specifically "religious" art is but one of those techniques. My hope, then, is that readers will be able to entertain the notion that the concept "religion," and the various rhetorical features that accompany this common classification, accomplishes as much as hallways and corridors, and that the selves made possible by the former are comparable to the privacy and domesticity made possible by the latter. Bringing to light some of the social and political utility that these specific sorts of selves hold for the modern, social democratic nation-state is the goal of all that follows.

Part I

Genealogy of credibility

There is nothing more difficult to convey than reality in all its ordinariness. Flaubert was fond of saying that it takes a lot of hard work to portray mediocrity. Sociologists run into this problem all the time: How can we make the ordinary extraordinary and evoke ordinariness in such a way that people will see just how extraordinary it is?

Pierre Bourdieu (1998a: 21)

Chapter 1

Form, content, and the treasury of devices

> In bidding a gracious farewell to Neville Chamberlain, Churchill nobly called him "the packhorse in our great affairs." Accepting the compliment, Chamberlain pointed out that the line comes from Richard III and not, as Churchill had alleged, from Henry VI. But no matter. The thing is not to be right about Shakespeare. The thing is *to be Shakespearean.*
>
> (Hitchens 2002: 123)

A couple of years ago I watched part of a U.S. Memorial Day celebration broadcast from Washington D.C. From the perspective of its participants, this is an annual celebration of benign patriotism, a ritual on the nation's so-called civil religion calendar, that commemorates those long since past who gave their lives for the sake of freedom and democracy. Although I would never contest those participants who characterize such holidays in just this manner – judging by my father, who is a Canadian World War II veteran, they quite sincerely intend to remember and thus memorialize fallen youths and, perhaps, their own fallen youth – Memorial Day, even "civil religion" itself (see chapter 12) can easily be theorized in a rather different manner than that which is offered by its participants. If the work of scholarship is something other than paraphrasing participants' self-reports (see McCutcheon 2001b: chs 8 and 9), then one might problematize the abstract notions of *freedom* and *democracy*, taking into account such things as the fact that, although representatives of various marginalized or minority groups do indeed win U.S. elections today, power and ownership are still reserved for a relatively small, privileged group whose sphere of activity is not limited to public office and the halls of representative democracy, then the rhetoric of freedom and rule of the *demos* that is celebrated on Memorial Day takes on new significance. Instead of seeing past wars as the defenses of abstract, inalienable freedoms and rights – as our politicians and the representatives of our official media-speak continually persuade us – we come to see them as the concerted exercise of imperial right and might, part of the inevitable clash of nation-states in a world of scarce resources. All the bells and whistles of nationalism – the fireworks, the flags, the uniforms, the somber speeches, the sentimental anthems played on lone bugles, and the effort to package it and present it back to ourselves benignly as mere patriotism – heighten emotions (i.e., Durkheim's "collective effervescence") and make possible the egalitarian illusion so essential to our modern sense of self and nation. After all, if a population is to be mobilized to risk great public expenditure, as well as risking the deaths of huge segments of its younger membership (traditionally drawn from the lower classes) in the service of private enterprise (after all, are not wars often fought over private ownership of productive land, private ownership of and access to trade routes, private ownership of and access to natural resources and trading markets?), then the *material gains and losses to the privately owned system* must be mystified, universalized, and thus dehistoricized, thereby represented as *moral gains and losses credited to some abstract "public good."* This is democratization in an ideological sense (perhaps in its only sense!): the gains added to, and the losses inflicted upon, the various parts must be portrayed as gains/losses to the Whole. Or, as Noam Chomsky recently phrased it in a lecture, with regard to public support, via tax dollars, of the high tech sector of the economy, the costs are socialized while the gains are privatized.[1]

I open with this brief reflection on the rhetoric of the Whole to make a simple point: what appears to the non-participant gazing in from the margins to be the playfulness and an ad hoc-ishness that characterizes all human attempts to know and act, appears to the participant as self-evident, universal, and utterly legitimate. To rephrase it, people go to extraordinary lengths to decorate, and thus make meaningful, that which is entirely ordinary. Instead of owning up to the mundane fact that people generally act in accordance with a set of specific, tactical and all too changeable interests local to our own social group, groups decorate and universalize these local interests by attributing them to everyone – everyone from our family, our class, our gender, and our race, to our nation-state, and finally, even to Human Nature itself. People even go so far as to attribute them to beings from other realms (e.g., the will of Allah) and even to time immemorial (e.g., Fate, Natural Law, Luck, Karma, Manifest Destiny). But the marginal viewpoint that allows an insight into some of the workings of culture, value, and social identity is the same marginal stance that ensures this critical insight will receive only a brief hearing, if at all, and then be either dismissed or demonized. Although all social formations are founded on contradictions of various sorts – something Marx told us so very long ago – their institutions function in concert to gloss over and constrain such social self-destruct mechanisms; they will not suffer gladly critics who are foolhardy enough to stick their fingers in the collective social eye by pointing them out.

As you by now might have no doubt guessed, containing social contradictions and gaps is made possible by something I term the rhetoric of religion – be it the work of the theologian or the liberal humanist, they both work tirelessly to avert our gaze from the local to the universal, from this specific, conflicted human actor (whose subjectivity I take to be a function of complex and competing structural constraints) to the Holy/Human Spirit writ large and timeless.[2] Despite the theological and humanistic pre-occupation with conceptualizing religion as the realm of ahistoric and deep meanings which must be respected, decoded, and then appreciated, religion, in this book, is more an issue of discursive form, medium, and structure. In the background of each subsequent chapter is precisely this issue: how contestable rhetorical form makes possible certain specific meanings and social institutions. Specifically, the institution examined herein is the North American study of religion as it has taken shape over two academic generations. While it may be so obvious as to make mentioning it unnecessary, the book's title – *The Discipline of Religion* – is therefore an explicit and unoriginal Foucaultian *double entendre*, for the topic of the book concerns both the institutionalized academic pursuit variously known as religious studies, the academic study of religion, comparative religion, the history of religions, etc., *as well as* the rhetorical technique whereby "religion" acts as a normalizing constraint, thus playing an important role in helping to reproduce large-scale social identities. Of crucial importance is that readers recognize the perhaps subtle, but nonetheless significant, difference between my title and, say, such a seemingly related title as *Disciplining Religion* – as in Ellen Messer-Davidow's recent book, *Disciplining Feminism* (2002). As Messer-Davidow's subtitle, *From Social Activism to Academic Discourse*, makes evident, her study documents the process whereby a dynamic form of cultural practice (specifically, a type of political critique) becomes an institutional practice, maybe even an academic commodity. Such institutionalization is evidence of long sought after legitimacy, some might argue, or, as others would no doubt counter, sufficient evidence that a form of potent oppositional speech and practice had been thoroughly co-opted and brought within the fold. Regardless which side one takes, both presume that a dynamic element of social life preceded its institutionalization, such that *Disciplining Religion* would connote that the spontaneity, creativity, authenticity, etc., of this thing we call religion was somehow constrained by its reinvention as an academic pursuit. Nothing could be further from the point argued across the following chapters.

Regardless of whether this academic pursuit is described by its members as a discipline proper (often defined by appeals to a common method or theory, as in the sociological method used to study a host of different social phenomena) or a cross-disciplinary field (in which a shared object of study unites scholars each employing different methods of inquiry to study it, as in such area studies as Women's Studies or Culture Studies), it is the normalizing, political role played by both of these discourses and their tools that is the object of my attention, thus making the onetime heated discipline vs. field of studies debate of minor consequence to the chapters that follow. In collapsing this discipline/field distinction, I hope to press the work of such important contemporary writers as the University of Chicago's Jonathan Z. Smith a little further; for, when Smith rephrases his (in)famous words from the opening lines of his book, *Imagining Religion* (1982) and writes that the concept "religion" is a "second-order, generic concept that plays the same role in establishing a disciplinary horizon that a concept such as 'language' plays in linguistics or 'culture' plays in anthropology"

(1998: 282–283) I agree completely, yet I am curious about the political "disciplinary horizon" that such conceptual tools help to establish outside of the strict intellectual and social boundaries of the university. In other words, while I believe that Smith is entirely correct in concluding that "[t]here can be no disciplined study of religion without such a horizon" (282), I am left wondering if there can even be a social sense of "we" – whether the "we" denotes a group of scholars who study religion theologically, humanistically, or even social scientifically or, more importantly perhaps, a group of people who think they share deep-seated, non-empirical commonalities capable of minimizing their obvious, empirical differences – without the concept religion and the self/state complexes it makes possible. *The Discipline of Religion*, then, connotes both an institutional site of intellectual toil as well as the practical effects of the concept itself, effects that make possible certain forms of political organization and self-constitution.

In stressing this wider, disciplining effect of homogenous form over supposedly free-floating, pre-social, competing content or meaning (with this chapter's epigraph in mind, one might go so far as to maintain that content [e.g., text] follows form [e.g., context]) I think both of the late Marshall McLuhan's well-known and oft-repeated dictum, "The medium is the message," as well as Frits Staal's more recent conclusion that Vedic ritual (indeed, ritual *per se*) is meaningless, patterned activity (1989; cited in McCutcheon 2001b: 205, 209–210) that takes on meaning only in hindsight. As Staal concludes, *rituals are not about anything* (i.e., they have no referential meaning or content); if they signify anything at all, it is simply following the rules (form) properly. Meaning is thus a hindsight production and more importantly perhaps, an inherently contestable concoction. Meanings are social artifacts, the tips of changeable and long since past worlds. As the journalist Christopher Hitchens concludes in his criticism of Churchill, "the thing is not to be right about Shakespeare. The thing is *to be Shakespearean*."

This alternative approach can be applied throughout culture studies, ensuring that the critic's gaze consistently falls on what Roland Barthes once termed "that which goes without saying" – the constraints within which meaning can be made to happen – rather than on the search for meanings or what the participants say about their own meanings. To make the point, take the example of a popular song which flirts with the issue of structure and meaning: Bruce Springsteen's 1984 hit, "Born in the U.S.A." The first two verses read:

> Born down in a dead man's town
> The first kick I took was when I hit the ground
> You end up like a dog that's been beat too much
> Till you spend half your life just covering up
>
> Born in the U.S.A.
> I was born in the U.S.A.

I was born in the U.S.A.
Born in the U.S.A.

Got in a little hometown jam
So they put a rifle in my hand
Sent me off to a foreign land
To go and kill the yellow man

Born in the U.S.A.
I was born in the U.S.A.
I was born in the U.S.A.
I was born in the U.S.A.
Born in the U.S.A.

For some listeners, it is difficult to hear this song's simple, hard-hitting chorus –
repeating "Born in the U.S.A." to the steady, lone drum beat – as anything but
a celebration of unbridled national pride. This reading is confirmed when you
take into account the album cover, picturing in the foreground a white t-shirt
and jean-clad man – presumably Springsteen himself – from behind, with a red
ball cap sticking out of his back pocket and the U.S. flag's broad red and white
stripes in the background. Perhaps this is why, as described by Chris McNulty,
the song caught the attention of U.S. President Ronald Reagan – and/or his
handlers – during his successful 1984 re-election campaign. As McNulty tells it,
"On a campaign stop in New Jersey," Reagan

> cited a local hero named Bruce Springsteen, who had released a hugely
> popular rock album earlier in '84 called *Born in the U.S.A.* "America's
> future," said Reagan, "rests in the message of hope, in the songs of a man
> that so many young Americans admire, New Jersey's own Bruce
> Springsteen. Helping you make these dreams come true is what this job of
> mine is all about". ("Reagan and the Record Business," available in 2000 at
> http://users.drew.edu/~cmcnulty/)

Whether or not Reagan had actually heard the song is not really important.
Given the rhetorical context inhabited by politicians, either he or one of his
handlers clearly understood the meaning of this hit – and thus profit-producing
– song: it *is* a "message of hope" in the American Dream. After all, what else
could being born in the U.S.A. stand for? In the light of such a reading, the
album cover thus bears an uncanny resemblance to George C. Scott's well-
known film portrayal of the U.S. General George S. Patton, addressing troops
with an enormous U.S. flag in the background.

Well, as might be expected, McNulty finds a rather different meaning/refer-
ence in the song, derived largely from his reading of its verses' content, not the
chorus's catchy hook.[3]

While Reagan may have been correct in commenting on Springsteen's popularity, his remark on Springsteen's "message of hope" was way off target, as his music contained no such message. However, Reagan was not alone in this error, and the popularity of Bruce Springsteen had as much to do with the nationalist fervor encompassing the nation as it did with the content of his music.

Although I appreciate this one writer's attempt to interpret the song, and thus explain its success in light of larger structural factors (e.g., resurgent U.S. nationalism in the mid-1980s), what catches my eye in the above statement is his claim that Reagan had *misread* the song. Reagan's reading was "way off target" he says, for the song "contained no such message" of hope. Reagan and others were simply wrong in hearing the song as they did. In a similar vein was the *Chicago Sun-Times* rock critic, Richard Roeper, who wrote:

> Is it even worth trying one more time to point out that, while Springsteen indeed has written and performed songs about his love for this country, his most famous anthem, "Born in the U.S.A.," was not the jingoistic parade anthem Ronald Reagan's people claimed it to be, but a heartbreaking, lung-ripping wail of anguish from a disillusioned Vietnam veteran.
>
> (2000)

So, what do we have here? On the one hand there is a "jingoistic parade anthem," and on the other there is "a heartbreaking, lung-ripping wail of anguish." On the one hand we have strong allusions to General Patton and on the other we have a disillusioned Vietnam vet parading his ass in front of the flag. Despite the distance between these two readings, in both cases it comes down to a matter of politics and hermeneutics and, whether you acknowledge it or not, you simply pick the reading that accords with your previously held inter-ests. "To each their own," "There's no accounting for taste," and "Live and let live" thus become the mottos of social groups intent on containing these essen-tially unmanageable and arbitrary interpretive and political differences.

Unless we, as supposedly enlightened liberal intellectuals, are willing to assume that Reagan's handlers were, well, let's be honest, complete morons, we must change our gaze and try to account for how the benign arrangements of words and sounds can take on such divergent meanings. Rather than thumping our chests with national pride while singing along with, say, John Mellencamp when, at a mid-October 2001 concert to raise funds for victims of the September 11, 2001, air attacks on New York City, he sang his 1983 hit, "Pink Houses," we could instead be asking how it is that a song which includes verses that certainly appear to lament the lack of opportunities for many inner city blacks, the plight of women in dead-end marriages, as well as the apparently fleeting, if not outrightly misguided, dream that anyone can indeed grow up to be president could be sung (almost twenty years after it was written) as a rousing, nationalist anthem for the working classes. The apparent irony was all the more profound when the television cameras panned by the crowd attending the concert, as it enthusiastically joined Mellencamp in singing the song's final words which, in another context, would be difficult to hear as anything but a stinging indictment of the crowd itself – of how the very people who suffer from domestic economic and political policies are also the ones who continually pay the costs for the state's military conquests. The easily found pessimism, even cynicism, of the lyrics meant little to the cheering audience of simple, working-class people – an audience filled not only with family members of New York City firefighters and police killed in the World Trade Center collapse but with "simple men" whose tax dollars were paying the bills for the violent retaliation on Afghanistan. The early 1980s, working-class dissent of both Springsteen's and Mellencamp's anthems has today thoroughly been contained, appropriated, and commodified.

With "Pink Houses" in mind, my colleague, Ted Trost, brought to my attention Malvina Reynolds's (d. 1978) song, "Little Boxes," made popular in the early 1960s by the influential U.S. folk singer, Pete Seeger. Its opening verses are:

> Little boxes on the hillside,
> Little boxes made of ticky-tacky,
> Little boxes on the hillside,
> Little boxes all the same.
> There's a green one and a pink one,
> And a blue one and a yellow one,
> And they're all made out of ticky-tacky,
> And they all look just the same.

> And the people in the houses
> All go to the university,
> Where they were put in boxes,
> And they came out all the same.
> And there's doctors and lawyers,
> And business executives,
> And they're all made out of ticky-tacky
> And they all look just the same.

Folk music legend has it that Reynolds's got the idea for the song forty years ago, while driving on the interstate, past the brightly colored and newly constructed hillside, suburban homes of Daly City, CA (near San Francisco). The song is therefore easily heard as a biting indictment of the kind of cookie-cutter suburban, middle-class life that developed in the U.S. in the 1950s (the same sort of world/time period parodied by director Tim Burton in his 1990 film, "Edward Scissorhands," featuring plenty of green, pink, blue, and yellow suburban houses). Interestingly, though, since then the song has sometimes been used as a quaint children's song (I suspect the second verse is not sung in such settings), thus lessening its potential political impact considerably. According to Cathy Fink, writing on one online resource for parents in the Washington area:

> Some of my favorite music for families isn't the newest, or the slickest, but it is wholesome, heartfelt and inspires kids and families to sing-along. Wonderful songs with simple production can be very inspiring. Let's start with Malvina Reynolds. Malvina started writing songs in her 40s. Pete Seeger took a liking to her song, *Little Boxes*, and it, along with many others became a classic.
>
> (http://www.washingtonparent.com/articles/0112/music.htm.)

On the one hand, then, we have an anti-conformity anthem and, on the other, a quaint children's classic with a catchy tune.

What's more, despite folk music's usual preference for celebrating the ordinary, unsung lives and loves of working-class people, the song's apparent disdain for middle class values can actually be read as erasing the lower classes from the map entirely. For, as one contributor to an online discussion group has recently observed:

> I was around in the fifties and I saw the houses people lived in, and factory workers lived in ticky tacky, doctors and lawyers lived in varied dwellings, not ticky tacky at all. I specifically remember commenting to my wife in the early 60s as we drove along the tri-state, these are the slums of 20 years from now. You need to read up on the effects of the interstate system, of which these ticky tacky houses all looking the same were the product, and which, to repeat, held working class overwhelmingly. Perhaps a few managers just out of college and straining at the bit to get out of them. My brother, who ended up assistant finance manager for Checker in Kalamazoo, [MI,] only lived in ticky tacky (all just the same) at a time when he was working two jobs (the second a clothing sales clerk evenings) to pay off his college loans. All his other houses were quite different from the houses around him, and no ticky tacky. The song stinks, and stinks badly.
>
> (http://www.marxmail.org/archives/Mar99/seeger.htm)

The meaning of the song is therefore not as apparent as it at first might appear. What for one is a politically left song of dissent, is for another a quaint and wholesome children's song, and for yet another, well, it stinks – and stinks badly.

Simply put, the production of seamless meanings and identities, and thus the containment of competing meanings and identities, should be our object of study, not the justification of any one specific local meaning or identity. We must be wary of simply invoking our authority as careful hermeneuts to elevate one interpretive frame above the rest, as if we are in the position to declare which meaning is right and which is wrong for, in so doing, we are engaged in the self-serving activity of declaring one among many social worlds as right, truthful, normative and all others as wrong. In service to one social world we sacrifice our ability to study the processes whereby competing worlds bump and grind against each other. As James Ross, a journalism professor at Northeastern University in Boston, has remarked in his study of diverse Judaisms around the world, it is "nearly impossible to define who is a Jew. Perhaps a more meaningful question is: 'Who decides who is a Jew?'" (2000: 13).[4] This is a promising shift in focus, but sadly it is often not made by scholars of religion. Instead, as archaic as his work now appears to some, we still see remnants of Rudolf Otto's famous pronouncement from the opening lines to chapter 3 of *Das Heilige*, where he makes it clear that his work will only be understood by those who have had for themselves "an intrinsically religious feeling" (1950: 8). The shift from Otto's complex assertions that "rationalizations of religion," such as scholastic theories, "are methods by which the fundamental fact of religious experience is, as it were, simply rolled out so thin and flat as to be finally eliminated altogether" (27) is brought about by posing a rather simple but profound question: "how does he know?" Having asked just this show-stopping question, Greg Alles goes on to ask, "Is it not equally possible that religious experiences are evoked by ideas, expectations, and social contexts?" (2001: 326). Only if we take seriously the role that context, history, grammar, and structure play in all claims to know will we find assertions concerning genuine experience troubling. Taking such discursive settings seriously means that it is not difficult to read what Alles refers to as the "notorious fence that Otto constructs about his entire analysis" (325) as nothing but a politically effective rhetorical device whereby "Otto declares people who disagree with him incompetent and thereby makes their objections irrelevant" (326).[5]

For those who do not immediately see the links between pop music, popular culture, contesting identities, and the study of religion – links that are more than apparent to those who see all as equally inventive and ordinary sites of contestation and social formation – it is easy to find other, more recent examples of the quest for authentic, indigenous meaning that are taking place closer to our disciplinary home. Finding examples should not be difficult if we trust Alan Wolfe who has recently remarked (in a review essay on works on religion in the U.S.) that "[m]any recent books want to know *what faith means to the faithful*" (2002: B8; emphasis added). As an example, take one of the books Wolfe examines, Robert C. Fuller's *Spiritual, But Not Religious: Understanding Unchurched America* (2001), in which Fuller portrays the distinction between *being religious* and *being spiritual* as a matter of choice, a choice in which participants' sense of what is important about institutional religion's functions is taken at face value. Instead of going beyond mere self-reports to theorize the disparate cultural practices he groups together under the rubric "unchurched spirituality" as being evidence of the triumph of a socio-political system that, as Chomsky commented, "isolates everybody,"[6] Fuller sees "the unchurched" as triumphing against materialist culture and achieving "as mature a spiritual orientation to life as can be reasonably expected in our contemporary world. ... They hope for beliefs and practices that might help them sustain such a state of wonder and thus make spirituality possible in an otherwise secular world" (12, 174). Unsure of what to make of historically embedded human subjects making claims about their "hopes" and their "mature spirituality," I opt instead for a theoretical context in which these rhetorics can be translated into practical discourses.

As another example, take what some see to be the troublesome fact that their religious texts have equally been used by those with whom they disagree – sometimes vehemently. For many U.S. readers, the case of Biblical justification for the onetime practice of owning slaves hits pretty close to home, but there may be no better – because more recent – example than the effort to reorganize the country of South Africa after years of often brutal, state-sanctioned apartheid policies and practices. That the text of the Bible, as read in the Reformed tradition, played an important role in legitimizing race politics and anchoring the Afrikaner sense of nationhood has long been recognized and needs no further demonstration here. What is curious, however, is the manner in which some contemporary South African scholars are attempting to rescue their text from its previous uses and interpretations. Insomuch as the rescued text plays a key nationalistic role in helping to establish the "new South Africa" – by means of reconciliation commissions and public displays of confession, guilt, and forgiveness – we could almost say they are actively repatriating the text. With no choice but to resort to precisely the same hermeneutical practices as their predecessors – although driven by very different politics – these scholars are locked in the same vortex[7] as interpreters of "Born in the U.S.A"; they are hunting for timeless standards and values, a meaning and content that somehow transcends their specific context or present-day structural setting.

For instance, consider an article that appeared in the South African academic journal, *Religion & Theology* (published by Brill of the Netherlands), "Will It Happen Again?" (Snyman 1999). Snyman, an Old Testament scholar at the University of South Africa (Unisa), observes the same old hermeneutical tendencies in the work of post-apartheid, South African theologians, what he labels as the fetishization or the objectification of the Biblical text, as he finds in their conservative Reform predecessors. He argues that this common practice results from a literalist, or what he also calls a naively realistic, reading insomuch as such approaches fail to see textual interpretation as also and always the result of the reader and the reader's context. Instead of seeing the Bible for what it is, an ancient book open to varying interpretations, the Reformed tradition saw it as a timelessly meaningful text that, once translated literally, could be read and understood by virtually anyone with common sense (1999: 400). In his words, such "[o]bjectification ignores the human contribution to the reading process" (393).

But, ironically or not, anti-apartheid forces presume just as much! As evidence, Snyman cites the case of then assistant archbishop Desmond Tutu who, at a meeting at the University of Pretoria in 1981, quite understandably argued for a Biblical basis (i.e., legitimacy) of his particular brand of liberation theology. Quoting Loader (1987: 9), Snyman writes:

> the bishop claims to preach what the Bible says and appeals to us to believe him (and not Aristotle) on the strength of the Bible; what are we to do then with the narrative of the book of Joshua? Here God's underdogs become the upperdogs, and the Canaanites should become God's favourites if he has to be seen as the God who sides with the underdog.
>
> (1999: 297–298)

Snyman concludes: "Whereas liberation theology found inspiration in the Exodus theme, apartheid theology, whose foundation also rests in liberation ([Dutch liberation] from the British), found inspiration in the events following the liberation of the Jews. Similar to the Jews' oppression of the Canaanites, the Afrikaners designed laws to keep the 'Canaanites' at bay" (398). The moral of Snyman's tale? Grounding the legitimacy of one's political position upon some proclaimed authoritative interpretation of the Biblical text prevents a full reconciliation in the new South Africa because "the same hermeneutics that made a theological justification of apartheid possible is still firmly in place" (398).

This is an interesting argument and I agree completely with Snyman – up to this point, that is, for I fear that part of the story has escaped his analysis. That a liberal theologian such as Desmond Tutu should reproduce this reading/authorization technique ought to come as no surprise; after all, like those who preceded him, he too is an elite member of a community that employs readings of this text to sanction a specific set of current practices. It is just that he is a member of a group that does not share the particular interests of those Reformed Church predecessors. So, although Snyman's use of Tutu as an example brings the point home nicely, I am not sure that Tutu is guilty of anything, for this is in fact how such texts are used by people in his position; like all readings, his is an interested reading that is rhetorically deployed in the service of an ad hoc political position (whether or not it is a dominant or oppositional position, and whether or not we happen to agree with it). What ought to attract our attention, however, is that a scholar of religion such as Snyman *hopes for it to be otherwise*. Although he calls for an "indispensable," radical re-reading of the text – a practice supported, he argues, by the Society for Biblical Literature's "Bible and Culture Collective" (which produced *The Postmodern Bible* [Oxford University Press, 1995]) which holds that "there is no reading of the Bible that is innocent" (Snyman 1999: 380) – *he falls considerably short of making the endless hermeneutical quest itself a piece of data*. Instead, much as the reified "meaning" of the supposedly innocent Bible text is routinely invoked to produce an extra-contextual standard against which the credibility of some current human practice can be measured, he invokes an extra-textual, reified, and thus innocent "morality" that can be used to adjudicate between readings and practices. For instance, take Snyman's example of the "discrimination" of women in the Reformed tradition (385–388); that he even conceives of the non-ordination of women as "discrimination" is evidence either that he is part of a generally liberal political group who, in his own words, when reading texts such as the Bible "will draw out those ideologies that best fit their own political frameworks" (394), or he has access to extra-textual guidance such as trans-human "morality" which can be used to supplement our reading of a text. Presuming, as Snyman says he does, that all readings are utterly interested (i.e., locked within an historical situation), then the latter option is simply a rhetorical move to conceal the former. To say it a different way, discrimination is a social judgment not, as he seems to suggest, a social fact. While I happen to share some (perhaps many) of Snyman's political interests, that does not make our judgments right or obvious or natural; it just plots me as a member of his social group with shared interests and a basis for organization to work toward promoting those interests.

When it comes to recovering after apartheid, Snyman correctly sees the arbitrariness of political judgments grounded in this or that reading of the Biblical text. However, failing to take seriously the ad hoc nature of social life, he goes looking for yet a new extra-contextual source for judging action. For example, we read:

> A moral judgment on the theological justification of apartheid will only be possible when one is able to see a difference between the context of the story world, the world of the production of the Bible story, and one's own world.
>
> (385)

> … ideologies must be made explicit and put under scrutiny, even when one has the moral high ground.
>
> (400)

> As the ruling elite of Israel never really asked moral questions about the effect the deeds in these stories had on the victims, later readers from the Afrikaner community never question the effect of their reading of the Israelite history on the other inhabitants of South Africa.
>
> (401)

To put it frankly, I am not convinced that "a moral judgment" is any different from, say, Tutu's theological judgment. Of course if we presume that this thing some of us call Human Nature exists, a liberal humanist sleight of hand on a par with the Christian notion of the soul, then the self-evidency of the rhetoric of morality goes unquestioned, as does the social world it helps to smuggle in. However, the sort of alternative approach to the problem of meaning-making that is being argued for in the following chapters finds that, like Tutu, Snyman is also after "a new hermeneutical stance" (394), one that – as already quoted – recognizes "the human contribution to the reading process" (393). My difficulty with all this is that *all the reading process* is *is a human practice*. Human practice does not *contribute* to anything; it's all there is! So, as he goes on to say: "A lack of any consciousness of human involvement is fed by a lack of historical consciousness." But "human involvement" leaves the door open for other sorts of factors that also play a role in interpretation, as if humans participate in something larger than themselves – something extra-historical – when they read and write. But if interpretation is a thoroughly historical, contestable, human activity, then there can be no other factors, no values external to the human act since values are the result of human acts. Like interpretations of a text, morality too is thus a thoroughly historical and contestable artifact. Perhaps the opening words to his essay are thus more significant than he anticipated: "I am not sure whether we have overcome this fetishisation, routinisation, and bureaucritisation in our efforts to come to grips with our apartheid past" (380). Coming to grips with history rests on such routinization – the ability to organize a present and a sense of self that is juxtaposable to some distinct, chronological Other. Without such routinization we would see no need to "come to grips" with anything in particular, suggesting that Snyman is simply after a new type of routinization and not its end, as he suggests. If all reading is interested – is the enaction of a particular routine, a specific repertoire – then there is no non-reified reading and interested routinization is the inevitable means by which we discipline both unruly texts and unruly pasts in the service of some specific present.

If indeed meaning – like one's appreciation of everything from beauty and wine to jokes and hairstyles – is in the eye of the beholder, then there is nothing to be gained from the scholar *qua* critic entering the interpretive fray, intent on finding out what a text "actually means." After all, as Willi Braun has most recently commented, these local or indigenous meanings "are as numerous as a thousand flowers in the garden." But advocating a "come one come all" liberal relativism is hardly the answer for, as he goes on to comment, "the plurality of meanings does not stand in symmetrically 'balanced' relationship to each other for those who have and hold a meaning" (2001a: 170). He continues:

> To be sure, they may be regarded, in one sense, as "provincial" insofar as "other" "provincial" meanings are recognized, even tolerated, but this recognition and tolerance of "other" meanings generally does not de-mean or relativize "my/our" provincial meaning-complex. The thousand flowers in the garden thus reveal themselves as a thousand provincial absolutes, not as a thousand "sympathetic relativisms," as Gellner puts it (170–1).[8]

Braun then posed the following question: "What, then, is the scholar to do if he or she frets to do something more interesting and intellectually challenging than merely count and catalogue the flowers of meaning in the garden?"[9] He answers his own question by shifting our gaze from the meaning to the meaning-making: "I suggest to my students that we might learn a lot more about religious meanings by paying attention not so much to the flowers in the garden but to the gardener and the gardener's human processes of planting, cultivating, fencing off, and reaping meanings" (171).

Preoccupation with determining such meaning, as in the case of deciding what Springsteen's or Mellencamp's songs are *really* about, or which Biblical interpretation is morally sound, thus requires the arbitrary elevation and acceptance of one provincial set of rules to the self-appointed status of the absolute – an elevation authorized by appeals to our "careful" and "close" reading of the text's "deep structures", where text is assumed to be a unified and homogenous document in a one-to-one correspondence with "what actually happened" or "what an author actually thought and intended." It is a reading that, as Foucault pointed out some time ago, equates "meaning" with "finality" (1990: 153), a profoundly anti-historicist association. Although it may be understandable that the people we call religious use their texts in this fashion – endeavoring to be ever "faithful to the text" or to the "author's intentions" or to the text's "spirit" – this is precisely what the study of religion has traditionally been about as well. As phrased most recently by Jonathan Smith, the discipline has been propelled by

> the etymological conviction, still regnant, that there is something of surpassing value hidden "beneath" the words, a something that is essential, as opposed to the verbally accidental, and that may be uncovered only by decipherment.
>
> (2001b: 134)

Instead of holding what Smith here characterizes as the "rhetorical conviction that values the givenness of the 'real' concealed 'behind' the words," would it not be more interesting to focus on the problem of meaning-making, what Smith called "verbal accidents," and ask such questions as, "How could this one song or this one text *be made to mean* such different things for such different listeners and readers?" In both the case of politically conservative and liberal pundits, "Born in the U.S.A." is liked and the song is played and purchased, but for very different reasons; those reasons are indicative of interests and varied interests reproduce varied socio-political worlds, which in turn provide the structural context that makes possible further interests and interpretations. So, as phrased by Tim Murphy:

> "What consciousness does on its own is of no consequence," said the young Marx. ... [C]onsciousness is neither cause nor interesting effect of what religion is or does. The issue is signification, not the awareness of signification; the issue is the rules which govern meaningfulness, not the

ontogenetic appropriation of these rules; the issue is how things mean not how they come to mean for a particular person or group.

(forthcoming)

If these things scholars call text, ritual, myth, etc., are behavioral sites where rhetorical rules are enacted and policed, sites where groups are continually remade, then it follows that varying contents can be attached to the same myth-ritual-text complexes, so that in different discourses contents of assorted political stripe will be authorized by means of common techniques. After all, an appeal to "the will of the gods" says nothing about just what this "will" might be. As already suggested, in the history of the U.S., such a rhetoric helped to normalize the institution of slavery but it also helped to legitimize the civil rights movement. Although, for what are no doubt a host of happenstance factors, I happen to side with the latter over the former, I can still recognize that the persuasiveness of my position has little to do with some inherent logic, morality, or its obvious correctness but, rather, to such structural factors as changing rhetorical situations, changing demographics, and changing socio-political interests, changing economic forces, etc. While the content changes, these structural forms and factors endure. We should therefore not be surprised to see the same techniques up and running throughout culture: up to this point we have seen them at work in Memorial Day celebrations, Staal's study of Vedic ritual, popular music, and Biblical interpretation. Elsewhere I referred in passing to the case of former U.S. Vice President Al Gore's answer to a 2000 town hall audience question about the way he makes foreign policy decisions; as I recall it, he said something like, "I ask myself, 'What would Jesus do?'" And then there was George W. Bush's remark during a Republican primary debate that same year concerning "Jesus Christ" being the "political philosopher" who had most influenced him. How so? "Because he changed my heart" was his reply. Whether intended or not, these are masterful, political answers; they work well because, in the middle of a Presidential primary debate (or, for that matter, in the middle of any debate or even a conversation around the proverbial office water cooler), no one is going to stand up and say, "Hey, wait a minute; when you mentioned Jesus just now, did you mean Crossan's Jewish peasant, or maybe Borg's subversive sage, possibly Meier's Jesus with four brothers and at least two sisters, Mack's wandering cynic, Funk's 'Jewish Socrates,' or maybe you meant Johnson's 'real Jesus' who defies all historical specificity?" Substantive (a.k.a. subversive) questions like that just are not asked in polite society; much like "character-" or "values-talk," "Jesus-talk" works extremely well in our public discourse. It has no need to clarify any specific content for, being utterly devoid of specific content, *it means all things to all people*. Although later chapters will tackle the popular but troublesome notion of "civil religion," Robert Bellah was correct when, over thirty years ago, he observed that the public use of God-talk was effective precisely because it "means so many different things to so many different people that it is almost an empty sign" (1990: 170).[10] Or, to phrase it another way, if you have to ask "Which Jesus?", then you damn well know that you've got the wrong Jesus. Should one wish to be counted among the members of the group, then the only appropriate response to the use of such codes is to avoid contesting the level of content and simply nod your head knowingly and in silent agreement.[11]

Because the rhetoric concerning the utter uniqueness of the ivory tower has always struck me as just as misleading and self-serving – both for those whom it protects and for those who wish to dismiss what academia contributes to wider social life – one would expect to see these same rhetorical techniques up and running in academe as well. Case in point: in 1997 I was fortunate to have an article accepted for publication by the *Journal of the American Academy of Religion* (1997a). Apart from receiving several kind emails from readers of that article (sent mostly by younger scholars, mind you), I received an angry email from a scholar at Pepperdine University. Given that I had argued in that essay that the scholar of religion came not to inform the world on deep meanings and transcendent truths, he basically asked why "the good people of Springfield" (the city where I lived and taught at that time) were even paying me to do what I do. Presuming that religion was somehow an essentially good force, or at least an other-worldly and therefore utterly extraordinary impulse with whose true nature he was apparently all too familiar, my correspondent took offense at my suggestion that religion was an ordinary component of socio-political existence and, as such, was susceptible to the very same methods of research used throughout the rest of the human sciences. Despite continued debates concerning whether Plato's writings constitute philosophy proper or an extended political manifesto (and whether these two are even different to begin with), my email correspondent presumed that the nature of "the good" had been settled long ago and that scholars in the employ of taxpayers should be getting on with the business of realizing that good in public life.

I cite this personal example because this email tells us much about writing theory from the demographic, if not political, margins within academia. As I have concluded from other responses, representatives of the dominant discourse in our field are easily able to suspend the usual requirements of scholarly discourse when responding to work that arises from an oppositional or minority position (see McCutcheon 2001b: 145 ff.). While the members of a dominant group are the ones to establish and police the normally transparent rules by which the game of academia is played (think, if you will, of the conformity established by the institution of peer evaluation as used in refereeing journal articles, or the fact that lesser known writers sometimes must submit a copy of their c.v. along with their submissions to journals and conferences, or even the time honored tradition of reference letters – what the cultured elite once called "letters of introduction"), they are also the first to suspend these rules when it suits their purposes. The irony – I will not call it an "injustice" for it could not be otherwise – is clear: in supporting their work with appeals to evidence and argumentation, critics are easily dismissed for being too "aggressive" and not playing nice despite the supposedly "come one, come all" nature of the liberal, public square. Form not only wins out over content, it establishes the environment in which claims are allowed to be understood as meaningful or persuasive. Offer the wrong response, wink when you should nod, bow when you should curtsy, and the gatekeepers will collect up their toys and go home, taking their context with them.

What have I learned in all this about the rhetoric of the discipline and the politics of writing from the provinces? Well, for one thing, recommending that scholars study religion as an all too human practice – rather than a private experience – does not win you friends either among Christian theologians (who study religion as a transcendent message inspired by a fleeting Holy Spirit) or liberal humanists (who study religion as the expression of some timeless Human Spirit). In the words of the literary critic, Stanley Fish – writing on the tactics employed by seemingly well-meaning types who, nonetheless police the status quo –

> the guardians of orthodoxy rise up in a combination of outrage and incredulity – outrage at the very fact of an assault on truths so perspicuous that no one could, or should, deny them; incredulity at the spectacle of intelligent credentialed men and women who seem unaccountably to have forgotten what everyone knows and shouldn't have to say. (1999: 52)

These guardians presume that those behaviors we call religion are informed by a special impulse or feeling that is somehow manifested in human affairs (they've dutifully read their Schleiermacher, Otto, Tillich, and Eliade). The origin of this impulse is variously known as God, the Sacred, Meaning, or Human Nature. Despite the fact that, as one moves across the list – moving from God to Human Nature – there appears to be an apparent declining "religiosity," or increasing secularity, to these posited sources of impulses, they are but different names for the same thing, or, to be more precise, clever names that refer to nothing. After all, suggestions that religion is an ordinary rhetorical device are met with condemnation – not too strong a word, I think – from both the religious/political left *and* the religious/political right, indicating that, despite their apparent differences, some foundational presumption or technique shared by both must be in jeopardy.

What these otherwise different viewpoints share is that in each case the historical, material world of happenstance human doings is being portrayed as the local setting of necessary and cosmic events that defy re-presentation and expression, events that are understandable only within the context of the lone human being's interior life. For example, when it comes to talking about this thing religion – in the words of a U.S. Supreme Court Justice Stewart – it is generally thought by those on both sides of the political divide to inhabit "the inviolable citadel of the individual heart and mind";[12] what we have here is a classic example of Liberalism. By intentionally choosing the uppercase "L" I mean to make clear that

I am not talking about liberal as opposed to conservative political positions as we today define them (e.g., classifying people based on whether they argue for more or less "big government"), but, rather, to the wider and older political philosophy presupposed by both contemporary liberals and conservatives alike.

Liberalism denotes a tradition of political thought that understands human beings as: (i) individual moral agents who ought to be free of, or who can rise above, essentially oppressive structural constraints, and as (ii) reducible to universal yet interior mental or emotive processes. To appeal to Fish once again, in Liberalism

> what counts is the moment of private inspiration in which the superior consciousness rises above its surroundings and proclaims an atemporal truth. ... [T]he person is [thereby] reduced, or exalted, to the status of pure mind, a bodiless agent whose paradigmatic act is the act either of forming an expression or expressing it. Everything else is accidental, in the strict philosophical sense; everything else is dross.
>
> (50)

When first reading that passage – a passage which, for Fish, characterizes the supposedly apolitical stance of traditional literary criticism's quest for the essence of creativity and meaning of Literariness – three things immediately came to mind: (i) the writings of countless phenomenologists of religion intent on "taking religion seriously" by personalizing some aspect of contestable human practice, thus removing some "it" from history; (ii) the current popularity of equating the academic study of religion to the practice of religious pluralism, an effort which resolves material diversity and dissent by appealing to the abstract universality of some disembodied "faith," "drive," or "hope" we all supposedly share; and (iii) the infectiously quaint nationalistic paintings of Norman Rockwell, specifically, his "Freedom of Speech," a 1943 cover of the *Saturday Evening Post*.[13] Despite going some distance to quiet the guilt of those who occupy positions of privilege and to soothe those who do not, none of these strike me as particularly appealing since they effectively gloss over the role played by material difference and contestation, as well as the effects of unanticipated structural imposition in human affairs, while rushing to resolve conflict by arguing its existence away.

Given my own personal politics, I happen to agree with the substance of some of the claims (content) that assorted theologians and humanists authorize by their appeals to the rhetorics of faith or Human Nature (form). But, because I have no idea how to adjudicate the truth of either their or my own claims, *as a scholar of religion* I am a little more timid than they are in making grandiose claims about the sort of Human Nature that somehow unites all people (past, present, and future) with little old me.[14] Knowing the trouble second-wave feminists got into when Third World women and women of color stood up to say that they did not recognize themselves in these generally upper class, Euro-

North American, white feminists' claims about "woman," one would think that today we as scholars would be a little more timid in making such universal claims about "the triumph of the Human Spirit." Armed with the hunch that parts all too easily slide into Wholes, some scholars of religion focus their attention instead on the way groups negotiate the distinctions of fact/value, contingent/necessary, History/Nature, and local/universal. Or, to phrase it more accurately, because they understand value to be fundamentally a negotiable, historic item, they are intrigued by the manner in which material interests are encoded in supposedly timeless values and principles – values and principles which all too obviously arise from specific, provincial situations but which are used as if they were atemporal, established truths with application in all possible situations.

With a tip of the hat to the reflexive anthropologists, I thus accept that claims to knowledge are tactical and conditional and that they are based on perspective, on viewpoint, on interests; the "close" reader will have already seen that I do not fear using the first person singular pronoun. However, because my viewpoint is not necessarily yours and because social life is not homogenous, I also maintain that those who occupy one local position may see something that others do not, making incremental social change, even active resistance, a very real possibility. Even Foucault, whom some have criticized as having a deterministic or nihilistic social anthropology that makes social change impossible, made it clear that both the state and the self are the site of multiple, fractured, and potentially competing disciplines – competition which allows for change and effective opposition. To elaborate on an example I have used elsewhere (2001b: 107–108), although people become tennis players insomuch as they act within a specific set of rules, neither are all people acting within that one rule set nor are tennis players acting only within that one rule set even when they *are* acting as tennis players. To pick an easy example, high profile players are also simultaneously acting like business people, celebrities, and, if their frequent glances to their coaches and family members in the stands mean anything, they are also acting like students, sons and daughters, and lovers. Although we are all insiders to various socio-semantic worlds, they are not all the same world and multiple overlapping worlds are always present. So, "as much as we are all immersed within a framework, we are not all swimming in the same conceptual pond" (McCutcheon 1991: 256). To know anything is therefore to know just a bit of something and certain bits are produced within, and productive of, certain institutional places. For instance, I try to persuade my students that, despite living in the age of so-called inclusivity, the utility of a definition is in its ability to exclude items from consideration. This act of exclusion (call it focus, if you will) is, of course, directed by one's pre-observational theoretical context as well as one's political interests. I think of Nietzsche at this point, who argued in section one of the second essay in his *On the Genealogy of Morals* (1969) that knowledge is the product of necessary exclusion, making totalized knowledge an ideological fantasy. The part (empirical) is hardly the Whole (a non-empirical reification) but we continually overlook the gap between them, to the advantage of the groups whose interests we pursue.

If, as Foucault argued, "[d]isciplines have for their function the reduction of gaps" (1977a: 179), then what is so utterly fascinating about human beings is the manner in which we deploy a host of such disciplinary techniques, without noticing them, to deal with the inevitable gaps between parts and Wholes (whether the "we" is constituted by so-called religious fundamentalists, moral absolutists, nationalists, scientists intent on unlocking Nature's code, or members of a bowling team). Instead, there is an admirable certainty encoded within the manner in which most people enact – myself included – a certainty that, when seen against the background of what I assume to be the ad hoc nature of the physical/cognitive world, is profoundly interesting. How is it that just this opinion, just that behavior, just these narrative sequences, or just this way or organizing ourselves gets sanctioned and reproduced? How does one go about making the move from a viewpoint to The Viewpoint? How is it that a part (and which part?) gets portrayed and authorized as the Whole? I happen to think that not only the social practices that we group together as religion have something important to do with this but, more importantly perhaps, the very presumption that these practices ought to be grouped together as religion plays a role as well. To rephrase, the very activity of grouping together and classifying this or that *as* religion (whatever the content of the "this or that" may be) is among the most important of all disciplinary techniques.

If you think that in making these claims I am criticizing religion and self-identified religious people, saying that "anything goes" in our relativistic universe, or that my own analysis of religion finally wins the day as true and accurate, then you have taken my text in directions of your own. For, as I wrote elsewhere, the role of culture critic entails being a bit like Dorothy's dog, Toto; culture critics fully participate in, but also peek behind, the curtains that normally pass for just part of the scenery; they look for what makes the scene possible, the manner in which we make things stand out as significant.[15] Now, of course we cannot live without benign scenery passing unnoticed in the background – who but a madman could give equal attention to all pieces of sensory information? But every now and then someone will stumble into town and see the scenery not as inevitable but, due to his/her peculiar perspective, as the contingent context that makes differing places conceivable, a view that makes it possible to represent "mere scenery" in a new way, as the medium that allows different organizations of the all-too-ordinary-world to come into relation, rise to dominance, be contested, and pass out of being; in the process, something stands out for a short while as meaningful and familiar.

It is this itinerant critic who treats our claims, our behaviors, and our institutions as artful, ad hoc, inventive, accidental, marvelous, mundane, and, most important of all, historical and thus political re-presentations that briefly transform the ordinary into the extraordinary, the unruly into the manageable, the isolated into the unified, and the self into the nation. The following chapters attempt to do just this at a variety of otherwise routine sites in the discipline of religion, addressing not only the problem of how talking about "religion" becomes meaningful but how it helps to make certain sorts of people meaningful and credible. It did this – better put, a relatively small group of people disenfranchised from other dominant groups helped to make themselves and others *into* a new group – by artfully fabricating a rhetorical and institutional zone and doggedly patrolling its boundaries against incursions mounted from out here in the territories. In a previous work (1997b) I focused my analysis on the technique of conceiving of religion as an utterly unique object. I now realize that this is but one of many interconnected rhetorical devices that deserve further scrutiny. For, along with the much repeated rhetoric of uniqueness we also find the related jargons of centers, experience, indigeneity, expertise, mystery, crisis, evil, and authenticity. In tackling these rhetorics as they circulate in one academic field I have in mind a remark of Foucault's: "For those of my generation, meaning does not appear on its own, it is not 'already there,' or rather, 'it is there already,' yes, but under a certain number of conditions which are formal conditions" (1999: 88). Not taking meaning for granted, this book, then, is a further step toward examining some of those formal conditions of meaning-making at a specific site. It therefore presses writers such as U.S. Supreme Court Justice Stewart in a new direction for, when he goes on to conclude in his 1963 school prayer majority decision, "We have come to recognize through bitter experience that it is not within the power of government to invade that citadel," my reply is that it may well turn out that governments in modern social democracies not only construct the domain of the citadel in the first place, but that the fiction of the private citadel's autonomy and interiority, much like the fiction of a cloistered nun's piety, is a necessary political device for the smooth running of a certain form of national government. This book is thus an effort to begin to assemble Lease's catalogue for grappling with social breakdowns. It attempts to collect a "treasury of devices, techniques, ideas, and procedures … [all of which] constitute, or help to constitute, a certain point of view"; it is my hope that amassing such a catalogue "can be a very useful tool for analyzing what's going on now – and to change it" (Dreyfus and Rabinow 1983: 236).

Notes

1 Delivered in New York's Town Hall Auditorium, January 22, 2002, and broadcast on CSPAN's "Book TV." The speech was sponsored by the U.S. media watch group, Fairness and Accuracy in Reporting (FAIR).
2 See Judith Perkins (1995) for a persuasive account of how discursive pre-conditions enable humans to think and experience their subjectivity. The social nature of experience is argued in further detail in McCutcheon 2001b: 7–8.
3 See McCutcheon 2001b: 210–211 for a similar analysis of the alternative rock group Blues Traveler's equally complex and self-referential song, "Hook."
4 Although Ross's book can be read as a politically liberal challenge to the exclusive right of Jewish "ultra-orthodox authorities" to set standards of group status and membership – hence making his book an example of the insider "bump and grind" I

am describing – his attempt to shift the question from the presumption of stable identities to social processes whereby identities are contested is still a useful example of the shift I am advocating. My thanks to my colleague, Steve Jacobs, for bringing Ross's book to my attention and for hosting Ross at the University of Alabama for a public lecture (January 2002).

5 In her 1999 article, in which she replies to Robert Sharf's earlier claims (e.g., 1998) that discourses on experience in Buddhism were European imports, Gyatso draws on a rich Tibetan literature on experience as evidence that such discourses are not solely the product of imperialism. However, she does not contest his conclusion that rhetorics of experience are boundary maintenance mechanisms; her article is mainly a description of, and commentary upon, Tibetan Buddhist understandings of experience. For a useful survey on approaches to the problem of religious experience, and the growing field of cognitive studies of religion, see Andresen 2001 (especially the editor's introduction).

6 Instead of mere reporting, such an analysis (or theory-based redescription) of these participant claims would help to make sense of why pollsters, merely repeating participant self-disclosures, conclude that "Americans are among the most religious people on earth" (Fuller 2001: 154). If, as my later chapters argue, the discourse on religion and faith are linked to the rise of the nation-state and maintenance of large scale social identities, then who would be surprised to learn that the most successfully reproducible modern nation-state is among the most "religious" nations on earth?

7 As I have cited in print before, the tongue-in-cheek term, "hermeneutical vortex," was coined in Michael Pye (ed.), *The Continuum Dictionary of Religion* (New York: Continuum Publishing Co., 1994).

8 Braun is citing Gellner 1992: 50.

9 At this point, his endnote reads: "Even Clifford Geertz, among the very best hermeneutic anthropologists, spoofs this gathering and appreciation effort as an exercise in going 'round the world to count the cats in Zanzibar' (1993: 16)" (Braun 2001a: n. 13). Geertz's quotation – citing Thoreau's own comment from the conclusion to *Walden*, "It is not worth the while to go round the world to count the cats in Zanzibar" (n.d.: 283) – is useful here for it emphasizes the sheer arbitrariness of studying just this, and not that, meaning. However, Thoreau's original comment pertained not to arbitrariness but to the uselessness of searching in faraway, overseas, and exotic climes when the real focus of each person's search ought to be directed inward, to "obey the precept of the old philosopher, and Explore thyself" (284). "What is the meaning of that South-Seas Exploring Expedition," he asks rhetorically, "but an indirect recognition of the fact that there are continents and seas in the moral world, to which every man is an isthmus or an inlet, yet unexplored by him" (283). Thoreau thus represents the very concern with enduring and universal self that this book seeks to problematize.

10 I would add that it is an empty sign. Jean-Jacques Rousseau, to whom we trace the concept "civil religion," was cognizant of this as well: "The dogmas of civil religion," he wrote in Book IV, chapter 8, of *The Social Contract* (1762), "must be simple and few in number, expressed precisely and without explanations or commentaries" (1982: 186). For elaboration, see chapter 12 of the present book.

11 That not all U.S. voters are appreciative of public references to "Jesus" is more than obvious. Demographics dictate, however, that such rhetorics are powerful, the alienation they prompt in some voters notwithstanding.

12 These words can be found in Justice Stewart's majority decision in the case of Abington v. Schempp (374 US 203 [1963]) – the U.S.'s classic "school prayer" case. Fish's second chapter, "Sauce for the Goose" (1999: 34–45) wonderfully demonstrates the manner in which this rhetoric privileges religion within such an air tight

zone of isolated human experience so as to ensure that any normative claims as to how the world ought to work which arise from a so-called religious discourse will easily be brushed aside by Liberal claims to represent the public, inclusive good over exclusivist, private intuitions and matters of conscience.

13 This well-known painting shows a confident looking, flannel-shirted, working-class man standing alone, speaking his mind at what appears to be a town hall meeting. He is surrounded by seated people stretching their necks to watch and listen to him, two of whom are men who are likely of a higher class since they are wearing jackets and ties.

14 Note that liberal humanists talking about "human nature" are hardly interested in the easily observed empirical, biological, and behavioral similarities that are commonly used to differentiate *Homo sapiens sapiens* from other animal species. Although it may seem fairly safe to assume that ancient peoples procreated, were born, digested food, excreted, and died in much the same manner as my contemporaries, moving from this apparently brute biological similarity to positing some non-empirical commonality, meaning, or value that transcends the differences of space and time is another matter altogether. Although we might all have tear ducts, we don't necessarily all cry at the same thing or "mean" the same thing by our tears. In fact, liquid flowing from tear ducts is not always crying. So, if by "the human condition" one means "man's [sic] quest for meaning," then this is something entirely different from the utterly neutral, biological imperatives of birth, change, and death.

15 It is telling that Blues Traveler drew explicitly on the wizard behind the curtain in the music video for their song, "Runaround," in which the band was hidden off-stage, playing and singing for a front band comprised of suitably stylish but untalented rockers.

Chapter 2

God's people defending their ivory towers

Reassessing the study of religion's emergence in the U.S.

The place of the study of religion within the modern publicly funded university is a topic that continues to provoke discussion. The debate is greatly complicated by the failure of some participants to discriminate between religion and the study of religion as special cases and those things we call religion and the study of religion as simply being subsets of ordinary, human practices. In one form or another, this debate has raged for quite a number of years and shows no signs of dying down anytime soon. As in the case of many intellectual and/or academic controversies of this nature, some clarification of the argument can be found in tracing a bit of its history and vocabulary, determining more precisely the lines of the conflict and just what has been, and perhaps remains, at stake for either side. This and the following chapter will attempt just that, looking first at the early-twentieth-century emergence of the field in the U.S. and its subsequent re-emergence in the late 1950s and 1960s.

Although there have been a number of recent books addressing the discipline's initial North American emergence and the continuing controversy over the role of religion in public education (e.g., Cherry 1995; Hart 1999; Marsden 1994; Nord 1995), in this chapter I wish to examine just one particular account: Robert Shepard's *God's People in the Ivory Tower: Religion in the Early American University* (1991). Despite Shepard's own analysis of the field's emergence in the early parts of this century, I believe his work provides valuable data for rewriting this history in light of rhetoric and access to resources.

Shepard plots the institutional history of the early years of religious studies programs in six American institutions: Boston University, Cornell University, New York University, University of Pennsylvania, University of Chicago, and the Harvard Divinity School. While devoting his first chapter to a brief historical survey of the somewhat lesser known early programs at the first four schools, Shepard reserves the bulk of his text for a more detailed examination of the promising rise and eventual decline of the early-twentieth-century programs at Chicago and Harvard. After analyzing the pivotal roles played by the founders of these two schools in bringing their own comparative religion programs into existence (William Rainey Harper at Chicago and Charles W. Eliot at Harvard), the training and meager employment opportunities of their graduates (a sadly familiar tale for contemporary Ph.D.s; see chapter 6 in this book), and the motivations and research interests of their faculties, Shepard concludes his study with a chapter chronicling the conflicts and cooperations between these early, and largely unsuccessful, *Religionswissenschaft* programs (roughly translated as " the science of religion" though, in the U.S., often trans-lated as "history of religions," as in *Religionsgeschichte*) and their long established divinity school counterparts.

Shepard's analysis is an attempt to investigate more closely the well-known and suggestive interpretations of the rise and fall of the early field made by such writers as Joseph Kitagawa, Erwin R. Goodenough, and Eric Sharpe. Conventional wisdom has it that the initial success of American comparative religion – relying as it did upon the crucial European advances and liberal Protestant optimism for the essential complementarity between science and religion – quickly gave way in the 1930s to the spirit of Christian exclusivism and neo-orthodoxy. This decline in the early North American field has in turn been linked to the social pessimism that followed World War I and the Depression, a pessimism that anticipated the impending second European war. By examining the early years at these six American institutions, Shepard intends to "narrow the gap" in the historical knowledge of how the young disci-pline was nurtured, yet, unfortunately, not weaned. To accomplish this goal requires not simply such generalized social reasons as those offered above but, in Shepard's words, a systematic examination of the "institutional and social envi-ronments of the people who tried to push ahead the discipline" (8). It is precisely this analysis that promises to set his study apart from the others.

Because, in Shepard's opinion, the nature of this gap in our knowledge surrounding the fate of the young discipline is primarily the result of the failure to integrate the personal, institutional, as well as the social influences of the era, the most profitable method to employ to close it is the sociology of knowl-edge. So, as Shepard puts it, his aim is to make a contribution to the "broader question of the relationship of knowledge to its social context. Scholars do not formulate ideas ... in a vacuum" (6). Although he does employ a comparative method – specially useful in the more detailed case histories of Harvard and Chicago – despite his interest in context, Shepard's study relies mostly upon an individual narrative history of each successive university based upon assorted biographies, institutional histories, personal correspondence, enrolment statis-tics, and academic publications relevant to the school in question. His variation on the sociology of knowledge approach mainly yields information on the rela-tionship between the beliefs and careers of *individuals* – be they philanthropists, administrators, teachers, or students – and the programs they founded or with which they were involved.

Unfortunately, this method precludes from the outset questions concerning the influence of the larger socio-political world of which these individuals and programs were a part, making Shepard's contribution to the sociology of knowl-edge more akin to a history of great men and their great ideas (though a limited number of women do figure in the story). Apparently, events in the structural environment (i.e., the economic, political, and cultural world) of the university played little or no part in the lives of these individuals (i.e., content wins out over form). For example, the relationship between the malaise of the post-World War I European world, increasing U.S. isolationism, and the rise of neo-orthodoxy is not explored, nor is the fate of costly education during bleak fiscal times; all are serious shortcomings when he turns his attention to discerning the significance of such data as student enrolment statistics. While acknowledging that such methods as intellectual history, institutional history, and the sociology of knowledge are interrelated, it is not altogether clear from the outset which of these Shepard intends to practice. Like many scholars of religion who emphasize personal beliefs and individual agency over social practices and structure, his emphasis falls upon the association between personal beliefs and the shape of institutions and curricula and thus leaves largely untouched the structural connections between material interests, socio-rhetorical context, and personal beliefs. In this way, his history of the field counts as entirely orthodox.

What *is* clear (and of great use) is that Shepard has gathered much evidence to track the initial and possibly premature excitement with which North American scholars welcomed the new European science. I say *North* American since some of the early faculty at Chicago, such as George B. Foster and A. Eustace Haydon, were Canadian Baptists originally trained at McMaster University, then situated in Toronto (and now in Hamilton, Ontario). In the case of Haydon, he received four degrees from McMaster between 1901 and 1907 before entering the ministry at the First Baptist Church of Saskatoon, Saskatchewan. Besides reading the work of European scholars such as F. Max Müller, many of these young teachers had been trained in Europe. For instance, Morris Jastrow of Pennsylvania studied under C. P. Tiele at Leiden in the Netherlands and George S. Goodspeed of Chicago studied at Freiburg in Germany.

One point put strongly by Shepard is the reliance of these young programs on the energy and personal appeal of a solitary, enthusiastic, and charismatic teacher – often ultimately to the detriment of the institution since, with their inevitable retirement or untimely death, the programs often were thrown into complete turmoil. For example, following William F. Warren's retirement at Boston University, his courses were shuttled among indifferent successors until the comparative religion program was reorganized and placed within, predictably perhaps, the Missionary Grouping of the Divinity school. And at Chicago, Goodspeed's early death ended his enthusiastic reorganization of the comparative religion program, which then, due in part to poor staffing (A. E. Haydon eventually became the head of the department and its sole lecturer for a number of years), slowly slipped out of the arts and sciences faculty and into – where else? – the theological school, once again as a supplement to the already existing Christian missions program. Lack of internal cohesiveness throughout the emergent discipline, as evinced by the lack of professional associations, avenues for publication, and standardized curricula, is surely to blame for the isolation of these spirited yet marginalized teachers. Such cohesiveness does not spring from nowhere and it is hardly to be expected in the case of an emergent group. However, since the North American discipline did triumph, some decades later, a question arises concerning just why it did eventually succeed in establishing and successfully reproducing a group identity. The opening chapters to this book will attempt to account for this by arguing that, over the course of several decades, practitioners of this emergent discipline gained significant ground by slowly and efficiently appropriating the very rhetorical techniques that their intellectual predecessors had battled against. As the old saying goes, "if you can't beat 'em, join 'em."[1]

Although he does not make the parallel explicit, Shepard does make his reader aware that the early enthusiasm of many of the initial administrators and teachers was accompanied by their pronounced disillusionment with, and alienation from, various forms of organized American Christianity. While virtually all those individuals whom Shepard examines were ordained ministers of one Protestant denomination or another, most intentionally left the confines of the institutional church in search of the intellectual and social freedom they believed could be found in an academic environment. Be it from their unwelcome and untimely critical views on supposed Christian superiority, their attraction to the historical-critical method, or, as in the case of Goodspeed, their dismal ministerial talents,[2] all of them were displaced from their own social worlds in one way or another, which made of them the raw material for a potentially emergent group.[3] Even in the case of such empire builders as Chicago's Harper and Harvard's Eliot, their profound sense of the unity of science and religion, or their belief in the essential complementarity of the world's religions, placed them significantly at odds with the accepted doctrines and practices of their own denominations. Eric Sharpe provides a useful example of such disillusionment with organized Christianity – Roman Catholicism in particular – in the case of Müller himself: he was a member of the Church of England largely because of its "greater freedom and more immunity from priestcraft," believing, as he did, in the inevitable decline of religion as a result of institutionalism (Sharpe 1986: 39). What we have here is an instance of the socio-rhetorical theory's presumption that emergent groups arise from onetime dominant but now disenfranchised groups. The early rise of the North American field is evidence of just such an episode in disintegration/reintegration, both on the level of the people who provided leadership in the early discipline but also on the level of the nation in which the discipline took effect.

With this second, structural level of disintegration/reintegration in mind, let me take a step back from Shepard's analysis for a moment to sketch the background of the argument I am trying to make, one to which we return more explicitly in this book's final chapters. What I am trying to suggest is that in early-twentieth-century America we can find some socio-political changes taking place that also took place in Europe four hundred years earlier. In both cases these changes were in part made evident in (and made possible by) a discursive contest between differing parties vying for control over the rhetoric of religion and the public authority that comes with such control. In other words, I believe there is a link between managing an emerging empire and the rhetoric of religion. The sort of social, economic, and political realignments that characterized the shift from feudalism to the invention of the early European nation-state have a rough parallel in the sort of social, economic, and political realignments that characterized the early twentieth century in the U.S. For it was during this period that the U.S.'s onetime policy of isolationism and only regional influence developed into a nascent worldwide, hegemonic role, one that escalated dramatically after World War II and which, after the end of the Cold War and under the guise of globalization, has now taken on truly global overtones. Shepard's study places us at the earliest phases of this change/contest. In both the case of early-twentieth-century America and early-sixteenth-century Europe, smaller-scale social groupings were coalescing (sometimes violently) and in the process were readjusting to the newfound ability to stretch what may have once been but one of many local identities (e.g., the members of many large and even mid-sized cities all over sixteenth-century Europe who saw themselves as belonging to an independent republic) over increasingly large and diverse populations and land masses (or, more likely, preparing to relinquish the sense of republican autonomy). We could add to this mix the late nineteenth century, when, along with comparative religion first taking shape as a discipline, we also find the European powers stretched out across the globe. Whether or not a newly discovered (a.k.a. conquered) group had a religion, a degraded form of the Christian religion, or a primitive form of Christianity was but one of the means to classify, cognicize, and thus govern these diverse populations (see Chidester [1996b] for an analysis of the case of southern Africa). Although these various historic periods are hardly identical, in all three cases the public discourse on religion played a significant role in political life – significant enough in the instance from the sixteenth century to necessitate seeing battles over religious doctrine as if they were the primary or even exclusive motive force in history (e.g., what we commonly call the Wars of Religion or contemporary scholars who study the Reformation and church history as if they were purely doctrinal affairs). I am suggesting that it was not a coincidence that the contest over who policed the rhetoric of religion took place in early-twentieth-century America, that comparative religion as a science was contemporaneous with the height of European colonialism, and that the realignment of political power we today call the Reformation took place on the eve of the nation-state's birth. Although I am not suggesting a strict cause/effect relationship, I am suggesting that the discourse on religion provided some of the necessary conditions for such socio-political changes.

In order for us to draw these parallels we must cease presuming that religion necessarily and solely denotes an inner world of unseen power and morality expressed in doctrine or ritual. Instead, we must historicize this very assumption, seeing "religion" instead as a discursive technique used in specific rhetorical situations, a type of social classification with significant political import. With this shift in mind, such things as the Reformation, the so-called religious wars of the mid-sixteenth century, and even F. Max Müller's public lectures in favor of a non-sectarian science of religion, can all be redescribed as practical contests for influence and control of the means of classification, which is none other than the means of producing knowledge. This knowledge proved useful in extending control over lands and populations and was fought in contests in which specific vernaculars and rhetorics proved useful to either side. As an early example of the contest for control of this rhetoric, take the case of the fourteenth-century humanists who successfully opposed scholastics by mastering the so-called classical languages of Greek and Latin, thus by-passing Aristotelean logic and gaining access to the "original meaning" of a text, all as part of their effort to exert control over the public reading, interpretation, and implementation of texts. On their quest for the proper meaning, the original intent, these humanists were able successfully to contest the authority of their confessional peers, an authority evident in the onetime "monopoly over the interpretation of texts claimed by university professors" (Tracy 1999: 44). Along with the obvious case of Erasmus of Rotterdam (1469–1536), Tracy uses as but one example the earlier Italian humanist, Lorenzo Valla (d. 1457), who worked as an independent scholar (thus outside the control of traditional institutions). By means of a different approach to the problem of meaning (i.e., his knowledge of classical languages and his effort to reconstruct what he took to be the historical context of the texts under study), he was able successfully to overturn long-held assumptions about the "proper" meaning of the *Codex of Justinian*, widely used in medieval Europe as the foundation for civil law (Tracy 1999: 44–45). Regardless what the *Codex* does or does not really mean, we see here an early example of how the contest over such things as meaning, origin, and intention was the site at which political contests (e.g., the workings of medieval European civil law) were waged. While I hardly wish to argue that such contests led directly to such a multifarious thing as the Reformation and the modern nation-state, I would argue that the context that made it possible to reorganize the individuals and social groups of feudal Europe into a new series of citizens with inbred national identities had something to do with the tactical skirmishes over what ancient texts meant and what counted as a legitimate interpreter. Much as in the case of the early North American discipline of religion, these skirmishes pitted humanists against confessional theologians.

So, what does this have to do with the classification religion? Well, at roughly this same time, in sixteenth-century Europe we also see the beginning of a significant shift in the manner in which the term "religion" is used. As argued by Jonathan Z. Smith (1998: 270–271), between the sixteenth and eighteenth centuries a change occurred, such that a concept/word that was once reserved for naming behaviors and membership within institutions (e.g., a member of a monastic order was once known as "a religious") comes to be universalized, interiorized, and thus privatized. A suitable example would be the onetime Greek professor and Luther's Wittenberg spokesman, Philip Melanchton (d. 1560), who, in 1549, gave assent to the partial restoration of Roman Catholic liturgy. "He did so," writes Tracy, "because he believed that outer forms of worship were 'indifferent things' [Greek: *adiaphora*] that could be accepted if essential doctrine was not compromised" (1999: 93). Obviously connected with the practical successes of various sixteenth-century Reformers' rhetorics (e.g., the subversion of an institution by privileging the lone reader accomplished by Martin Luther's quest for original meaning [the doctrine of *sola scriptura*] or, as Smith suggests, Huldrych Zwingli's and John Calvin's association of religion with personal piety), Smith describes how, by the eighteenth century, the onetime ritual, institutional contexts of such commonly found terms as reverence, service, adoration, and worship "have been all but evacuated of ritual connotations, and seem more to denote *a state of mind*" (271; emphasis added). As he then goes on to observe,

> [t]his shift to belief as the defining characteristic of religion (stressed in the German preference for the term *Glaube* over *Religion*, used in the increasingly English usage of 'faiths' as a synonym for 'religions') raised a host of interrelated questions of credibility and truth.

As Smith suggests, by shifting the ground from ritual to faith, from observable practice and institution to private feeling and sentiment, a whole new set of criteria were needed to adjudicate not the properness of following the prescribed ritual behaviors but the supposed authenticity, truth, or depth of one's experience. And of course, along with these new criteria came new institutions in which these criteria were debated, canonized, and applied, along with new collections of authenticity experts who interpreted and implemented the rules, as well as new forms of prescribed behaviors. Recalling Lease's thoughts on the need for a history of "religion" that could "trace how and why a culture or epoch allows certain experiences to count as 'religion' while excluding others" (1994: 472), we have here an early instance of the manner in which the very public and obviously political rhetoric of privatized faith and experience proved to be a highly effective means by which to organize an emergent, oppositional group intent on unseating long-established institutions, centers of political power, and modes of behavior and social organization.

This shift on the part of those marginal to, and thus disenfranchised from, the centers of traditional authority – a shift that demoted uniform exterior practice (e.g., ritual, institution, social rank, etc.) to the status of mere "indifferent things" by means of a rhetoric of interiorized faith (all of which is eerily reminiscent of William James's first Gifford Lecture, in which he criticized "conventional observances" as being mere secondhand, dull habits, and also similar to the phenomenological distinction between essence and manifestation) – was thus a useful rhetorical and political move for negotiating competing senses of credibility, rank, legitimacy, and value. It provided an escape from a dominant environment while also providing an alternative basis for authorizing oppositional meaning and for contesting identities. Given that the slow shift to the nation-state required tools for reclassifying, reorganizing, and remanaging ever more diverse and widely scattered populations, the universalization and privatization provided by the discourse on faith proved an effective technique of social engineering.

If this shift from confessional to humanistic scholarship, and the shift from understanding religion as a public mode of social organization to defining it as a personal feeling (what amounts to the move from a classical to a modern sense of *pietas*) occurred along with the sorts of dramatic shifts in social organization indicative of Europe in the sixteenth and seventeenth centuries, then perhaps the contests in early-twentieth-century America between Divinity schools and nascent programs in the study of religion can also be read in light of the practical demands placed on the growing (in this case, U.S.) nation-state. These demands ranged from an increasingly diverse population at home to dramatic changes in geo-political and economic clout. This was a context in which the apparently traditional Protestant hegemony was not up to the role it once played. A new, more widely applicable classification and organizational technique was needed. While the move from a policed orthopraxis to a controlled orthodoxy helped to produce discourses focused on ascertaining truth, the modern nation-state, the site of a dramatic number of potentially competing truth-communities, needed something else to help organize its population. It needed a far more vague, interiorized item and it found just that in meaning or faith. It is within this changing context that I think we can reassess the study of religion's early (and brief) rise in North America in the first decades of this century. It is against this historical background that we ought to read the rhetorical contests between theologians and early historians of religions.

Even though some of the North American field's early-twentieth-century founders may have been disenfranchised from the dominant denominational structure of their times, perhaps sufficient to convince them of the need to ensure that no one religious denomination determine the future of their schools and programs, nevertheless one must not overlook the fact that each university and/or its founders were securely placed within a particular Christian denomination: e.g., Quaker at Cornell and Pennsylvania, Presbyterian at NYU, Baptist at Chicago, and Congregationalist in the case of Harvard. Although challenged by these early comparativists, the denomination system was hardly ready to crumble. Sadly, this tension between stated non-denominationalism and the clearly Protestant Christian ethos is not a topic much explored by Shepard. To be fair to the founders of these schools, their statements that all religions find their ultimate expression in Jesus Christ and the Christian way (a common enough position among a certain element of the scientifically inclined, intellectually elite Christians of the nineteenth century) was radical enough in their day to qualify them as dangerous to the interests of the orthodox ("radicalism," of course, exists along a sliding scale). A case in point is Eliot, whose apparent faith in an immanent deity led him to remark in one of his annual reports, "true Christianity is not a body of doctrines, or an official organization to direct and control men's minds and wills. *It is a way of life*" (Shepard 1991: 53). We see here evidence of the trend Smith identifies as beginning in Europe some two hundred years before: Christianity is no longer defined by appeal to external institution and ritual behavior, and not even in terms of right belief in certain doctrines (beliefs people once seemed to have fought over). No, Christianity is now an inner disposition made manifest in the living of one's life.

To identify such a position with what one would today term the academic study of religion is highly problematic – though many contemporary scholars would likely be persuaded by Eliot's shift. Although there was once a time when one might have distinguished and thus favored non-sectarian yet still religious interpretations over those which were obviously sectarian,[4] one today distinguishes between two rather different options: naturalistic as opposed to non-reductive approaches (whether they are labeled theological or humanistic). If such early figures as those outlined in Shepard's volume are used as exemplars for the modern study of religion, then what one will fashion is a study of religion akin to the work of the non-denominational religious pluralist. Accordingly, the myth of origins told by Shepard is ideally suited to legitimize the work of contemporary liberal caretakers for the nation – the very people who, having been produced by the discipline, are now quite naturally its gatekeepers.

While one cannot rightly demand of Harper or Eliot an interest in matters that preoccupy the contemporary scholar, they did have contemporaries who were quite capable of distinguishing between these two competing approaches. The late Sam Preus, in his widely praised *Explaining Religion* (1987), traces a relatively coherent naturalistic tradition in the study of religion from Jean Bodin (d. 1596) to Freud. The work of still others, including Hume, Durkheim, Feuerbach, and Marx offered competing, naturalistic approaches to the study of religion. Contrary to this competing naturalistic tradition, Shepard's study assumes as normal that the interpretation of religion ought to be religious; i.e., that one studies religion, at least in part, in order to become a better person. Sadly, it is an assumption that goes wholly unquestioned by Shepard. Three minor but noteworthy exceptions in his study come to mind, all of whom appear to have been marginalized by their contemporaries. Two happen to be Jewish – Morris Jastrow, mentioned earlier, and, notably, Abram Isaacs at NYU who wished "to lay the stress on Hebrew as *literature*, not theology," a view which, Isaacs correctly recognized, "was apt to frighten away all but a few [students]" (26) – and the third, a woman named Elizabeth Moon at Chicago, was a doctoral student intent upon studying the relationship between the social sciences and religion. That the social and gender identities of these three people placed them firmly outside the mainstream, perhaps prompting them to be concerned with studying religion in a somewhat different fashion, should not go unnoticed.[5]

This lack of nuance in distinguishing these two different approaches to the study of religion spills over into the way Shepard (like many before him) names the field itself. It is therefore lamentable that he does not devote more attention to the significant (yet perhaps subtle) distinctions between such terms as non-denominational, non-sectarian, *Religionswissenschaft*, history of religions, comparative religion, the scientific study of religion, the academic study of religion, and religious studies; he appears to use various of these interchangeably throughout his text. Even if one grants that the persons he examines made their distinctions based upon criteria wholly different from our own (as in the case of George F. Moore at Harvard, who defended the creation of an "undenominational school of theology"), it still does not justify uncritical repetition of their vaguely defined categories. And even where Shepard attempts some definitional discrimination he does not succeed. As an example, take his comment that, by using the term *Religionswissenschaft* to designate the study established in the nineteenth-century university, he "[i]n no way [implies] a hermeneutical orientation to the study of religion as popularized by the famous historian of religion, Mircea Eliade" (7). After making this point, Shepard fails to elaborate upon how the study of religion in nineteenth-century America was, for lack of a better word, *non-hermeneutical*. Nor does he clarify just what he means when he goes on to characterize the early field as "objective and historical"; for, given the totalizing rhetorics of its early practitioners, this claim makes little sense. Shepard's synonymous use of a variety of terms and meager definitional clarity, while accurately reflecting the confused spirit of our predecessors, does not help the modern student all that much. In other words, by failing to problematize and theorize his data, Shepard's admittedly accurate description of the state of the early discipline hardly helps us to understand the contemporary field any better.

Before leaving the founders of these schools, two points remain to be made. First, in his efforts simply to describe faithfully rather than analyze and theorize his historical subjects as data, it escapes Shepard just how ironic it is that Harper and Eliot, who were so intent upon escaping the confines of institutional religion, became such successful builders of institutional empires of their own. Shepard therefore misses the opportunity to examine further the role alienation plays in emergent social formation. Second, both Harper and Eliot were astute enough to enshrine the new comparative religion within their schools without alienating the established Divinity schools with whom they were each long associated. These two topics deserve much closer study because contesting who had the legitimate voice to discuss "things religious" in public (a contest that equally redefined who got to count as "the public") seems to have been a crucial point at which an emergent institution defined itself in relation to a longstanding institution with which it was in competition for scarce resources. "Religion" – to borrow Foucault's words from another context – thereby comprised "the space that divides them, the void through which they exchange their threatening gestures and speeches" (1977b: 150).

It should be more than apparent that I am not convinced that *God's People in the Ivory Tower* is the "substantive analysis of the rise and decline of the nascent discipline" that its author had hoped it would be. While not wishing to underestimate the important contribution made by his extensive archival research, Shepard's account is far too sympathetic in its portrayal of the early field and offers little explanatory analysis concerning *why*, in Goodspeed's early words, "It ha[d] no ... popular favor behind it" (62). As important as it may be to describe *how* something may have occurred, one cannot conclude the account without attempting to explain *why*. Unlike Kitagawa, who attempts to address extra-academic influences, Shepard provides descriptive evidence of the rise and decline of the early field by means of enrolment figures and the personal correspondence of administrative decision makers, but fails to explain the possible causes of these contributing factors. His approach leaves a variety of questions unasked: What interests kept North American *Religionswissenschaft* from coming of age in the late nineteenth century? What was at stake for those early (and some would add modern) schools of Divinity – their faculty and administrators included – in not allowing new departments for the study of religion to develop? Why was sufficient government or private funding not forthcoming to secure the position of these latest additions to the university? Answering this might, in turn, help us to answer a more vexing question: Why did the funding, both private and public, later begin to flow so freely?

Although Shepard does not explicitly ask such questions, his descriptive data does suggest some interesting possibilities. Reading between the lines, I can take Shepard's history to narrate the failure of *Religionswissenschaft* in its attempts at establishing *credibility*. While interesting and well worth study in themselves, Shepard's reasons for this failure (the young discipline was too dependent upon the charisma and energy of individual teachers and administrators; scholarly associations and publications were not forthcoming; it failed to attract young scholars concerned to make it their life's work while succeeding in attracting a number of persons interested in it purely as a supplementary study), all overlook the pre-conditions of institutional power and influence that may well have ensured such lack of interest and support.

For instance, Shepard appears to assume it natural, or perhaps desirable, that wealthy benefactors played such an explicit role in founding and guiding these early programs. Without critical commentary, Shepard recounts how Henry Sage at Cornell and John D. Rockefeller at Chicago exerted their considerable influence in both the hiring and structural decisions of their respective institutions. The degree to which power, money, and divinity were merged in this era is evident from a story which Franklin I. Gamwell, a recent Dean of the Divinity School at Chicago, approvingly relates about Reverend Frederick T. Gates, the onetime Secretary of the Baptist Education Society who later became John D. Rockefeller's business and philanthropic aide. In his 1988 address welcoming Rockefeller's grandson – himself a benefactor to the Divinity School – Gamwell notes how, when addressing the Board of Trustees who administered the Rockefeller Foundation, the 73-year-old Gates had reminded them that:

> when you die and come to approach the judgment of Almighty God, what do you think he will demand of you? Do you for an instant presume to believe that he will inquire into your petty failures or trivial virtues? No. He will ask just one question: "What did you do as a trustee of the Rockefeller Foundation?"

Even when read as a joke, it is impressive just how successful Gates is in joining belief in God to responsible fiscal management. After going so far as to characterize this attitude as a "spirit of bold purpose," Gamwell reworks the story into an in-house joke, to the benefit of yet a newly dominant group: "for better or for worse, there is a decently large company of us who suspect that the gates of heaven will be guarded by one who asks: 'What did you do as a graduate of The Divinity School?'" (*Criterion* 27 [1988]: 8).

On yet another level, Shepard's description fails to investigate the more elusive instances of power and authority that plagued the early field. Take this quotation from Jastrow, for example:

> I venture ... to enter a plea for the recognition of the historical study of religion as a *legitimate* subject to be chosen by a student. ... I feel convinced that not much progress in advancing the historical study of religion at colleges and universities can be expected from now on unless the question of *official recognition* is seriously taken up.
>
> (123)

Shepard notes that the lack of *official recognition* implied the "dearth of meaningful, substantive, and enduring academic support," but fails to elaborate. What was Jastrow implying by *official recognition* and how does it differ (if at all) from Shepard's understanding of academic support? Had Shepard investigated further, his account might have shed some light on how the history of the academic study of religion is, to build on Jastrow's insight, the history of its quest for power, legitimacy, and credibility within the university and the nation, a quest frustrated at crucial early points by those whose influence over the public discourse on religion it threatened.

This history of contestation is nowhere more apparent than in Goodspeed's attempts at reorganizing the existing Department of Comparative Religion at Chicago into a Graduate School of Religion and Ethics, within which the degrees of Ph.D. *and* Th.D. would be awarded. In his own words, the aim was to devise a new department within arts and sciences that would be the "center for all the studies of religion in its various forms and fields which the university offers" (Shepard 1991: 98). Although his unexpected death renders purely speculative all estimates as to what extent Goodspeed would have succeeded in his attempt to centralize the university's hold on the early discourse on religion, it is fair to assume that it would have entailed quite a struggle with the Divinity school – the onetime traditional center of power on public matters of religion. In the words of the then Dean of the Divinity school, Shailer Matthews, responding to a memo from Chicago President, Ernest D. Burton, concerning the proposed changes:

> As I said rather bluntly perhaps over the telephone, I don't believe it practicable. … We have on the other hand given the matter very careful thought … [and] the plan as we have it involves the following general principles. First, the avoidance of building up two sets of religious faculties in the University. To establish a graduate school in Religion would mean just that.
>
> (109)

Shepard concludes that Matthews's argument for the priority of the Divinity school was "in one sense" (though he fails to detail any other senses) simply a recognition of the school's significant role in the production of Ph.D.s. Perhaps; but in another sense, one far less sympathetic to the Divinity School's interpretation of the situation, it reflects the very real threat a Graduate School of Religion would have held for Theology's control over education. So, although Shepard's description is correct – the conflict was certainly over issues of *production* – it was not simply the production of Ph.D.s but *producing and reproducing the authority that came with controlling what counted as public talk on religion*. It was thus the authority to produce an item of public discourse and to legitimize one's place in the competitive economy of public discourses that was at stake in the early years of our field. If this redescription is sound, then the successful movement of comparative religion into the university proper comprises one of the important, yet momentary, conquests of the late-nineteenth- and early-twentieth-century American university – the appropriation of a discourse from church regulation. However, so that we do not overemphasize the significance of this first of many exchanges between these two institutional adversaries, we must repeat that, even though it was renamed *scientific*, this new approach to the study of religion, as is clearly evident from Shepard's account, was still largely in support of Christianity. It remained Christian but without being devoted to the institutional limitations of various Protestant denominational standards.

Given this alternative reading, what could be understood as the various tactical, rhetorical skirmishes are, possibly without his knowing, well documented in Shepard's closing chapter, "The Seminary Influence: A Professional Role for Comparative Religion." Unfortunately, they are not understood in this way by Shepard and therefore receive little or no critical study. At Harvard and Chicago, the Divinity schools alertly and effectively responded to the challenge of competition in the discursive marketplace from the graduate religion programs in arts and sciences by instituting their own graduate degrees. By attracting students to their newly established S.T.M. and Th.D. degrees, the hegemonic churches effectively contained the newly emerging field by guaranteeing that potential *Religionswissenschaft* scholars took up careers either as ministers within the various Protestant denominations or as teachers in their own theological institutions. Shepard's explanation, that the "professional dictates of the seminary hindered the growth and development of comparative religion" (107), is based wholly upon a uncritical description of the missiological needs the seminaries were required to fulfill. However, if we inquire into just what lay behind such "professional dictates," his book appears to suggest that a struggle for control of the discourse on religion was raging in the late-nineteenth- and early-twentieth-century American university – a struggle all too apparent today, if the work of writers such as George Marsden is any evidence. At stake were economic and political power as well as the authority to speak on behalf of religion in a public context. Moreover, if one is willing to rethink arguments for the autonomy of religion and, instead, accept that nineteenth- and twentieth-century Christian missions and missionary training are part and parcel of a larger economic and cultural imperialism, then the battle for control over this discourse within the university as documented by Shepard is inseparable from a general campaign to control much more than professorial salaries and the right to make appointments and confer graduate degrees.

The rhetorical weapons used by early *Religionswissenschaft* scholars in this battle to gain the right to speak in a manner different from their colleagues – rhetorical weapons still commonly used in the long-standing battle – included such terms as scientific, serious, critical, academic, historical, objective, neutral, non-denominational, etc., all of which relied upon the ever increasing authority of the scientific worldview. Those utilized by the Divinity side, and those which at least for the moment proved more inviting, powerful, and victorious, revolved around appeals to the ineffable ultimacy of Christianity, which was, ironically, further entrenched by the descriptive evidence provided to missionary programs by this new and daring study of the exotic, "non-Christian" other. The eventual missiological appropriation of the methods and findings of these early comparative scholars – enabling the theology student to benefit from the "liberating powers of *Religionswissenschaft*" (Shepard 1991: 116) – provided generations of Christian theologians with the means to generate more effective knowledge of their target audience; it is precisely in this professional role that we find one instance of where knowledge and power meet.

I am suggesting that although the early comparative religionists, as well as people like Harper and Eliot, were pivotal in diagnosing the weaknesses of the denominational system in the United States, they apparently underestimated the resiliency – for the time being – and the extent of the church's dominance within the public discourse. For a variety of reasons the effectiveness of its influence over the population was in jeopardy over the coming decades and the unquestioned public authority previously exercised by sectors of the

Church was increasingly up for grabs. In the words of Bruce Kuklick, in such an "intellectual [and, to avoid duplicating Shepard's narrow idealist account, we must add, socio-political] environment, theology was unable to prosper, and it lost its hold on the literate, upper-middle-class public" (1989: 79). It is to the credit of the orthodoxy and their firmly entrenched influence that their rhetoric, for the time being at least, won out over the new humanistic science of religion. Much as in the case of earlier humanists who effectively challenged church rule, nineteenth-century theology never did rebound from the challenges of the universities.

So ends this first installment on the successful defense, on the part of God's people, of their declared territorial imperative over the public discourse of religion. Given Shepard's lack of interest in the redescriptive analysis concerning the social and material benefits that reward those who dominate a field of study and the underlying reasons for such calculated power-struggles between the Divinity Schools and the nascent comparative religion programs, his book falls short of providing a suitable example of the contributions to be made to the study of religion by the sociology of knowledge. Only if one accepts, along with Shepard, that the public study of religion is based on a distinction between sectarian and non-sectarian yet humanistic approaches can one join him in maintaining that "an academic, humanistically based identity eluded [comparative religion's] grasp until after World War II" (129). However, if one instead sees the issue as between descriptivists (whether theological or humanistic) and theorists who historicize "religion" itself, then one may yet believe that a coherent identity continues to elude the field. It is to some of the more recent settings of this same contest and elusive identity that the following chapters turn.

Notes

1   I am generally in agreement with Wiebe (1984) when he characterizes the dominant discipline as having had a "failure of nerve" when it came to following through on the early and rather bold methodological developments made by the study of religion's nineteenth-century founders. However, the irony I am trying to get at here, and one not examined by Wiebe (insomuch as he laments the demise of the nervy founders' methods), is that the "success" of the discipline is based precisely on *not* following the lead of the early discipline. If, as argued throughout this book, the very category "religion" functions as a technique in wide-scale social formation, then any emergent use of "religion" that fails to assist in nationalist reproduction is, perhaps, doomed to failure.

2   As noted by Shepard, a pastoral associate of Goodspeed's frankly wrote Harper at Chicago: "If he ever becomes a successful pastor, it will be through years of painful experience – this last year has been one of them" (93).

3   See McCutcheon 2001b: 29–30 for a discussion of Jack Lightstone's and Braun's work on the role played by the alienated Jewish scribal class in bringing about text-based Judaism.

4   That day might not be as far behind us as some say; for example, on several occasions over the last few years I have heard colleagues argue that such organizations as the

non-denominational, yet obviously Christian, American Bible Society (ABS) complemented the study of religion as practiced in public universities. The ABS – whose web site lists the number of Bibles distributed much as McDonald's lists hamburgers sold (e.g., for the fiscal year 1998–9 their web site lists: Bibles, 526,695; New Testaments, 2,015,817; Bible Portions, 4,927,065; and Bible Selections, 56,183,116) – has the motto: "Sharing God's Word with the World" and offers the following as its mission:

> The purpose of the American Bible Society is to provide the Holy Scriptures to every man, woman and child in a language and form each can readily understand, and at a price each can easily afford. This purpose, undertaken without doctrinal note or comment, and without profit, is a cause that all Christians and all churches are urged to support.
> The people and programs of the American Bible Society are centered on the Bible and its life-giving message of hope, justice, and reconciling love. We believe the Scriptures speak for themselves; we don't add doctrinal notes or comments. By honoring this historic focus on the Scriptures, the Bible Society is able to unite Christians from all traditions and strengthen the impact of the Bible's transforming power. ABS seeks to serve the Scripture needs of all by staying centered on the Word.
> (http://www.americanbible.org/about/about_us_more.cfm)

Despite the apparently important literary critical scholarship that goes on under the aegis of the ABS, the hermeneutical theory outlined in the above mission statement, along with the ABS's obvious missions purpose, should make it abundantly clear that the ABS is but one more piece of data for the study of religion as it is conceived in this book.

5   At this point I recall a conservative Roman Catholic scholar with whom I once worked in a public university; despite our obvious disagreements concerning the motivation for, and the goal of, practicing the public study of religion, this scholar proved to be an important ally when it came to identifying and contesting the liberal Protestant hegemony in which we found ourselves.

Chapter 3

Autonomy, unity, and crisis
Rhetoric and the invention of a discipline

> Decorative gestures add romance to a life.
>
> (DeLillo 1986: 9)

Despite its length, the point of this chapter is a rather simple one, although its implications are, hopefully, somewhat more complex and far-reaching. Beginning in the late 1950s, scholars of religion employed an effective collection of decorative displays to re-establish the study of religion as a credible academic pursuit. As documented by Robert Shepard, comparative religion flourished only briefly in North American universities prior to World War I; despite its longtime success in Europe, the field had to wait for another generation of scholars (foremost among them, Eliade) to reinvigorate it on this side of the Atlantic. My interest, therefore, in this chapter is to examine the rhetorical strategies deployed by a collection of self-named historians of religion in the 1950s and 1960s in their effort to recreate an institutionally autonomous, humanistically based, study of religion.

However, as stated in the introduction, I must note from the outset that what we term the history of religions is but one instance of what I refer to as the discourse on *sui generis* religion or the private affair tradition, an essentialist discourse that has now gained hegemonic status in the field. The discourse on *sui generis* religion is comprised of two central claims with four interrelated implications. The first claim, going back at least as far as eighteenth-century German Pietism, is that all observable aspects of those things classified as religions – most often summarized by means of the trinity of myths, rituals, and symbols – are but the external representations (i.e., "indifferent things"), historic traces of a prior, interiorized, pre-theoretical, personal experience. The second claim is that such non-empirical religious experiences are *sui generis* (utterly unique because they are self-caused) and thus distinct from the mundane factors that prompt all other sorts of experiences. Therefore, (i) the datum of the scholar of religion is socio-politically autonomous; (ii) in order to understand the so-called deep meaning (sometimes called the "depth dimension") of these numinous experiences, scholars must employ special interpretive (rather than explanatory) methods; (iii) institutionally autonomous disciplinary locations are needed for carrying out these unique studies in any satisfactory manner; and (iv) access to these deep meanings privileges the scholar of religion for intervening in current social or cultural affairs. Although I have identified the contours of this discourse elsewhere (1997b), I have yet to chronicle its rhetorical development and constitution from the 1950s to the present. This chapter is an attempt to remedy that.

The larger issue implied in this documentary project concerns not simply the plight of an isolated intellectual pursuit, variously known as comparative religion, the history of religions, the study of religion, religious studies, the science of religion, etc., but the ways in which human beings construct, maintain, and contest their social identities over time and place. Accordingly, re-establishing the study of religion is simply a case in point that allows us the opportunity to trace certain rhetorical moves that we should expect to find in all cases of emergent social formation that are communicated and maintained, at least in part, by means of written texts. Just as Benedict Anderson (1991) has examined the ways in which mass-distributed written texts assisted in enabling the construction of national identities, so too we can study the discursive/textual means by which a previous generation of scholars came to identify themselves as historians of religions.

One particular strategy, for instance, is the rhetoric of socio-political autonomy, part of an essentialist discourse that abstracts and insulates its participants, their pursuits, their social institutions, and their social stances from the historical realm of contingency. Identifying, then critiquing the rhetoric of autonomy – or the rhetoric of naturalness – was one of the primary concerns of Marx and Engels in *The German Ideology*; their critique "treats all [so-called] natural premises as the creatures of hitherto existing men [*sic*], strips them of their natural character and subjugates them to the power of the united individuals" (1988: 86). Such a rhetoric is ideological insomuch as it accomplishes the identification of heterogeneous difference and open-ended History with homogenous and teleological Nature, to rely once again on Roland Barthes's terms. This process relies on what Barthes termed the rhetoric of identification: "In the petit-bourgeois universe … any otherness is reduced to sameness" (1973: 165).[1] Such identification protects and privileges both the participants and their pursuits as if they were ahistorical, necessary, and unique.

The primary means by which scholars of religion gained this protection and social identity was by their ability to define their project as the study of "religious experiences," conceived as interior, personal, and utterly unique emotive states and dispositions not accessible to the reductive gaze of social scientists. Such reductionists, argued the "religious experience" scholars, have access only to the externals, the observable phenomenon, rather than the *noumenon*, the deep and ahistorical essence common to all religious phenomena. The reductionists, argued Wilfred Cantwell Smith in his 1963 work, *The Meaning and End of Religion* (1991; see also Asad 2001 for a re-reading of this classic work), for example, may have access to the observable cumulative tradition, but they have no understanding of the deep abiding faith that is somehow contained in or signified by that tradition. Accordingly, only by means of the trope "religious experience" were scholars of religion able to distinguish their pursuits, and their social groupings, from those of other intellectuals, in adjunct disciplinary fields, who were equally interested in studying "sacred" behaviors.

Social formation through discourses on founders

Another essentialist, rhetorical gesture employed in construction of "religion" as a disciplinary field is common in the formation and maintenance of social group-ings: claims concerning the socio-political autonomy of one of its founding figures. In the (re)emergence of the study of religion in the last three decades, Mircea Eliade is often valorized as the primary and generative figure associated with the field's rebirth in the 1960s (ironically, perhaps, critiques of the role he played in its founding equally reinforce this status!). Through their uniform portrait of the historical Eliade as a virtually disembodied, apolitical Great Man (see chapter 9), many scholars of religion engage in the kind of mythmaking so essential to the construction and subsequent legitimation of social identities. Although the myth of Eliade is not necessarily to be equated with the myths of other sorts of founders (e.g., Siddhartha, Socrates, Jesus, Muhammad, assorted Kings and Queens, as well as Parson Weems's now well-known tales of George Washington's early life all immediately come to mind) that we find scattered throughout the world's various social formations, the manner in which his defenders doggedly argue for conceiving of him as somehow removed from and uncontaminated by the political turmoil associated with interwar Romania suggests that there is an intimate connection between maintaining the group's social identity and its members' recurring efforts to posit a pristine, idealized representation of its founder. One might recall stories of George Washington's youth, for instance, in which we find the camouflaged claim: "We are a nation of truth-tellers." That such a social ideal, encoded in a myth, contradicts actual social practices must not be overlooked.

Although research into the historical Eliade hardly amounts to the same "publishing cottage industry and a revivified academic subfield" as does scholar-ship on the historical Jesus (Arnal and Desjardins 1997: 3), it is nonetheless noteworthy that since his death in 1986, there has been a small but growing interest in the life of Eliade. The section of Arnal and Desjardins's *Whose Historical Jesus?* that is devoted to socio-rhetorical criticism of "Jesus" discourses suggests that there may well be links between research on the historical/mythic Jesus and the historical/mythic Eliade. As Willi Braun phrases it, representa-tions of the past are

> deeply embedded in the contemporary social, institutional, and disciplinary settings that furnish the historian not only with the motivations and aims but also with conceptual and analytic tools for "doing history" in the first

place. [For example,] the historical Jesus would hardly exist as a figure of continuing interest, most certainly not in the reshapable and displaceable forms he has taken on in the history of Jesus research, apart from the socio-political and intellectual warrants for his existence that are inherent in the modern discourse about the historical Jesus.

(1997: 92)

One could easily substitute "the historical Eliade" for "the historical Jesus" in this passage: the historical Eliade would hardly exist as a figure of continuing interest were it not for the intellectual, social, political, and economic warrants that are inherent in the modern discourse on religion. In other words, and in suitably dialectical fashion, the rhetorical trope "Eliade the great man" functions as a shorthand for the ongoing campaign for the political and institutional autonomy of the field itself – a field he was in part responsible for founding in the late 1950s and early 1960s – while the supposedly apolitical field provides the necessary discursive conditions for the creation of the trope in the first place.

The myth of Eliade is therefore intimately connected to the life of the social formation we know as the history of religion, a social formation that has its authoritative texts (written by Schleiermacher, van der Leeuw, Otto, Wach, Eliade, etc.), sanctioned meeting times and places (every third week in November at the AAR/SBL convention), sacred sites (the physical and mythic space of the University of Chicago, for one) and myths of origins (stories of the 1893 World's Parliament of Religions held in Chicago[2] as well as references to the 1963 U.S. Supreme Court decision in the case of Abington School District v. Schempp). As quoted later in chapter 9, I believe Tim Murphy has it right: "What is at stake in these debates [on Eliade] is a struggle over what the study of religion itself should be. Eliade has become a focal point for the on-going identity crisis in the field" (1994: 383). Accordingly, writers focusing on Eliade most often are hardly historians; rather, "history" and "myth" are quite predictably fused; these writers are active mythmakers, hagiographers, and rhetoricians.

Therefore, frustration over the manner in which colleagues portray their claims (either about religion *per se* or the life of Eliade) has resulted in my transgression of some disciplinary boundaries. In the background of this chapter, then, I have in mind connecting scholarship on our field's historic origins with the kind of work currently developing in other fields, such as the study of Christian origins where scholars examine the rhetoric employed in acts of social formation (e.g., Humphries 1999). To this end, I derive some of my method from Burton Mack's work on the origins of early Christianities or, more properly, the earliest Jesus movements (e.g., 1995, 1996, 2000, 2001b). By understanding the Jesus movements as social formations that were/are imagined, constructed, and legitimized through the art of textual mythmaking, Mack has gone a considerable distance in helping us to develop a thoroughly naturalistic basis for theorizing on the beginnings of those social groups we call religions – going so far as to help us to see so-called religious movements as none other than ordinary social formations employing specific rhetorical techniques in their never-ending quest to reproduce and authorize themselves. Given the naturalistic presumption that no types of human behavior or institutions are privileged and exempt from study by means of social-scientific theoretical tools and vocabularies, I reason that Mack's tools and terms – such as the categories "social formation," "mythmaking," and the socio-rhetorical theory that unites them – can be of use in studying the techniques that made possible the mid-twentieth-century rebirth of the study of religion in North America. Situating the study of the formation and maintenance of an academic discipline within a wider, socio-rhetorical framework capable of drawing attention to the material benefits that derive from such formations should help to clarify aspects of the natural history of this discipline.

The preface harbors a lie

Because of the complexity of studying any large, and still developing academic discourse, some arbitrary simplification and focus is inevitable. So, I have selected the prefaces to three different, but widely read, collections of methodological essays, each of which record the proceedings of conferences held at the University of Chicago. I choose to examine these historic texts since they are useful examples of the attempt to create a manageable continuity and identity out of unmanageable heterogeneity – a strategy that the volumes as a whole attempt to achieve in the service of authorizing the autonomy of "religious studies" discourse.

To be honest, my selection of prefaces is not completely arbitrary. I specifically select prefaces with a comment from the opening to one of Jacques Derrida's own books (1976) in my mind. As Jean Hyppolite observed in the case of Hegel's preface to his *Phenomenology of the Mind*, seeing the genre of the preface as an unassuming introduction, a mere appendage tacked onto the main (and thus serious, substantive, etc.) body of a text is highly misleading. As my own preface should make clear, prefatory texts are more cunning than that and, therefore, all the more intriguing. The preface ostensibly occupies a place outside the text (pre-text, *Prae-fatio*: a saying beforehand) – although, as we all know, it is written after the text and functions not only as an introduction but more accurately an apology for the text, making the preface the site of much rhetorical work. Therefore, the preface cannot exist innocently or neutrally outside the text, for it presupposes, comes after, and defends all that follows it. Much like the notion of religion existing independently of socio-political structures, the presumed independence of the preface does important social work. So, if Derrida's translator, Gayatri Spivak is right, we should suspect that "the preface harbors a lie" (Spivak 1976: x).

Motivated by the hunch that the larger and seemingly coherent Whole of this discipline is merely an artful depiction, this chapter, then, asks what other lies might we uncover if we examine a sample of prefaces. The answer, ahead of time, is that prefaces are a prime site where various rhetorics are deployed to manufacture and privilege not only the data studied by scholars of religion (so-called religious experiences), but also one sense of the field itself.

Between the years of 1959 – three years after Eliade first arrived in Chicago – and 1985 – one year before his death and two years prior to the publication of the sixteen-volume *Encyclopedia of Religion* – three separate volumes of multi-authored methodological essays were published under the common title, *The History of Religions* (Eliade and Kitagawa 1959; Kitagawa 1967; Kitagawa 1985; hereafter each referred to as *HR* followed by the appropriate date of publication). Although the first volume arose as a collection of essays commissioned specifically for publication, the second and third volumes contained the proceedings of two subsequent conferences, one in 1965 and the other in 1983. Similarity in title (although each bears a different subtitle) immediately suggests that the editors – at least from the second volume onward – implied some form of continuity between the themes, aims, contributors, and implications of the three collections. This is confirmed when Joseph Kitagawa, who was involved in the editing and organization of all three collections,[3] explicitly notes that the final volume "follows the pattern of two earlier publications" (*HR* 1985: xvi). After briefly reiterating what he considers to be the "noble tradition" of the History of Religions at Chicago, Kitagawa concludes that after "Eliade's arrival in 1956, there arose a new interest in gradually developing the entire enterprise of the history of religions. In an attempt to sort out the issues, the first volume … was published" (*HR* 1985: xvi–xvii).

It is precisely in the light of this "gradual development" that these collections of essays should be read, as attempts to construct and authorize an emergent field by generating a self-understanding – the very theme of the second volume – built upon a common set of assumptions and a shared vocabulary articulated through a rhetoric of institutional and methodological autonomy and passively inevitable "development." In other words, the possibility of a discourse on religion emerges from such volumes. The number of times the essayists in subsequent volumes quote the writers from one or both earlier collections, as well as the number of times articles from the newly-born journal, *History of Religions* (1961), are cited, lends further credence to the view that the self-conscious construction of institutional identity – or the invention of a discursive tradition – achieved through the manufacture of this cumulative tradition, is one of the major effects of these publishing projects.

Prior to embarking on this analysis of the manner in which a cumulative tradition is manufactured, however, it may be worth our while to sketch the early context of the study of religion at the University of Chicago, the mythic Mecca of the modern study of religion in North America.

Joachim Wach and the autonomy of *Religionswissenschaft*

After he delivered his Haskell lectures at the University of Chicago in the 1956–57 academic year (published in 1958 as *Birth and Rebirth*), Eliade was asked by the Dean of the Theological Faculty, Jerald C. Brauer, to remain at Chicago to chair its program in the history of religions. The former chair, the German sociologist of religion Joachim Wach, had died unexpectedly while on vacation in Switzerland in 1955. Ironically, it was Wach who, in the spring of 1955, while both he and Eliade were attending the International Congress of the History of Religions (now known as the IAHR) in Rome, had invited Eliade to come to Chicago to deliver the Haskell lectures in the first place.

Although Wach seems to have had a greater interest in the particular socio-historical conditions of religious experience than did Eliade, he nonetheless thought highly of the Romanian scholar, writing that Eliade's 1949 book, *Le mythe de l'éternel retour*, was a "brilliant analysis of the attitudes toward time in various cultures and religions" (Wach 1958: 87). Despite some differences, Wach's and Eliade's understanding of the history of religions had much in common; both men agreed upon the utter uniqueness of religious experience, thereby guaranteeing the need for a distinct interpretive (rather than explanatory) method to determine its meaning, and the autonomous and humanistic disciplinary location for its study. Upon arriving in Chicago, therefore, Eliade found himself part of a young but clearly envisioned program that accorded well with his own view of both the data and the discipline.

Wach had arrived in Chicago in 1945, after teaching for a decade at Brown University in Providence, Rhode Island. The early advances made by practitioners of comparative religion within the American university had, to a considerable degree and for a number of reasons, been lost by this time. Under A. Eustace Haydon (d. 1975), the sole faculty member of the Department of Comparative Religion and Wach's immediate predecessor at Chicago, the program, already considerably weakened, lost its distinct disciplinary location as a humanistic study and simply became part of the theological program, complementing its missionary training curriculum. In the words of Kitagawa: "Comparative Religion finally ceased to exist as a department in the Division of the Humanities, and it was Haydon, fundamentalist-turned-sceptic, who brought the program into the Divinity School shortly before his retirement in 1945" (Kitagawa 1987a: 138).

Wach thus was cast into the role of chair of a rather weak and misunderstood program. Knowing his early efforts to differentiate the history of religions from other studies such as historiography, on the one hand, and normative pursuits such as theology and philosophy, on the other, Wach's new position provided an ideal opportunity to put into practice a project he had outlined in his *Habilitation* thesis of 1924, *Religionswissenschaft: Prolegomena zu ihrer wissenschafts-theoretischen Grundlegung*: the creation of disciplinary autonomy for *Religionswissenschaft*.

It is intriguing just how clearly we see the relationship between the socio-political autonomy of religious experiences and the disciplinary autonomy of the study of religion in Wach's early writings where he is concerned with the "emancipation of the history of religions (*Religionswissenschaft*) from the domination of the other humanistic studies" which he believes will occur through the "inner consolidation [or what I would redescribe as the social formation] of the discipline." After asserting, matter of factly, that the religious world is a "unique configuration of life, with laws and principles of its own," which occupies "an autonomous realm ... within human cultural life," Wach delimits the hermeneutical strategies necessary for an adequate understanding of this "specifically religious" aspect of human life (Wach 1988: 20). He claims that these interpretive practices can best be carried out only once they are *emancipated* and *liberated* from the *domination* of other disciplines – a rhetoric that suggests the uphill battle of the emergent field, a battle in which not only the rhetoric of autonomy but also of "crisis" were often drawn upon to rally the troops. In Wach's estimation, these other approaches to the data misuse and manipulate (even oppress) the research of the historian of religions for such inappropriate purposes as legitimizing a literary theory, a theology, or a philosophy. They obscure and deflect from what can only be interpreted as the sheer joy of understanding the religious Other.

Wach even goes so far as to lay the foundation for what Eliade would later call the new humanism, a theory concerning the ramifications of this new discipline for the researcher and society at large.

> As the inquiring mind discovers the essence of these modalities of life within the experience of life, this experience of life is itself enriched and deepened through the understanding of its modality, their nature and richness, their multiplicity and laws.
>
> (Wach 1988: 20)

The individualism, essentialism, and idealism of Wach's study are all evident here, as is his own interpretation of how personal/existential changes may occur as a result of such understanding. It is not a large move from this passage on the disembodied, apolitical mind encountering enriched "modalities of life" to Eliade's own thoughts on how the creative hermeneutics will enrich the dispirited West by reincorporating formerly lost archaic meanings and values. (On the politics of the new humanism, see McCutcheon 1997b.)

Judging by the early success of Wach's rhetoric of autonomy, his rhetoric of fact (where assertions rather than argumentation win the day), and his attendant thoughts on the crisis that will undoubtedly result should such a rhetoric not win the day, it is not surprising to see that over the coming years these themes and techniques become the backbone of the emerging social formation known as the history of religions. Gregory Alles's description is thus quite accurate: the Chicago school "insists upon religious meaning as a *unique*, *nonreducible* dimension of human life, a sort of meaning that invites us to comprehend it in its *uniqueness* and its *totality*" (1989: 108). But to these aspects must be added the view that a social crisis will result from any other approach to the data of religion. It is precisely upon this rhetoric of autonomy and crisis that a successful rebuilding of the study of religion depended.

Despite the possible irony, we can appeal to Martin Marty's work on American nationalism, *The One and the Many* (1997) to support this thesis. I say "ironic" because Marty's own work over the years has consistently supported the irreducible character of religious experience, a character that necessitates unique interpretive methods and the unique social contributions of scholars of religion to contemporary cultural issues. Despite being – or better put, because he is – part of this very social formation, he accurately describes the relatively standard "set of complaints and claims" that various leaders employ to sustain social groups:

> First, they say, our subculture has been misused or suppressed by the dominators. Hence we have all suffered a trauma, so we must enjoy a privileged situation during the recovery, if it ever comes.
>
> Second, our subculture has values of its own. Born of our suffering, these are different from and superior to "yours," although you were long positioned to voice and display yours, while until recently we were not.
>
> Third, because we have been depressed while our values have been neglected and suppressed, we seek liberation from suffering and must state its terms on our own. Our values need articulation, and we alone can offer it.
>
> (1997: 106)

Marty goes on to identify how this set of common complaints and claims – social engineering techniques, I would call them – can be found in the literature of a number of social movements; having briefly examined Wach's early writings, this is a list to which we can now add the emergent history of religions. Thus, along with the discourse on founders, we must add the rhetoric of autonomy and crisis to the means by which social formation takes place. In studying the history of religions in this way we have shifted the ground from studying some stable thing, religion or myth or ritual, to studying the ways in which social formations deploy such talk to promote its members' interests and their perceived affinity for one another. Therefore, far from having some sort of unimpeded access to the deep meaning of human existence, historians of religions routinely employed such claims in an effort to establish, legitimize, and extend their social identity, turf, and privilege in a competitive economy of the mid-twentieth century.

Imagining a community through rhetoric

As suggested at the outset, in my analysis of the discourse as it is created and objectified within printed texts I rely upon Benedict Anderson's much cited work concerning the relations between personal identity, nationalism, and print capitalism (1991). Examining the ways in which individuals construct personal and social identity through positing national allegiances, Anderson places great emphasis upon how printed (and therefore mobile) vernacular texts assisted in replacing the previously unquestioned religious modes of thought and identities (i.e., "I am a member of Christendom") with newly constructed nationalist modes ("I am Irish"). As described by one of his reviewers,

> for Anderson, nationalism could only arise historically when, and where, three linked cultural conceptions common to the great religions lost their axiomatic grip on human minds. The waning of these conceptions was fostered by a complex of developments, but was immeasurably aided by the growth of "print capitalism" – the explosive new combination of authors, printers, publishing firms, and book merchants that encouraged the rise of a literate audience through the use of vernacular print languages. Hence, the "sacred imagined community" became replaced by multiple national consciousnesses, and belief in the "Nation" became the bedrock axiom of cultural/political imaginings.
>
> (Heathorn 1994: 105)

According to Anderson, the old social identities depended upon three axioms that privileged certain elements within society over others: (i) the privileged status of so-called sacred languages believed to possess some sort of privileged ontological significance (e.g., Holy texts written in Arabic, Hebrew, or Latin); (ii) the belief that the privileges accorded select individuals (e.g., monarchs, ritual specialists, scribes) within strict social hierarchies were self-evidently proper and cosmically determined; and (iii) the identification of cosmogony (i.e., the view that the world as we know it, complete with its social divisions, came to be when the universe itself came to be) with what is today understood as history (a narrative reconstructive effort directed by contemporary needs and criteria). According to Anderson, only once the credibility of each (and the linkages between each) axiom was lost, could old social identities be re-constructed on a new footing.

What is important is Anderson's observation on the pivotal role vernacular languages play in developing, then representing, communal identity (nationalistic or, in our case, disciplinary), all of which is accomplished largely through the ability of an authoritative rhetoric, carried on through print-capitalism, to unite a formerly diverse and ambiguous community within the newly inclusive identity of an imagined "we." Of use, then, in the analysis of textual productions, will be a study of how their contributors are concerned to define and promote a social identity through rhetorics of essentialism, autonomy, and unity – in a word, mythmaking or mystification. To the degree that such mystification obscures actual material relations between human communities, one will therefore look for judgments that, literally, conserve the distributions of power and privilege associated with some past or idealized social formations.

This finally brings me to the prefaces of the *History of Religions* volumes. I will examine them for: a developing disciplinary vocabulary (i.e., a jargon or vernacular); their use of strategies of dehistoricization, unification, naturalization, and essentialization; their efforts to construct a shared intellectual and institutional lineage or genealogy – how they invent a tradition;[4] their preoccupation with philosophical idealism and political conservatism; their shared assumptions concerning the self-evidently *sui generis* status of religion,[5] the unique methods and privilege of the disciplinary location of the field, and the cultural benefit and social utility of the study. In short, how do these three prefaces produce and reproduce the discourse through various rhetorics and sheer assertion.

Establishing the discursive tradition: *History of Religions* 1959

In the preface to the first volume of methodological essays (co-edited by Eliade and Kitagawa), Jerald C. Brauer provides the rationalization for such a collection: the history of religions, he believes, is at "a critical point in its development" (*HR* 1959: vii). After lamenting the "uncomfortable" and "peripheral" position occupied by the discipline in the English-speaking world (its self-perceived status as the proverbial underdog), he asserts that it "is a most auspicious period for the history of religions to become one of the pre-eminent disciplines in university life." In suitably idealist fashion, Brauer maintains that the new-found success of the history of religions partly originates from "the new perspective that has been at work for the past quarter century and is now beginning to dominate the *mind* and *spirit* of much of Western mankind" (emphasis added). This new perspective "upholds the *uniqueness* and *givenness* of vast expanses of *human experience*" (emphases added) – not least of which would be religious experience. Echoing Eliade's classic formulation of the non-reductionist position in his preface to his *Patterns in Comparative Religion* (1958), Brauer concludes:

> Unlike the approach which seeks to reduce all experience and reality to a few basic ingredients or principles, this new perspective tries *to grasp a given reality in its own terms, in its own uniqueness, and in its own context. ... Religions are to be studied and understood for their own sake.*
>
> (*HR* 1959: vii; emphasis added)

Evidently, not only is the new success of the discipline due to this rhetoric of socio-political autonomy, but the assumption grounds the discipline's very existence. Without defining the datum, participants in this discourse are confident enough to discuss "its own" terms, uniqueness, and context. Again, Brauer argues that

> a perspective *dominates* in the history of religions that demands investigation from a point of view that takes seriously the *uniqueness* and *particularity*

of each historical religion. ... The discipline does not give up the search for universal types, but it has moved far beyond the possibility of locating these in a few clear moral, ethical, or national common denominators. It can be argued that the enterprise now seeks the *basically religious* by moving through individual historical religious experiences rather than by ignoring or moving around the peculiar or particular experience. Thus the discipline has much to contribute to modern self-understanding and will make its impact felt increasingly in university education.

(HR 1959: viii–ix)

In the preceding quotations one finds a useful introduction to the preoccupations of most (if not all) of the writers represented in all three volumes: the call for taking religion "seriously" (which generally functions as a codeword for the non-reductive discourse on *sui generis* religion); speculations, based upon no theoretical argumentation concerning just what counts as religion, on the enduring presence of the "basically religious"; the contemporary social utility of the findings of this discipline; the need to use historical investigation in the service of accessing deeper, ahistorical universals.

It is crucial to notice how Brauer rationalizes the development of the discipline: it is the result of such blind forces as the perspective, the enterprise, the era, mind, and spirit – bringing to mind Kitagawa's quotation of Cornelius P. Tiele's explanation for why comparative religions first arose in the nineteenth century. Writing in the last of the three *History of Religions* volumes (Kitagawa 1985) he writes: "*Religionswissenschaft* was not 'founded' in the sense implied by this term, but [Tiele asserts] that in the mid-nineteenth century *Religionswissenschaft* was 'called into being *by a generally felt want* in different countries [in Europe] at the same time and as a matter of course'" (*HR* 1985: 123; quoting Tiele's essay, "On the Study of Comparative Theology," in Barrows 1893: 568). Such historical factors as colonialism as well as economic and political imperialism, appear to play little or no role in such a passive reading of historical developments, a reading surprisingly similar to Eliade's comments on the way in which his so-called creativity simply sprang forth and was not constrained by his youthful context (1990a: 274). Attributing the field's rise to the nameless forces of the era or the benign spirit of the times are fine examples of how the rhetoric of autonomy shapes our present sense of our histories; in fact, we have no history, no beginning. Instead, we are impelled by an originating *Geist* that, much like an irruption of the sacred (a hierophany), or one of Vishnu's avatars, makes a brief appearance on the stage of history.

There is one additional theme peculiar to this 1959 preface. According to Brauer, not only is the history of religions at this time involved with questions of intellectual and institutional demarcation – of "mark[ing] out its own responsibilities and contributions," it is also entwined with issues of national identity and global cooperation – all of which are also issues of social formation, but at various overlapping levels of analysis. He maintains that the history of religions, as practiced specifically within the United States, is in a privileged position to act "as the middle ground between European culture and the culture of the Asian nations," largely because of the "unmatched financial resources" of the United States. "In this central situation American scholarship should be eager and willing to play a new role" (HR 1959: ix). Brauer thus argues not only for the privileges which arise from disciplinary autonomy, but also for the privileges that arise from the autonomous field's specifically U.S. location. He continues: "Because of the vast amount of research in the social sciences, American universities are especially well equipped to become great centers for the study of the history of religions" (HR 1959: ix–x). According to his logic, the discipline itself should benefit within its institutional setting from this irresistible movement: the history of religions could "become as universal and as necessary a study for the college or university student as mathematics or history."

Brauer's uncritical association between this discipline and the "unmatched financial resources" of the U.S. – the result of the rise of a particular political, economic, and military hegemony begun after the close of World War II – relies upon the strategies of dehistoricization, naturalization, and universalization. Just why this one nation-state is the leader is unproblematic to Brauer; he seems to suggest that it is natural that this one way is the universal way. Much as the highly successful movie, *Forrest Gump*, portrayed an orthodox sense of U.S. history as a series of disconnected, well-intentioned, almost naive and sometimes accidental, politically neutral interventions and episodes (i.e., instead of making history, history *happened to* Gump), Brauer conceives of the U.S.-based study of religion as a politically neutral force, moved by an undefined internal compulsion to mediate between these two things, Europe and Asia. Just because Brauer appears to be addressing simply what he believes to be the promising social applications of a supposedly disinterested academic method and discipline should not occlude the fact that, for him, the early successes of this new perspective of the history of religions are intimately linked to the successes of U.S. foreign policy and its markets overseas.

In a related vein, Kitagawa (HR 1985: 137) comments: "For the most part, American universities … were not concerned with inquiring into the historical, comparative, and phenomenological study of religion(s) until after World War II." Given such comments, coupled with the observation that the data with which nineteenth-century *Religionswissenschaft* scholars worked relied almost exclusively upon the ethnographic findings of the earlier European colonial/missionary age, it seems that a history of the specific U.S. contributions to this discourse during the Cold War period will uncover the material interests behind what have until now been viewed simply as issues of purely intellectual content and origination. With this in mind, one should recall that Eliade was allowed to remain in the United States, having been judged to be "indispensable to the security and welfare of the United States" (Eliade 1988: 213, n. 15). It appears that *Religionswissenschaft* has been not so much the handmaid to theology – as lamented by not a few historians of religions – but rather the handmaid to nation-building. Given this critique, it is not entirely clear, then, to what Brauer's "new perspective" refers. Is it the newly developing hermeneutic method these scholars are appropriating from philosophy? Or, is it the ever increasing hegemonic role played by the United States in world politics? Likely, it is both – though the latter remains unacknowledged.

I am not arguing here for a direct causal link between, for example, the Cold War and the rise of the history of religions in the U.S. For, as Donald Wiebe rightly points out in a recent essay in a collection on the Cold War and the study of religion, "there is no direct evidence [yet presented, I would add] that any direct support, whether from government agency or private foundation, is responsible for the entry of religious studies into the curriculum of college and universities in North America in the 1960s and no evidence that its research agendas were influenced to any great degree by specific Cold War values" (Doležalová *et al.*, 2001: 280). All I wish to identify is the considerable body of circumstantial or structural evidence that ought to prompt further studies of what the Cold War setting of such things as the police action in Korea, the war in Vietnam, changing U.S. immigration policies in the mid-1960s, the anti-government backlash among a younger generation of Americans, etc., all had to do with the sharp rise of interest with studying religion – and not just *being* religious – in a humanistic fashion on U.S. college campuses. Such structural issues hardly amount to a direct cause, of course, but we might be mistaken if we study social systems by looking for smoking guns in the hands of intentional agents. I am therefore inclined to agree with Luther Martin, writing in the same volume as Wiebe, who concludes that "the study of religion which was developed in the United States during this period must be seen as being in some way legitimated by the religio-political obsessions of that time, certainly in the selection of Asian and Third World 'religions' for its dominant subject matter" (220).

From stepchild to genius: *History of Religions* 1967

In his preface to the second collection of essays, published eight years later (Kitagawa 1967), Brauer revisits several themes of his earlier preface, but the former urgency and insecurity (i.e., the "critical point in [the discipline's] development") is lessened considerably. This should be expected, because teaching humanistic courses *about* religion (rather than teaching this or that religion itself) in American public institutions had begun in earnest after the U.S. Supreme Court's decision concerning the place of prayer in public schools in the Schempp case in 1963. In the majority decision, Justice Clark differentiated between the confessional study of religion and what he refers to as the "objective" study of religion:

> It might well be said that one's education is not complete without a study of comparative religion or the history of religion and its relationship to the

advancement of civilization. It certainly may be that the Bible is worthy of study for its literary and historical qualities. Nothing we have said here indicates that such a study of the Bible or of religion, when presented objectively as part of a secular program of education, may not be effected consistent with the First Amendment.

(quoted in Welch 1971: vii)[6]

Although the history of religions as a systematic approach still had to contend with competing approaches and disciplines (e.g., anthropology, classics, sociology, philosophy, psychology), after the Schempp decision its practitioners could be confident that they were involved in a legitimate, almost judicially sanctioned, scholarly activity. As Jonathan Smith insightfully pointed out, the decision functions as a virtual cosmogony for the field. However, a certain sense of urgency still haunts this second preface, as well as the entire volume, since the favorable decision in the Schempp case could not be confused with the continuing work of establishing the history of religions as not only the *autonomous* but also the self-declared *pre-eminent* location of the public discourse on religion. As Brauer remarks, although the history of religions was formerly the "Stepchild in the field of religious studies ... [t]oday it is beginning to come to the front as *one of the most provocative ways* to study religion" (*HR* 1967: vi; emphasis added).[7]

Brauer is still concerned to remark on the lineage of this provocative discipline, but its onetime shaky past now recedes considerably. What moves to the fore now is that the University of Chicago and its early Department of Comparative Religions, under the guidance of George S. Goodspeed, is conceived as forming an important part of the field's cosmogony. The 1967 volume, Brauer informs his readers, marks the 150th anniversary of the Divinity School at the University of Chicago. At this time there appears to be little need of relying upon the legitimacy and prestige of the formerly celebrated group of older European intellectuals for carrying on the task of defining and establishing the discourse.[8] Whereas the 1959 volume largely relied upon well-established, predominantly European scholars,[9] the 1967 volume is exclusively written by past and present professors and students at the University of Chicago, making it somewhat akin to an overly ambitious version of the promotional pamphlets some graduate programs now distribute in which they list their graduates and copies of their curriculum vitae.[10] Acknowledging that "something is lost by not inviting the best scholars throughout the world to contribute" to the conference, Brauer assures his readers that "something is gained" by limiting the discourse to "only those men who have been educated or are now teaching at a single theological center of America long noted for its scholarship and its education of theological professors" (*HR* 1967: vii). In addition to what Brauer believes is gained (e.g., an overview of the influence of a series of generations of scholars at one institution), he thinks it will help to assess the "particular genius, if any, that a given institution possesses," and assist in placing these scholars into the midst of contemporary theological debate. Moreover, it will add significantly to the momentum of the growing U.S. (and the specifically Chicagoan) influence in the world of scholarship. Where the field of studies in religion was once dominated by Europeans, U.S. scholars (and specifically Chicagoans) seem at this point ready to exert their new-found influence.

Thus Brauer places Chicago's history of religions program onto the map of international comparative religions through the device of genealogy. He details a number of international and domestic scholars whose names can be associated with Chicago's Haskell Lectures (begun in 1895). As well, the Barrows Lectures afforded many Chicago professors the opportunity of traveling in India and Asia to lecture and participate in the "exchange of ideas," not to mention the promotion of the home institution. After naming several of the more prominent members of Chicago's recent program (Wach, Eliade, Kitagawa, and Charles Long), Brauer concludes his genealogy by informing the reader of the many professors from abroad who have visited Chicago.

After such an extended and self-assured effort to situate and authenticate the Chicago program, Brauer immediately introduces the particular methodological theme of the 1967 volume, namely the problem of understanding meaning that, he observes, inevitably leads to the problem of self-understanding: "In one sense, the volume represents an attempt at self-understanding on the part of the History of Religions as a particular discipline" (HR 1967: ix). The traditional problem of *Verstehen*, a favorite topic of Wach's, intimately linked to the "development of a methodology adequate to interpret and understand the data of religion," is also, then, associated with the self-definition of the discipline – or, more accurately, one particular school's understanding of itself as "the discipline." At this point, the discursive field can once again be identified; there is here a relation between self-evident religious data, interpretive precision, and disciplinary self-definition. Furthermore, such a methodology aimed at developing understanding both of the data and of one's self, according to Brauer, "tends to see the present from a perspective supplied by an analysis of the religious forms and vitalities of the past" (HR 1967: ix). Like in his earlier preface,[11] Brauer writes of a generic, amorphous past, but this time goes so far as to outline explicitly how this undifferentiated and therefore politically autonomous past as well as the wholly undefined "religious forms" are influential in the present. This is but one example of the conservatism of this rhetoric.

According to the 1967 preface, then, there is a greater confidence within the discourse, and a concerted move to distance it from its European origins and to control and establish the Chicago program as autonomous and exemplary. Brauer quite effectively argues for the priority of Chicago scholars and thereby goes a long way in constructing the modern Chicago tradition that we today take for granted. I refer to this history as constructed, since in order to create the appearance of continuity (from which the authority of lineage is derived), Brauer must not only gloss over significant intellectual and contextual differences between Wach and such predecessors as Goodspeed and Haydon at

Chicago, but he must also minimalize or completely ignore the very real discrepancies between Wach's academic and socio-political world in Germany in the 1930s (from which he was expelled by the Nazis in 1935) and that of Chicago in the 1960s. Not only does Brauer's use of the title "History of Religions" gloss over great disparities within the many approaches to the modern study of religion and elevate just one as pre-eminent, but the first attempts are made to associate the University of Chicago exclusively with this now privileged, autonomous approach.[12]

Weaving a unified tapestry: *History of Religions* 1985

The final preface to be considered was written by Joseph Kitagawa (*HR* 1985). Although entitled "Introduction," this text functions the same as Brauer's two previous texts: it attempts to contextualize the essays and is preoccupied with creating a credible genealogy and constructing a coherent tradition.[13] By now it should be apparent that efforts to construct a coherent and authoritative tradition involve mastering and controlling the dynamic tension between homogeneity and heterogeneity, past and present – defusing historical flux and difference in favor of some posited, essential similarity.

This tension between homogeneity and heterogeneity is identified from the outset in Kitagawa's preface to the 1985 essays. The volume, he writes,

> is not meant to imply that its contents present a neatly packaged account of the historical background, contemporary state, and future outlook of the discipline of the history of religions (*Religionswissenschaft*). ... Thus, the volume does not advocate any party line.
>
> (*HR* 1985: xi)

Within a few lines he further elaborates this heterogeneity and neutrality thesis by adding that the discipline "has never tried – and is not likely to try – to develop a rigidly defined methodological orthodoxy." Rather, Kitagawa claims that the "various perspectives" of the "leading scholars and practitioners of the discipline" who have contributed essays ensures that the book – like the discipline itself – is more akin to a "richly brocaded 'scholarly' tapestry."

Kitagawa is correct in his analysis if by its perceived heterogeneity one interprets this volume not to present radically diverse viewpoints on the subject of the study of religion, but rather to disclose undetected fracture points in the regnant discourse. This last volume of *The History of Religions* thus betrays better than any other the inevitably artificial nature – the constructedness – of this supposed discursive unity. With the addition of such contributors as the late Ninian Smart as well as Kurt Rudolph – both of whom in some ways promote a different approach to the study of religion – various discursive strategies must be employed within Kitagawa's preface to minimalize and diffuse their divergence

on certain methodological and theoretical issues. The discipline is now dominant enough to allow a certain element of dissension; a degree of security is
evidenced by the inclusion of some dissenting voices and a return to the model
of mainly including the work of famous Europeans, but it is a tightly controlled
dissension. As will be argued in later chapters, the very category of "religion"
may accomplish as much for the European-based, social democracies.

In other words, strategies are employed to divert questions which might
concern objections to foundational assumptions, and to circumscribe objections
within the realm of the acceptable. However, the usefulness of reading both
Smart and Rudolph to espouse truly oppositional ideologies is limited since
their very presence within such collections suggests that they yet share with
others within this regnant discourse key assumptions regarding the "universal
character of religious phenomena" (HR 1985: xi) and the ability to differentiate
religious experiences and behaviors from other sorts of behaviors. Therefore,
much as Noam Chomsky has characterized U.S. political conservatives and
liberals as hawks and doves who are united insomuch as they both leave
unquestioned certain basic assumptions regarding the divine right of the U.S.'s
world hegemony,[14] so, too, the debate within these "various perspectives" in the
history of religions is so narrow as to leave untouched the shared idealist and
essentialist assumptions, let alone their socio-political implications. In the
words of Marc Manganaro, writing on the ways in which a uniformitarian
agenda is concealed within a rhetoric of encyclopedism in the works of J. G.
Frazer, T. S. Eliot, Northrop Frye, and Joseph Campbell, a "profusion of voices
may stand out as diversity, but they ultimately move toward the system or idea
that unites, destroying variation in the process" (1992: 17).

Potential variation is thus eliminated by Kitagawa's aesthetic rhetoric which
suggests the complex but ultimately unified nature of the discourse. He writes:

> To take an analogy from art, by the eighteenth century, there had already
> been hung a richly brocaded 'scholarly' tapestry, woven with threads from
> the Hellenistic, Jewish, Christian, and Islamic traditions, embroidered with
> threads from the Renaissance, and embellished with a growing knowledge
> of non-Western religions and cultures. To be sure, the nineteenth- and
> twentieth-century pioneers of the history of religions were conscious of this
> tapestry, but they attempted to weave their own patterns.
>
> (HR 1985: xi)

The image of a tapestry that weaves (i.e., subsumes) difference into uniformity
and identity nicely demonstrates the liberal pluralist position that dominates
the field and its sense of the minor place of historical difference. In spite of the
supposed autonomy and integrity of the isolated threads, the overall totalized
pattern and order of the tapestry nonetheless conforms to accepted or so-called
legitimate models. This is an example of the rhetoric of unity and totalization
whereby the complex relations of human beings are reduced to, or contained

within, a uniform weave. It is significant that, despite the supposed richness of the weave, the debate within this volume leaves untouched any substantive discussion with social scientists and materialists.

For Kitagawa, then, scholars of religion are crafty weavers for whom the datum of religion is self-evident; they need give little thought to the mechanisms whereby they set the limits to their tapestry. The effect of this rhetoric is that the relations of these early weavers to issues of theoretical or socio-political relevance (i.e., local or world politics, imperialism, or colonialism) remain obscured – not just unaddressed but unidentified. Rather than understand academic discourses as products of a theoretical and socio-political world, these weavers are artists motivated simply "by their concern with the ... universal character of religious phenomena."

Before leaving the aesthetic, pluralist image of Kitagawa's tapestry (an image that reappears in the prefatory texts of the *Encyclopedia of Religion*, as well) it must be noted that the absence of works of, or references to, a variety of otherwise widely read contemporary writers on religion from virtually all the essays collected in all three of these volumes demonstrates the mere illusory nature of this plurality of voices and undermines Kitagawa's claim that the volumes do not represent a strict "party line." For example, many of the writers denounce reductionism but not a single "reductionist" enters the debate or is quoted at any length.[15] Rather, in the use of the term reductionists – as in the use of other terms such as social scientist, historian, and even theologian – a group of Others is massed together as an easily identifiable oppositional camp that is self-evidently dangerous to the history of religions, itself thereby portrayed as a monolith as well. There is a definite strategic advantage to not looking one's foes in the eye, to not addressing them by name, to generalize and essentialize them into a homogenous crowd.

Kitagawa continues to develop his constructed lineage in the remaining pages of his "Introduction." The early disciplinary difficulties in Europe are noted (the study was housed in theological schools and was distrusted for its evolutionary assumptions). In the U.S., such nineteenth-century events as the institution of the American Lectures on the History of Religions (1891) and the still much celebrated World's Parliament of Religions held in Chicago (1893) are raised up as examples of the humanistically oriented historical study indicative of the North American scene.[16] These assemblies of writers and scholars served the function, however inadequately, of unifying the early discourse. Much like Brauer before him, Kitagawa notes that it is only after World War II that the history of religions' particular brand of historical-comparative work – and that of related disciplines (e.g., comparative mythology) – became successful in the United States. Describing the pre-World War II American ethos as culturally provincial (a time when denominational control over the public discourse on religion was largely unchallenged), Kitagawa echoes a strong Eliadean theme: intimate *confrontation* with the Other, following World War II, increased the desire to *understand* that Other. Pressing beyond his analysis, and recalling the last chapter, we can say that the humanistic approach to cross-cultural and universal meaning provided a new and widely applicable classification technique that allowed it to dethrone sectarian theology. Predictably, just what the specific association is between the largely European war, the impending rise of American global influence, and the subsequent rampant increase in state-funded and controlled departments of religion is left uninvestigated by Kitagawa; instead, the field is compelled by an inner compulsion to understand. If Foucault's insights into the intimate relations between knowledge and power have any value whatsoever, they will shed much needed light upon the ironically provincial nature of the desire to *understand* and thereby *control* the "exotic" Other.

In this "new context" of disciplinary success, the three central problems that confront the discipline still revolve around rationalizing and further entrenching its autonomous disciplinary status: (i) its cooperation with other disciplines; (ii) its explicit self-identity; and (iii) the effective communication of issues (i) and (ii) to colleagues, students and society in general by taking on the role already suggested by Brauer, namely the scholar of religion as a publicly engaged intellectual. To justify the place of the history of religions within the university, Kitagawa appeals to the distinct methodological contributions to be made by approaching data "not as objects of study in themselves but as integral parts in the whole history of the religious experience and expressions of humankind" (*HR* 1985: xiii).[17] To do so, he maintains, the historian of religions examines and presents to students "exemplary data," and "exemplary features of religion." As with many writers in the field, Kitagawa does not recognize that a previous judgment and some criteria operate behind these assertions; the exemplary status of the data is simply proclaimed and assumed not to be based on judgments on the scholar's part.

Although Kitagawa's text does defend and rationalize the need for an autonomous disciplinary location for the history of religions, coming two decades after the establishment of the first public programs in the history of religions, Kitagawa naturally is far more interested in ways to articulate and sustain the discourse rather than to create it. Although the issues are intimately linked, communication with its disciplinary neighbors – or, as Ninian Smart puts it in his contribution to this volume, its "conversation partners" – figures more prominently for Kitagawa than the issue of self-definition. This change in focus is evidence that previous rhetorical efforts have successfully established the disciplinary location from which both Smart and Kitagawa call for the communication and the sharing of methods with long-established peer disciplines. In spite of the successes of the 1960s through the early 1980s, it should not go unnoticed, however, that the question of identity continues to occupy a place in the text.

Kitagawa ends his essay with an Eliadean lament for the recent inability of the history of religions to reach a "wider audience." Understandably, he cites Wach and Eliade as two examples of modern scholars who were able to write less technical essays accessible to the general reading public. After detailing examples of what he considers to have been several previously successful popularizations of the discipline aimed at the field of public education (an initiative now being pursued energetically within the American Academy of Religion and among certain European professional societies), Kitagawa observes appreciatively that "there are today signs of renewed interest in these enterprises" (HR 1985: xvi). As he goes on to suggest, the popularity of the field with both students (to provide a way to staff and thus perpetuate the discourse) and the general public (to continue to act as its funding source) is essential to its continued existence, prosperity, and privilege. In Kitagawa's slightly different words, the discipline's

> grand vision of trying to understand the profound religious dimension in human experience and history must be presented to challenge the imagination and the intellect of both scholarly and lay audiences. The discipline's health and survival require articulate and effective communication of what it is and what it can be.
>
> (HR 1985, xvi)

His emphasis upon challenging both imagination and intellect accord well with idealist assumptions operative in the field.

It is just this "health and survival" of the autonomous discipline that is the implicit focus of these three collections of essays. The appeal to its royal lineage as well as the use of a variety of rhetorics are the primary means by which Brauer and Kitagawa quite successfully build a sense of the modern history of religions centered in Chicago. If one were to see the texts within these collections as part of a seamless, homogenous unity bearing no scars, betraying no ideological battles internal to the discourse, then the implicit aim of the authors of these prefaces to portray the discourse as essentially a privileged whole would have been attained. Then Kitagawa's repeated emphasis on the need for unity in the discipline and his stress upon the severe dangers of ambiguity (both in method and in the very name of the discipline) would be interpreted only at face value and not receive any critical investigation.[18] Likewise, Eliade's attacks on specialized methodological and theoretical pluralism within the field could simply be interpreted as they traditionally have been, as a romantic nostalgia for the days of such encyclopedists as Müller and Frazer.

But this rhetoric of unity can be read much more critically. In the words of the feminist historian Joan Wallach Scott, such a disdain for heterogeneity and specialization can be evidence of

> a deep anxiety about challenges to elite versions of history. In fact, I would like to suggest that discussions of specialization are often (not always, but often) objections to democratization – to the appearance of varieties of interpretation, varieties of histories, and histories of diverse philosophies,

all of which threaten the uniformity, the continuity, and homogeneity that orthodox historians have traditionally sought to impose.

(1989a: 686; see also Scott 1989b)

Her message seems to be that to accept at face value such a rhetoric of unity and continuity is to miss identifying the dangers that heterogeneity and pluralization – in a word, fragmentation – pose to the dominant discourses. Following Wallach Scott we can conclude that the threat is not so much to this abstract thing, religion, as it is to those who benefit from representing themselves as a uniform collection of like-minded, orthodox guardians and cultural gatekeepers. The concept "religion" is their technique for maintaining a very specific form of institutional order – the discipline of religion in both senses of the term.

It should be apparent, then, that it is not my intention to suggest that the history of religions is itself an unproblematic whole. However, because a sufficient number of themes and techniques are shared across these prefaces, e.g., the repeated appeals to autonomy, the social role and privilege of the discipline, even a number of theoretical terms associated with Eliade's work are used quite often, it seems sensible to read them as part of a self-consciously coherent, developing discourse. Much as in Carrasco's *Religious Studies News* interview, cited in my own opening, examples of the Eliadean terminology abound in these essays: the terror of history (Ricoeur 1985; this and all of the following references are to essays in the specific *HR* volume); the socially redemptive role of creative hermeneutics and the new humanism (Bolle 1967; Ashby 1967; Jerome Long 1967; Ricoeur 1985); the importance of the myth of the eternal return (Kitagawa 1967; Ricoeur 1985); the relations between myth and memory (Charles Long 1967); a preoccupation with the analysis of religious symbols, i.e., such as the cosmic tree (Bolle 1967; Jerome Long 1967); use of "the sacred" as a technical but undefined term (Kitagawa 1967; Meslin 1985); attacks on cultural provincialism (Bolle 1976); the *coincidentia oppositorum* (Altizer 1967; Ashby 1967); hierophanies (Meslin 1985); the history of religions as a total discipline (White 1967); the priority of the archaic over the modern (Jerome Long 1967; Charles Long 1967; Kitagawa 1967); the intuitive nature of definitions of religion (Kitagawa 1967; Bianchi 1985); the irreducibility of religion (Ashby 1967; Kitagawa, 1985).

The work of Eliade, through his own synthetic efforts and encyclopedic readings, therefore provides for these writers a technical vocabulary which, functioning as a vernacular, contributes to the creation and maintenance of a disciplinary identity. Although his influence in the 1959 volume is understandably minimal, by 1967 and especially by 1985, Eliade's morphological approach to the study of religious symbols is employed by a number of writers as the unquestioned basis for their own analysis. All this is best summed up by Ricoeur's phenomenological study of various conceptions of time where he writes: "Let us take as a starting point and basis for comparison the model of mythical time elaborated by Mircea Eliade in *Patterns in Comparative Religion* and in *The Myth of the Eternal Return*" (HR 1985: 19).

The rhetoric of crisis and boundary maintenance

Although on the surface the apparent profusion of voices in the three volumes appears indicative of lively and diverse debate, upon closer analysis this debate turns out to be simply a collection of minor skirmishes over inessential points. Chomsky's words apply well here:

> Controversy may rage as long as it adheres to the presuppositions that define the consensus of elites, and it should furthermore be encouraged within these bounds, thus helping to establish these doctrines as the very conditions of thinkable thought, while reinforcing the belief that freedom reigns. In short, what is essential is the power to set the agenda.
>
> (1991: 48)

At no time in any of these volumes is the agenda of the history of religions questioned, nor is the reason for taking Eliade's work as "our starting point and basis" questioned. The self-evident power of sheer assertion over argumentation is never called in question. The need for defensible theories of human minds, behaviors, and institutions is never entertained. Rather, each writer unquestionably subscribes to the irreducible uniqueness of religious experience and religious phenomena and the privileged position of this one approach to understanding it. In fact, the discipline-wide preoccupation with issues of methods, rather than theories, constitutes sufficient evidence of the unarticulated territorial imperative that underlies these volumes. All contributors set out to discuss which *technique* of analysis suits the data of the field, yet not one attempts to defend the logically prior set of assumptions – the grammar – that determine just what constitutes the "it" under study. No one entertains that something is data precisely because of a prior theory – a theory which is not simply expressed by or manifested within the datum under study but which is the product of a pre-existent scholarly community. In the beginning wasn't the datum; it was the curious observer. As represented in these three volumes, the study of religion is not only apolitical and acontextual, it is apparently atheoretical as well.

That not all scholars of religion are in agreement should be evident from one final strategy of containment employed by Kitagawa within his preface to Kurt Rudolph's Haskell lectures (Rudolph 1985): the rhetoric of crisis that was evident in Wach's earlier thoughts on domination, emancipation, and liberation. Commenting on Rudolph's essay concerning the autonomy of the discipline, Kitagawa uses the opportunity to heighten the reader's sense of the potentially disastrous implications of losing the crucial debate on autonomy by speaking of the "crises of autonomy and integrity that threaten to fragment the discipline and disperse its remnants among the human studies." Rudolph also echoes this theme in that same essay when he writes that "several signs indicate that the history of religions is experiencing a crisis." As well, after commenting on how other specialties are encroaching upon the history of religions, he argues that "this entanglement threatens to dismember and demolish the discipline" (1985: 43–44).

These comments on the impending crisis echo Brauer's early strategic description of the "urgency" which confronted the discipline in 1959. Due to the effects of World War II and the Cold War, the world in 1959 was described as "bewildered" by Kitagawa (*HR* 1959: 30). With the decline of western Europe's worldwide hegemony, Cantwell Smith in that same volume speaks of the "new world situation" (*HR* 1959: 33, 46), which brings to mind Brauer's rhetoric of the "new perspective," Kitagawa's "new context," perhaps even Franklin D. Roosevelt's "new deal," let alone George H. W. Bush's "new world order." Although such idealists might not wish to recognize this, they, like Eliade, are prompted to reconfigure the discipline by means of their talk of urgency, crisis, and newness – a reconfiguring prompted by changes in concretely material factors, namely the redistribution of global political, military, and economic resources. For instance, for Eliade one of the main motivations for the urgent need to understand the Other (or, as phrased by Cantwell Smith, the need to befriend the Other) was his often written observation that in the 1950s the east was for the first time "re-entering history." The incredibly egocentric (and, ironically, in spite of all ornaments which suggest otherwise, Eurocentric) nature of such a judgment is betrayed when one problematizes his use of the term history as if it were a uniform thing, and simply asks, "*Whose* history?" As Christian missions in the global age seem to have given way to liberal humanist initiatives to dialogue with a tightly constrained Other (an activity that retains striking aspects of the earlier missionary enterprise), the now firmly re-established study of religion seems to a large degree deeply rooted in attempts to realign and revive European-North American world hegemony in the face of the rising east.

Describing such a situation as a crisis and then relying upon images of fragmentation and dispersion are all crucial for maintaining the facade of homogeneity and control. To refer again to the recent debate on the supposed crisis in the field of history, Wallach Scott offers a most helpful insight into the agenda which underwrites the disciplining effects of the rhetoric of crisis:

> For those who think their position is or ought to be hegemonic, the appearance of critical challenges constitutes a "crisis." By representing themselves simply as the guardians of "History" [or, in our case, *sui generis* religion or the history of religions], they deny the possibility of fundamental disagreement about the boundaries of the field, instead representing those who challenge these boundaries as outsiders ... [and] as either ignorant or wilfully destructive enemies.
>
> (1989a: 682)

Eliade's apparently lifelong distrust and fear of what he often referred to as dilettantes in the study of religion has much to do with such boundary maintenance.

Such supposedly provincial dabblers are those judged by the self-designated guardians of orthodoxy to be ignorant, or, in Eliade's terms, devoid of deep passion. According to historians of religions, they are no doubt comprised of those who do not take religion "seriously" enough.

The main difference between the strategic deployment of the rhetoric of crisis in the field of history and in the history of religions is that in the former, according to Wallach Scott, such imagery is used by the faithful to characterize and thereby combat the contemporary threats made on orthodoxy by such developments as post-modern and feminist critiques. Part of the strategy, then, is to juxtapose the chaotic present and unstable future with the nostalgic past characterized as a peaceful, uniform, and uncontested intellectual landscape. However, in the case of the history of religions, at least according to its leading representatives, the crisis appears always to have been present, if not in the form of the theoretical and institutional menace of theology and philosophy, then in the form of perilous reductionism and the social sciences.

Although participants in the regnant discourse may wish to project these various and ever-changing challenges into one transcendent and recurring crisis, it is clear that the motivations for, and implications of, the battles for institutional autonomy waged by F. Max Müller and C. P. Tiele in the nineteenth century should not be so quickly homogenized with such later developments as Wach's call for autonomy – Wach, after all, was highly sympathetic to theologizing the data of the discipline – and Eliade's and Kitagawa's calls for integrity. To identify these individual historical debates as part of one universal crisis in the discipline simply serves to universalize and essentialize the enemies of the field as well as to provide one starting point for the invention of the tradition, a strategy employed in so many contemporary ethnic-nationalist clashes: the shared historical battle against the Other. The official picture of this academic field, then, is of a group of like-minded, well-intentioned, and serious scholars working perilously close to two great dangers, reductionism and confessional theology – a picture with some resemblance to the Cold War-period portrait of Europe as helplessly situated between two threatening super-powers.

Conclusion: trading in territory for maps

The three prefaces display a number of recurring rhetorics, themes, and strategies: the use of explicit or implicit genealogical strategies, the repeated appeal for the autonomy of both religion (in the form of religious phenomena embodying universal religious experiences) and the disciplinary location for its study, the association between disciplinary identity and unique methods, and the social relevance of the discipline. All of them function to limit, authorize, and contain the developing discourse. The entire discursive field, at least the most significant portions of it, exist and are reinforced within all of these texts.

At the same time, strategies of containment or damage control have also been identified as operating to limit – even camouflage – lapses within the discourse. The supposedly monolithic nature of this discourse, symbolically represented in the recurring title "history of religions," therefore has been undermined not only by demonstrating the ideological rifts present within the texts, but also by identifying the mechanisms that are used to create the facade of homogeneity and unity. To mistake all three volumes as part of a coherent and continuous "tradition" or uniform tapestry is to be seduced by the rhetoric of essentialization and dehistoricization. An interpretation which portrays these three books – covering a period from the early Cold War to the excesses of late-capitalism – as part of an extended and identical tradition undervalues and ignores the constructed nature of all social formations; it also glosses over the changing socio-political world of those writers and the people they attempt to re-present through their texts.

That the history of religions is far from the only scholarly activity whose influence was intimately dependent upon an essentialized and mystified object of analysis should be clear. Evolutionarily stagnant "primitives" of an earlier generation of anthropologists (see Kuper 1988), monolithic "society" for an earlier generation of sociologists, uppercase "Literature" for many literary critics, classless and genderless "Man" for a host of humanists and social scientists, all served as tropes for asserting a particular group's social privilege. Upon closer analysis such claims concerning all-inclusive, universal signifiers betray local-ized skirmishes over access to resources, power, and prestige.

The question we must ask is whether such mystification is inevitable. As some self-reflexive, post-modern scholars have suggested, the human sciences might be inextricably locked within the essentialist/political project. I would suggest that the recent move toward cross-disciplinary scholarship on human communities overcomes some of these problems by shifting the focus from inductively available, self-evident data to the role of the scholar in providing deductive-based theories that actively classify, organize, and categorize. For example, instead of organizing a disciplinary identity based on "the sacred," the contemporary academic study of religion is moving toward constituting itself around a collection of theories concerning how and why human beings organize themselves through the use of this or that technique or process. Evoking Jonathan Z. Smith's often quoted phrasing, this constitutes the move from studying the actual lived "territory" of ineffable human experiences (whether they be religious, ethnic, or gendered experiences) to the "maps," classificatory schemes, grammars, and taxonomies that scholars devise in their effort to compare and explain human behavior (part of that which is the human penchant to create and authorize taxonomies!). Shifting the focus from self-evident and self-authenticating data to the discursive systems for which this or that instance of human behavior counts as data (i.e., is made into data), enables the field to continue as a more self-reflexive endeavor, open to two ironic insights: (i) there is nothing necessarily interesting about that which we as scholars find so curious; (ii) the rhetorics used to authorize our interests and taxonomies deserve just as much critical study as any other group's behaviors. We scholars of religion ought to become our own data.

Scholars who recognize that they are themselves implicated in their efforts to classify, will be more open to critiques that examine the socio-political contexts in which their scholarship is inevitably carried out. At least so one hopes. Although this will by no means ensure that scholarship becomes the neutral enterprise it was once thought to be, it will serve to strengthen the human sciences by opening them to social and material critique. Sadly for some, perhaps, this will also lessen their influence to the degree that such criticism lessens the self-declared authority scholars once enjoyed. Perhaps something is lost when such empty claims as Eliade's "the sacred is that which is not profane" are no longer accepted as a meaningful basis of study; lacking such rhetoric, historians of religions will no longer be able to make their contributions to public debates as the wise guardians of previously lost, archaic meanings and values. Much more is gained, however, when the rhetoric of tautology is seen for what it is – potent decorative gestures that, in addition to adding romance to a life, are intellectual and political side-steps, distracting attention from much larger material issues. Only once we understand their rhetorical role will we not just hone the tools with which we conceptualize our data, but we will also be able to examine critically "the historical conditions which motivate our conceptualization," thus providing us with a "historical awareness of our present circumstance" (Foucault 1982: 778).

Notes

1 What Barthes named the rhetoric of tautology is painfully evident in Mircea Eliade's *The Sacred and the Profane*, where he defines the sacred as that which is not profane! – "tautology is a faint at the right moment" (Barthes 1973: 166).

2 See Burris 2001 for an effort to contextualize and examine, among other expositions of the late nineteenth-century, the 1893 World's Parliament in a manner that does more than simply celebrate it as a triumph of early liberalism and religious pluralism.

3 Eliade co-edited the 1959 volume and is listed, along with Charles Long, as Kitagawa's collaborator in the editing of the 1967 volume. The last volume, although edited by Kitagawa alone, is the product of a number of people who recorded various aspects of the 1983 conference. Along with Kitagawa, Gregory Alles co-wrote the Afterword which largely is a summary of the verbal and unpublished conference responses to the various essays published in the volume.

4 Such exercises in the formulation and articulation of a lineage (what else is a cosmogony or a genealogy?) are useful in establishing identity and credibility based upon the presumed authority of those represented as part of a genetic tradition. In the words of Eric Hobsbawm, writing the introduction to *The Invention of Tradition*, "all invented traditions, so far as possible, use history as a legitimator of action and cement of group cohesion" (1992: 12). Of importance is the recognition that, as already suggested by Braun, what is represented as undisputed history is "not what has actually been preserved in popular memory, but what has been selected, written, pictured, popularized, and institutionalized by those whose function it is to do so" (Hobsbawm and Ranger 1992: 13).

5 Again, to apply Hobsbawm's insights on nationalism to the study of religion, the rhetoric of self-evidency can be seen to be operating when members of this discourse refuse to define just what they mean when they refer to "religion" or what it is that makes experiences, behaviors, or institutions religious. Such writers find the self-evidency or intuitive nature of these characteristics "so 'natural' as to require no definition other than self-assertion" (Hobsbawm 1992: 14). That such writers then champion inductive, rather than deductive, methods of research should, then, come as no surprise.

6 Abington, Pennsylvania, School District v. Schempp, 374 U.S. 203, 225 (1963). In this passage, the use of "comparative religion" and "the history of religion" appears not to indicate disciplines but rather two ways of studying religion, their history and their comparison. Further, it is important to note that Justice Clark – like the regnant discourse in the field – appears to conceive of religion in a rather positive and uncritical light, drawing particular attention to the ways in which religion has been associated with the "advancement of civilization."

7 Significantly, Brauer, then professor of Christian Church history at Chicago, maintains that the history of religions' methodology "will soon prove influential in all dimensions of theological study" (HR 1967: vi). Writing in the same volume, Kees Bolle asserted that Jesus Christ was the *sine qua non* of faith and that "Christian faith is not a general or generalizable something. It is as specific as the task of theology itself is inalienable and irreplaceable by the History of Religions" (HR 1967: 110). The question of the demarcation between the history of religions and Christian theology arises in not a few other places in these volumes, e.g., when Michel Meslin employs the category of "sin" as a comparative category (HR 1985: 42).

8 The same technique was used in establishing their quarterly journal, *History of Religions*. Eliade recalls: "in the winter of 1960 we began to write to a number of European colleagues, asking them to contribute" (1988: 208).

9 Contributors to the 1959 volume were: Joseph Kitagawa (Chicago), Wilfred Cantwell Smith (Toronto, Harvard, McGill), Raffaele Pettazzoni (Rome), Jean Daniélou (Paris), Mircea Eliade (Romania, Paris, Chicago), Louis Massignon (Paris), Ernest Benz (Marburg), and Friedrich Heiler (Marburg). One can observe the success of this strategy of established authority at work when, just six years after the publication of this volume, Charles J. Adams was confident enough in the success of this volume and the self-evident authority of its contributors to recommend it to the readers of his *A Reader's Guide to the Great Religions* (1965). At the conclusion of his own essay on "primitive religions" he notes that the "scholar's represented there are the leaders in the field at the present time, and for this reason their views on methodology have unusual interest and importance" (1965: 30).

10 Besides Brauer, those who contributed were: Eliade, Kitagawa, Charles Long, Kees W. Bolle, Thomas J. J. Altizer, Philip H. Ashby, Charles S. J. White, Charles J. Adams, H. Byron Earhart, Jerome H. Long, and Paul Tillich (who participated in a joint seminar with Eliade at Chicago in the winter and autumn of 1964). The European roots of the Chicago program are still partially apparent in the posthumously translated essay of Wach's, originally published in *Zeitschrift für Missionskunde und Religionswissenschaft* in 1935, that introduces the volume.

11 "One way in which man seeks to understand the present is to see it in relation to the past out of which it comes" (HR 1959: vii).

12 To his credit, Charles Long, in his essay "A Look at the Chicago Tradition in the History of Religions: Retrospect and Future," acknowledges that Wach and Haydon both wrote on the topic of the need for a distinct discipline but, he adds, "for quite different reasons" (HR 1985: 92). However, Long fails to elaborate on this point. Instead, much as we find in the Afterword to the 1985 collection of essays, Long must emphasize the imagined whole which transcends and unites the individual,

historical parts of this divergent tradition. The rationale for such unification is provided in the Afterword: "Because it persists in the midst of change, the concern for the whole can serve as a fixed point from which to view the discipline as it is situated in the flux of time" (HR 1985: 146). Being historically situated, it is intriguing how these writers can acquire such privileged knowledge of the subject of the above sentence, the "it" or the "fixed point" which persists in spite of the "flux of time."

13 This volume comprises essays originally read at a University of Chicago conference in May 1983. Mircea Eliade's and Paul Ricoeur's contributions to the volume originally were keynote addresses. The essays by Michel Meslin (University of Paris-Sorbonne), Ugo Bianchi (University of Rome), Ninian Smart (University of California at Santa Barbara), and Charles Long (University of North Carolina, Chapel Hill) were oral presentations which, at the conference, were followed by the remarks of various respondents. Kurt Rudolph (then working at Karl Marx University, Leipzig) was unable to attend and so his paper was read *in absentia*. Joseph Kitagawa's essay was written for a different occasion but included in this volume.

14 In spite of their apparent differences both are nonetheless birds of a feather. See *Necessary Illusions*, for Chomsky's example of the debate over U.S. policy in Nicaragua in the 1980s. Even though the media doves question the efficacy of Reagan's policy toward Central America, they do not question such supposedly fundamental issues as self-evident American right to impose regional arrangements on its neighbors (1991: 60–61).

15 Donald Wiebe's essay, "Is a Science of Religion Possible?" (1978) is cited by Kitagawa (HR 1985: 143 n. 45), but only for its references which discuss the ambiguous use of the term science of religion.

16 Rudolph, unlike Kitagawa, finds little time for emphasizing the importance of the Chicago Parliament. According to him: "Only thanks to the guiding lights and overwhelming majority of the members of the International Association for the History of Religions [IAHR] have the most recent world congresses of this body avoided slipping into congresses of religion after the model of the Parliament held in Chicago in 1893" (HR 1985: 74).

17 As with others, for Kitagawa the autonomy of the discipline is intimately related to its methods: "if the history of religions is to make its distinct contribution to the cooperative inquiry into religion(s), its scholars must bring to bear on the cooperative endeavor the perspectives and approaches of their discipline, which is an important alternative to other disciplines" (HR 1985: xv).

18 Other examples of the rhetoric of unity are: the often made remark concerning the hermeneutic need to subsume the parts within a whole; Friedrich Heiler believes that the unity of religion (in the singular) transcends history, doctrine, and cultus (HR 1959: 152); Byron Earhart, like Kitagawa, wants to develop a unified interpretation of Japanese religious history which ignores historical rifts in the data (HR 1967: 195); Charles Long talks of establishing a world culture and, total truth (HR 1967: 82–83); Philip Ashby also speaks of world culture (HR 1967: 158); Ugo Bianchi (echoing Pettazzoni [HR 1959]) writes that we need urgently to link and to harmonize the two approaches of phenomenology and history (HR 1985: 57); and reminiscent of Eliade, Kurt Rudolph asserts that the history of religions is a universal discipline which "holds the entire globe before its eyes" (HR 1985: 116).

Chapter 4

Classification and the dog's breakfast

The American Academy of Religion's research interest survey

> There is always a little thought even in the most stupid institutions.
>
> (Foucault 1988a: 155)

With some of the techniques of discursive control and constraint used in helping to establish this discipline fresh in our minds, I turn now to an analysis of a contemporary document: the American Academy of Religion's (AAR) annual research interest survey that divides, and in some cases then subdivides, the study of religion into four main areas. Although this chapter was first inspired by the AAR's 1997 research interest survey, since that time the survey has not changed in any significant way as far as I can tell (though it is now available to members on line; while the content has remained, the form has changed). In these surveys the discipline is divided into four parts: historical periods, geographic areas, traditions, and approaches and/or fields. My aim in this chapter is to examine the AAR research interest survey as a case study in the way a discipline is understood by some of its practitioners, an understanding that betrays the general bankruptcy of critical intelligence that has now come to comprise the dominant manner in which religion is studied in a public setting. Although one should of course not put too much stock in the significance of this one survey – a survey possibly devised to determine which members mailing list to sell to which advertiser/publisher/book seller – the confused and seemingly arbitrary nature of its classificatory scheme confirms some of the problems already documented in the previous chapters.

The problem of the survey involves issues of demarcation and classification – what we as scholars study and how we study it. It is a problem of understanding the relationship between theories, methods, and data, three distinct yet related levels of analysis. This problem will be more than apparent if, instead of scanning through the survey to find what applies to one's own work – i.e., if one does not simply implement the taxonomy to plot and thus legitimize oneself – readers instead examine the survey as a whole and inquire into its rationale and impact. Read in this manner it will become apparent that the survey – and quite possibly the field itself – lacks coherence and is, instead, a dog's breakfast of inductively based self-evidencies. The portrait that emerges from this survey can accurately be described in the words from Charlotte Allen's *Lingua Franca* cover article on our field (1996; see also 1998): the study of religion, she concludes, is "a shapeless beast, half social science, half humanistic discipline, lumbering through the academy with no clear methodology or *raison d'être*" (see McCutcheon 2001b: ch. 1).

As most recently offered, the survey is as follows:

Periods

- Prehistory
- Ancient
- Medieval
- Modern
- Contemporary

Geographic areas

- Africa: East/West/South
- Africa: North/Egypt
- America: North
- America: South/Meso/Caribbean
- Asia: South/Southeast
- Asia: Central/North/East
- Asia: Middle/East/West
- Europe: East/West
- Oceania/Australia

Traditions

- African
- African American
- Ancient Greco-Roman
- Ancient Near Eastern
- Buddhist
- Christian
    - Catholic
    - Orthodox
    - Protestant
- Confucian
- Gnostic
- Hindu
- Indigenous
- Islamic
- Jain

- Judaic
- Native American
- New religions
- Popular and folk religions
- Postmodern
- Secular modern
- Shinto
- Taoist
- Zoroastrian

Approaches and/or fields

- Anthropology
- Archaeology
- Arts
- Comparative
- Cultural critique
  - Gay/lesbian
  - Gender
  - Ideological
- Cultural studies
- Ecumenical studies
- Education
- Ethics
- History
- Literature
- Liturgy/worship
- Myth
- Pastoral care/counseling
- Performance/ritual studies
- Phenomenology
- Philology
- Philosophy
- Psychology
- Rabbinic studies
- Sacred texts & literatures
  - Hebrew Bible
  - New Testament
  - Pali Canon
  - Qur'an
  - Talmud
  - Vedic
- Science
- Sociology

- Theology (Christian)
  - Historical
  - Practical
  - Systematic
- Theory of religion

The problems with this survey are numerous. To begin with, take its section on *Traditions*. Despite the many criticisms that have focused on the continued use of this vague, Cantwell Smithean category, we may well have little choice but to continue its usage; despite the fact that the majority of the world's population has no functional equivalent to our classification "religion," members of our profession continue to presume that certain social formations are easily divided into these relatively stable units known as religious, as opposed to political traditions or family traditions. Such a critique notwithstanding, the logic of this category is lost on me. First off, the Eurocentric, Christian bias in this and other categories is glaring – something which is hardly news to those who attend the annual AAR/SBL meetings. Whereas, for example, the heterogenous complexes known by the short-hands Buddhism, Hinduism, and New Religions are each presented as single entries, each being an apparently monolithic thing, the entry for Christianity is further sub-divided into Catholic, Orthodox, and Protestant (the 1997 survey included "Other" as a fourth sub-division of Christianity). Such excessive attention to what are, from other points of view, minor sectarian differences[1] is reminiscent of R. C. Zaehner's old comparative religion textbook where Christianity received five chapters (Early Church, Eastern Schism, Medieval Theology, Protestantism, and Catholicism since the Reformation). At least Buddhism, which is at least five hundred years older, received three chapters in Zaehner's book.

Should we be in the business of reproducing particular social worlds, such as a Christian view of the world, then the navel-gazing that comes with emphasizing "us" and our ways is quite understandable. Unfortunately, we in the academy are supposedly doing something other than that, despite the fact that drawing the Euro-Christocentric bias to people's attention has somehow lately been seen as passé or based on a strawman argument. This navel-gazing is apparent right across the curriculum, informing how we construct entire fields of knowledge. As but one example, take the highly developed taxonomy of the Blackwell Book Service, the service that supplies many of our libraries with their books. When, for example, a U.S. university librarian pre-selects the areas in which she or he would like automatically to receive new books or descriptions of new books, Blackwell classifies the religious traditions of these books' topics as follows: Judaism receives 7 sub-headings (including Conservative, Orthodox, Reform, and Other Judaism); Buddhism receives 4 (Theravada, Mahayana, Zen, and Other); Islam receives 3 (Sunni, Shi'ite, and Other); African Religions, Ancient Religions, Hinduism, Jainism, Primal Religions, Shinto, Sikhism, and Zoroastrianism have no sub-headings whatsoever. Christianity, of course, receives *55 separate sub-headings* – everything from a special focus on many of the denominations to areas devoted to such topics as eschatology, patrology, and saints. Luckily, there is a category for "Non-Christian Sacred Books," including 9 non-Christian entries.[2] Of course almost all sub-headings include "Other," that wonderful technique for including everything you've either never thought of or simply forgotten, and thus left out – a technique which is the opposite of one sub-category in Borges's fictional list of animals drawn from a "certain Chinese encyclopedia": "included in the present classification" but which is in line with another of his sub-categories: "*et cetera*" (quoted in Foucault 1973: xv). The difference between the book service list and Borges's list is that, unlike Foucault's laughter upon first reading the latter – a laughter prompted by his realization of "the stark impossibility of thinking *that*" – the former is sadly typical and reinforces "all the familiar landmarks of my thought, *our* thought, the thought that bears the stamp of our age and our geography" (quoting Foucault once again). That the book service classification system and the AAR survey do *not* prompt laughter is what ought to attract our attention!

Just as with the book service, the AAR's category *Tradition* includes a number of sub-categories whose interrelations are not entirely apparent: whereas some sub-categories are geographic (African), others are historical (Ancient Near Eastern), nationalist/ethnic (African-American or Native American), and yet others are the more traditional "world religions" (Buddhist or Islamic). Such a mixture suggests that the explicit relations between the concepts by means of which we organize our data are of little consequence. Despite this odd combination of sub-categories, what I find most troubling about this grouping is how Postmodern and Secular Modern find their way into it. Placing these two categories under *Tradition* suggests that, despite their inability to win in the Courts, Creationist arguments concerning the religion of secular humanism have somehow triumphed in the academy. If, however, *Tradition* in this case does not refer to a particularly religious tradition (as it does in all the other sub-categories), then I am not sure how other sorts of traditions were ruled out of this category (for example, flipping a coin at the start of a college football game).

Equally troubling is the rationale behind the category entitled *Approaches and/or Fields*. One must beware of the way in which the seemingly inclusive "and/or" covers up for poor thinking, for here we find a truly disquieting mix of humanistic and social scientific disciplinary rubrics and methods (Anthropology, Comparative, History, Sociology, etc.), analytic constructs (Arts, Myth, Literature, Ritual), and theological practices (Liturgy/Worship, Pastoral Care/Counseling, Rabbinic Studies, and Christian [as opposed to other sorts?] Theology, further subdivided into Historical, Practical, and Systematic). As if this was not bad enough, last and likely least comes Theory of Religion, reduced to one among many options in this category, as if developing theories to direct one's research on religion somehow operates on the same cognitive or institutional level as Rabbinic Studies, Theology, or Pastoral Care. In fact, to place Theory of Religion alongside such phenomenologically based categories as Sacred Texts, Worship, Ritual, and Myth, is sufficient evidence both of the bankruptcy of critical thinking skills in the field and the extent to which gate-keepers will go to constrain a pursuit that might otherwise topple their current dominance. It is comparable to a survey in Psychology that might list Behaviorism or Psychoanalysis (a theoretical system and a method) alongside Ego (an analytic category) and Schizophrenia (a term for organizing data in need of study). If members of our field cannot distinguish theories from methods, from analytic constructs, from the various data we define, sort, classify by means of the previous three, then there is little wonder that some departments have had difficulty justifying their continued existence.

The chaotic scholarly smorgasbord that results from unarticulated theories, vague definitions, and the presumption that our object of study is elusive and personal, can be witnessed in the AAR's 2001 list of Program Units.[3] Arranged hierarchically (from the permanent "sections" to the temporary, three-year experimental "Consultations"), they are:

Sections

- Academic teaching and the study of religion
- Arts, literature, and religion
- Buddhism
- Comparative studies in religion
- Ethics
- History of Christianity
- North American religions
- Philosophy of religion
- Religion and the social sciences
- Religion in South Asia
- Study of Islam
- Study of Judaism
- Theology and religious reflection
- Women and Religion

Groups

- African religions
- Afro-American religious history
- Asian North American religion, culture, and society
- Black theology
- Bonhoeffer: theology and social analysis
- Chinese religions
- Christian spirituality
- Christian systematic theology

- Church–State studies
- Comparative studies in Hinduisms and Judaisms
- Confucian traditions
- Critical theory and discourses on religion
- Eastern Orthodox studies
- Europe and the Mediterranean in late antiquity
- Evangelical theology
- Feminist theory and religious reflection
- Gay men's issues in religion
- Hinduism
- Indigenous religious traditions
- Japanese religions
- Kierkegaard, religion, and culture
- Korean religions
- Lesbian-feminist issues and religion
- Men's studies in religion
- Millennialism studies
- Mysticism
- Native traditions in the Americas
- New religious movements
- Nineteenth-century theology
- Person, culture, and religion
- Platonism and neoplatonism
- Pragmatism and empiricism in American religious thought
- Reformed theology and history
- Religion and ecology
- Religion and ethics in health care
- Religion and popular culture
- Religion and science
- Religion in Latin America and the Caribbean
- Religion, film, and visual culture
- Religion, Holocaust, and genocide
- Ritual studies
- Roman Catholic studies
- Schleiermacher
- Theology and continental philosophy
- Tibetan and Himalayan religions
- U.S. Latino/a religion, culture, and society
- Wesleyan studies
- Womanist approaches to religion and society

Seminars

- Constructions of ancient space

- Modern historical consciousness and the Christian churches
- Practice of Christianity in Roman Africa
- Rastafari in global contexts: religion and culture
- Studies in Yogacara Buddhism
- Tokugawa religion seminar

Consultations

- Anthropology of religion
- Augustine and Augustinianisms
- History, method, and theory in the study of religion
- Law, religion, and culture
- Religion and disability studies
- Religion and human rights
- Religion, ethics, and society in contemporary East Asia
- Religion in Central and Eastern Europe
- Religion, culture and communication
- Religions, medicines, and healing
- Western esotericism from the early modern period

We see here multiple, overlapping, and sometimes competing rubrics based on the names given to religions and their sub-divisions (Yogacara Buddhism), geography (North American Religion), ethnic/nationalist groups (Chinese religions), historic eras (Modern Historical Consciousness), influential Christian (generally Protestant) theologians (Bonhoeffer), analytic tools (Ritual Studies), and the all-encompassing category of themes (Arts and Literature).

What is fascinating about this "come one, come all" approach is (i) its ability to allow the field virtually unlimited growth because (ii) the field is utterly deregulated insomuch as it has a complete absence of any explicit rationale (an absence which provides the necessary conditions for such rampant growth). As Jonathan Smith has commented, this rampant growth coupled with a lack of rationale is evidence that "[we] may not always know what we are doing, but we are doing exceedingly well at it!" (Smith 2002: 7).[4] There is something oddly capitalistic about the field's growth economy; based on an undefinable inner essence, there necessarily develops a proliferation of competing approaches, none of which will ever be deemed adequate or superior since the object of study is undefinable and invisible. Infinite growth inevitably follows; proliferation for proliferation's sake is the rule; a thousand flowers bloom and wilt. Although I have commented critically elsewhere on the continued prominence of the politically suspect world religions model (1997b: ch. 4), it would at least be a relief to see, say, the sections reflect each of the so-called major world religions (as in the book service taxonomy), under the assumption that each requires a sustained analysis by an ongoing group of scholars. Instead, we see only Buddhism, just the *History* of Christianity (not Christianity itself, of course, since that's just too complex a thing to study all at once), North American religions (which could be literally anything, so long as it happens in North America[5]), Islam, Judaism, and Religion in South Asia (which, again, could contain any number of things) in the permanent section category. Hinduism luckily receives group status, (alongside Wesleyan Studies?), whereas work on the history of the field is now part of an experimental consultation.

With this last mentioned consultation in mind, in 1999 the Program Committee of the AAR denied the request of a group known as the History of the Study of Religion (first formed as part of the AAR in 1988) for what could have been a routine renewal of its status[6] – a similar situation had arisen during its regular review in 1992 but the group was reviewed once again and then renewed for another five-year term. It was not so lucky at the end of that period, however. Despite the positive comments of the AAR's external reviewer,[7] one of the reasons for ending the group, according to the letter communicating the decision of the Program Committee (see the consultation's site, www.netrax.net/~galles/hmt) was that its focus was unnecessarily narrow. Although one would think that a group dealing with the history of the field would warrant the most permanent – section – status, instead, its focus was judged too narrow, whereas ongoing groups examining, for instance, but one mid-twentieth-century German Protestant (Bonhoeffer), a nineteenth-century British Protestant brother team (Wesleyan Studies), and a lone eighteenth-century German Protestant (Schleiermacher) are not. Despite Foucault's thoughts on the presence of some sort of logic in all institutions, looking for it in the list of program units, as well as the Program Committee's decisions, might be too much to ask.

If we really must presume there to exist some underlying logic we must keep in mind, to quote one of Foucault's asides, that "schools of rationality balk at having their history written, which is no doubt significant" (1988a: 83). Such historicization calls into question previously assumed certainties, making it rather dangerous. For example, if, as the utter diversity of AAR program units seems to suggest, religion conceived as deeply personal feeling, is whatever you make of it, then by definition it cannot have a history. This, in turn, further propels the growth economy model, for every new "Religion and ... " proposal must be acceptable, since the professional organization must contain every conceivable personal preference that falls within its ill-defined party lines. The now mammoth, alienating size of the annual meeting (rumored to be nearing 10,000 participants/attendees) is a direct result of this. But, if scholarship on the history and continued identity of our field as a whole does not count as among the most inclusive, and active sub-fields within our profession, then I have trouble defending the status of the Academy's current sections listed in our call for papers.

In an effort to help members of the field to rethink the study of religion's rationale, goals, and identity, I suggest that future surveys – and, along with them, the way we classify our data and think ourselves into being scholars – be reorganized in a rather different manner. By publishing an earlier version of this chapter in our field's widest circulating professional newsletter (*Religious Studies Review*) my goal was to prompt a debate on just how research in our field is actually carried out. Future surveys did not change in any significant degree and, apart from a kind letter written to me (containing a copy of the construc- tively critical reply to my article she had written and unsuccessfully submitted to *RSN*; see the appendix to this chapter for a copy of my response to her), the article raised no debate whatsoever. Because I continue to be persuaded that these are important issues, and because nobody likes to be ignored, I once again offer the following suggestions.

That the classificatory scheme that I propose comes with certain values is part of what is involved in the act of classification; classification is not neutral. It is an exercise based in higher order intellectual, institutional, social, even political values and agendas. Such agendas drive our research by directing our questioning gaze. As observers and participants we are actively constituting this world through innumerable pre-observational judgments, assumptions, anticipa- tions, and curiosities, all of which are encoded in the way in which we divide up the pie of our world. It falls to the scholar to articulate, systematize, and, when it is necessary, to defend these broad theoretical frameworks that control the problematics of the field; in the final analysis this amounts to articulating, systematizing, and defending the field itself for a scholarly field of study is constituted by its problematics. As phrased by Jonathan Z. Smith in a 1990 *JAAR* essay, it is in part our job as scholars to "expose the set of tacit under- standings which inform, but are rarely the objects of, our corporate discourse about religion" (1990a: 5). Such exposure is all the more important when we are attempting to identify the contours and limits – its historical conditions – of the discipline by means of research surveys. Perhaps this rearticulated scheme will prompt some of this critical dialogue and make a contribution toward greater clarity in our institutional self-definition. It is a scheme that, in part, informs the way in which my co-editor, Willi Braun, and I understood the field to operate when we devised our *Guide to the Study of Religion* (2000; on the rationale for the *Guide*, see Braun and McCutcheon 2002).

First in our new survey must come the category *Theories*, since theories of human minds, individuals, social formations, texts, and institutions are what drives our research. These theories can be in one of a number of areas and each area undoubtedly has a number of subdivisions. For example, we might identify several such widely operating theoretical frameworks: Intellectualist (concerned with studying people's attempts to explain the causes of events in their world), Emotivist (concerned with studying the affective aspect of human experience and behavior), Symbolist (concerned with how symbol systems make meaning possible), Holistic (concerned with system-wide analysis such as structuralism), Ideological (concerned with how undisclosed techniques constitute all social relations), and, finally, Naturalistic (concerned with studying human minds, beliefs, behaviors, and social groups as products of biological or genetically determined constraints).[8] Although debate on just what gets to count as a theory is obviously important, offering these six frameworks to begin with at least gets us talking about the ways in which scholarship proceeds. It begins with curiosity and questions that arise from observing the unexpected. The very fact that we first expect this or that to take place suggests that we are not naive innocents but that we come on the scene with anticipations and, if not explicit, then at least implicit or tacit, theories. As scholars, can we be responsible enough to bring them to light? Without reverting to the proverbial, and suitably arbitrary, "Because it's there," can we answer someone when they ask us the simple question as to why we climb the academic mountains that we do?

Second in this alternate survey would come the category *Methods*, for, depending on the theory that shapes one's problematic, one will use different tools. This category could include: Anthropological, Archaeological, Economic, Feminist, Hermeneutical, Historical, Linguistic, Literary Critical, Morphological, Phenomenological, Philological, Philosophical, Political, Psychological, Sociobiological, and Sociological. Each of these categories can be used in one or more theoretical contexts to organize a specific set of tools that are used to study different aspects of human minds, beliefs, behaviors, symbolic systems, and social institutions. That theology is absent from this list will perhaps strike some as a glaring omission. Given my conception of the field, a conception I have argued for in detail elsewhere, theological methods of interpretation and commentary are part of the mythmaking carried out by elite members of the social formations we study. Accordingly, theology is data – *not* method – for scholars of religion. Also, the comparative method is absent from the above list because I assume it to be the basis of all claims to knowledge – to know something is to know it in relation to something else. We are thus all comparativists from the start.

Which brings us to the last category – and the order of these three categories is crucial – *Data*; I specifically place this last because an aspect of the ambiguous world is of interest to us (i.e., is data for just us) *only because* we already have this or that set of questions about how human minds or societies work. The category of *Data* could, of course, be further divided into such sub-categories as Traditions (by which I mean the usual but nonetheless troublesome classification of some social formations by such names as Buddhism, Christianity, Hinduism, etc.), but I would prefer such sub-headings as Cultures (further subdivided), Texts (oral or written), Theologies, Practices, Narratives, Historic Periods, or Geographic Regions, or possibly a sub-category to represent the discipline itself as a datum for our study.

Instead of the dog's breakfast served up in the current survey and the current program units, such a new classificatory scheme would enable us to acquire a new view of the field and ourselves as laborers in it. For example, a scholar filling in such a survey might first select Naturalistic followed by Psychological (maybe even going so far as to distinguish Cognitive from such other sub-categories as Freudian, Jungian, Behavioral, Abnormal, etc.), and then indicate that she studies a particular practice of a particular group of people in a specific region in just this time period. The relationship of her work to a sociologist studying the same people's behaviors in the same time period, or another psychologist using the same methods but to study a different group of people, would then be more than apparent.

Such a revised survey would indicate that the field is based on theories – thereby possibly putting to rest the nagging inductivist or descriptivist fallacy. It would clearly identify the ways in which our various scholarships do or do not intersect. It might also communicate that we as scholars are interested not in studying self-evidently meaningful religious people but are pursuing questions that we are trying to answer by means of our study of these people, their behaviors and social formations. As I have stated it elsewhere, none of us studies religion; instead, some of us use the taxon "religion" to classify and distinguish certain sorts of beliefs, behaviors, and social systems we find curious. As Durkheim wrote on the opening page of his Introduction to *The Elementary Forms of Religious Life*, our study is not simply a purely descriptive act "for the sheer pleasure of recounting the bizarre and the eccentric" (1995: 1). Instead, these classifications are directed by large, controlling questions, questions based on our theories of how minds, bodies, and societies work. As Durkheim writes just two pages later, "even the most specialized scholars must choose a hypothesis and take their inspiration from it if they want to try to account for the facts they analyze – unless they mean to confine themselves to a task of pure erudition" (1995: 3). That these comments on explanatory theorizing occupy Durkheim's thoughts on the very first pages of his now classic book suggest just how fundamentally important they were to some of our predecessors. The challenge will be to convince most of our colleagues of their importance.

Based on my understanding of research as being more than pure erudition, artful interpretation, and value neutral description, I find the rationale of the AAR research survey puzzling and, by extension, the rationale of the current field itself curiously vague but all too understandable. To help get us back on track I offer this suggestion for rethinking our basis for classifying and organizing the study of religion, and in the process for rethinking ourselves as scholars. Such a rethinking makes it clear that there can indeed be a logic and a coherent shape to this field of study but it is not a logic dictated by the inherent meaning of our data and discerned only by the careful interpreter. Instead, it is a logic of our own making, established by *our* questions, *our* tools, and *our* theories.

Appendix[9]

28 January 2000
Dear …
Thank you very much for sending me a copy of the unpublished letter you sent to Tim Bryson back in 1997; forgive me for not replying sooner. A snowy day in

Missouri provides me with an ideal opportunity to catch up on some correspondence.

Apart from the various things I could comment on, the one thing I would
like to say is that I place theory, rather than data, first in my list precisely
because I wish to put in the forefront the various motivations and choices that
compel us to think that what we do is worth doing. For instance, I fully agree
when you say, in the first paragraph on p. 2, "One starts with a field, a people, a
myth, a social structure, etc., *deemed worth studying*" (italics mine). As you make
more than clear, prior to the piece of data we all think to be first, there is in fact
the value judgment that the "it" of our study is "deemed worth studying." This
judgment is obviously based on many unarticulated criteria; since we are not all
psychologists adept at identifying these assorted motivations, I believe that
scholars can at least be expected to identify the political and intellectual (i.e.,
theoretical) factors that motivate them to study this (i.e., a datum), in just this
fashion (i.e., a method), rather than that, in just that fashion. So, in my work, I
press scholars to clearly articulate the theoretical and political interests or
parameters that permit them to specify a particular problematic. Despite what
the phenomenologists have told us, placing data first in the AAR survey over-
looks that the world does not come prepackaged for our intellectual
consumption. Scholars, like all human beings are deeply involved in the act of
classification.

Another point has to do with your particular understanding of religion as a
lived event; clearly you understand the study of religion in the hermeneutic
tradition. Given my stance, to "understand" the meaning of the lived experience means one must already have tacitly agreed upon, and thereby have
reproduced, the discursive parameters of just one of the many possible
"meaning" worlds. Since each "experience" and each "world" comes with an
active politics that delineates what and who gets to count as meaningful and
significant (what J. Z. Smith aptly calls the "economy of signification" policed
by ritual behaviors), the hermeneutical quest smuggles into the academy an
indigenous politics that has little to do with any so-called essential features of
the phenomena to be explained; after all, these supposedly essential features are
"deemed worth studying" only when a specific, local economy is accepted as
inevitable or beneficial and thereby reproduced.

Because, in my estimation, scholars play by their own set of discursive rules
(which obviously bring with them a specific politics of their own), I have little
interest in reproducing the politics of the signification systems I study. My
interest is to explain how it is that any given system of signification can come
to be seen as natural and authoritative in the first place. Therefore, I have little
interest in pursuing a hermeneutical quest. Of course, should one go along with
the modernist *Verstehen* school and presuppose that so-called religious experience is an essential feature of human nature or the enduring human spirit (a
rhetorically efficacious abstraction that homogenizes historical/material difference; on the politics of liberal humanism see Stanley Fish's new book, *The*

Trouble With Principle), then my warnings will be seen as misguided, since religious experiences are easily understood to be simply given and in no need of explanation. Perhaps this is what Ivan Strenski had in mind when, in a 1998 article, he resurrected Schleiermacher's reactionary romanticism by lumping Gary Lease, Fitzgerald, and myself together as religion's "despisers." All that we as scholars should apparently be doing is an exercise in catalog production based on the system of classification employed/authorized by the people we study: ordering these obviously religious experiences based on their assorted types and then proceeding to understand how their transhistorical meaning can be found amidst their varied historical expressions.

I, however, am far more timid than this for I balk at thinking that my local system of classification is universal (i.e., that there is such a thing as religion as opposed to some people who use "religion" to classify and move around in their world). In my opinion, scholars ought to take responsibility for the classifications they use and the first step toward this is identifying the parameters that allow them to engage in their studies in the first place.

It was nice to have met you at the NAASR session, and, once again, thanks very much for sending me a copy of your letter. A call for an open conversation on how such a survey (and with it, how the field) ought to be arranged is something I fully support. However, I assume that things will change little in the AAR – after all, just last week I learned that the History of the Study of Religion Group was removed from the program (the AAR program committee chose not to renew its status as a group), suggesting to me that any activity which contextualizes either religion or the study of religion (either within an historical or theoretical setting) is doomed to be marginalized by the gatekeepers of our profession.

Notes

1   I am reminded of a foreign student (of Indian/Hindu ancestry) who once came to my office at the University of Tennessee, puzzled as to why the Southern Baptist students in our world religions class got so worked up while discussing certain doctrinal issues during our class on Christianity – especially during our unit on Roman Catholicism. (As an aside, having grown up in southern Ontario, surrounded by Catholic, European immigrants to Canada, I was fascinated to learn in Tennessee that Roman Catholics are not true Christians. My childhood friends who were altar boys will no doubt be pleased to learn this.) His sincere puzzlement was refreshing: to him, their impassioned debates were over exceedingly minor variations on essentially the same theme. From his viewpoint, Christians all shared so much in common that he could not understand why they saw themselves as so different and why they placed such importance on matters which struck him as inessential. Needless to say, his non-participant viewpoint and observation could not be fully expressed in the class – he was literally the only observably "different" student in that class, as I recall, and this was not lost on him – yet it was a breath of fresh air to hear him articulate it in my office.
2   Those entries are: Jewish, Islamic, Hindu, Buddhist, Tibetan, Taoist, Chinese, Sikh, and "Sacred Books of Other Religions."

3 My thanks to Gene Thursby for providing me with an electronic copy of this list. Due to the time required to produce a book such as this, the list of AAR Program Units is predictably slightly out of date.

4 Smith's comment was made in his analysis of the "2000 Census of Religion and Theology Programs." The census was sponsored by, among other associations, the AAR, and funded by a major grant from the Lilly Endowment Fund "Strengthening College and University Programs in Religion and Theology." The conjunction "and" in the initiative's title should make it clear what such a census is designed to accomplish.

5 What is the difference, say, between a paper presented in the Buddhism section, and one on Buddhism in Toronto presented in the North American Religions section and a paper on Buddhism in Vietnam presented in the Religion in South Asia section? Is this not an unnecessary reproduction of services? Should there perhaps be a "Schleiermacher read in the German original" section as opposed to some other Schleiermacher section?

6 The following year the AAR Program Committee accepted, on a three-year trial basis, a reconceived consultation on History, Method, and Theory in the Study of Religion, comprised largely of the same people who supported and led the History of the Study of Religion group. The reconfigured group met for the first time during the AAR's 2001 annual meeting in Denver, CO.

7 As published on the consultation's web site, the anonymous referee's letter concludes: "It is self-evident, or it should be self-evident, that the AAR needs some sustained attention to the history of the study of religion. In my judgment HSRG [the History of the Study of Religion Group] is playing a significant role in filling this gap at the Annual Meetings."

8 My thanks to Tom Lawson and Luther Martin for their suggestion of just these categories.

9 As mentioned earlier in this chapter, at the November 1999 meeting of the North American Association for the Study of Religion, I met a scholar who told me about a reply she had written to the earlier version of this chapter that was published in one of the field's professional newsletters, *Religious Studies Review*, in 1997. Her reply was never published by *RSN*, but she kindly mailed a copy to me. Because her reply to my article raised issues that, I believe, still might be raised in response to this chapter, and because no profession-wide discussion of this topic has yet taken place, I reprint that letter in its original form as an appendix to this chapter.

Part II

Techniques of dominance

Discipline "makes" individuals; it is the specific technique of a power that regards individuals both as objects and as instruments of its exercise. ... [Disciplines] are techniques for assuring the ordering of human multiplicities.

Michel Foucault (1977a: 170, 218)

Chapter 5

The good, the bad, and the ugly

Looking past the violence of cults and fanatics

> Everything we need that is not food or love is here in the tabloid racks. The tales of the supernatural and the extraterrestrial. The miracle vitamins, the cures for cancer, the remedies for obesity. The cults of the famous and the dead.
>
> (DeLillo 1986: 326)

The general absence of social theorists from among the ranks of so-called experts usually appearing in the media suggests that there is considerable distance to go if we are to become more engaged intellectuals – an engagement that will surely help to offset the sensationalism that almost always characterizes print and televised media coverage of events for which we can legitimately claim some expertise. But lamenting the ever-present sensationalism of tabloid journalism may arise from clinging to the belief that the media is – or somehow ought to be – a neutral purveyor of benign information, an ideal it might better embody if only cooler heads prevailed and we were invited to appear on "Larry King Live." If the media's task is indeed simply to communicate generic content and meaningful information – as opposed to providing information in the service of building specific sorts of worlds (i.e, rhetoric or propaganda) – then scholars will likely hang their heads and wring their hands every time a so-called cult expert appears on television, following some unanticipated or shocking event. But if the media, no less than any other institution, functions to assist in the smooth reproduction of an apparently seamless, larger social group by portraying the world in ways conducive to one group's various interests, then we should expect nothing less from it than to employ common rhetorical devices that assist them in this endeavor.

Most recently, the tremendous effort that has been expended in the media in classifying a small sub-group of politically engaged, oppositional groups of Muslims as "radicals" or "fanatics" – rhetorical efforts reinforced by equally energetic attempts to portray so-called mainline Muslims as not politically engaged whatsoever, but, instead, as peaceful and tolerant of whatever status quo happens to surround them – is but one example of the manner in which political and media commentary deploys a series of rhetorical devices in the service of reproducing a specific sense of both "us" and "them" (whomever these two groups happen to include). For instance, take the message from the President of the Association of American Colleges and Universities that ran soon after the September 11 attacks in the AAC&U's periodical, *Liberal Educator* (Schneider 2001). Carol Geary Schneider remarks that

> Americans now find themselves at war. And our enemy, extraordinarily, is a far-flung, if deviant, movement within Islam. From Palestine, to Pakistan, to the Philippines, there are many thousands, collectively professing an antagonistic understanding of their own religious commitments and drawing from these commitments the determination to conduct a "holy war" against the American Satan.
>
> (2)[1]

That the social movement we call Islam, like *all* social groups – from families to nation-states – is indeed comprised of many historic and contemporary sub-groups, some of which contradict each other, many of which represent people with competing interests, and all of which fall across a wide, loosely connected spectrum, is lost in such efforts to isolate "radical fundamentalist Muslims" from the complexity of the social group we today call Islam. Instead, a very specific sense of peace, tolerance, and normalcy is reproduced by means of these assorted classificatory techniques, classifications by means of which we conveniently disallow from the realm of credible and meaningful human practice all those behaviors which fail to reproduce one specific set of local interests.

In a fascinating reversal of usual liberal values, Schneider, writing in an avowedly "liberal" periodical, goes on to observe that, after September 11, 2001, "we in the academy ... *confront the limitations of the respectful pluralism* which for the most part governs our approach to both liberal education and a pluralistic society" (2; emphasis added). Having made the unusual disclosure – unusual for a liberal humanist, that is – that a "respectful pluralism" governs our approach *for the most part*, she elaborates:

> As a humanist, I wanted my students to "stand inside" very different ways of looking at the world; I wanted them to understand how and why and with what results such different views were held. It was not my goal to have my students argue for or against the views of medieval popes or mystics; all I asked was that students be able to take others' times and places seriously, on their own terms. ... But respectful engagement stalls when opponents have no interest in dialogue. And when incommensurable differences hold life-altering consequences, as they so plainly do now, they force us beyond the practices of empathetic exploration and dialogue into the less familiar humanist domain of evaluation, judgement, and decisive action.
>
> (3)

Apart from having the resounding ring of a call to arms, Schneider assumes it to be a foregone conclusion that the differences are incommensurable, that the debate is limited to issues of innocence and guilt, and that when the truly difficult work of understanding a real live Other who is unwilling to play by "our" set of rules comes along, humanists do not need to scrutinize the historicity of the rules but, instead, must lead the way in circling the wagons and calling for war. Simply put, all cultural contact comes with "life-altering consequences," it's just that such consequences do not usually impact on "us"!

Failing to have the complexity and interconnectedness of all acts of social formation brought to their attention, along with conveniently overlooking the ever-present intolerance of all social ideologies – liberalism included – readers of such articles are thus confirmed in their presumptions that social identity is homogenous, self-evident, and eternal, that we are good, that they are evil, that we are innocent, that they are guilty (Burton Mack's "myth of innocence" is alive and well), and that behaviors and interests that diverge from our sense of the status quo are simply the result of insanity or fanaticism. Confirmed in our self-satisfying, almost narcissistic, beliefs, it is easy to nod our heads in agreement with writers such as the director of character development programs at the John Templeton Foundation who, in that same issue of *Liberal Educator* wrote: "Our challenge as educators is to discern how best to help our students develop a relationship with what they hold to be Sacred. ... Perhaps at the core of 'spirituality' is a mysterious relationship that opens our hearts to questions of intimate meaning and ultimate truth" (Schwartz 2001: 35). As humanists prepared to make judgments and take decisive action, none of this is really all that much of a challenge, to be honest, or a mystery, for we all know well in advance that a rather narrow party line of "what they hold to be Sacred" will get to count in our classrooms, in our legislatures, and in our courts; those ultimate truths that we find unpalatable will luckily be found to be just plain old wrong, fanatical, and an attack on civility and freedom.

Because many people in North America are quite understandably still feeling the repercussions of this most recent media feeding frenzy – a frenzy prompted by admittedly horrendous and, for millions of people prior to September 11, 2001, literally unimaginable events – it may help to look back a few years, hoping that a little distance from the eerie glow of our picture tubes will allow our eyes to become accustomed to a less captivating and thus all the more curious picture. Such a critical distance may also be beneficial in our analysis of other social interactions continually taking place worldwide, for the speed with which the post-September 11 rhetoric of "terrorist" and "fanatic" was adopted by governments was astounding (but, lamentably perhaps, hardly surprising). Although early on some international commentators and politicians were intent on distinguishing "freedom fighters" from "terrorists," since then this grey area has largely been lost in the "you're either with us or against us" rhetoric of many politicians. The world, it appears, is now populated by civil, peace-loving people of good nature and noble intention, on the one hand, and evil, dangerous freedom-hating fanatics who have no rationality or respect for life and liberty, on the other.

To gain some much needed distance from the current events, take, for example, the national U.S. magazine cover articles that soon appeared after the Heaven's Gate "cult" suicides in Rancho Santa Fe (just outside San Diego, CA) were announced on March 27, 1997. *Time*'s and *Newsweek*'s April 7, 1997, covers featured grainy blowups of the group's wide (wild)-eyed leader, Marshall Applewhite (or "Do" as he was most recently known to members of the group). That he was quickly and effectively portrayed as being abnormal, even clinically insane, is apparent not just from these close-up photos. In my undergraduate class's discussions on this event as well as the media coverage of the event, one of my students at the time pointed out that in the second paragraph of *Time*'s feature article the bodies are likened to "so many laboratory specimens pinned neatly to a board," a comparison that suggests that the leader of the group, Applewhite, was some sort of a lab-coated mad scientist – or worse, a vivisectionist. Having established his – and by extension his followers' – lunacy by means of caricature, these articles then attempted to explain it all by resorting to amateur, Freudian psychologizing, suggesting that Applewhite's behavior was caused by his alleged homosexuality – "Imprisoned By His Own Passions" is the supplementary *Time* article devoted to this series of speculations.

Although they are to be congratulated for opting not to reproduce the tabloid photograph of Applewhite on this early April 1997 cover (instead, interestingly enough, it pictured the silhouette of a lone man pictured from behind, peering upward into the starry heavens), the editors of *U.S. News & World Report* nonetheless subtitled their cover article, "How *Reasonable People Can Hold Unreasonable Beliefs*." No doubt this subtitle referred to the startling disparity between the seeming normality of the group members in their video-taped last messages to their family and friends, clips of which were being repeatedly played on the TV news magazine shows, on the one hand, and their patently "abnormal" actions, on the other. Within a month of what one of my undergraduate students correctly termed their "departure" (for, instead of "suicide," the emic terms "departure" or "graduation" are phenomenologically accurate since they accord with the group members' own self-descriptions; as I will soon demonstrate, the much celebrated phenomenological bracket slips pretty quickly when confronting such "abnormal" events), HarperCollins published the first "instant book" (a.k.a. tabloid exposé) on Heaven's Gate authored by the staff writers of the infamous *New York Post* (Hoffmann and Burke 1997). The book comes complete with chapters on the "mysterious lives" of the "UFO cultists," their "frightening secret computer files," their "castration shocker," Applewhite's "stunning sexual secrets," his supposed "steamy sex trysts with a student," as well as the "chilling after shocks of the mass suicide." As but another example of Mack's myth of innocence, the book employs a "strangers in our midst" motif to communicate its information, but this stranger in our quiet little subdivisions is not sent to save us: "As whacked-out as their talk of space beings and body-shedding might have been," write the authors, "nobody in the neighborhood besides real-estate agents really knew about the claims, simply because the group was quiet" (27). As will become apparent, as "whacked-out" as such tabloid journalism at first appears, it is surprisingly similar to what also appeared in the so-called mainstream media.

Identifying such grossly oversimplified caricatures of this admittedly curious social formation entails pointing out that few, if any, of this group's beliefs and behaviors were all that "unreasonable" when compared to those of other groups whose legitimacy is beyond question. But, such an observation would likely highlight, and thus draw into question, the key techniques whereby our own group has reproduced itself by classifying and constraining dissenting *behaviors* and ways of *organizing and acting* (as opposed merely to putting up with certain dissenting *beliefs*): the rhetoric of cult and fanatic, a rhetoric that "effectively distances them [i.e., those who employ the term] from the unsettling activities" (Muesse 1997: B-6). As argued in more detail throughout the following chapters, such rhetorics are practical techniques dominant groups use to classify, demarcate, and constrain competing social worlds, techniques deployed in the simultaneous effort to know and control potential competitors while reproducing oneself.

What I have in mind when theorizing such techniques is something very much akin to Mack's notion of a myth of innocence; it is nicely communicated by one of Don DeLillo's characters, a university professor in the novel, *White Noise* (1986). Describing his classroom analysis of the genre of car crashes in U.S. cinema, he says:

> "The movie breaks away from complicated human passions to show us something elemental, something fiery and loud and head-on. It's a conservative wish fulfillment, a yearning for naïveté. We want to be artless again. We want to reverse the flow of experience, of worldliness, and its responsibilities. My students say, 'Look at the crushed bodies, the severed limbs. What kind of innocence is this?'"
>
> "What do you say to that?"
>
> "I tell them they can't think of a car crash in a movie as a violent act. It's a celebration. A reaffirmation of traditional values and beliefs. I connect car crashes to holidays like Thanksgiving and the Fourth [of July]. We don't mourn the dead or rejoice in miracles. These are days of secular optimism, of self-celebration. We will improve, prosper, perfect ourselves. Watch any car crash in any American movie. It is a high-spirited moment like old fashioned stunt flying, walking wings. The people who stage these crashes are able to capture a lightheartedness, a carefree enjoyment that car crashes in foreign movies can never approach."
>
> "Look past the violence."
>
> "Exactly. Look past the violence, Jack. There is a wonderful brimming spirit of innocence and fun."

(218)

Looking past the admittedly alluring, graphic, and thus hard-to-ignore content of tabloid violence, we see the state of innocence that is made thinkable by means of such representations of violence. Like a shopper patiently waiting in a grocery store's checkout line, idly perusing the covers of *The National Enquirer* or *The Star* or *The Weekly World News* and shaking his or her head at the most recent exploits of Michael Jackson or Elizabeth Taylor or the preacher who spontaneously combusted without burning a page of the Bible he held in his hand, a profound sense of normalcy and contentment is produced in juxtaposition to the odd, the dangerous, the extreme, the fanatical. Celebrity, in other words, makes possible anonymity.

This point is pressed again a little later in DeLillo's novel – a novel whose protagonist is a famous Hitler studies scholar who, oddly enough, doesn't know German (hence his ever-present anxiety and insecurity) and who is also much concerned with the topics of death, disintegrating families, forgetfulness, the disillusion of identity, and a toxic cloud hovering over the city – when another character expounds to the protagonist the same theory of social formation, but this time using the human emotion of fear, prompted by a hypothetical grizzly bear attack:

> "[I]t is a grizzly bear, enormous, shiny, brown, swaggering, dripping slime from its bared fangs. Jack, you have never seen a large animal in the wild. The sight of this grizzer is so electrifyingly strange that it gives you a renewed sense of yourself, a fresh awareness of the self – the self in terms of a unique and horrific situation. *You see yourself in a new and intense way. You rediscover yourself. You are lit up by your own immanent dismemberment*"
>
> (229; emphasis added)

The point I am trying to press is hardly novel: the "normal" self is experienceable and meaningful only insomuch as it is continually juxtaposed to, and in relationship with, the alien, idealized, or even extreme and dangerous Other, be it in the form of a highly choreographed car crash in a darkened movie theater or a grizzly bear attack out on the trail. Applying this to the topic of this current chapter, the ideal of the politically neutral media, the innocence of domestic life, and the fanatical evil "Other" all coordinate to perform an essential socio-political task: helping to make our otherwise messy day-to-day lives manageable and knowable.

The argument I develop in this chapter, then, is fairly straightforward. To repeat: what the rhetorics of cult and fanatic, the rhetoric of religion, the genre of movie car crashes, the exhilaration inspired by a surprise encounter with a bear, tabloid newspapers, and the daydream of media objectivity – not to mention the homey, comforting nostalgia spun around such U.S. holidays as Thanksgiving and the Fourth of July – all have in common is that they each reproduce at a discrete social site Mack's notion of a myth of innocence. As he has phrased it, social groups are reproduced by deploying, and acting within the deployment of, classification schemes that

function ... at a certain distance from the actual state of affairs experienced
in the daily round. They articulate a displaced system (imaginary, ideal,
"sacred," marked off) as a counterpoint to the ways things usually go. The
inevitable incongruence between the symbol system and the daily round
provides a space for discourse. It is the space within which the negotiations
fundamental to social intercourse take place – reflection, critique, rationalization, compromise, play, humor, and so forth.

(1991: 21)

The myth of innocence, then, is a socio-rhetorical technique that creates a fluid
sense of a manageable, everyday life by artfully juxtaposing it to some posited
incursion from beyond, a moment of unambiguous and pristine origination,
some Eliadean irruption of the sacred from beyond the otherwise messy and
ambiguous world of history and happenstance. It is a myth that arises from, and
in turn continues to make possible, a very particular historical world by helping
to portray fragmentation as seamlessness.

Mack, along with a small number of contemporary scholars of religion, has
astutely picked up on a point made by Emile Durkheim (and which I have cited
before in an essay on redescribing "religion" as social formation [2001b: 31]):

A society can neither create nor recreate itself without creating some kind
of ideal by the same stroke. This creation is not a sort of optional extra step
by which society, being already made, merely adds finishing touches; it is
the act by which society makes itself, and remakes itself, periodically.

(1995: 425)

Whether this counterpoint or ideal be a tale about an idyllic past or some evil
Other, whether it be found in the Gospel of Mark's narrative of an unblemished
savior (as examined by Mack), a movie car crash, or the elaborately choreographed
violence of a Sam Peckinpah or a Quentin Tarantino motion picture, all of these
are highly controlled narrative sites of abstract, caricatured Otherness that make it
possible to imagine and then act within the normal, the safe, the innocent, the
meaningful, the credible, and thus the utterly necessary moment of the present –
despite the fact that this is a present in which we only happen to have found
ourselves. Alluding to Lévi-Strauss's work on the manner in which posited binary
opposites make our social worlds thinkable and inhabitable, Bruce Lincoln is
among this small group of contemporary theorists; as he has recently phrased it:

in widely disparate times and places, people have found binary categories
like hot and cold, moist and dry, male and female, high and low, east and
west powerful instruments of thought and discourse: items that are "good to
think," although I hasten to note that in this and related contexts, "good"
surely represents a technical, and not a moral, judgement.

(2001: 326)

The posited good, the bad, and the ugly are thus all interconnected discursive sites; they are all artful moments that conspire to make meaning possible in the discursive interstices they and their opposites create.

If only a small number of theorists begin not with, for example, the meaning of goodness or the horror of violence but, instead, with the socio-political grammar and system of classifications that make such meanings and judgments possible, then all too predictably the cult experts appearing in the mainstream media after the Rancho Santa Fe deaths were just as enthralled by the content of violence as were their tabloid counterparts. It was just that their placement as talking heads on "serious" television news shows, rather than as telephoto color photographs on the tabloid racks in the supermarket, made their claims sound all the more learned and thus persuasive. For almost all were just as intent on cari-caturing the Other so as to sanction our sense of shock and repulsion, and thereby establish our innocence. (The anthropologist Tanya M. Luhrmann's fine article from that time, published in *U.S. News & World Report* [1997] is a pleasant exception that proves the rule; see also her ethnographic study of witchcraft in contemporary England [1991].) That the members of the Heaven's Gate group, despite initial media and police reports, turned out *not* to be disillu-sioned and disaffected males between the ages of 18 and 24 – an initial conclusion undoubtedly based on the way they were dressed and their short hair, all of which fit nicely with the widely circulating misconception that young males are particularly apt to have bouts of despair and are therefore open to cult indoctrination – is sufficient evidence that there was more to this "cult" than initially met the eye of investigators and subsequent commentators.[2] All this is not to say, however, that the various differences between this and other groups are non-existent or inconsequential. Some of the differences are glaring and any sufficient analysis of both this group and their subsequent media coverage must take them into account. Of all the differences that most attract my attention is the one fundamental point where Heaven's Gate diverged radically from almost all other marginal or oppositional groups: in annihilating themselves they actu-ally *acted* on their dissenting *beliefs*, making this group all the more dangerous to the current status quo. Although I hardly agree with most of his statements, iron-ically enough this was also the estimate of Applewhite himself; in a recruiting videotape, clips from which were frequently played on national television following their deaths, he acknowledged that his followers would be understood as members of a "dangerous cult" because, in his words, "we threaten the family; we threaten the established norm of family values."[3] Drawing on his under-standing of the message of Jesus (e.g., the group often highlighted sayings concerning the need to leave your mother and father, such as Matthew 10:37, Mark 10:29, Luke 14:26), Applewhite pursued the analogy between what he understood to have been the political danger posed by Jesus some two thousand years ago and what he also perceived to be the threat of his own movement to the contemporary status quo. His argument seems to have been that, like his understanding of Jesus enacting oppositional views, his own late-twentieth-century group not only imagined but enacted an alternative to the nuclear family model so celebrated in contemporary U.S. culture; once this socially dangerous action went public it was necessary for the gatekeepers of normalcy to expend tremendous material and rhetorical resources so as to constrain and discipline the perception of the group long after they left their "vehicles" behind in favor of a space ship in the tail of the Hale-Bopp comet. It is precisely these disciplining practices that simultaneously make possible both transgressor and rule-follower. It was thus socio-politically necessary to uniformly portray their enaction of dissent as inconceivable for any sane human being.

Before suggesting how this single but nevertheless key difference between dissenting groups (i.e., enacting oppositional beliefs) can provide the basis for rethinking how we study the workings of culture, consider the many striking similarities between Heaven's Gate and other so-called mainline traditions (Muesse 1997 makes a related argument; see also Wessinger 2000). From what I can gather, like all social systems, the beliefs of Heaven's Gate members were a complex synthesis of divergent elements: post-World War II science and science fiction were both fundamental to the group, along with contemporary conspiracy theories (references to the U.S. government hiding alien bodies and to Waco found their way into their much publicized web site's literature),[4] contemporary political issues (their criticism of the conservative rhetoric of family values), and various well-established doctrines drawn from a host of sources (from mainline Christian scripture, Theosophical literature, Hinduism, etc.). As with the historically early phase of all social movements, then, their beliefs and practices arose from a variety of seemingly disparate sources (suggesting that calling any social group "syncretistic" is utterly redundant, and adds nothing to our descriptions[5]). What's more, these sources are far from exotic; they are basic components of contemporary U.S. popular culture. Are not conspiracy theorists prominent on both the U.S.'s political Left and Right? In fact, after only a short search on the web you will find articles conjecturing that the U.S.'s Central Intelligence Agency (CIA) was behind the Heaven's Gate deaths. And there may very well be just as many, or more, people in the U.S. who claim to have seen a U.F.O. (let alone having been abducted by one and probed) as claim to have seen the Virgin Mary or been visited by angels. Yet marginal or oppositional belief systems – most notably, those that act on dissent – are constructed in a sufficiently different manner, and come with sufficient different consequences, so as to prompt many seemingly informed commentators to drop the much-celebrated phenomenological, descriptivist stance routinely assumed when describing the beliefs and behaviors of well-established social formations.[6]

An example of just how quickly the thin veneer of value-neutral description can be peeled away, in favor of policing the limits of normalcy in the face of what is obviously a fanatical threat – by means of the deployment of socially effective sets of binaries – is found in an already cited episode of ABC television's late night news program, *Nightline* in which, ironically perhaps, the reporters went to greater lengths to describe the group than did their expert panelists. The experts interviewed were: Martin Marty, the well-known scholar of U.S. religion and liberal pundit; Bruce Epperly, Professor of Divinity at Georgetown University; Cynthia Kisser, the outspoken former executive director of the "real" Cult Awareness Group, a cult watch organization that filed for bankruptcy in 1996;[7] and Robert Ellwood, the author of a number of religious studies textbooks and Professor at the University of Southern California. At several points in the thirty minute show, both in Michelle McQueen's opening background segment and in host Chris Wallace's questions to his guests, the reporters make clear that the distinctions between a religion and a cult are slippery at best. For example, although she acknowledges that the Heaven's Gate beliefs can certainly be seen as odd, McQueen reports that the then upcoming holiday of Easter celebrates the death and resurrection of a god/man, a belief that is equally fantastic to the claims of a spaceship riding along with a comet. And in his opening comments Wallace not only makes it clear that the episode is not intended to "denigrate or trivialize" anyone's beliefs but he goes so far as to observe that, when it comes to discussing Heaven's Gate, it is "too easy to dismiss them as cooky." Despite this warning, this is pretty much what his commentators all proceed to do, if only by means of their inability to see the local and the so-called normal as equally complex and artful.

For example, because cults cannot be identified simply by the *content* of their belief system (after all, even supposedly normal people believe in angels, halos, U.F.O.s, astrology, ghosts, luck, destiny, etc. – a point made clear in McQueen's opening report[8]), we must identify them by the *form* in which they reproduce their belief systems. Kisser therefore offers the following list of what she characterizes as the dangerous cult practices in evidence in the case of the Heaven's Gate group:

- they got up early in the morning;
- they worked long hours for the organization;
- they were probably fatigued;
- they used mental and meditative exercises that probably put them in an altered state of consciousness;
- they employed an insider vocabulary – "They used 'loading zone' for the parking lot," she noted.

Summing up she said, "you control language, diet, sleep, communication with the outside world, those are powerful techniques." Indeed, they are; but they are also employed by pretty much every social system in the everyday labor of recreating itself, making her observations banal. For example, after viewing this episode with introductory level university students I was told by one astute student that both families and the U.S. military do all of these things. The banality of Kisser's observation thus left me wondering if the reasoning that led her to understand "parking lot" as a natural kind, perverted by "loading zone," was an instance of what she called "critical thinking" – as in her claim that, "if we don't teach people to be better critical thinkers these type of things are going to occur over and over again." I would rephrase this to say that, unless we teach a brand of critical thinking that assists students to see how rhetoric such as Kisser's functions in a social group, then comments such as hers will continue to be broadcast over and over again.[9]

Although superior to Kisser's comments in some ways, true to his liberal sentiments Marty's contribution to the panel tipped a hat to "them" as being similar but then quickly circled the wagons by confirming that they are in fact radically different from us. A strategy he used twice – and one which his nineteenth-century predecessors would have found familiar – was to distinguish birth from maturity, thus lodging the so-called cult in some posited immature stage of psychological and social development. For example, although in their birth phase all religions seem to make "extremely demanding calls … the big difference is that the mainstream religions are weathered, tattered, and usually a little mellowed." What starts out as, in his words, an uncompromising, zealous, and fanatical movement ends with its members taking a second look and reconsidering their priorities, such that they choose life over death. He returns to this theme again when he answers Wallace's question concerning the place of killing oneself in the "established religions." Marty replies that, yes, "in the early days" of religions, voluntary martyrdom is sometimes present but "the [modern, he implies] Church doesn't celebrate it." Dominance is a sign of development and thus maturity (i.e., to the victor go the spoils). Marty employs other techniques as well; elaborating on the topic of self-inflicted death, he later alluded to the group having some sort of maladaptive death wish, as in when he characterized the group's members as having "cheated" the "game of life" by "getting to another world prematurely." Epperly – equally interested in establishing the normalcy and fairness of believing in a specific type of invisible being and the deviance of cheaters – picked up on this topic by terming the group members escapist and accusing them of not facing up to the problems of the world and not discovering God in the world. Marty added, "I'd rather stick around and not give up on the world before God does," and, following Epperly's brief comment of agreement, off-camera Marty added somewhat jovially, "Bruce *and* I are going to stick around" (emphasis added). Such a comment makes sense since Marty and Epperly are, obviously, members of the same group; by their rhetoric you shall know them.

Another rhetorical technique that helped to establish the social conjunction "and" highlighted in the above quotation is the "yes but" that enables a simultaneous admission yet evasion – a sly two-step, if you will. On several occasions Wallace poses a question that relies on a comparative analysis in which striking similarities are all too obvious, despite the labels "cult" or "fanatic" and "mainline religion" or "established religion." For instance, following Kisser's less than illuminating list of dangerous cult mind-control techniques, he asks Marty "isn't there a history of control, discipline, and martyrdom in mainstream religion?" After briefly acknowledging that, yes, indeed, religions often offer a host of control and discipline opportunities judged by members to be beautiful – his example is a spiritual retreat, but, to complicate matters we could add to the mix such practices as the cloistering of medieval women – he then quickly adds, that "target practice with a pistol and Russian roulette are very different; there's a big difference between the two." Likening a spiritual retreat to target practice and Heaven's Gate to Russian roulette is a puzzling analogy. It is puzzling because I am not sure what it tells us about the actions of the people outside of Rancho Santa Fe, or the actions of people who go on things called "spiritual retreats." Watching Marty flippantly say this I could not help but ask the screen, "Ok, there's a big difference. But what is it?" From my vantage point the difference is obvious, though I'm sure that it is not the one Marty had in mind (the difference he saw? – they are violent and we are peaceful, perhaps?): in one case the content of a person's beliefs and their actions are completely disconnected (i.e., they're shooting blanks) and, in the other case, they are not. In one, dissent is internalized, displaced, and spiritualized and, in the other, it is enacted directly, brutally, and violently. In fact, such an enactment is so at odds with the status quo that television viewers and magazine buyers have little choice but to see it as fanatical, idiotic, and gruesome (it goes without saying, perhaps, that those wars we finance and fight which we see as righteous are never understood in this manner); for in putting into practice dissenting ways of organizing and understanding self, one has attacked what many take to be settled about their own world and selves. In the truest sense of the term, then, such representations are self-defense techniques.

On another occasion, after Marty simply declares that the difference between a cult and a mainline religion is that the latter allows criticism and free thought (I hear echoes here of the tired, old distinction between tradition-based religions and the so-called individuality and rationality of modern religions[10]), Wallace asks Epperly, "There's not a lot of democracy in a lot of religions, is there?" Doing a lively two-step of his own, Epperly replies:

> Well that's true but I think that the difference between mainline religions and cult-like religions involves the question of authority and self-criticism; most mainstream religions see the major authority in God and not in any individual who claims to be a messiah or a savior as Do did. Another issue is self-criticism, that indeed mainstream religions recognize the possibility that persons, even leaders, can make mistakes and there's always the need to ask questions. One wonders what would have happened if enough people asked questions in the Heaven's Gate group [emphasis added].

Now, one could choose to refute Epperly's claims by pointing out that a group of 24 in 1975, gained 30 more members after a meeting in Oregon, reached almost 100 in 1976, dropped to about 80 and then, in the late 1990s ended up with 39 suicides; apparently, then, quite a few people did indeed ask some questions and, for whatever reason, they departed the group before its members departed their vehicles. But what is far more interesting is the manner in which he acknowledges a structural similarity among these social groups by answering "Well that's true ..." and then immediately evades the implications of these far-reaching similarities and, instead, creates the illusion of rational choice within our social groups by seeing in *some* religions some notion of self-criticism. Despite softening his rhetoric by opting for "cult-like" as opposed to "cult," Epperly is nevertheless a fascinating study in the manner in which members of dominant social groups are fundamentally incapable of entertaining that members of another group are just as deeply invested in the worlds of meaning made possible by their own rhetorical arts.

Such commentators are incapable of doing as much since their own stable and uniform but nonetheless provincial and contingent social identities are premised on the extreme Otherness of those who organize themselves differently; the death of the Other thus brings about the demise of self, so a massive and highly defensive response is inevitable and necessary. Recalling Foucault's opening words from his *The Order of Things* (1973), what is fascinating about these commentators is their inability to entertain that their claims about some supposedly unmediated experience of God are just as rhetorically loaded as Applewhite's claims about seeds and space ships. "We know our God directly," Epperly seems to be saying, "while they know only the flawed messenger." This is the height of rhetorical technique practiced deftly by skilled, elite members of a dominant group – after all, coming out of anyone else's mouth it would sound downright silly. Through their skillful means, they are able to overlook the utter humanness and historicity of these things we call religion, skipping right over the fact that their own beliefs are forever locked in the very same world of mediation, translation, writing and reading. They trust their "major authority" only because they can take for granted the seamlessness and thus credibility of but one history of cultural transmission.

Not long ago, the editor of the *Bulletin of the Council of Societies for the Study of Religion* lamented the lack of informed scholarly commentary in the media following the attacks of September 11, 2001. "I have been dismayed," Craig Prentiss frankly wrote in his editorial,

> by the frequency with which I have seen newspaper and periodicals turn to "expert" scholars of religion for insight, only to find those "experts" providing obscurantist responses that differ little from those we might expect from any Sunday school teacher or theologically inclined person on the street. Distinguishing the academic study of religion from the practice or promotion of religion has become a well-worn mantra among nearly all of us, but judging from quotations in wire-service articles and the major news weeklies (with few notable exceptions), one would be hard pressed to make that case.
>
> (2002: 2–3)[11]

As the preceding look at an episode of *Nightline* makes clear, Prentiss's lament is just as appropriate for other scholarly interventions in the media. If we are to do something other than serve as Sunday school teachers and thus avoid doing the unflattering "yes, but" apologist's dance and, instead, take seriously the fact that the members of marginal and oppositional groups are complex people – like all of us – working out issues of social formation, then just what do such groups believe, how do they accomplish their group identity, and what role do our representations of them play in our own acts of social formation? To begin to answer these sorts of questions we can say that, in the case of Heaven's Gate, they seem to have believed that their leaders/teachers periodically visited the earth from another, idyllic realm; that their own physical bodies were mere "vehicles" which contained immaterial "seeds" that would outlive the body; that, with the proper teachings, these seeds might someday escape their material surroundings, be reunited with their departed leaders (in this case, Bonnie Nettles [d. 1985], known most recently as Ti); and travel to a better place (i.e., The Evolutionary Level Above Human or, as they also referred to it, the Kingdom of God). Such a belief system – one that juxtaposed internal with external, immaterial with material, etc. – should not strike the comparativist as all that odd. Or, if it does, then one would have to admit that all self-identified religious people hold equally "unreasonable" beliefs: from Jains maintaining that karma results in matter accruing to, and thus weighting down, their jiva, to Hindus maintaining that the earth is periodically destroyed by the dancing Shiva and refashioned by Brahma, to Jews maintaining that a deity has given them land as part of an ancient contractual and hereditary agreement, to Christians maintaining that an incarnate deity will return at the end of time to save the righteous and damn sinners to torment, and finally to people from across virtually all cultures who engage in one or another form of body scarification as a sign of one's coming of age. We can even add to this list liberal humanists claiming that some invisible quality, Human Nature they call it, inheres in just our species. How are these common beliefs and practices any more reasonable, or any less incredible?

However, scholars should not be content simply to extend to Heaven's Gate the same phenomenological privilege routinely extended to those beliefs and practices to which we have become accustomed (or those which many of us may in fact practice/believe in ourselves). Given the above example from *Nightline* we can say that it would indeed be something if they at least just did this. Although our work in, as the old saying goes, making the strange familiar and the familiar strange by means of such fair and balanced description is important, it can only take us so far, for it fails to push beyond mere description and comparison to cultural analysis and explanation. Scholars should therefore not be content simply to use the comparative method to identify the individual similarities and differences between these various social formations. They can move beyond description and comparison and attempt to explain *why* it is that these people *acted* on these otherwise unexceptional beliefs and just what role the common belief/practice binary plays in our everyday efforts to re-create our wider groups by not acting on dissent. For, discussing the 1997 events from Rancho Santa Fe in my classes made it apparent that for many students it is the fact that these people died that makes this case peculiar and disturbing – not that they believed in seeds and space ships. However, keeping Bourdieu's advice in mind concerning the need to study the extraordinary as ordinary, what I have found most puzzling about these events is *not* that the members died – after all, as Durkheim long ago informed us, religious suicide is "the crowning logical step" of world-denying asceticism (1995: 37).[12] Rather, as suggested earlier, what is far more intriguing is that billions of human beings in the history of the world have professed remarkably similar beliefs *yet they did not act on them in this logical fashion*! Now *this* is truly perplexing.

Therefore, what may be most intriguing of all is why more people who profess to believe very seriously in a better realm elsewhere and a body that contains, even imprisons, a spirit, a soul, an atman, or a jiva, a self, or a seed, *don't do this more often*! Although we know of certain people from diverse cultural settings who have engaged in one or another form of what we generally refer to as self- or world-denying behavior (one thinks of such a diverse group as Hindu sannyasins, Jain monks, Christian saints and martyrs who could easily have escaped their captors, protesting Vietnamese monks in the 1960s [see McCutcheon 1997b: 167 ff.], or even Jews long ago under siege by the Romans at Masada), it is obvious that such behavior is far from common. However, the dualistic belief system (matter/spirit) that informs this behavior *is very common* and usually safely constrained within the realm of faith, feeling, privacy, etc. It therefore falls to us to try to explain the intriguing disparity between common beliefs and uncommon practices. It is a disparity comparable to that of snake handling among some Pentecostal Christian groups in the Appalachian region of the U.S. Despite the fact that large numbers of Christians throughout the world agree that the Bible is inerrant and the inspired word of God, only an extremely small minority of self-identified Christians take seriously the signs of a "true believer" as found at the close of the Gospel of Mark, two of which are handling snakes and drinking poison. That Christian snake handlers exist is indeed an interesting social phenomenon; however, why there are not more of them might be *far more interesting*.

One scholar who has tried to offer an explanation for why the Heaven's Gate members collectively ended their lives – or, as she might phrase it, why their belief system collapsed in upon itself – is Catherine Wessinger of Loyola University. In her comparative study of contemporary millennial groups that have opted to put into practice their dissenting beliefs (2000), Wessinger argues that, by setting goals for the group which, in practice, were impossible to attain (e.g., their ascension to the Level Above Human) the group's ultimate concern was radically called into question. Because group's are organized around their ultimate concern, or so Wessinger argues, calling this concern into question can lead to the (sometimes violent) dissolution of the group. In her words:

The students had been taught to depend on their Older Member as the sole means to enter the Kingdom of Heaven, but Do was getting old and would certainly die. To preserve their ultimate concern, the class decided to take violent action. ... Ti and Do had set an impossible goal for their students and the Heaven's Gate class decided to commit group suicide to preserve their ultimate concern. ... [T]he radical dualism of their catastrophic millennial worldviews contributed to the overreaction of the believers to any sign of opposition or disagreement from outside society.

(2000: 243, 268)

Wessinger's argument hinges on her sense of how groups go about concocting their ongoing identities. Relying on Paul Tillich's alluring but, as I will go on to demonstrate, explanatorily empty notion of an ultimate concern, she defines an ultimate concern as "the most important thing in the world for an individual or group" (5; see Baird 1971 as well). She then elaborates:

Religion is an expression of an *ultimate concern*. ... The ultimate concern is the religious goal people want to achieve. ... The ultimate concern is determined by a religion's cosmology. ... A *cosmology* is a view of the universe and its source.

(5; emphasis in the original)

Wessinger argues, in a wonderfully circular fashion, that although an ultimate concern predates a religion it is nevertheless a product of a religion's cosmology. As just stated, "religion is an *expression* of an ultimate concern [and] ... the ultimate concern is *determined by* a religion's cosmology" (emphasis added). To find this sort of argument persuasive, it seems to me that you must approach the study of social groups just as a traditional phenomenologist would study religious symbols or rituals. For the seeming circularity of this way of thinking disappears once one recognizes that "ultimate concern" takes on metaphysical loadings in the work of those who employ the category. In other words, if "ultimate concern" is analogous to some pre-socio-historical *essence*, then "religion" is its *manifestation* in the contingent, historical world (the abode of "indifferent things"), providing the historical context in which the ultimate concern is expressed. Only then can this transcendent ultimate concern – as Wessinger states it – first be *expressed* within and then *determined by* the specificity of this or that religion's cosmology.

If my reading is persuasive, then such an approach to studying social formation is unproductive because it fails to take seriously the anthropocentric nature of all social life and scholarship on social life. Smuggling in from beyond the fray this notion of an ultimate concern does not help us if we are trying to explain social groups and their standards of behavior as thoroughly self-made and not mere expressions of timeless principles or impulses. Thus, the essence/manifestation (hermeneutical) circularity that lies in the background of

Wessinger's analysis is but one more instance of the binary, rhetorical technique groups employ to concoct their discursive spaces, suggesting that Wessinger's examination of millennial groups is as much an instance of group boundary maintenance – maintaining an "us" who do not act violently in that manner, thus steering clear of millennial fever – as were the contributions to the *Nightline* panel. Recalling Mack's, Durkheim's and Lincoln's earlier comments concerning the manner in which binary pairs of counterpoints have no content in themselves but, instead, are deployed to set discursive limits within which meanings can be staged, we can conclude that "ultimate concern" and whatever its necessary opposite may be (Tillich once went on at length to distinguish an ultimate concern from mere nationalism or patriotism), are just such counterpoints. They are defined only in light of each other, are meaningless on their own, but, once accepted, set discursive limits. After all, the adjective "ultimate" is meaningful only in light of surpassing some identifiable but lesser standard, as in the mathematical notation "n+1"; by definition "ultimate" eludes identification because it is inevitably at least one more (i.e., greater than) of whatever you're doing or talking about. It is therefore invisible, hopefully existent, anticipated or even dreaded, but it is not part of the hectic world of actual social life. On the one end, then, we have the concept of ultimacy, on the other we have the sheer noise and hubbub of lived social life and social experience, and in the midst of this binary we concoct an ordered, meaningful, and habitable space.

If her work was simply concerned with studying how it is that some groups do and do not act on dissenting views – a question intent on investigating how social formation actually proceeds – then Wessinger would not have ended her chapter on Heaven's Gate by normatively characterizing them as a brand of "catastrophic millennialism [that] had the effect of radically devaluing earthly existence." "One hopes," she concludes, "that Heaven's Gate is now closed and will not be reopened ..." (2000: 246). Maintaining this hope is something I am not prepared to do; despite having no interest in passing through the Gate, I have no interest in entering the fray of competing worldviews and trying to adjudicate on which fantastical beliefs and practices are more sensible than others. After all, I entertain plenty of my own fantastical beliefs.

Although Wessinger's attempt to explain group members' decisions is premised on a troublesome notion – "ultimate concern" – nonetheless, I think that she is on the right track in attempting to explain the reasons for their actions. It is important to recall that Wessinger's book is trying to explain why certain millennial groups *sometimes* act violently. To do this we need to take the advice seriously that we found in DeLillo's *White Noise*: we need to "look past the violence" since labeling an other's actions as "violent" tells us far more about us, our interests, and our classificatory schemes than it does about some essential character of the action being described. In other words, as I would try to rephrase it, the shortcomings of her study (explaining actions based on a group's ultimate concerns) helps us to move in the direction of investigating why dissenting, marginal groups sometimes (but only sometimes) put into practice their dissenting beliefs. I suspect that such a project will require us to try to explain the commonly entertained abrupt distinction between belief and practice, two historical items which more accurately function together (as in the more accurate notion of praxis).

One possible explanation for the widely perceived (perhaps necessarily perceived) disparity between belief and behavioral systems involves exploring the role played by the development of subsequent interpretive communities and traditions that narrativize and thus mystify their sense of their own historic beginnings, a practice that serves to circumvent the more extreme practices of the earlier, marginalized social forms from which the now dominant group happens to have arisen. Such an explanatory account will not focus on the actual origin or even the continued attraction of some posited pure or pristine belief/practice systems but, building on the work of cognitivists and sociologists in our field, it will instead focus on the procedures of transmission, elaboration, repetition, and adaptation of these social systems over time and place. After all, injunctions against the majority of people actually acting on the extreme forms of world- or self-denying belief systems that we often associate with the early years of various social formations are the products of later traditions. In fact, the injunctions against widely practicing overtly oppositional behaviors, injunctions that we associate with later interpretive traditions, actually presuppose that earlier community members did in fact act on these belief systems at least some of the time – otherwise the injunctions would be pointless.

That the processes of cultural transmission and elaboration began quickly in the case of Heaven's Gate – that scholars *already* have something to study – should be obvious: former members of the group quickly appeared all over the media interpreting the group's actions. I can think of two nationally televised interviews in particular, one on CBS and the other on ABC, where the utter incredulity of the interviewers (Lesley Stahl and Diane Sawyer, respectively) prompted onetime group members to elaborate significantly on the group's beliefs. (As an aside, their incredulity is itself something we need to think about, for, coming from a largely Christian-influenced culture, it is all the more intriguing that interviewers and the wider public had great difficulty understanding how people could leave their families for the sake of a social group – it is almost as if no one had ever read the Gospel recommendations to deny oneself and leave one's land, mother, father, children, etc.) As a result of this small body of commentary, tradition, and story telling we learned that the previously mysterious quarters and five dollar bill found on each body were part of the group's response to earlier police charges of vagrancy. We know this not from primary sources but from a post-origins commentary tradition.

By focusing on the processes whereby social formations develop and are transmitted from early, marginal, and more extreme forms to more fully dominant socialized status, we might also be able to explain why it is that virtually all social systems continue to house a small, more extreme element that continues to practice various forms of self-denying behaviors associated with the movement's origins phase (a nineteenth-century anthropologist would no doubt call such behavior a survival). For instance, despite the fact that almost all contemporary Christians marry in elaborate, church sanctioned ceremonies, a very small but highly respected number still follow the early injunctions against marriage as well as the Gospel recommendation to leave one's family (e.g., Roman Catholic priests, monks, and nuns). Also, despite the fundamental importance of the classical Indian varnashrama-dharma system, a small number of highly respected individuals still renounce identity, family, and doing their dharma (e.g., sannyasins). Despite the early sangha's example, modern Buddhists the world over generally do not beg for alms – yet a small, respected number still do. Were such behaviors simply the result of the onetime extreme social and political marginalization of these various groups' historical antecedents, then, using the once popular secularization thesis, we would no doubt predict that such behaviors would disappear altogether as the early social formations slowly and successfully reformulated themselves as part of mainstream culture. But they have *not* disappeared; instead, they amount to Durkheimian ideals (often said to be unattainable by most group members) in each of these groups.

We might explain the continued but marginalized presence of such extreme behaviors within such groups – as well as the need for cults and fanatics within so-called normal society! – by means of the strategy of mythmaking, a strategy so important to the gradual process of institutionalization and traditionalization, a process by which mundane, practical behavior takes on new significations. As one means for constructing, authorizing, and maintaining the social formation over time and space, it seems that contemporary social movements physically embody for their members their own originary rhetorics in the here and now, for all to see yet *not* for all to imitate. For if they were all to imitate them, then the social formation would cease to exist altogether, or at least as we now know it. Appealing one last time to DeLillo's *White Noise*, I think of the apparently disbelieving nun who treats the protagonist's wounds near the novel's close. Answering his pestering questions concerning the beliefs, the dress, and the actions he thinks she *ought* to have, wear, and undertake, she replies bluntly:

> As belief shrinks from the world, people find it more necessary than ever that *someone* believe. Wild-eyed men in caves. Nuns in black. Monks who do not speak. We are left to believe. Fools, children. Those who have abandoned belief must still believe in us. They are sure that they are not right to believe but know that belief must not fade completely. Hell is when no one believes. There must always be believers. Fools, idiots, those who hear voices, those who speak in tongues. We are your lunatics. We surrender our lives to make your nonbelief possible. You are sure that you are right but you don't want everyone to think as you do. There is no truth to fools. We are your fools, your madwomen, rising at dawn to pray, lighting candles, asking statues for good health, long life.
>
> (319)

Without accepting this character's sense of diminishing belief (once again, the secularization thesis rears its ugly head), this nun who understands the importance of *appearing* to believe – "Our pretense is a dedication" she says – reinforces a point made earlier in this chapter, when I also cited DeLillo. Building on Sister Hermann Marie's insights we can argue that the present credibility and certainty of what is in fact an ever changing, fragmented, and adapting formation in part relies upon a tenuous link between (i) the perceived, heterogeneous, contingent present, (ii) the posited homogenous, mythic past, as well as (iii) the Other (whether dangerous or innocent) in the here and now. By means of this coordination a moment of mythic origins is continually remade in the present by being literally written on the bodies of those members who eat and breathe and embody the myth/ideal in the here and now.

Much as with the choreographed violence of cinema car crashes and the fanatical cults who populate the tabloid racks, this literal embodiment of the mythic ideal in turn authorizes the normalized and therefore mitigated present, an ad hoc, contestable, and tradition-based present that otherwise might bear little resemblance to some pre-traditional mythic origins. This is not to suggest, however, that the tradition-based present is somehow hypocritical, insomuch as it fails to live up to the ideal. It is the exact opposite, in fact. By definition it must *not* resemble its self-proclaimed origins or ideals too closely for, if it did then it would never have survived long enough to have become a tradition in the first place – hence the participants' widespread presumption that few, if any, members can actually perform the extreme behavior presumed to accord with, for instance, how Jesus's disciples might have actually lived or how the members of the sangha first moved across northeast India. Each social formation would come to an end as we know it if indeed all their members were to become renunciants or if all their members acted on the beliefs they seem to hold so dear.

So, much like DeLillo's character who proclaims that "Nostalgia is a product of dissatisfaction and rage ... a settling of grievances between the present and the past" (258), I am arguing that the myth/ideal embodied in the historic present by a small number of group members who embody an origins tale or enact Otherness is a socially necessary nostalgia that both expresses and sows seeds of insecurity and discontent within the dominant group, thus fueling new cycles of social formation. I have in mind here the sort of crisis rhetoric that can easily be heard coming from the mouths of those who firmly have a grip on the reins of power, the siege mentality that fuels new cycles of social formation. Applied to aging U.S. yuppies (i.e., Young Urban Professionals), we find no better example than Don Henley's 1984 rock song "The Boys of Summer," where he sings about seeing a Dead-head bumper sticker on the back of a luxury Cadillac automobile.[13] Giving the impression that he passed this car on the road, the singer reflects on how he thought to himself that one can never look back, suggesting not only that he ought not turn around to look at the car but that, as made evident in the famous title of Thomas Wolfe's 1940 novel, *You Can't Go Back Home Again*. Therefore, it is rather ironic that a luxury car bears a totem best associated with a critique of the kind of status and excessive consumption that the car (and its owner's lifestyle, I presume) represents. However, despite his admonition, "looking back," much like gazing at the Other, is the fuel of social formation. By symbolically re-embodying a moment when the group recalls itself to have been politically marginal, under attack, alienated in practical, material terms, and thus forced to engage in extreme forms of physical behavior either as a form of political protest, social experimentation, or actual combat, a small number of contemporary group members and ritual specialists can portray a onetime social trauma for their now satiated and privileged peers – a time when "they" too were hungry and marginalized. It is a technique that seemingly allows one to leap outside one's self, outward into a dangerous Other (i.e., Heaven's Gate or the grizzly bear attack) or backward into a very specific past so as to symbolically destabilize, and thus re-energize, the now normalized present, thus desperately propelling forward a renewed sense of the group and the self within the group. "We were once in Egypt." Neither the Other nor this past is some authoritative archetype, as once argued by Eliade. Like the bumper sticker on the Cadillac, it is a discursive device in the present that juxtaposes security with inevitable insecurity, as a means for destabilizing the apparent sense of having arrived by holding out one's eventual destination as if it was perpetually beyond one's reach.

Therefore, renunciation, extreme forms of world- and self-denying behaviors, along with representations of fanatical cults are not built-in institutional self-destruct mechanisms or the evidence of a defeatist attitude where participants cannot bear to face the problems of the real world. Instead, when we take into account the injunctions that the tradition has developed to contain and mitigate their more extreme effects, we can redescribe the isolated instances where they are still practiced as social survival mechanisms whereby members of a contemporary social formation call their own dominance into question by imaginatively confronting the Other or leaping to their own mythic, emergent state. Mixing DeLillo with another novelist, David Lodge, we can say that wild-eyed men in caves, nuns in black, and monks who do not speak, create "an alternating current of fear and reassurance that charges and relaxes ... [a social] system in a persistent and exhausting rhythm" (Lodge 1992: 9).[14] Without extreme, minority behaviors embodying the myth/ideal, there is no tradition that extends over time and place. However, if everyone practiced such behaviors, there would equally be no tradition, for everyone would have moved on to form their social identity in a new way – say, catching a space ship in the tail of a comet. There is only a tradition that extends over time and place when the inevitable anxiety and dissent of social life can be displayed harmlessly and thus displaced. Despite their minority status, renunciants and cultists are equally important insomuch as they step forward to live the outcome of the myth of origins, to provide a vicarious site for those who internalize dissent and disjoin belief from practice, and to embody the ideal in a way the rest of the group cannot, suggesting a love/hate relationship between the laity and its ritual specialists, between anonymity and celebrity, and between normalcy and fanaticism – a relationship that Freud understood well. "No matter what you say about them," a commentator might be heard to say, "you can't call them cowards," offering his grudging respect for outlandish actions.[15] Despite what insiders may think, then, there is an inevitable gap yet necessary relation between tradition and origin. What's more, the origin is not an item of history but, an item of ongoing discourse for it is constantly reinvented by each new cycle of social formation, forever serving new purposes.

The moral of this long detour is that, rather than Marty's normative and dismissive analogy:

> spiritual retreat:target practice::Heaven's Gate:Russian roulette

we can generate a counter proposal based on a theory of social/self formation – a theory capable of discussing far more than supposedly spiritual matters, and one based on something other than a self-interested liberal Protestant hunch about what constitutes normal versus abnormal religion. Following our social theory, then, we can argue that:

> abnormal cults:normal society::renunciants:religious traditions::cinema car crashes:a "wonderful brimming spirit of innocence and fun" (DeLillo 1986: 219).

As Mack was already quoted as saying, each pairing articulates a displaced system, "a counterpoint to the ways things usually go. The inevitable incongruence between the symbol system and the daily round provides a space for discourse" (1991: 21). In each of the above cases, a posited normal range of activity is made possible by means of a posited extreme.

Some readers may find it preposterous to make such comparisons between, say, Heaven's Gate and other established religions, let alone the modern cinema. For such people there is an almost intuitive common sense to talking about angels, gods, souls, and even demons instead of space aliens, seeds, and mother ships – even though, for the scholar, they are all sites of human behavior and meaning-making and, thus, all are equally curious. As scholars it falls to us to remind such people that the Heaven's Gate community does not have the benefit of two thousand years of hindsight, sympathetic, participant mythmaking, let alone a cultural atmosphere highly sympathetic to it. Surely one does not have to rehash the disdain that dominant cultures of the day had for the originators of what are now known and accepted as the great world religions. So, in embarking on these comparisons, we must not, for example, compare contemporary Christianity or Buddhism to Applewhite's movement, for the former social formations benefit from at least two millennia of historical development, elaboration, and successful contextual accommodation. Instead, we must maintain what Jonathan Z. Smith has termed the principle of parity

(1990b: 106), and see in Heaven's Gate an emergent social formation comparable in a surprising number of ways (though of course not identical) to the earliest phases of other social formations that did or did not eventually develop institutionalized structures to carry them into a future. (Just how and why those institutions eventually developed is part of the problem to be explained and not to be taken for granted!) After all, Heaven's Gate is a very young movement and has only recently leaped into the wider cultural imagination of North Americans. What might it become in fifty or one hundred years, let alone two thousand? Will it retain members, rise again, and thus devise the necessary institutional structures to exist over time? Will the already developed commentary tradition develop further? Will others see lights in the sky and attribute them to Do and Ti's return visitations (early on, some news sources reported that this had already happened)? Or was their actual, physical protest against the natural world, as opposed to a merely symbolic protest against the social world, sufficient evidence that this group has now passed from history's stage, leaving only its ongoing role of allowing "normal" and "civil" and "reasonable" selves to continue to be manufactured at their expense? What insights can we gain from its early growth, its appeal, and failure to reproduce over time that can be applied to study the beginnings of social formations removed from us in time and culture? Better yet, what insight can be gained from our continued fascination and disdain with cults?

If we see ourselves as more than just color commentators for bizarre cultural practices – as I have argued elsewhere, this is a role of limited interest (2001b: ch. 8) – then we currently face the challenge of applying our critical tools to help explain those aspects of human behavior that seem unpalatable as well as those that are palatable. To quote Smith again (this time talking about the deaths at Jonestown in 1978, but saying something equally applicable in this case), for there even to be a human science, we as scholars must be able to remove groups like Heaven's Gate, or people like Marshall Applewhite and his followers from "the aspect of the unique, of … being utterly exotic. … We must be able to declare that [this event] … was an instance of something we have seen before. We must perform an act of reduction. We must reduce [it] … to the category of the known and the knowable" (1982: 111–112). Despite their rhetorical power, "fanatic," "cult," "ultimate concern," "hero," and "coward," are theoretically vacuous categories for scholars interested to do more than just reproduce the social worlds made possible by those who wield these rhetorical techniques. Deploying these classifications in cases such as Heaven's Gate is understandable, given that its members' actions against their own biological selves are easily understood as a biting critique of the larger social world to which others of us unthinkingly or unproblematically belong. Their suicides are thus easily seen as an attack on us. But failing to look past the violence prevents us from taking into account that, by directing their dissent inward, toward the actual elimination of their biological selves, their so-called deviance from the mainstream not only offends against the very existence of the mainstream but, ironically perhaps, further reinforces the mainstream. Much as Judith Perkins has observed concerning suicide in literary romances from antiquity, such action actually serves to promote expected societal roles (Perkins 1995: 103; see also McCutcheon 2001b: 36); exempting oneself entirely from the historical, natural world by means of suicide leaves intact the social and natural worlds against which one was presumably protesting. Suicide is indeed a protest but, ironically, a reconfirmation as well.

Coming to see the irony and complexity of such actions and our efforts to understand them will hopefully prompt scholars to realize that they have far too often failed to live up to their critical potential. Instead of simply spinning rhetorical webs suited to the tabloid racks, an activity that reproduces but one sense of normalcy while securing one's place as an enlightened protector of common sense and good taste, scholars could instead be theorizing the world of competing passions, making them known and knowable human behaviors that are no more exotic than their very own web spinning activities.

Notes

1 This issue of the journal, although planned long before the September 11 attacks, was published soon after and contains this Presidential article and an editorial, both of which were written after the attacks. Although I was aware of the articles, I must thank Jack Llewellyn for bringing the President's text to my attention.

2 As reported by Wessinger (2000: 231) of the 30 group deaths: 19 were men and 20 were women and their ages varied from being in their 20s to their 30s, 40s, 50s, 60s. The oldest was 72.

3 All quotations from this episode were transcribed by the author from the March 31, 1997 episode of ABC's *Nightline* entitled, "The Thin Line Between Faith and Fanaticism."

4 Although the original web site is no longer available, mirror sites are still up. See, for example, <http://www.clas.ufl.edu/users/gthutsby/rel/gate/>.

5 If all social groups, regardless their historic phase of development, are a complex mixing and blending, borrowing and appropriating, then the continued use of "syncretism" to describe some groups is evidence of just how resilient the myth of homogeneity continues to be. After all, the term as used to describe others (e.g., such as Haitian voodoo being understood as a syncretistic mix of Roman Catholic with various African practices) has meaning and utility only in light of the presumed uniformity and seamless identity of the historically prior source cultures (as if those things we call "Roman Catholicism" and "Africa" were themselves uniform social identities).

6 One of the conclusions reached by Wessinger (2000) in her study of this and other groups that resort to violent action is that they must be studied as religions, and their members afforded the same respect as when the members of other religions are under investigation. Despite moving some considerable distance in her attempt to understand these Others, I still detect in her book many of the traditional social strategies used to classify and constrain dissent (to be addressed below). After all, classifying them as religious and not political movements still allows us to spiritualize and thus dismiss them and their practical concerns.

7 In a news release at the time, Kisser was quoted as saying: "We've been backed into this corner … simply because of the massive amount of litigation we have had to

face in the approximately 50 cases brought by Scientologists against us since 1991. If you get sued 50 times over four years the odds are that you're going to suffer losses at some point" (http://www.icon.fi/~marina/can/canpage/canc.htm). The onetime Cult Awareness Network, or what is now referred to by some as the "real" CAN, was replaced by the New CAN which promotes what it describes as religious freedom and tolerance (see http://www.cultawarenessnetwork.org/) while criticizing the former organization for its criticism of such groups as Scientology.

8 For example, Saler reports that, based on recent Gallup and *Time* magazine polls, "about one in four adults in the United States 'believes' that intelligent beings from outer space have been in contact with humans." Moreover, when asked "whether or not they believe that 'some of the unidentified flying objects reported are really space vehicles from other civilizations,'" 54% of the respondents in 1985, and 57% in 1988, and 54% in 1990, answered in the affirmative (2001: 47).

9 Near the conclusion of the *Nightline* episode she returned to the rhetorically useful, but sadly empty, jargon of critical thinking, saying: "if critical thinking was taught in the schools, and I think if seminarians were taught a little bit about the practical aspects of how cults execute their control mechanisms, the world would be a lot safer."

10 See McCutcheon 1997b: 108–109 for a related critique of how this same rhetoric is deployed in one of our field's best-selling world religions textbooks.

11 As if to counter this sad trend, in this issue of the *Bulletin* Prentiss published two particularly insightful pieces on the events of the Fall of 2001, written by Paul Johnson (2002) and Bruce Lincoln (2002b).

12 Or, as phrased by Muesse: "the rational way in which they approached their deaths made them seem even more irrational" (1997: B6)

13 For those who do not know, "Dead-head" is the self-designation for fans of the non-mainstream rock band, The Grateful Dead. The Dead, as they were often called, were generally associated with non-commercial, live performance music. For their fans (many of whom would follow them from concert to concert), they were representative of an alternative U.S. culture which recalled ways of expressing alienation and organizing political opposition characteristic of the 1960s. Seeing a "dead-head sticker" on a luxury car is thus a symbolically loaded image easily found today.

14 I should say that David Lodge's narrator is here describing the pre-flight trauma of the character Philip Swallow – the excitement and fear that always accompany his preparations for airline flights. I have used the quotation to describe social formation since I believe it nicely summarizes the dialectical relationship between emergent and dominant states. Even when it is successful, social formation is an insecure, "persistent and exhausting rhythm," where the future well being of the group is continually at stake.

15 I have in mind the comedian Bill Maher, host of the late-night television show "Politically Incorrect." He was much criticized for commenting on his September 17, 2001, broadcast that – picking up on a remark of his guest, the conservative political commentator Dinesh D'Souza – no matter what you thought about their actions, one could not label the September 11 attackers "cowards." So soon after the attacks emotions ran far too high to allow such a comment to go uncontested. Perhaps Maher's fate was sealed when, on a bit of a roll, he went on to juxtapose piloting a jet into a building, with the guaranteed result of one's own death, to U.S. troops seated many hundreds of miles away from their targets pressing buttons and launching missiles. "We have been the cowards lobbing cruise missiles from 2,000 miles away," Maher said. "That's cowardly. Staying in the airplane when it hits the building, say what you want about it, it's not cowardly." Drawing attention to the tremendous loyalty and commitment (whether or not one agrees with the loyalty or the commitment) required to bring about the attacks on New York and the

Pentagon, along with the jet that crashed in Pennsylvania, means calling into question the scripted roles of sane good guys and fanatical bad guys that were widely used to make sense of this situation. Fanatics do not have commitments; after all, they're fanatics! Calling this logic into question is just not allowable, and some of Maher's sponsors (Sears and FedEx), a number of local stations that carry his show (one in Washington D.C.), along with the White House's spokesman, Ari Fleischer, quickly rose to discipline him for such a statement. For example, although acknowledging that he had not seen the broadcast, Fleischer said that Americans "need to watch what they say, watch what they do, and this is not a time for remarks like that; there never is." If "there never is" a time for remarks such as Maher's then what are we to make of the much celebrated freedom of speech for which, we were repeatedly told, U.S. forces were fighting in Afghanistan?

Chapter 6

Alienation, apprenticeship, and the crisis of academic labor[1]

On the bad days, I wonder why I'm committing six to eight years to this. ...
Why am I postponing having a family, financial security, geographic flexi-
bility, and relationships for something that seems so uncertain?
  University of Chicago Divinity School graduate student (Spiegler 1997: 43)

Our generation of graduate students was told, "Don't worry, in the 1990s
there'll be a wave of faculty retirements and jobs will reappear."
Unfortunately they haven't, and too many of us have heard, or lived, tales of
adjunct-hell. ... For years we have all been wringing our hands over the state
of the job market – but who will *do* something?
  Yale University religious studies graduate student (Dugdale 1997: 13)

Preamble

I recall revising an earlier form of this chapter late one evening in Terminal C
of the Lambert-St. Louis International Airport in Missouri, laptop on my lap,
harsh lighting overhead, a cup of airport coffee at my feet, and two hours to kill
due to a flight delay. Like so many Canadians before me, I moved to the U.S.
(in 1993) to find work in a university; my Green Card application came
through in February of 2001. Because of relocating in a new country, with
different credentialing standards, my wife, who was a teacher of deaf and hard of
hearing students in Canada, had to develop a new career – a fact that, for
several years now, has necessitated us living in two different (sometimes neigh-
boring) states and visiting as often as possible. I state this from the outset not to
gain sympathy – for life is generally pretty good – but rather to help place
readers who may be disconnected from the life of an average, young academic in
the late twentieth century into the very real situation that I examine in the
following chapter. We are hardly the first or the last to live this generally odd
life, yet I know that I am lucky to have just these, and not other, problems.

  With a tip of my hat to the recent trend toward openly self-reflexive scholarship, then, I open this chapter with a few pieces of my own story of
disenchantment, migration, and professionalization – signaling, hopefully, that I

too am a piece of data for a rhetorical theory of social formation. So, in keeping with my interests in redescriptive scholarship, I hope that, by the end, my analysis wins the day over mere venting and storytelling; while the latter may help lonely hearts feel better for a while, only the former will help to change the situation.

Background

In November of 1996 I participated in a joint North American Association for the Study of Religion (NAASR)/Society for the Scientific Study of Religion (SSSR) panel held at the SSSR's annual meeting in Nashville, Tennessee.[2] The panel was devoted to diagnosing some of the current ills facing the study of religion, one of which is the nearly three-decade-old problem of the depressed academic job market in the humanities and social sciences. The reasoning behind the panel was that perhaps there exists a link between the way in which scholars of religion decontextualize their data (what I call the rhetoric of autonomy), on the one hand, and the way in which many of our colleagues routinely minimalize the economic and social woes currently facing the academy.

This topic was suggested by an article written by the literary critic Cary Nelson entitled, "Lessons from the Job Wars: Late Capitalism Arrives on Campus" (1995a).[3] When I first read Nelson's article in the autumn of 1995, I held a temporary, J-1 work Visa and was beginning my third yearly contract position as a full-time instructor in a religious studies department in the U.S. Despite feeling increasingly qualified for tenure track work, over those three years I found few jobs to which I could credibly apply (and those I did find were mostly in the U.S.). Having made it no further than to a few impersonal, twenty-minute interviews conducted by employers at the annual meeting of the American Academy of Religion/Society of Biblical Literature (AAR/SBL), I was seriously considering what it would mean to have earned a Ph.D. as an end in itself rather than as a means toward continued participation in a profession of research and teaching. In hindsight, I would say that I was prime material for the label of disenchanted.

What struck me most about Nelson's article was not only that someone was taking seriously my experiences as a young academic but, more importantly, that someone was studying how these experiences resulted from a blatantly absurd job market – a market in which pre-professional candidates must meet such professional standards as peer-reviewed publication, excellence in teaching, and the public presentation of their research at conferences before even gaining entrance to the profession. It was and still is a market in which candidates may very well have a more extensive publication record than many of the people interviewing them. It is a market in which, at many schools, it takes far superior credentials to get a job interview (let alone the job!) than it might have taken one's interviewers to have been awarded tenure. Although many have

commented on the evils of grade inflation, the need to improve student reten-
tion rates, and the drawbacks of income compression for senior faculty, few have
chronicled the credential inflation that now governs entrance to the profession
(though Bérubé has tackled this topic [1995]). That such credential inflation
can indeed be linked to a deflation in the quality or creativity of the research
now being published is, of course, a topic that should also be addressed;
however, to posit a necessary link between credential inflation and quality
deflation all too often works in the hands of the old guard to minimize and
dismiss, rather than address, the very real pressures currently facing younger
scholars.

The rhetoric of autonomy

Although there may have been a day when university professors were able to
initiate students into what was then considered the life of the mind, free from
the messy pressures to publish in peer-reviewed journals and deliver papers at
public meetings, that day is long over. (Though, I would seriously question
whether such a day ever actually existed.) No longer can we simply be quirky
though inspiring teachers; from the outset, younger scholars are now expected
to excel in research, teaching, and service, all the while paying off massive debts
and wondering what the future of tenure will be.

To put some flesh on the bones of this argument, consider this rapid fire list
of how things have changed in the U.S. over the course of a couple decades. (I
must preface these statistics by saying that I would hope any Canadian reader
will not dismiss my comments due to their U.S. context, for a surprising number
of friends from graduate school have at one time or another also moved south to
find employment. Whether or not this counts as a "brain drain," the problem is
serious enough to have attracted some national prominence in the last federal
election in Canada; my wife and I, watching the leaders' debate televised in the
U.S. on C-SPAN noted that the issue was raised by the pro-labor, New
Democratic Party [NDP]. However, until provincial and federal governments
increase their investment in the future of higher education, graduate students in
Canada would be well advised to think seriously about the likelihood that they
too will end up teaching in the U.S. state university system where salaries,
retirement packages, and health care benefits can sometimes be rather different
from what they have come to expect in Canada.)[4]

In 1970, 68% of Ph.D. graduates found teaching positions; since 1980 it has
hovered around 51% – and this does not take into account the number who do
not finish graduate school, how long it takes to get a teaching position, or
people currently working well below their means/credentials. Despite this
dramatic drop in career placement, between 1970 and 1993 the number of
Ph.D. degrees awarded *increased* from 29,500 to 39,750 (according to the
National Research Council). A recent study by the American Association of
University Professors (AAUP) found a 30% drop in faculty appointments at

U.S. public universities between 1991 and 1995 – a 12.1% drop was registered at private institutions. Between 1992 and 1995, an Indiana University survey found the average graduate student debt went from $16,310 to $26,800 (U.S.). Overall graduate and professional student borrowing from the federal government increased from $4.4 billion in 1993 to $7.7 billion in 1995. While they account for 14% of university enrollment, graduate students are saddled with 28% of all higher education debt. (These figures are all taken from Spiegler's sobering article.)[5]

Unfortunately, too many of our colleagues who currently enjoy positions of seniority and privilege in the field – who are insulated within this thing we call "the profession" – fail to recognize the drastically changed economic and political setting of the modern, corporatized university. For example, all too often they subscribe to the individualist myth and pass judgment on job candidates who have been on the market for several years, presuming their inability to land tenure track employment says something about the candidate's quality as a scholar rather than something about the structural constraints that have made them a job applicant rather than a job holder. In fact, many of our colleagues only recognize the drastically changed context of academic labor when current market pressures infiltrate their own universities' and departments' policies on such topics as the amount of research required to be awarded much coveted course reductions and promotions to full professor along with inflation-induced salary compression; in such instances the ground shifts out from under a generation generally freed from many of the pressures now facing younger scholars.

In most cases, however, the pressures of the labor market are far removed from tenured professors and a number actually worsen the problem by harkening back to a nostalgic golden age to which they think we can somehow return – a crippling nostalgia when consumed by pre-job market, idealistic graduate students. Commenting on events surrounding the contentious, 1996 teaching assistant strike at Yale, Andrew Ross, Director of the American Studies program at New York University, elaborates:

> To academics who subscribe passionately to the liberal ideal of disinterested scholarship, academic membership, and collegial autonomy, all of this economic and political turbulence is highly distasteful. Consequently, a psychology of denial has set in and is now entrenched within the comfortably tenured strata of academe. This has taken its toll. Not only is the possessive investment in the privilege of tenured seniority a prominent obstacle in the path of solutions to the crisis of academic labor, but tenured faculty's resistance to change has become one of the causes of the crisis itself.
>
> (Ross 1996: 27)[6]

Take, for example, the troubling editorial that ran in the main Canadian journal in the field, where the out-going editor, John Sandys-Wunsch, noted that "[t]hose of us who went to university in the 1950s can remember many teachers who never wrote a book of great consequence but who gave us the sort of education that goes with you for the rest of your life" (Sandys-Wunsch 1996: 140). As much as I agree when he states that it is hardly a good idea to force graduate students into the publication production line (prompting them to become pre-professionals, in other words), I cannot help but feel that Sandys-Wunsch's lamentation over this lost paradise hardly helps the situation; in fact, it provides sufficient evidence to support Ross's thesis. Whether it is good or not that pre-professionals are forced to seek, for example, peer-reviewed publication, current market forces dictate that if they wish to feed themselves by means of the skills they have worked on so long, and gone into such financial debt to acquire, they have little choice but to play by the profession's rules long before they are treated and reimbursed as professionals. Had many of us not become proficient at meeting the unrealistic expectations of the pre-professional life, we would not be doing what we do today – but, ironically perhaps, our meager successes only raise the bar that much higher, all of which hardly helps our peers who are sane enough *not* to live the absurd lives required of younger scholars.

Precisely how do views of a mythological golden age hinder, rather than help, the situation in which we now find ourselves? Simply stated, they place teaching assistants, adjunct faculty, A.B.D.s, and newly minted Ph.D.s in a double bind: while they are increasingly judged by rigorous professional standards, the self-appointed gatekeepers of the profession (by means of their control over journals, institutions, professional organizations, teaching positions, etc.) continually identify them as "mere" graduate students. To appeal to Sandys-Wunsch's editorial once again, after lamenting the lost paradise where we once apparently pursued the contemplation of disinterested ideas (I have visions of reclining, toga-clad graduate students, eating grapes and discussing Plato, truth, and beauty – a myth of grad school many of us likely shared at one point in time), he turns his attention explicitly to address the graduate student papers that are now routinely submitted to periodicals throughout the field:

> I do not object to papers from graduate students; it is a good way for them to try their wings and I have done my best to make sure that they get solid evaluations. It matters little that most of them are rejected, and justly so. I am sorry if it is held against a new Ph.D. that he or she does not have any "publications."

There could be no better practical example of the way in which, as stated by Ross, "tenured faculty's resistance to change has become one of the causes of the crisis itself." Despite the fact that graduate students and new Ph.D.s are, in many cases, highly competent writers and thinkers who often have had one or more successful careers prior to entering doctoral study, they are here characterized in a patronizing fashion as mere fledglings who sit perched on the edge of the nest, about to try their unsteady wings.

In this vein Sandys-Wunsch quotes Milton to characterize graduate students as "these berries harsh and crude." Such a stereotype strikes me as grossly unfair and part of the problem that must be addressed. As an editor, I have read and assessed my share of manuscripts written by international scholars at all points in their careers and can confidently say that the age of the berry often has surprisingly little to do with the taste of its jam! Moreover, the puzzling scare quotes around "publications" in the above quotation in fact betray the common refusal to recognize graduate student scholarship as *real* scholarship: graduate work is quaint but hardly serious, or so this position might argue. It should be of particular interest, then, to those who hold such an elitist view that Brian Malley, as a doctoral student, received the 1996 Society for the Scientific Study of Religion award for most distinguished article (as opposed to a *graduate student* essay award) for his essay on cognitive theorizing in the study of religion (Malley 1995).[7] That there is a relatively good chance that few of the profession's self-appointed gatekeepers have read much in the emergent field of cognitive studies of religion and ritual (which now boasts its own journal, published by Brill of the Netherlands) is sufficiently strong evidence for placing value on the work of younger scholars who are often key players in breaking ground in new areas of research.

Double standards, catch-22s, and "damaged goods"

Despite Sandys-Wunsch's possibly well-intentioned apology (in the popular and technical sense of the term) for the way in which he and many others address graduate student contributions to the field, *it happens to matter a great deal* that the profession's nostalgic gatekeepers hold to such an elitist view of the field and the knowledge it produces, *while in many cases* depending upon such graduate students to teach, grade the work of, and generally interact on a daily basis with large numbers of the undergraduate students who make our institutions possible. It is almost a classic example of how only members of dominant groups possess the necessary resources to engage in luxurious nostalgic appeals to an archetypical past as a means for contesting (or arguing away) current conditions and practices that conflict with their interests: as DeLillo was quoted as saying in the previous chapter, "Nostalgia is a product of dissatisfaction and rage. It's a settling of grievances" (1986: 258). This double standard matters a great deal not only to those who are caught by it (graduate students and sessional lecturers and instructors) but also to faculty since their very salaries are often dependent upon the presence of such graduate students who are treated as co-workers when it comes to grading and producing student credit hours for their departments (i.e., labor), yet treated as second-class apprentices when it comes to rewards (i.e., salary, job security, health and retirement benefits). Moreover, as suggested by Yale doctoral student, Kathy Newman, this also matters a great deal to administrators and the institution of the university itself for it is only through the graduate school that the university can exist over time: of all the professional schools housed in the university it is "only the graduate school [that] trains students for a life within the university's ivory towers" (Newman 1996: 102).

Although this double standard can be described as a necessary condition of all forms of professional apprenticeship, once it becomes apparent that there may literally be few if any jobs for which these so-called apprentices are training, the rhetoric of apprenticeship can be redescribed as an explicit form of exploitation; the utter irony of all such exploitation is that the groups upon which institutions most depend are the very groups most often exploited, making the rhetoric of apprenticeship a powerful force for ensuring that pre-professionals do not question their place in a complex system. Without low paid teaching assistants and part-time instructors who dream of full-time work, many faculty would be teaching two, three, or maybe four times more courses and students than they now do, and for not much more money either. Moreover, without graduate and teaching assistants there would be no faculty members to teach tomorrow's students and provide the necessary credit hour statistics that justify the existence of administrations and universities in the first place. Without graduate students and the research they carry out, many institutions would lose significant amounts of public and private funding. In the words of Nelson, although "the purpose of the graduate department is [ostensibly] to produce new teachers" they are in fact "a cheap labor pool" (as quoted in Spiegler 1997: 44). With the very real market pressures on the one hand, and elitist assumptions concerning the second-class nature of pre-professionals, on the other, candidates currently on the job market find themselves in a catch-22: they need professional credentials (e.g., publications, conference papers) to get a job and a job to get professional credentials.

It was Nelson who helped me to understand better not only the paralysis I once felt when caught in this catch-22, but also the frustration and alienation I was beginning to experience when confronted with the work conditions that are supported by nostalgic images of a once purer and dignified profession (recall that Marx and Engels understood *all* wage labor as exploitation) and my anger at the prospects of over-qualification and under-employment. And it was the novelist, Richard Russo, who reminded me of the empty victory that could result from excelling in an absurd labor market. In his novel, *Straight Man*, his protagonist – an aging Chair of a small English Department in a fictional mid-level U.S. state university – looks back over his career and admits that "promotion in an institution like West Central Pennsylvania University was a little like being proclaimed the winner of a shit-eating contest" (1997: 27). Given the sheer lunacy of playing by rules once reserved for seasoned scholars, I could see the risk I ran of becoming but another instance of what Nelson referred to as "damaged goods": the disillusioned, bitter, and severely over-worked and under-employed itinerant scholar who has paraded his or her c.v. before far too many hiring committees.[8] As much as one might wish simply to live the idealist life of the mind, pre-professionals have little choice but to internalize a professional discourse – to professionalize themselves – long before they leave graduate school; this is a brutally practical requirement unknown to those lucky enough to have gone to university in the 1950s and 1960s when the question was not *whether* you would get a job but *which* job you would accept. Just who and what gets to count as a professional is thus a function of the market.

The life of the mind, free from messy market constraints that determine who will eat and who will not, is simply a luxurious myth we can no longer afford to accept. Perhaps this factor can help to explain why a generation of academics has turned away from formalism and intellectualism and, instead, is interested in the material conditions and rhetorical techniques that make worlds of meaning possible and persuasive. Since it had been made obvious to them that they were up to their necks in the shit-eating game – and that the only thing worse than winning was coming in second – they turned their attention to scrutinizing the game's rules – who sets them, why we play by them, and the implications of not playing by them.

The myth of education for education's sake

It is particularly troubling that many doctoral students fail to anticipate the manner in which they will be thrust into the job market upon graduation. Internalizing the idealist myth of "education for education's sake," they can sometimes actually be hostile to those who point out the ways in which the university system simultaneously depends upon them and exploits them. It should come as no surprise, then, that some doctoral students are unwilling to confront their situation. Although tenured professors and university administrators have much at stake in reproducing the hierarchies at the heart of the university (e.g., salaries and social status), doctoral students not only have significant material investments at stake (e.g., loss of wages in other careers compounded by mounting student loan debts), but they also have their future to consider. To put it another way, their current situation makes sense only in light of their hoped for future income, job security, and social status – all of which are merely hypothetical, even in a seller's job market. (But, as we all know, it is always the other person who won't get a job or tenure.) Confronting the possibility of a future in which their hard earned Ph.D. degrees have no direct bearing on how they will come to feed and house themselves means that their efforts in the here and now may have little point. Simply put, it is in their best interest to support the hierarchical system that exploits them since it is only in light of how this system *might* reward them in the future that their current status is bearable and thus meaningful. This is yet another mythmaking technique that is related to a nostalgia for an ideal past: a hoped for future that makes the present bearable.

Doctoral students, then, are at the peak of the educational apparatus: they are both the end product of an elaborate and expensive institution *and* they are

the means by which that institution will reproduce itself (both as teaching assistants, future professors, and taxpayers). Because they are both product and
producer, they have the most to lose in addressing the exploitative nature of
their institution; they are deeply invested in this institution for both their
current identity and their future life. As product and producer, doctoral students
are therefore an ideal example of one specific site where an institution reproduces its own conditions of possibility. To cope with the sometimes outrageous
material situations in which they find themselves, doctoral students thus seem
to have little choice but to accept the myth that education marches to its own
drum beat and can only be judged by standards internal to education itself
(higher education is therefore understood as *sui generis*). Accordingly, they
sometimes cling to the notion of their education being socio-politically
autonomous and an end in itself, while they pay ever increasing tuition costs,
accumulate debts that some of them will slowly pay off over a lifetime, and
teach increasing numbers of undergraduate students in support of departments
that will eventually disown them so as to maintain their own graduation rates. I
have trouble imagining a more potent example of false consciousness than
claims concerning this disembodied life of the mind; after all, a library card, a
mediocre library, and someone to talk to over coffee are all one needs for this
type of education. Instead, being a graduate student entails playing a well-
defined role in an elaborate education industry. Failing to see this, failing to
understand both the university classroom and its commodity – education – as
historical processes, is to reify an all too human institution and thereby gloss
over its contradictions and shortcomings.

"It could have been worse": the myth of apprenticeship

Despite the fact that Nelson is himself from an academic generation for whom
landing a job of choice was almost considered a right (he was hired in 1970 at
the University of Illinois, at a time when the current market forces were just
beginning to be felt in academia), he correctly sees in the intervening decades
that the increasingly competitive job market signals much larger social, political, and economic issues in need of immediate attention. Therefore, his
contribution to the analysis of job applicant experiences comes by means of his
refusal to reify the university and education; trouble in the academic job market
is therefore neither an interiorized feeling of the applicant nor an isolated
phenomenon in academia. To support his point, Nelson writes:

> In the twenty years between the abolition of free tuition at the City
> University of New York and the massive cuts in the budget proposed for the
> State University of New York by the new Republican governor in 1995,
> signals abounded. We might, for example, have asked how the
> International Monetary Fund's austerity policies for developing countries

helped establish a cultural environment relevant to education's future in America. We might have asked whether Margaret Thatcher's effort to abolish tenure in British universities and turn higher education over to technological rationality reflected not only local politics but also widespread cultural tendencies in the postindustrial world. We might have wondered whether the increasing ethnic and racial diversity of California's postsecondary student population was linked in any way to the public's unwillingness to fund higher education out of tax revenues. ... We might have asked whether the increasing reliance on industry to fund research in the sciences might have implications for the humanities. We might have wondered what the policy implications of the New Right's cultural attacks on higher education since the 1980s might be. We might have questioned whether the decertification and disempowerment of unions that began with Reagan's handling of the air controller strike would prove prophetic for the rights of nonunionized employees in other sectors.

Nelson concludes:

> people concerned about higher education might have been interrogating its structural and semiotic relations with other cultural domains and economic and political forces. We might, in short, have been involved in an ongoing cultural analysis of education and in taking actions that such analysis suggested.
>
> (Nelson 1995a: 120)

Instead of engaging in such historically based cultural analysis and critique – which, after all, is the role of the social critic – many scholars continue to be complacent and rationalize the deeply institutionalized exploitation commonly associated with non-ranked or pre-tenure-track work by conceiving of it as a necessary form of professional apprenticeship. As Nelson has remarked elsewhere: "Universities persist in claiming graduate students teach as part of their doctoral training, not as employees. Yet higher education is pervasively dependent on cheap instructional labor. ... In the case of graduate teaching assistants ... the learning curve peaks years before the work ceases" (Nelson 1996: 8).

Understanding sessional lecturers and full-time instructors exclusively as apprentices, as opposed to cheap itinerant labor, therefore borders on artful self-deception. However, should people continue in this self-deception, then, as suggested by the University of Illinois English professor, Michael Bérubé, we should call their bluff and actually begin treating them like apprentices: "take graduate students out of the classrooms in which they work as graders, assistants, and instructors; maintain their stipend support at its current levels; and give them professional development and training that does not involve the direct supervision of undergraduates" (Bérubé 1996: 75). Then, he concludes, we'll see how long universities can "survive without the labor (which is strictly not 'labor' [according to those who advocate the apprentice thesis]) of its grad-uate student teaching assistants."

Furthermore, it is just this self-deception that has prevented many in academia from understanding that contemporary instructors and lecturers in many instances have no hope of ever participating in the profession for which they are supposedly training; there are no guarantees whatsoever that the skills they are learning as so-called apprentices will ever gain for them permanent, let alone full-time, employment. Instead, their migrant lifestyle, overload, lower division teaching, low salary, and poor (sometimes non-existent) benefits function to subsidize the higher salary, lighter teaching load, and smaller, upper division class size of more senior faculty members who also happen to be largely free of the pressures to publish. Many adjuncts have little or no private office space and many are unwelcome at (a.k.a. uninvited to) faculty meetings, thus playing no role in governance over the institution in which they labor. But, as bad as it is, we all know it could be worse. Recognizing how bad it could be is, of course, a sensible way of being thankful that one was spared more extreme circumstances; but it is also a powerful coping strategy that often prevents us from (i) identifying just how bad it has indeed been and (ii) doing something about it. In other words, when it comes to changing an institutional arrangement, group members are usually paralyzed, for a complex system of stratification exists whereby things could always be just that little bit worse. As in all social systems, where privileges are not shared by all, there is, then, a very real incentive to stay quiet, keep to yourself, put up with it, and just be thankful for the little piece of the pie that comes your way. (Is that not how profes-sors generally deal with salary inequities?) In part, this is precisely what Nelson means by the complacency that characterizes many members of our profession.

Cutting across rank and finding common interests

If we overcome this complacency – a complacency that amounts to little more than complicity – and peer behind the veil created by the rhetorics of autonomy and apprenticeship we will witness the creation and perpetuation of both an under-class of itinerant and perpetually over-achieving workers who often teach the majority of undergraduate students as well as departments where salaries rarely reflect actual teaching loads and research output. It should come as no surprise, then, that in today's increasingly conservative economic and political climate, the existence of such top-heavy departments is increasingly difficult to defend. Given that senior faculty members' salaries and teaching loads are sometimes so efficiently subsidized by the credit hour output of poorly paid itinerant workers, it is little wonder that many members of our profession are so well insulated from, and therefore ignorant of, the changing economic realities of the modern university.[9] The shared interests of full professors and sessional lecturers therefore go either unnoticed or even ignored.

As I write this I think of the August 1997 United Parcel Service strike in the U.S. Although it involved a number of complex issues, the one that received most public attention and which served as an effective rallying point for garnering the support of other unions was the manner in which part-time labor is often abused to the advantage of corporate interests. Contrary to what some might have thought, one of the main issues during this strike was not that part-timers were stealing work from full-timers but, on the contrary, that the future health of the industry – which is, after all, the future well-being of not simply its profits or market share but, more importantly, the well-being of its work force – would in large part depend on whether employers and shareholders were willing to invest the financial resources needed to create more full-time, long-term work opportunities. The UPS job action therefore makes it clear that shared interests do in fact unite part-time and full-time labor. Closer to home, this means that common interests also unite tenured professors of every rank with those who in our field are considered equivalent to part-time labor: graduate teaching assistants and graduate or post-graduate sessional lecturers.

In the summer of 1997, Mary Burgan, General Secretary of the AAUP (American Association of University Professors), wrote all members, in part to draw attention to this issue of part-time labor:

> We can see the effects of this disregard of the social responsibility of institutions as we look around us to discover that tenure-track lines are disappearing and that more and more of our courses are being taught by part-time faculty. We look in departments where each semester brings a bewildering array of "temps" to transmit independent units of information or skill, rather than to teach courses in a coherent, on-going curriculum. Many of us barely know these exploited colleagues of ours, and in accepting their anonymity, we participate in the lessening of community that threatens the "post-modern" university. Thus our tradition of academic freedom through tenure is eroded by a silent attack that is more successful in disrupting the faculty than any frontal assault in the past has been.

Part-time labor in the university is a thorny issue and clearly the tip of a very large iceberg. While part-timers comprise an exploited group of our colleagues who deserve support, they can also represent an institution's lack of commitment to the long-term requirements of teaching and research. Moreover, as Burgan rightly observes, discussions on part-time labor touch on a host of other issues of direct relevance to all who teach and research in the university: academic freedom, the future of tenure, faculty governance over the curriculum, fair and equitable monetary compensation and benefits for all university workers, the overall coherency of our curricula, and even, I might add, the use of various distance learning technologies that dramatically increase the student:teacher ratio while dramatically decreasing the cost of educating each student.[10] Taking into account the complexity of the issue, Burgan concludes her letter by noting that the AAUP has "set standards for fair treatment of part-time faculty, even as we expend out best energies on striving to close down campus dependencies on part-time teaching as the 'fix' for economic problems."

Having long failed to see the degree to which the future of all those involved in higher education was intertwined, some tenured professors are slowly awakening to find themselves perched atop a surprisingly unsteady system where class sizes continue to increase, where corporate inspired "downsizing" has eliminated support staffs, supplies, photocopy budgets, and sessional positions, and where administrators are understandably expecting that levels of "productivity" in the least be maintained or even increased (as measured by such markers as graduates, majors, overall number of students taught, grants received, books published, etc.). It is at their own peril that some fail to see that we are all in this together.

And what has all this got to do with the study of religion?

At the NAASR/SSSR panel we found ourselves in the position to engage in the kind of public critique recommended by Nelson and to apply it to the academic study of religion; from the ridiculously competitive job market to such interrelated issues as systemic budget cuts in the humanities and social sciences, academic downsizing, the implications of corporate devised "classwares," quantitative measures of faculty productivity, and newly developed web courses that threaten to marginalize the role of professors, the implications of declining student enrollments, and attacks on the institution of tenure, we find ourselves in the midst of a complex problem not unfamiliar to scholars of religion accustomed to defending their institutional niche. In the context of the United States, one need only mention the onetime plight of scholars of religion at both the University of Pennsylvania and San Diego State to understand the ways in which these social, political, and economic constraints can impact actual people's lives. In Canada, the University of Lethbridge and the University of Alberta come to mind as but two similar examples where departments were threatened with closure, actually closed, or substantially restructured.[11]

However, far too often scholars who see themselves as champions of a religiously pluralistic, liberal agenda, see in such attacks on religious studies departments – or even on religious people in general – evidence of the so-called secular world's fear and disdain for the abiding message of religion in the modern world. Unwilling to accept the validity and implications of the so-called deep, essential, or ultimate knowledge and truths afforded by their particular way of studying *and* practicing religion, the academy – or so this line of reasoning goes – attacks the enclave of wisdom found in the religious studies department, a department which, when situated in the public university, finds itself particularly vulnerable to such ideologically and economically driven attacks.

The idealism that drives this sort of analysis is at least partly responsible for the general silence among scholars of religion when it comes to addressing such practical issues as the plight of adjunct lecturers and the future of graduate students.[12] I find this sort of analysis sorely lacking for not only does it presuppose an implicit theory of religion as a socially autonomous, personal feeling, it also takes what Nelson rightly identifies as the systemic or structural nature of the problem and misrepresents and constrains it as local and isolated. It is yet another instance of the way in which scholars of religion isolate, dehistoricize, and decontextualize their data – data which in this case is not some human belief, practice, or institution *but their very own profession.* In other words, it is an example of the confusion and lack of intellectual rigor that results not only from asserting the supposed socio-political autonomy of the religious datum (i.e., the sacred, the *mysterium*, the numinous, etc.), but also the autonomous status of the very field that studies it. As argued by Bruce Lincoln and Cristiano Grottanelli over a decade ago, "the discipline 'History of Religions' managed to marginalize itself in the name of autonomy. Its connections with history, anthropology, sociology, political science, and other relevant fields are scarce, while its ties with theology – however much they are denied – remain strong, if implicit, covert, and distorted" (Grottanelli and Lincoln 1985: 8).[13]

In light of claims concerning the special problems faced by the study of religion, I found it heartening to hear some of the comments of one of our panel members, Warren Frisina, former assistant executive director of the AAR. Near the opening of the published version of his paper, "Religious Studies: Strategies for Survival in the 90s," he states that

> we are not alone in facing these difficult times. All of the arts and sciences are under attack, and it is important to acknowledge that difficulties in our field are symptomatic of larger trends rather than special instances of the old academic discomfort with religion. ... I suspect that our current problems are better understood if seen as part of a pattern which is larger and more pervasive than anything specific to religion. Today's challenges have more to do with whether or not the entire system of higher education needs to be radically rethought, and whether we can play a role of making a case for the importance and effectiveness of higher education in the humanities.
>
> (1997: 29)

There may be little peculiar about the institutional and economic troubles experienced by, on the one hand, job candidates in our field, or, on the other, departments in the study of religion. Simply put, religion departments are by no means the only departments that are scurrying to defend their continued existence in the university.

Conclusion

Perhaps we will begin to solve the current problems facing the field if we are first able to reconceive the study of religion not as a special case but as one among a number of fields engaged in the theoretically based study of human beliefs, behaviors, and institutions. In turn, this will require us to redescribe religion not as a privileged instance of private human experience but as a public technique of social formation. In this way will we engage in the kind of culture critique recommended by Nelson.

In setting out to theorize the practices and institutions generally known as religion as but one set of strategies for accomplishing the never ending work of reproducing social formations we will be able to communicate with other scholars about an observable, public, and enduring aspect of human behavior. Undoubtedly, such work means that we might lose the basis for our current cultural authority (as self-proclaimed experts on the numinous), but what is lost will more than be gained in our new ability to contribute to culture critique and analysis. Leaving behind self-serving rhetorics that, like colored ribbons at conferences, merely divide and rank those who are actually involved in the same activity, we will hopefully develop a vocabulary applicable to the study of many other institutional settings, and in so doing, we will develop new conversation partners and new social networks within the academy. We will find that our newly acquired tools will enable us to study the very institutions in which we carry out our research and teaching, as well as study the groups that fund (and rely upon) these institutions and the ways in which sets of competing social values are evident in their funding choices. Only once this theoretical context is established will the rhetoric of autonomy be set aside and only then will scholars of religion be able to address the material conditions that provide the context for the behaviors they study as well as their own work and the institutions in which their scholarship takes place. Until such a time we will no doubt continue to speculate on so-called secular conspiracies that aim to derail the pure pursuits of religious scholarship.

Postscript

Not long before completing the first draft of this chapter, I came across an article written by one of my former colleagues, Charles Hedrick, of Southwest Missouri State University, that was published in 1976 while he was a graduate student. At that time in the mid-1970s, the possible long-term nature of the job crisis was only beginning to settle into people's minds. What is *encouraging* about his article is that it not only offers an early and frank portrait of the job crisis but goes on to offer some practical, easily implemented suggestions whereby departments might remedy the situation. What is *disturbing* about the article is that it still reads as if it were written yesterday; few, if any, of its suggestions have been followed and, nearly three decades later, its portrait of the unemployed graduate student is still remarkably accurate. Recalling the epigraphs that opened this chapter, both of which are from contemporary graduate students, these closing comments from the mid-1970s frame this chapter in a rather sad but appropriate manner, for it seems as though we have learned little and done even less in the intervening years – sufficient evidence for the complacency that often attends the privilege of attaining rank in our profession.

I can therefore do no better than close by quoting Hedrick's own conclusion, and hope that serious, sustained attention at all levels of the profession will finally be given to the situation in which we find ourselves:

> I hope the reader will forgive an obvious platitude: these are difficult times that call for bold action. It is not enough to *counsel* new graduate students about their bleak prospects for employment. Some way must be found to *aid* the currently unemployed Ph.D. to bridge the gap between the academic community and the rest of the world, and to lessen or preclude future employment crises. At the very least the present situation demands that graduate schools take an aggressive role in the placement of their graduates.
>
> (Hedrick 1976: 5)

Appendix[14]

An open letter to department search committees

Given the characteristics of the current North American job market in the humanities and social sciences, where each year the number of qualified candidates far exceeds the number of tenure track openings, search committees sometimes fail to follow reasonable advertising and hiring procedures. In so doing, they increase not only their own workload but the workloads of all those who apply for positions. Overly detailed application requirements, coupled with vaguely defined job advertisements, suggest that search committees often do not define their departments' needs before venturing into the job market. A casual survey of current job descriptions will suggest the manner in which candidates are sometimes confronted by virtual wish lists that few, if any, actual applicants could ever satisfy.

To begin addressing this we would like to propose the following minimal recommendations:

1   Before advertising for a position, a department should decide what are its specific requirements and needs. That is, search committees should decide what they want and advertise for it clearly, rather than placing a vague or excessively wide description of the position in their advertisement and only making their actual decisions after candidates have submitted their application materials. Applicants should know in advance that they have a reasonable chance of obtaining a position if they are going to go to the trouble and expense of applying.

2   Departments should use a layered application system instead of requesting all application materials from the outset. To request of all candidates a full dossier is not only an unnecessary expense and inconvenience to the applicant, but it results in an excess of initial information and paperwork for already busy department search committees. A first round should include

only a *curriculum vitae* and a cover letter from the applicant that includes a list of her/his references. Moreover, if this is all that is initially requested, candidates should comply and avoid submitting unrequested materials. In this day and age of couriers, faxes, and electronic mail, additional information can easily and quickly be requested and submitted in subsequent rounds of the search.

3   As soon as possible, candidates should be notified of the receipt of their application materials and again be notified as soon as they are definitely out of the running. To this end, candidates can be pro-active by including with their application materials a stamped, self-addressed postcard. In addition, it would be courteous if, in the final form letter sent to unsuccessful applicants, they were notified of the successful applicant's name and credentials.

We believe that because some search committees have not followed these simple and minimal recommendations, it has tainted the hiring process in general; vague, ambiguous, and excessively wide job descriptions have increased the time and effort of hiring committees as well as candidates by generating a surplus of job applications that can force search committees to take short-cuts in their selection process. Such poorly articulated job descriptions suggest that the successful candidate will be selected on the basis of some mysterious qualification that will only be known to the committee when they intuit it. Surely, as a community of scholars we can expect our peers not only to be able to identify the actual needs of their departments in advance but also to be able to articulate and advertise these needs clearly and to be able to address all applicants with courtesy. Of course, to do this will require all department members to engage in frank discussions of their individual conceptions of not only the needs of their own department but the future of the field as well. Only if such admittedly involved but necessary conversations are carried out prior to advertising a position will the search process be more efficient, fair to all applicants, and of greater benefit to the overall health of our field.

Notes

1   After presenting an earlier form of this chapter at a conference in celebration of the twentieth anniversary of the Graduate Centre for the Study of Religion, University of Toronto, in 1996, it was first published as "Late Capitalism Arrives on Campus: Making and Remaking the Study of Religion," in the *Bulletin of the Council of Societies for the Study of Religion* 26/1 (1997): 3–7. In the present, revised version I have also included a small portion from a review essay also published in the *Bulletin*, "'But Who Will *Do* Something?': Diagnosing Some of the Ills of Academia," 27/2 (1998): 11–14.

2   The panelists were: Gustavo Benavides (Villanova University), Warren Frisina (then the Associate Executive Director of the American Academy of Religion), Darlene Juschka (then of the University of Toronto and now Director of Women's Studies, University of Regina, Saskatchewan), and Charles Reynolds (Department Head, University of Tennessee at Knoxville). Several of the papers from this panel

appeared throughout 1997 in the *Bulletin of the Council of Societies for the Study of Religion* (*CSSR Bulletin*).

3 For a profile of Nelson, see the *Chronicle of Higher Education*, 43/36 (May 16, 1997): A10 – 12. See also Nelson's other works that pertain to the issue of graduate education: 1995b, 1996, 1997a, 1997b. On the economics/cost of graduate education, see also Watt 1995. For a critical response to Nelson's indictment of the Modern Language Association's lack of leadership in responding to problems in the job market, see the response by the MLA's President, Sandra Gilbert (1996).

4 As an aside, as a Canadian doctoral graduate from 1995 I happen to be among a group being tracked by Statistics Canada. I receive detailed phone surveys from the government every few years that ask such questions as how my U.S. wage compares to a Canadian wage in my field, whether I would consider returning to Canada, and why it was that I came to the U.S. in the first place. For a primer on Immigration and Naturalization Service (INS) regulations for non-U.S. scholars intent on working in the U.S., see Lapel and McCutcheon 2001.

5 Although it is unclear the degree to which these statistics reflect numbers across the field, see the January (1997) issue of the AAR/SBL's *Openings* or the February (1997) issue of *Religious Studies News* for a report on the statistics from 1996's employment center in New Orleans. In brief, ratios of available positions to applicants vary from the rather favorable 1:0.67 in Islamic Studies and 1:0.78 in Women's Studies in Religion, to 1:3.5 in Early Christianity and 1:4.6 in Theology and Philosophy of Religion. Further, the disproportionate amount of our field that is yet concerned with Bible Studies, Theology, or the study of Judaism or Christianity is also reflected in these numbers: 46% of the job opportunities and 66% of job applicants were in these combined areas. My thanks to Miki McBride-Sala of the AAR/SBL's Employment Information Services Center for making these numbers available to me.

6 See this issue of *Social Text* for a number of useful essays on the December 1995 labor conflicts between the Yale administration and some of its teaching assistants. One particular issue addressed by a number of the writers is the manner in which administrations generally subvert student unions by defining graduate and teaching assistants as students and not as employees. The National Labor Relations Board charged Yale with acting illegally by punishing teaching assistants who withheld undergraduate grades during the December–January strike (*Academe* 83/1 [1997]: 5). Regarding the Yale strike, see the essays collected in Nelson 1997c.

7 For those not acquainted with *Method & Theory in the Study of Religion*, it was begun by Ann Baranowski and John Morgan in the late 1980s while they were both graduate students at the University of Toronto's then named Centre for Religious Studies (now known as the Graduate Centre for the Study of Religion). The peer reviewed journal, which has gained a devoted international readership, is published by Brill Academic Press of the Netherlands.

8 That I was in fact fortunate enough to be hired in a tenure track line at Southwest Missouri State University beginning in the Fall of 1996 – just as my three-year lectureship at the University of Tennessee was expiring – and that I was then fortunate enough to move to my current position at the University of Alabama in 2001, does not lessen the point I am trying to make. To take the position in Missouri, my wife and I once again had to live apart, pursuing our two careers, since Springfield, MO, provided a far from suitable setting for her career (audiology, specializing in cochlear implant research). I raise this point simply to emphasize what many in the field are all too familiar with: that there sometimes is a surprisingly high social cost to "succeeding" in the careers we have chosen. Whether we decide to pay this cost is, of course, our own personal decision, so those who pay it have little basis to "sing the blues" – though widely operating institutional constraints (such as the job

market and such investments as missed wages due to graduate education) often make the decision for us, making "personal choice" a slippery concept.

9 Concerning the sometimes even more dramatic disparity between full-time salaries based on discipline, see Nelson, "Superstars" (1997b). As an aside, it is a sobering exercise to calculate the number of students taught by, on the one hand, part-time instructors in some departments and, on the other, tenure track and tenured faculty. Because large enrollment, bread-and-butter undergraduate courses often fall in the laps of part-timers – leaving smaller, upper division classes to full-time faculty – their role in subsidizing faculty salaries, teaching loads, *and* a department's overall credit hour figures is sometimes staggering. Moreover, if religious studies majors are drawn from these lower-level, entry courses, our adjunct instructors are likely among our most important recruiters. In my experience I have seen a very small number of part-time workers teach between 30% and 50% of a department's undergraduate students – while, in some cases, these adjunct faculty members have little or no advanced training in the profession and little or no input into the department's curriculum or its future.

10 While encouraging the use of computer technology to increase access to higher education, the AAUP's director of governmental relations, Ruth Flower, noted that we must beware the ways in which "surfing" can threaten traditions of critical thought and argumentation. She concludes that "we should not change the experience [of higher education] to something more distant, something less engaging, something less enticing than a full pursuit of learning" (1997: 95).

11 See the special issue of *Method & Theory in the Study of Religion* (7/4 [1995]: 295–416), guest edited by Gary Lease, for detailed and sometimes provocative reports on the institutional well-being of three U.S. departments (Santa Cruz, Penn, and Arizona State) and three Canadian departments (at the Universities of Lethbridge, Alberta, and Toronto) in the mid-1990s. See also Christine Downing's report on the situation at San Diego State (1993) and Stephen Dunning's update on the situation at Penn (1997).

12 Dugdale (1997) and Tite (2002) are two of the very few articles to appear in our discipline's professional periodicals that directly address some of these issues. Of significance is that both articles were written by graduate students – one is forced to wonder where the senior, tenured voices are in this debate (the "full bulls," as a senior colleague once called them). As should be evident, the authors who have influenced my own thinking on these topics have not been scholars of religion but, for the most part, literary critics who have freed themselves of the myth of autonomy that once dominated their field and that still dominates our field. As an aside, the editors of the AAUP's *Academe* should be complimented for keeping their readers' focus on just these issues; most recently see the issue almost completely devoted to part-time appointments and the future of the university (84/1 [1998]).

13 The degree to which scholars of religion marginalize themselves politically in their search for institutional autonomy is argued in my "A Default of Critical Intelligence? The Scholar of Religion as Public Intellectual" (2001b: ch. 8).

14 The following, co-written with my then co-editor at the *Bulletin of the Council of Societies for the Study of Religion*, Tim Murphy, appeared as an open letter in our inaugural issue (26/1 [1997]). It is reprinted here, with Tim's and the CSSR's kind permission, in hopes that it will prompt more discussion than it did when first published.

Chapter 7

"Like small bumps on the back of the neck ... "

The problem of evil as something ordinary

Theology as ordinary human data

When I first read the quotation from the late Pierre Bourdieu cited earlier in this book – concerning the effort it takes to make ordinariness interesting – I was struck by the importance of his misleadingly subtle point. It is important for three reasons, I think: first, it takes seriously the participants' unreflective understanding of their own social worlds – after all, our object of study throughout the human sciences is people simply doing what they happen to be doing, not people interpreting or communicating the meaning and significance of what they are doing. Second, Bourdieu helps scholars to focus their attention on the techniques whereby some people (scholars included) sometimes actively represent a subset of their behaviors (i.e., *what they happen to be doing*) as important, meaningful, and worthy of reproduction and transmission (i.e., *what they must or ought to be doing*). Finally, both of these points reinforce the notion that scholars are not in the business merely of paraphrasing a group's own articulate or reflective understanding of themselves; instead, we bring our own curiosities, value systems and classifications, and sets of anticipations (i.e., theories) to bear on our human data, leaving us responsible for making this or that mundane cultural act significant and interesting in a whole new way.

For scholars concerned with studying those assorted cultural practices easily understood by most everyone in society to be obviously important – I'm talking here about those things we call "religion" – Bourdieu's comment has profound implications. If we presume those beliefs, behaviors, and institutions usually classified as religious to be nothing more or less than instances of completely ordinary social formative behavior, then the trick would be to develop an interest in the ways that such routine social acts come to stand out as privileged in the first place. The trick, then, is not simply to reproduce the classification scheme, value system, and hence socio-political world, of one's informants (i.e., the so-called religious people themselves), but to bring a new language to bear, a language capable of redescribing the indigenous accounts of extraordinariness, privilege, and authority as being ordinary rhetorical efforts that make extraordinariness, privilege, and authority possible.

In a word, the trick would be to make participant rhetorics and indigenous self-classification one's *data*. I am therefore part of a scholarly tradition that sees theology and its practitioners as nothing more or less than native informants;[1] they are but one more group whose reports and actions are in need of study and theorization. For instance, I recall that the Protestant process theologian and advocate of liberal religious pluralism, John Cobb, once spoke at a university where I was teaching; I found it rather odd attending his talk for I did not see myself there as Cobb's colleague and dialogue partner, as many in the room no doubt did. Rather, I attended the lecture much as an anthropologist might attend a ritual ceremony – as an observer gathering descriptive data for later theoretical reworking. With this in mind, I recently came across Freeman Dyson's review essay on John Polkinghorne's most recent book on the compatibility between religion and science (*The God of Hope and the End of the World* [Yale University Press, 2002]). Dyson, an emeritus Princeton physicist, finds Polkinghorne's thoughts on the end of the world, and the inability of science to adequately inform us about it, interesting but not because they illuminate us as to some actual future state of affairs. No; instead, he asks, "What are we who are not Christians, or we Christians who are not theologians, to make of all this?" His answer?

> We are in the position of anthropologists observing the rituals and liturgy of an alien culture. As anthropologists we try to understand the alien way of thinking and we enter into the alien culture as far as we can. We make friends with individual members of the alien culture and listen to their stories. ... We do not for a moment imagine that their detailed vision of a world to come, with heaven and hell and eschatological verification, the vision that they find emotionally satisfying or intellectually compelling, is actually true.
>
> (2002: 6)

Sadly, too few scholars of religion are capable of studying people in this fashion.

The scholar of religion as I am portraying him/her studies people – and the "detailed vision of the world" they produce – in just this fashion; accordingly, they conceive of and study people called theologians as elite ritual and textual practitioners, as a generally privileged, influential class of mythmakers.[2] Although not all of the scholar of religion's data will come from the ranks of such theologians (after all, not all of the people and groups we study are involved in the articulate, systematic reflection and rational expression on the meaning, context, or implications of "the faith"), *all theologians are fair game as data*. It is for this reason that I decided to open a recent book (2001b) with an epigraph taken from David Lodge's novel, *The British Museum is Falling Down*: "I don't have any myself, but I believe in other people having religion"; I believe in other people employing the classification of religion for the simple reason that, without such people, their claims, and the institutions they establish and reproduce by means of these rhetorics, scholars such as myself would have nothing to study. Having said this I should point out that scholars such as myself are often chastised for not getting their hands dirty by studying the real thing, religion, "on the ground" as it were. However, after the 2001 meeting of the American Academy of Religion in Denver, CO, where I happened to attend a paper in which the author engaged in some amateur psychologizing of me and my work, and after being told of another scholar that same year who referred to me in his paper as a "vulgar Smithian" (whatever the intention, I take this as a tremendous compliment), I had an epiphany. I realized that these people are studying me while I study scholars who, in turn, say that they are busy studying religious people. Therefore, such critics are even further removed from the genuine article, the "real thing" – the source of the Nile – that they wield when judging my work (the "real thing" is a rhetoric that sells Coca-Cola just as effectively as a scholarly discipline, by the way). I now feel considerably better about myself.

Answering the *how* and *why* questions

When meta-theorists do descend from either Denver's or Mount Olympus's heady heights to study religion "on the ground," just what is it about people's behaviors that they study? To make a complex answer simple, I can say that we study *how* it is that they believe and behave and, having gathered this descriptive information, we go on to theorize as to just *why* it is that they believe and behave as they do, leaving to others the speculative endeavor of ascertaining what it means either to them or to us for them to believe and act as they do. To accomplish this we draw on descriptive and comparative skills followed by explanatory theories concerning such things as the workings of human brains, bodies, and social formations to study why it is that people invest such tremendous amounts of intellectual creativity and social energy talking about invisible beings or the origins, purpose, and fate of the universe. Although some scholars – known variously as phenomenologists, historians of religions, or simply liberal humanists – are equally interested in investigating the descriptive where, when, what, who, and how of religious traditions (i.e., they pursue detailed descriptivist information and are generally concerned with what religion *means*, either to the participant or for humanity in general), the scholar I have in mind draws on the descriptive how as data in need of theorizing. Unlike theologians, assorted other religious practitioners, and even liberal humanists – all of whom take the existence of religious beliefs as given, inevitable, necessary, or self-evidently meaningful and good (though they differ dramatically as to what this meaning may be) – scholars ought to go beyond mere description and comparison to inquire as to *why* people find such beliefs, behaviors, and institutions attractive, compelling, effective, and worthy not only of reproducing (theory) but, more importantly, to inquire as to *why* people group such behaviors together by means of their taxon "religion" (meta-theory). For sure, not everyone studies human behavior in this way but, when studying this thing we call religion in a publicly funded context – a "public" comprised not just of members of assorted complementary and contradictory religious traditions but also agnostics and atheists who equally pay taxes to support the education system – it strikes me that this is the only viable option for our field. Despite their intimate relation, then, there is a tremendous gulf between public scholars of religion, on the one hand, and theologians and humanists, on the other (see McCutcheon 1999 on this point, as well as 2001b).

To phrase it as I do in my own introductory classes, whereas theologians (if we can use this term for not just Christians or theists in general, but for all forms of elite, systematic participant reflection on the meaning of their participation in those social movements we commonly name as religions) study the gods, scriptures, and origins, then scholars of religion study groups of historically embedded people who talk about the gods, scriptures, origins, etc. Because of this distinction, the famous lines from Alexander Pope's poem, *Essay on Man* (1733–1734), are particularly useful to me (but, I must add, useful only to a point[3]): "Know then thyself, presume not God to scan. The proper study of Mankind is Man" (Epistle II). As should be clear by this point in the book, scholars of religion do not study religion or the gods whatsoever – as counterintuitive as that may sound, I think it worth stating. Instead, they use a tool (the category "religion" itself is one such tool, the comparative method is another, as are the explanatory theories they bring to their work) to demarcate, name, and study a relatively small range of the complex collection of observable, cross-cultural, and eminently ordinary human doings that are available to us through such artifacts as written and oral texts, architecture, archeological sites, ritual behavior, social institutions, etc. Whereas religion may have something to do with salvation or damnation for a theologian, for the scholar of religion "religion" (which I now purposefully place in quotation marks) is a tool with a specific history and possible analytic utility for scholars studying but one aspect of the complex range of human behaviors. Other than human reports we can hear, the human systems of classification used to create and then convey information, the human texts we can read, the human actions we can observe, and the social institutions that make these reports, taxonomies, texts, and actions possible, what else is there for scholars in the human sciences to study? As phrased by Willi Braun,

> There is no religion in-it-self apart from people who do things that both those who do them and scholars of religion call "religious," though with different meanings of the term "religious." In that sense, religion does not exist; all that exists for our study are people who do things that we classify as "religious." … Thus, even when we study objects that in the religious doings of religious people represent themselves as artifacts from the world of the gods, it is *people* who make this representation.
>
> (2001a: 163)

Updating Pope's language and jettisoning his theological agenda, I can simply say: "The only study of Humankind is Human Beings."

What should be clear is that the theologian/humanist and the scholar of religion I am describing have two completely different starting points – a point that deserves to be highlighted, given the manner in which scholarship on religion is often misunderstood by our colleagues in the university. Whereas the former presumes religion to contain a world of self-evident meaning and value somehow apart from, and therefore which impinges upon, the world of mundane human doings, the latter presumes all meaning and value (including the social practice named theology) to be a thoroughly human, historical, even ad hoc concoction. This presumption makes the latter approach thoroughly anthropological (or, as Braun phrased it, anthropocentric; see 2001a: 162).

Given this way of distinguishing between these two groups, I must now refine my terms; it should be clear that I find it misleading to talk about the study of religion vs. theology; after all, as already suggested, phenomenologists and other liberal humanists intent on studying the various manifestations of the enduring Human Spirit or *Geist* (notably as manifested in the so-called Great Works of Literature) have much in common with so-called theologians: all are equally invested in studying what the scholar of ancient Greek religion, Walter Burkert, simply terms "non-obvious beings" (i.e., "things" you don't bump into). Although I would be the last to suggest that such things as "society" or the "nation-state" were real in the same way that my laptop, or the chair I'm now sitting in, are real, unlike the humanist or theologian, I see "society" "economy," and "the nation-state" – not to mention "God," "sin," or "heaven" – as *heuristically useful, everyday rhetorical fictions* that people in certain groups use to organize and negotiate their way through the complex worlds (both social and natural) that envelope them. Others long before me have made this same observation about our chief tool "religion" (most notably, of course, Jonathan Z. Smith and, just above, Braun). This taxon, "religion," and the set of representations and social arrangements that we are able to name and identify when using it (e.g., the presumption that "faith" is somehow a private, privileged insight into reality), is a way that people inhabiting certain socio-linguistic families (those traceable to Latin – from which we get our term "religion"[4] – or those influenced by the European world through its history of conquest) name, divide up, and act out their world. Whereas for the theologian, religion or faith has something to do with salvation, human shortcomings, or communication with an unseen world, the scholar of religion understands the term "religion," or such rhetorical pairs as sacred/profane or belief/practice and private/public, as one way that certain human communities concoct cognitively and socially habitable worlds. Although not all human communities concoct their worlds by means of grouping together discourses involving such things as a belief in non-obvious beings, tales of absolute origins, tales of end-times, ritual behaviors, etc., some of us do just that. But why?

If you are not curious about this specific "why" question, then perhaps you should not be a scholar in the academic study of religion. If all you are curious about is where and when and by whom Hindu death rituals are enacted (description), whether Buddhist rituals are similar to Christian rituals (comparison), or what it means to a Muslim when they make pilgrimage to Mecca, then perhaps the academic study of religion is not your home, for it is precisely this question, "Why?" that sets the anthropologically based study of religion apart from both its theological and humanistic counterparts. Whereas both of these are concerned with the never-ending hermeneutic quest for elucidating meaning and significance, the study of religion, as I propose it be practiced, is concerned with what the late Michel de Certeau termed an anthropology of credibility (1997: viii) – with examining and then explaining the conditions and socio-rhetorics that enable a group to portray a piece of social data as meaningful, significant, and credible in the first place, rhetorics such as sacred/profane or private/public that make seemingly stable "selves" and "groups" possible. This different focus – a meta-focus when compared to the quest to discover meaning – raises a host of questions and opportunities peculiar to the public study of religion as something ordinary and historical.

To summarize, then, I provide the following assumptions that drive the anthropological study of religion as I understand it.[5]

Social world and the natural world

The backdrop for all human doings is the natural world comprised of generic stuff that we bump into when we try to cross either a street or the hotel lobby; because I presume this natural world to be a complex place of competing judgments and interests, I also presume that no human community knows what is *really* going on in it (i.e., metaphysical reductionism simply makes no sense to me as an explanatory option; following Don Wiebe of the University of Toronto, I advocate methodological reductionism; on this critical distinction see Tite 2001). Instead, whether we are relying on individual hunches or socially authorized traditions that began long before we came on the scene, we all recall just this or that past event, and anticipate this or that possible future event, all in an effort to narrativize a meaningful social world which is never quite in perfect step with the natural world.[6] As a quotation from Burton Mack made clear in a previous chapter, the play between these two provides room for groups to exist. Thus, collections of what I seem to recall Foucault simply calling biological material exist as a human "we" by narrativizing themselves into *themselves*. I think here of the opening lines of Joan Didion's 1979 collection of essays, *The White Album*: "We tell ourselves stories in order to live," she writes,

> The princess is caged in the consulate. The man with the candy will lead the children into the sea. The naked woman on the ledge outside the

window on the sixteenth floor is a victim of accidie, or the naked woman is an exhibitionist, and it would be "interesting" to know which. We tell ourselves that it makes some difference whether the naked woman is about to commit a mortal sin or is about to register a political protest or is about to be, the Aristophanic view, snatched back to the human condition by the fireman in priest's clothing just visible in the window behind her, the one smiling at the telephoto lens. We look for the sermon in the suicide, for the social or moral lesson in the murder of five. We interpret what we see, select the most workable of multiple choices. We live entirely, especially if we are writers, by the imposition of a narrative line upon disparate images, by the "ideas" with which we have learned to freeze the shifting phantasmagoria which is our actual experience.

(2001: 11)[7]

The collection of such shared, narrativized "ideas" I term a world, following William Paden, who notes that, unlike the more philosophically idealist terms worldview, philosophy, or viewpoint, "world" connotes "the operating environment of linguistic and behavioral options which persons or communities presuppose, posit and inhabit at any given point in time and from which they choose courses of action" (Paden 2000: 335).[8] We might place this "world" in quotation marks when using it in this manner so as to draw attention to the fact that this is the contestable, ad hoc social lens or template by which we plot ourselves in relation to a select few aspects of what I referred to above as the natural world, a world whose many aspects are the raw material out of which our "worlds" are made.[9] As an aside, given this presumption, one of the goals of a liberal arts education is to persuade students that the natural world is far more complex than suggested by their inherited "worlds" and our academic models of these "worlds" (see Smith 1991: 188 and Smith n.d.).[10]

Pluralistic methodological reductionism

Because of this presumed complexity of social worlds, a variety of tools will be necessary to start talking about them in an academic manner – which means, first, describing them, but then situating them within their contexts, explaining their attraction to people, accounting for both their endurance and change over time, etc. I therefore support pluralistic methodological reductionism ("Given my methods of analysis, religion functions to … "). I would be quite mistaken to think that, once the work of studying social formations is exhausted (as if it could ever be exhausted), *either* there would be nothing left for colleagues using other scales of analysis to study *or* that there would remain some refined distillate called experience, consciousness, belief, the sacred, or Human Nature, that we could only study by means of some special methodology from outside the human sciences.[11]

Mythmaking vs. theorization

Any system of thought and practice that fails to presume 1 and 2 is a candidate for the status of data. Reflection on the deeper truth or meaning of religion (whether that reflection is theological *or* humanistic) attempts to bypass the historically grounded nature of all human attempts to know the world around us, making them instances of mythmaking and thus candidates for theorization. It is for this reason that I think it sensible to exclude certain approaches from the pluralistic methodologically reductionist study of religion as carried out in the "world" of the public university. Those approaches to be excluded (i.e., those approaches which are themselves instances of data) are those that (i) presume the natural world either to be the tip of an unperceivable, supernatural or ahistoric "world" or to be in perfect correspondence with any given "world" and (ii) presume that the underlying principle, workings, meaning, or purposes of any world can be fully known by those possessing special, gifted, intuitive, or privileged knowledge/wisdom.

Totalizing discourses are data

Finally, there are no final or complete explanations; explanations, like all cognitive endeavors, are products of specific social contexts, concerns, and "worlds"; when correctly understood in their technical sense, theories and explanations are a part of a specific, academic (as opposed to a folk) discourse about the natural world. We must therefore never fail to recognize that scholars are just as deeply involved in the art of rhetoric, contestation, and social formation as anyone else. It is just that scholars do not necessarily draw on the same rhetorical techniques to accomplish their acts of social formation. As Bruce Lincoln has most recently phrased it, "scholarship is myth with footnotes" (1999: 209).[12] Therefore, it is a useful rule of thumb to say that it is the people we study who typically propose final, universal, total, metaphysical explanations (e.g., "At the end of time ...," "God's will is that ...," "The meaning of life is ...," etc.).[13] Because scholars in the study of religion are methodological reductionists, their explanations are purely a function of their interests and the theories they propose and apply ("Given my theory of social formation, rituals function to ...," etc.). This means that scholars of religion must own up to their own curiosities, instead of mis-portraying them as eternally interesting and obviously relevant questions (that one sense of disciplinary lying identified by Smith [n.d.]). As anyone who has made idle conversation at either a wine and cheese party or a bus stop can tell you, *nothing is self-evidently compelling or interesting*. Things are compelling, interesting, or boring only in light of shared systems, grids, interests, and lenses of meaning, value, and significance – in a word, in relation to specific and structured "worlds" – that are produced and reproduced in social groups. That not just every "world" counts as a participant in the institution we call "academe" should go without saying.

Case in point: the problem of evil

As a way to demonstrate what can be accomplished by agreeing that our work on human doings is driven by these assumptions – and as a way to illustrate Bourdieu's comment as applied to the field of data named "religion" – I would like to examine a specific piece of human activity. Rather than ask questions concerning what it means to the actors, how it works within their context, or whether this sort of behavior is good or bad, I would like to suggest that the meta-focus of the anthropologically-based, socio-rhetorical study of religion allows us to formulate general theories to investigate the historic precedents and effects of cross-culturally observable human behaviors. The general theories of human minds, behaviors, and institutions that we employ in this activity thus enable us to interact with our colleagues throughout the human sciences. As opposed to being what I – following Burton Mack – have termed caretakers for the behavior under study,[14] I would like to provide the following as a case study in applying a different sort of scholarship to the study of religion, an approach that makes scholars active and public culture critics. I would therefore like to turn our attention to the seemingly privileged or unique genre of Christian theological writing traditionally known as "theodicy" to demonstrate what is to be gained by the socio-rhetorical approach to the study of religion as a particular form of ordinary human practice.

Theodicy described

The term "theodicy" is generally credited to the German philosopher, Gottfried Leibniz (1646–1716); it is a compound derived from combining two ancient Greek words, one referring to a divine being or god (*theos*) and the other referring to justice (*diké*): a theodicy is therefore a systematic discourse on the justice of a divine being. Although when strictly used the term applies only to those belief systems that posit some sort of moral, supernatural being who controls the universe (i.e., ethical monotheism), it is nevertheless widely used to denote any human attempt to deal with the fact that events in the natural world do not always unfold according to plan or anticipation. An example of this wider usage of the term can be found in the work of the early sociologist, Max Weber, who used the term to name any attempt to grapple with the problem of human suffering. For instance, although many Buddhist systems hardly posit a loving God ruling the universe (although countless, compassionate *bodhisattvas* are central to many Mahayanan Buddhist groups, such as Japanese Pure Land Buddhism), philosophers of religion have no difficulty speaking of a "Buddhist theodicy"; after all, as is made clear from the origins tale concerning Prince Siddhartha's disillusionment and subsequent awakening, the problem of human suffering and disquiet (Pali, *dukkha*) is one of the central topics in Buddhist thought. Also, even though a "Hindu theodicy" may strike some as an awkward choice of terms, others will undoubtedly answer that the interrelated notions of *karma, caste,* and *dharma* provide a powerful way of explaining why events in the world happen as they do. (This comprises an Intellectualist approach to studying theodicy.) In fact, Weber called the law of *karma* "the most radical solution of the problem of theodicy" (1993: 147). However, despite this wider usage for the term "theodicy," even a quick glance makes it clear that Muslim, Hindu, and Buddhist writers, for example, have not been nearly as concerned with this issue as have been Christian writers.

Within the history of Christian theodicy writing, the problem of evil comes down to what many others before me have named as a trilemma: three related premises any two of which can be held but to the exclusion of the third: (i) God is all-good; (ii) God is all-powerful; and (iii) evil exists. For example, holding (i) and (ii) logically excludes (iii); in this case the observable evil in the world (whether natural evils such as rock slides or moral evils such as genocides) is explained away as merely the result of our inevitably limited, human viewpoint. Participant reports from this perspective would likely take the form of, "Yes, but in God's eyes ...," "The time will come when we will see ...," or "These seemingly evil events are actually tests ..." (as in the ancient Hebrew tale of Job). Holding (ii) and (iii) would exclude (i); in this case a malevolent but powerful God would be responsible for evil events. Holding (i) and (iii) would posit a well-intentioned God who was incapable of preventing certain harmful events, events caused by Fate, human freewill (as in the case of the largely U.S.-based process theology movement), or possibly the actions of some other deity (as in the case of Zoroastrianism). It should be apparent that, in the history of Christianity at least, all three of these combinations have struck various participants as appealing explanations for evil, since evil events have been variously attributed to the inscrutable will of God, as tests for human worthiness, as the corrupt, rogue actions of Satan, or as the prideful acts of human freewill traceable to Adam and Eve's self-centered rebellion. Despite the seeming logic of the trilemma, often mutually exclusive options arise in the same theodicy; reporting on why he was bitten by a rattlesnake during a Pentecostal ritual ceremony, a snake handler in the Appalachian region of the U.S. informed the documentary film-maker that "It was God's will but the devil's work" – a theodicy that let one have one's cake and eat it too, for it effectively frees belief in a loving deity from responsibility for capricious events *while simultaneously* attributing to this same being absolute power and control.[15]

Although this partial list hardly exhausts the many different solutions that Christian writers have offered for this thing they call the problem of evil, it nonetheless provides a descriptive starting point for our redescriptive efforts.

Theodicy redescribed

Prior to embarking on a redescription of theodicy, it is important to state explicitly that theodicies are part of an emic, insider discourse that scholars freely accept as part of their first level, descriptive lexicon, a rhetorical term used to demarcate a specific indigenous discursive domain of interest to them. Insomuch as scholars are inevitably members of specific social worlds and are thus understandably intent on reproducing the material conditions that make their worlds possible, I assume that they will have great interest in making pronouncements on whether this or that is good, bad, or evil. However, *qua* scholars I would assume that they have no stake in reproducing any specific rhetoric of evil but, instead, are intent on studying its workings and impact.[16] Sadly, virtually all academic treatments of theodicy – from textbooks and encyclopedia entries to the work of contemporary philosophers and, of course, theologians – are concerned simply with grappling with the problem of evil and offering solutions to it *rather than* theorizing as to just *why* human beings even bother to grapple with this thing they call the problem of evil and what is accomplished by their use of the term. Where we *do* find attempts to explain the existence, attraction, or function of theodicies and rhetorics of evil, they usually follow along the lines of Ronald M. Green's thoughts as found in his entry on theodicy in the *Encyclopedia of Religion*: there is, Green asserts, "essentially a moral motivation" behind formulating theodicies, for they "draw upon and deepen our moral self-understanding" (1987: 441). As evidenced by Green's comments, there are few, if any, attempts to talk about the problem of evil that are not themselves instances of mythmaking. Relying on the presumed existence of an inner, "essential moral impulse," Green's explanation only mystifies our topic, for what we as anthropologically based scholars are trying to account for is not *how* independently existing moral impulses are expressed and deepened but *why* human communities presume the existence of such things as inner or immutable moral impulses and *how* such rhetorics are employed for very specific, tactical, socio-political gains. Green does not help us in this endeavor because he presumes the existence of that which we as scholars of religion are trying to explain. The tremendous difference between solving, and studying why people attempt to solve, the problem of evil will hopefully become evident as we proceed with our redescription.[17]

To begin a redescription of theodicy as something ordinary, we need to recall that, as suggested by my earlier revision of Pope's quotation and my appeal to Braun, the study of religion is not concerned with extraordinary discourses on the gods but with studying ordinary groups of people in their everyday lives and their classificatory activity. When redescribed in this manner, the rhetoric of evil can be seen as both a problem in cognitive intelligibility and a problem in political justification. I will deal with each in turn.

First of all, a theodicy is an ill-fated (recalling Lease) attempt to create a seamless, totalized world by eliminating the divergence between a wishful *belief* in a rational, coherent, meaningful natural world, on the one hand, and those daily *observations* of the empirical, natural world (once again, everything from rock slides to genocides) that contravene that wish. Recalling Didion, it is the attempt to have our narratives walk in step with the world of disparate happenings. Recalling Mack, it is an attempt to eliminate the divergence between discursive counterpoints. Redescribed in this way, theodicies are one of the ways in which human beings systematically address the perceived anomalies in their expectations for how the natural world works. To drop the narrative metaphor used by Didion and, instead, to appeal to one derived from biology, theodicies are symptomatic of cognitive nausea; for, according to recent studies, motion sickness

> occurs when there is a conflict between the motion we experience and the motion we expect to experience. ... Nausea arises when the brain receives unanticipated sensory inputs – for someone new to boats, say, feeling the ground beneath him pitch up and down, or, for someone in a virtual-reality helmet, seeing oneself move through the world while one's body knows it is standing still.
>
> (Gawande 1999: 36–37)

Moving from the biological to the cognitive, we can say that theodicies are evidence of cognitive queasiness. To appeal to Foucault once more, they are one of the points at which our perception of the world as a heterotopia is transformed into a utopia (1973: xvii).

Given that a belief system that provides a context for our expectations is part of a larger social "world," then theodicies mediate between our "world" (i.e., our systems of socially reproduced knowledges and expectations) and the nagging observation that the natural world we regularly bump into does not conform to our expectations; because theodicies work much as shoe horns once did, to make the natural world fit our social "world" (or vice versa), we can conclude that they are part of a doomed totalizing discourse and are evidence of "worlds" conflicting with the world. Where we find a theodicy we therefore find a disciplining technique, an attempt to make an ambiguous situation totally intelligible, knowable, and thus controllable. They are like the horizontal or vertical control buttons on old television sets, used for manual fine tuning when the picture flips and makes us queasy.

If we presume the utter complexity of the natural world (the world of "actual experience," to borrow Didion's phrasing[18] or Foucault's heterotopia), then it is inevitable that all human communities will develop a series of mechanisms to address the lack of fit between their "worlds" and the world. An important point arises here: although scholars using the scientific method are equally engaged in constructing a world and actively constructing scientific theories to mediate the lack of fit between their "worlds" and the natural world, their classification systems are not totalized but ad hoc and they do not authorize themselves by appealing to destiny, necessity, or the gods. Although such scholars are indeed deeply engaged in making the world intelligible and knowable, they presume that their master narrative is a thoroughly historical product, a step-by-step toolkit driven by practical interests, as Foucault once described it (1980: 145; on this point, see also Clifford 1988: 23). Theories are thus acknowledged by their makers to be tactical, contextually specific, ad hoc, and open to being discarded when their practical utility fails. "The role of theory," writes Lawrence Kritzman in his introduction to selected interviews with Foucault, "is therefore not to formulate a global analysis of the ideologically coded, but rather to analyze the specificity of the mechanisms of power and to build, little by little, 'strategic knowledge'" (Foucault 1988a: xiv). Theodicies, which I understand to be equally ad hoc and tactical (that is, when thoroughly historicized and redescriptive), are understood by their users to be total, global, all-inclusive, and necessary. Whereas historically embedded tacticians employ the former, the guru or the prophet employs the latter. We must be careful, therefore, to distinguish the differing ways humans grapple with perceived anomalies: we can develop theories or we can develop theologies and, more specifically, theodicies. "Like small lumps on the neck," then, both theories and theodicies are "a symptom that all is not well" (Eagleton 1992: 26). Each responds to this in a rather different manner.

The efficiency of theodicies in particular in addressing anomalies, disjunctions, contradictions, and outright surprises, lies in their ability smoothly to posit, and thereby contain and control, two contradictory premises: (i) the natural world is rational; and (ii) its rationale is a mystery beyond comprehension. Take for example, the following quotation from the *New York Times*:

> "All those people died for a reason" [said a 16-year-old sophomore at Columbine High School outside Denver, CO, site of the April 20, 1999, shootings]. "God was with them every step of the way," she went on to say, "He chose them for some special reason."
>
> (Rimer 1999: col. 4)

As the student makes clear in her attempt to understand what I would certainly agree to be a tragic event (a statement not so much about the event's essential character as it is about the social world and set of practical interests this young lady and I likely share), *there was a reason* for the many student deaths at Columbine High School in Colorado, but it's just that it was "some special reason" known, it seems, only in the mind of God. The oxymoronic presumption of "unknowable rationality" functions because "God" or "mystery" plays the role of an empty signifier, which is, by strictest definition, devoid of content because it is, after all, "special" or, to us, utterly unknowable. "Mystery" thus provides a rhetoric that acts, as I have once before quoted Robert Sharf as commenting, much as the rhetoric of "experience." It is "a mere placeholder that entails a substantive if indeterminate terminus for the relentless deferral of meaning. And this is precisely what makes the term experience [and I would add, theodicy] so amenable to ideological appropriation" (1998: 113).

Recalling the words of Gary Lease, those social institutions we commonly call religions – most notably, we can now add, by means of their theodicies – attempt "to be totally *inclusive* of all paradoxes by establishing *exclusive* meanings." Because, as we have assumed, historical life is rather more complex than any totalized model, Lease predicts that, despite theologians' best attempts to completely rationalize the natural world, the dissonances and conflicts that inevitably arise will eventually cause "the societal system to *breakdown* and the 'structures' [i.e., 'worlds'] which allowed such a paradoxical mutuality to dissolve" (1994: 475). One set of such rhetorical structures are, then, theodicies. As cited early on in this book, Lease immediately goes on to suggest that embarking on writing a history of the rise and decline of a social formation requires one to "catalog [the] strategies for *maintaining* paradoxes, *fighting* over dissonances, and *surviving* breakdowns." Such a catalog comprises a map of the many social sites where such rhetorical devices as theodicies are developed, deployed, and contested.

As suggested by Sharf and in Foucault's comments on utopian discourses, such devices are not simply cognitive interfaces, to be studied – in the manner of a nineteenth-century scholar – as mere intellectual processes for answering some inevitable "why" questions. They are necessarily also an exercise in overt political justification and an exercise of power. Appealing to Foucault once again – and pressing beyond his purely linguistic example to our social example – whereas utopias "run with the very grain of language and are part of the fundamental dimension of the *fabula*; heterotopias … desiccate speech, stop words in their tracks, contest the very possibility of language at its source; they dissolve our myths and sterilize the lyricism of our sentences" (1973: xvii). Both of these two redescriptions – the intellectual and the socio-political – are necessarily related for, insomuch as a theodicy can be understood as mediating between the natural world and social "worlds" – thereby allowing participants to gloss over or contain and integrate anomalous experiences and observations – then theodicies are also the conserving mechanisms whereby this or that "world" is authorized as being satisfactory, sufficient, and in a one-to-one fit with the natural world. They constitute intellectual and political fine tuning. Intelligibility, meaning, and communication are therefore intimately linked to social legitimacy (this is nothing other than the old knowledge/power equation). *Theodicies therefore rationalize, in both senses of the term ("to make rational" and "to legitimize").* Because semantic and social "worlds" are neither innocent nor disconnected from their builders, theodicies are political insomuch as they enable participants to actively portray any one particular "world" – along with the interests that shape this "world" – as being just or unjust, changeable or inevitable, bearable or unbearable, necessary or contingent, or simply – to borrow the infamous words from Voltaire's character, the metaphysico-theologico-cosmolo-boobologist, Dr. Pangloss – "the best of all possible worlds."[19] Even a casual reader of Voltaire's biting satire, *Candide* (1966), easily sees the sadly comic lack of fit between Pangloss's "world" and the incredibly tragic situations in which he and his young student, Candide, repeatedly find themselves. Even the naive Candide has sufficient ironic sense to appreciate the lack of fit; early on in their travels, after they have been arrested – "one for talking and the other for listening with an air of approval" – Candide is flogged and Pangloss hung, all as part of an elaborate *auto-da-fé*: an "act of faith" or public ceremony of repentance designed to protect the city from further earthquakes (a ritual, as it turns out, which does not work).[20] Candide, stunned by the whole affair, simply remarks, "If this is the best of all possible worlds, then what are the others like?" (1966: 12).

Although it is only a short tale, *Candide* nicely demonstrates how people (such as its author, Voltaire) with different interests and political commitments actively contest the status of competing social "worlds" by means of differing theodicies (cosmogonies and apocalyptic tales can be redescribed in precisely this way as well). For, when read in his historical context, Voltaire's Pangloss is clearly a critique of Pope's (1688–1744), and, before him, Leibniz's, well-known "philosophical optimism." Voltaire, it seems, correctly understood the wider implications of their brand of complacent optimism: it is not only naive but it also amounts to little more than a politically conservative apologia for the regnant status quo. After all, active social change of any sort is not really encouraged when, in the last lines from Epistle I of Pope's *Essay on Man*, we read those often cited lines:

> All Nature is but Art, unknown to thee;
> All Chance, Direction, which thou canst not see;
> All Discord, Harmony, not understood;
> All partial Evil, universal Good:
> And, spite of Pride, in erring Reason's spite,
> One truth is clear, "Whatever is, is RIGHT."

Or, as Voltaire phrased it himself, near the close of an article in his *Philosophical Dictionary* (1764), in which the writings of Leibniz and Pope are specifically critiqued (belittled might be a more apt description):

> This system of *All is good* represents the author of nature only as a powerful and maleficent king, who does not care, so long as he carries out his plan, that it costs four or five hundred thousand men their lives, and that the others drag out their days in want and in tears.
>
> So far from the notion of the best of possible worlds being consoling, it drives to despair the philosophers who embrace it.
>
> (1972: 74)[21]

Although not all theodicies share/promote the same politics (obviously, Voltaire's parody was oppositional to both Pope's and Leibniz's political writings), *all theodicies are at their root political* and, much like mythologies for Roland Barthes, intent on conserving a particular "world." Insomuch as they portray one possible "world" as *the* World (whether that "world" is conservative or liberal, dominant or oppositional), they are by definition ideological for their function is to portray the part as the Whole. As evidence of this we need look no further than the lines from Pope's poem already quoted; they provide an example of the very totalizing of which Lease spoke earlier; all viewpoints, we are persuaded, are partial, limited, and subsumed under one harmonious, coherent, universal totality. It is a totality which, upon closer examination, is none other than yet another part dressed up as the Whole. This is the ideology of liberalism at its best; it is a profoundly political stance that seeks non-empirical, essential unity amidst empirical difference.

So, when redescribed as rhetorical devices, *theodicies* become *sociodicies* (i.e., discourses on the status and legitimacy of this or that "world") and the so-called problem of evil then becomes the problem of the rhetoric of "evil." By this I simply mean that, for the scholar of religion, the *presumption* that evil exists (and must therefore be addressed, somehow, as an anomaly in an essentially good, meaningful, and ordered world) is itself the datum in need of dedicated study. So, instead of asking, along with Harold Kushner's popular book on the problem of evil, "Why do bad things happen to good people?," the scholar asks two very different questions: "Why and how do people presume that the world *ought* to be coherent, sensible, intelligible, meaningful, or good in the first place?" and "What practical, historical ends are served by this or that application of the good/bad pairing and thus the rhetoric of 'evil'?" Although it may seem obvious to many that former U.S. President Ronald Reagan's references to the former Soviet Union as an "evil empire" were artful rhetorical devices in the service of reproducing a very particular social world in contest with another, the ease with which, say, post-September 11, 2001, commentators on virtually all sides of the political divide, on both sides of the Atlantic, invoked similar rhetorical conventions, culminating in George W. Bush's widely quoted "axis of evil" comment (in reference to the current governments in Iraq, Iran, and North Korea), suggests that answering these two questions is far more difficult than it might first appear. It is difficult work because the assumption that drives this sort of redescriptive work is that all descriptions are linked to value judgments and thus identifying this or that event as "evil," inevitably takes place within ambiguous, ever changing historical, social "worlds" – worlds shared by the one posing the questions as well as those making the claims. The designation "evil," then, tells us far more about a particular social "world" we occupy, and the interests of the classifiers, than it tells us about the act being classified.

Once again, the academic study of religion – when religion is conceived as but one more cultural practice – turns out to be an exercise in (i) determining the limits of what social groups understand as credible and (ii) identifying the mechanisms used to police and contest those usually invisible limits. It is a conclusion seemingly related to Green's own conclusion: "theodicy's deepest impulse," he writes, "is not to report the bitter facts of life but to overcome and transform them" (1987: 440). But upon a closer look, Green is still engaged in *mythmaking* rather than *explanation*, for the "facts of life" (i.e., events in the natural world) in themselves are neither bitter nor sweet – they just are. Theodicies are thus one of the means by which communities plot and process the generic stuff of experience *as* either bitter or sweet, since experience "in the round" – as Mack phrased it – is thereby ranked in comparison to a utopian ideal, in Durkheim's sense of the term. Also, Green's sense of "overcoming and transforming" – something that sounds surprisingly close to my notion of making a social world fit the natural world – arises from a view of theodicies as expressions of private, essentially moral impulses and motivations, rather than seeing theodicies as structural mechanisms that enable communities to posit and act out this thing we come to know as morality.

Conclusion

As described in this chapter, scholars study the way people artfully deploy and manipulate such classifications and social focusing devices as discourses on evil, origins, end-times, and non-obvious beings. The Christian doctrine of predestination would be another wonderfully rich site for such a redescription, especially given John Calvin's interest in this topic; taking into account his role in the practical governance of sixteenth-century Geneva, his interest in an utterly homogenous and unified past-present-future strikes me as an obvious site of political rhetoric. As will be argued in the coming chapters, the very classification "religion" might itself be the most important device in the socio-rhetorical lexicon of the nation-state. If so, then the self-identified scholar of religion may turn out to be among the more important ideological managers of our society. Or, to put it another way, because not all events in the natural world equally attract our attention (remember, the world's a busy place and I've only got so much attention to focus), such things as doctrines, creeds, traditions, myths, and rituals constitute the mechanisms whereby groups concoct and reproduce their "world" by exercising and managing what Jonathan Z. Smith terms an "economy of signification." It is a hectic economy efficiently managed by cognitive and social classifications that delineate this from that, important from unimportant, saved from damned, good from evil, and, finally, us from them. As scholars we therefore examine a rather specific group of narrative, behavioral, and institutional devices employed by people like, but not just, theologians, devices that represent and contest differing conceptions of who gets to count as part of the social "we."

What should be clear is that scholars of religion as described in this chapter are not in the business of nurturing, enhancing, or – despite the caricatures of those who wish to make the academic study of religion essentially a theological pursuit – criticizing the communities they study; this is the business of the various groups' members, theologians included. Neither are we in the business of proposing final, definitive, totalized narratives, theories, or histories. In a word, we don't engage in the trade of closures. Instead, our work presumes the ambiguous, ad hoc nature of all social activity – our own scholarship included – making the academic study of religion tactical, problem-oriented, and ironic. The anthropologically based scholar of religion's contribution is therefore made as a scholar of classification and social rhetoric – both of which are all too human, historic activities with discernable beginnings and discernable consequences.[22]

Given this conclusion, I repeat that, unlike the theologian, for the scholar of religion *qua* anthropologist of credibility, there is nothing religious about discourses on religion and nothing evil about discourses on evil. Religion is simply the classification some of us give to various collections of artful but all too human devices that help to portray any given world in which we happen to find ourselves as the "world without end." To quote Voltaire writing in his *Philosophical Dictionary* (1764):

> The problem of good and evil remains an inexplicable chaos for those who seek in good faith. It is an intellectual exercise for those who argue: they are convicts who play with their chains. As for the unthinking mass, it rather resembles fish who have been moved from a river to a reservoir. They do not suspect that they are there to be eaten in lent: nor do we know anything by our own resources about the causes of our destiny. Let us put at the end of nearly all chapters on metaphysics the two letters used by Roman judges when they could not understand a lawsuit: *N. L., non liquet,* this is not clear.
>
> (1972: 74)

Amen.[23]

Notes

1   I rely here on Jonathan Z. Smith: "From the perspective of the academic study of religion, theology is a datum, the theologian is a native informant" (1997: 60). Smith elaborates: "In the same spirit in which I welcome the study of the totalizing mythic endeavors, the *univers imaginaires,* of an Ogotemmêli [see Griaule 1965] or an Antonio Guzmàn [see Reichel-Dolmatoff 1971], I would hope, some day, to read a consonant treatment of the analogous enterprise of Karl Barth's *Church Dogmatics.*"

2   By "mythmaking" I simply mean those discourses which dehistoricize and decontextualize. On this alternative use of the term "myth" see McCutcheon 2000a; on the relations between mythmaking and the Althusserian term "social formation," see Mack 2000 and McCutcheon 1998.

3   Given the approach advocated in this book and this chapter, Pope's words have only limited use, of course. (On the politics of Pope's theodicy, see below.) When we take into account the rest of the *Essay on Man* (Pope 1950), his other writings, as well as his historic context (1688–1744), it is obvious that he is not advising against metaphysical speculation and theology but, rather, warning against (mis)using human reason to pry into the inscrutable ways of God. For instance, compare Pope's counsel to that which is found in Milton's *Paradise Lost* (VIII: 72–75):

> … the great Architect
> Did wisely to conceal, and not divulge
> His secrets to be scann'd by them who ought
> Rather admire.

It should be clear that, despite my use of Pope, I follow neither him nor Milton in their counsel against the use of human reason.

4   Despite my disagreement with the late Wilfred Cantwell Smith's well-known criticism of the category "religion" for its misplaced emphasis on the external, cumulative tradition at the expense of what he understands as the prior, inner, personalistic faith of the believer (a rhetorically loaded distinction), his survey of the history of the category "religion" is still one of the most widely read (1991). For a more useful survey see Jonathan Z. Smith 1998.

5   The following four presumptions are derived from my brief rejoinder to Bryan S. Rennie, author of *Reconstructing Eliade* (1996); the rejoinder appeared as McCutcheon 1999. They elaborate what I have also published in McCutcheon 2001b: 37, n. 1.

6   To establish this point with students, I tell them a story about a dinner party one summer evening at my brother-in-law's home in Niagara Falls, Ontario. Several times throughout the course of the evening guests moving from the house to the patio, and vice versa, unknowingly walked straight into the patio door, knocking the screen out. In fact, as I recall, my late-father-in-law did it more than once. Although each time was funnier than the last, and each guest more embarrassed (and inebriated) than the last, each instance was an example of how the guests' expectations for how the external world functioned were not quite in step with the natural world itself.

7   Traditionally, "phantasmagoria" was a term applied to a late eighteenth- and nineteenth-century European lighting effect whereby a lantern projected light through various layers of colored gauze, and later colored sheets of glass, providing viewers with a constantly shifting image (sometimes projected around live actors). Understandably, the phantasmagoria was often associated with ghostly images and used by mediums for seances. For example, in Lewis Carroll's 1869 poem, "Phantasmagoria," the second stanza reads:

> There was a strangeness in the room,
> And Something white and wavy
> Was standing near me in the gloom

As pointed out by Roxanne Euben, however, in the critical theory tradition of Adorno and Benjamin, what she calls the phantasmagoria effect "comes to indicate the concealment of mystification of the mechanisms by which an image is produced, so that the image appears as reality" (1999: xiv; see also Adorno 1981: 85). As used in her quotation, however, I take Didion to employ "phantasmagoria" to signify the busy world of competing sensations, images, values, perceptions, happenings, etc., which is, according to her, "our actual experience." All of this must be classified, narrowed down, and ordered for something to count as sensible, meaningful, and thus memorable. This editing and ordering is accomplished by means of narrativization. For Didion, then, the phantasmagoria effect, as Euben phrases it, would be to mistake any one specific narrative line, as in the tale of the naked woman on the window ledge, as the brute fact of the matter, instead of seeing it as the result of a specifically strung together collection that reflects specific interests, contexts, etc.

8   We must be careful to distinguish "world" (as in operating environment) from "ideology" (when ideology is taken in its weaker sense as meaning "a system of ideas"); ideologies (when understood in the more critical sense) are the devices that actors employ to re-present some given "world" as the World. I will elaborate more on this below.

9   On the roles selection and archiving play in the production of "history," see Braun 1999.

10 As suggested in the opening of the book, where I tamed an earlier generation's hopes for writing natural histories, I am not so bold as to think there is anything necessarily natural or inevitable about the so-called natural world. I fully realize that the strategy of naturalization can be a power technique for authorizing one particular social world. All I mean by the social/natural distinction is that we must always keep in mind that there is an inevitable gap between bumping into extra-subjective things and the social conventions that determine whether it is good or desirable to continue bumping into them. That the social/natural distinction is itself a social, historical artifact goes without saying; nonetheless, it is a heuristically useful distinction.

11 On the social (and hence political) nature of discourses on "experience" see Sharf 1998 and Scott 1991.

12 The full quotation reads: "If myth is ideology in narrative form, then scholarship is myth with footnotes." By this I believe Lincoln means to suggest that differing discursive communities concoct themselves by means of differing rhetorical techniques; connecting one's ideas and arguments to a historical tradition of scholarship by means of footnotes is a technique that authorizes one's own work by weaving it within an already recognized body of work (something this very citation of Lincoln has already accomplished for my own essay). Myth without footnotes – in other words, narratives that actively obscure their own historicity by appeals to, for example, the time of origins – is what Lincoln labels ideology. See chapter 10 in this current book for elaboration on Lincoln's thesis.

13 Speaking of the "meaning of life," Monty Python's film by the same name comes to mind. What makes the film particularly comic is that it takes a topic of seemingly universal import and provides a number of clearly skewed, partial, and even idiotic takes on it, thereby effectively disarming the totalizing rhetoric of all "meaning of life" discourses.

14 On critics vs. caretakers in the study of religion, see Mack 2001a and McCutcheon 2001b, especially chapters 8 and 9.

15 This quotation comes from the anthropological film on U.S. Pentecostal snake-handling churches in the Appalachian region, *Jolo Serpent Handlers* (Karen Kramer Films, 1977).

16 I recall a recent regional meeting of the American Academy of Religion where, as a member of a panel, I was asked if I believed there was anything that was simply evil. Earlier at this meeting a Chair of an influential Department of Religious Studies in the southeast had told an audience of Department Chairs from schools in the region that the work of Holocaust deniers was evil; moreover, we were also told that there were limits to scholarly empathy. These two experiences confirmed for me the ease with which scholars fail to distinguish between, for example, their professional selves and their nationalist selves. To rephrase it another way, it is easy to conceive of one who agrees that yes, there is such a thing as outright evil, but whose examples of such evils would quickly alienate him or her from others in the room (i.e., rhetorics of evil are social techniques). For example, with world hunger and global poverty being what it is, it is easy to imagine someone thinking that academics living the life of the mind who are free to fly or drive hundreds of miles so as to sit around in a conference hotel discussing evil while sipping coffee and eating danishes and melon cubes is itself pretty damned evil. But I fear that my dialogue partners would not be willing to entertain that they and their discourse might be part of the problem. So, to avoid the endless spiral of contesting meanings and adjudicating evils, this book recommends a significant shift in our discourse.

17 "Redescription" is a term derived from Jonathan Z. Smith; see in particular his essay, "Sacred Persistence: Toward a Redescription of Canon" (1982: 36–52).

18 I assume that Didion means here raw, uninterpreted brute happenings that have yet to be narrativized and structured. As such, they are meaningless and unrelated in a technical and logical sense. In other words, I do not read Didion to be recommending that we shrink from the problem of narrativization by prioritizing some supposedly authentic thing called experience.

19 In the French original, Pangloss is described as a teacher of "*métaphysico-théologo-cosmolonigologie*"; the French *nigaud*, whose phonetic equivalent "nigo" appears in this comical compound, translates as "boob."

20 Readers must keep in mind that *Candide* was written in the wake of the great Lisbon earthquake of 1755 where it was first thought that more than 100,000 people had perished.

21 Reading these lines I could not help but think of an article in *Religious Studies News* in which a professor is interviewed about having had her class on medieval women mystics taken hostage, on February 12, 2002, by a former student of her university. After learning from her that the former student said he had a bomb (it turned out he did not), that a number of student hostages were gradually let go, that he had a disjointed series of demands to make, etc., the interviewer – a modern-day Dr. Pangloss – asks: "Was there a 'teachable moment' in the incident, either as it unfolded or later?" (Anon. 2002b: 12). My thanks to Steve Berkwitz and Jack Llewellyn for suggesting I read this article.

22 I can do no better than cite as examples some of Bruce Lincoln's work, especially 1989, 1994, and 1999.

23 An earlier version of this paper was delivered to the Faculty of Theology at Georgetown University, November, 1999. My thanks to Professor Francisca Cho for kindly arranging my visit to her campus.

Chapter 8

The jargon of authenticity and the study of religion[1]

> [U]niversal humanity ... is ideology. It caricatures the equal rights of every-
> thing which bears a human face, since it hides from men the unalleviated
> discriminations of societal power: the differences between hunger and over-
> abundance, between spirit and docile idiocy. Chastely moved, man lets
> himself be addressed through Man: it doesn't cost anyone anything. But
> whoever refuses the appeal gives himself over as non-human to the adminis-
> trators of the jargon, and can be sacrificed to them, if such a sacrifice is
> needed. ... Self-righteous humanity, in the midst of general inhumanity, only
> intensifies the inhuman state of affairs.
>
> (Adorno 1973: 66–67)

The night before the closing plenary session of August 2000's Congress of the
International Association for the History of Religions (IAHR) – a Congress
where the now ever-present topics of globalization and post-colonialism were
discussed against the backdrop of the South African seaside city of Durban – I
was flipping through the channels on the television in my hotel room. Apart
from some local South African programming and the international version of
the Atlanta-based Cable News Network (CNN), to my surprise I happened
across Dan Akroyd starring in a 1997 Canadian-made movie on the development of the Avro Arrow, a Canadian jet fighter developed in the early 1950s
which was reportedly capable of doing Mach 2 – a plane that was well ahead of
its time. The movie, simply entitled "The Arrow," chronicles how the development of this jet was abruptly and mysteriously ended in 1959 by the Canadian
government and soon after all of the prototypes were completely dismantled
and destroyed, and a U.S. missile system was purchased along with U.S.-made
jet fighters. Although conspiracy theories abound concerning the causes for the
government's decision, we can at least say for certain that one of the effects of
this decision was that the high tech industry packed its bags and, like Canadian
Geese (or Canadian retirees wintering in Florida), flew south.

Given that it does not take much to prompt most Canadians to tell you how
much we differ from Americans, you probably see why the events surrounding
the so-called unfulfilled promise of the Avro Arrow occupy such a prominent
place in the hearts of the some of the people who live north of the 49th parallel.

And, you can likely guess why it was narrativized into a television movie for their – or should I say "our"? – domestic consumption. That this 40-year-old story was only recently filmed suggests that the recurring threat of Quebecois separatism lurks somewhere in this film's message of pride in a nation whose promise, like that of the Arrow, is as yet unfulfilled and thus ill-defined. The Canadian inferiority complex is thus nicely expressed and, at least temporarily, overcome in the tale of the ill-fated Arrow.

So there I sat in my hotel room: a Canadian born within twenty minutes of Buffalo, New York, working since 1993 in the U.S. public university system, watching television in a luxury hotel in the resort city of Durban in a room paid for by a much appreciated grant from my former university, allowing me to wield a dollar that dwarfs the South African Rand. With the rhythmic surf of the Indian ocean pounding right outside my window, there I sat, reconstructing my own national identity as a displaced, disaffected Canadian, fully capable of conversing in English with virtually anyone in Durban due to an accident of British colonial history, an accident helped along significantly by disaffected Loyalists who emigrated to Upper Canada rather than join the colonies' rebellion against King George III. Durban, so very far removed from my "home and native land" in southern Ontario, had thus become a site of Canadian nationalist production and consumption.

Before my personal revelations turn this chapter into a heart-warming episode of "Oprah," I'd like to step back from my narrative to say that all of this was marked as information in need of reflection, rather than as the self-evidently meaningful world in which I moved and had my being, in large part because I have read the work of Bruce Lincoln. Much as in the case of my exposure to the work of Jonathan Z. Smith, I mostly read Lincoln's works out of their chronological order, coming first across his *Discourse and the Construction of Society* (1989) ten years ago and then moving on to such works as *Myth, Cosmos, and Society* (1986), and *Death, War, and Sacrifice* (1991), then of course his 1994 book, *Authority: Construction and Corrosion*. With his recent *Theorizing Myth* (1999) – a book examined in more detail in a subsequent chapter – Lincoln has confirmed for me his place as one of the few scholars of religion who takes seriously the challenge of studying this thing many of us call religion as an ordinary form of human practice, as a socio-rhetorical technique used to create, contest, and re-create credible worlds. It was precisely due to his work that I found myself becoming my own data that summer evening in Durban – an awfully long way to go to look in the mirror.

As I read him, three crucial assumptions drive much of Lincoln's work. In his own words, those assumptions are: (i)

> When one permits those whom one studies to define the terms in which they will be understood, suspends one's interest in the temporal and contingent, or fails to distinguish between "truths", "truth-claims", and "regimes of truth", one has ceased to function as historian or scholar. In that

moment, a variety of roles are available: some perfectly respectable (amanu-ensis, collector, friend and advocate), and some less appealing (cheerleader, voyeur, retailer of import goods). None, however, should be confused with scholarship.

(1996b: 227)

This is nothing other than a strong stand on the difference between participant and non-participant perspectives and projects, the old insider/outsider problem. Because Lincoln is interested in doing something other than reproduce the social worlds under study, he further assumes that (ii),

> as objects of experience and of 'scientific' knowledge, primordial origins and perfect centers remain notoriously elusive. They are constituted as objects of discourse, not knowledge, by bricoleurs who collect shards of information and prior narratives, from which they confect the fictions that satisfy their otherwise unattainable desires while doing their ideological work. When students of myth ... succumb to this temptation and engage in a discourse of origins and centers, the results are particularly ironic.

(1999: 95)

Here we see his commitment to a theory of social formation as tactical, prac-tical adhocery – a theory that applies to his own work as well. Building on the last line I have just quoted, comes the third assumption:

> If myth is ideology in narrative form, then scholarship is myth with foot-notes.

(1999: 209)

Here we see the profoundly self-reflexive nature of his work, meaning that scholarship is itself equally ad hoc; although not all discourses are characterized by the same rhetorical features and not all contribute to the same social iden-tity, they all have political, and, simply put, ideological effects. What sets scholarship apart, however, is the insistence that, quoting Lincoln's second "Thesis on Method," it is a "discourse which speaks of things temporal and terrestrial in a human and fallible voice, while staking its claim to authority on rigorous critical practice" – the footnotes he talks about – whereas that practice we call religious is a "discourse whose defining characteristic is its desire to speak of things eternal and transcendent with an authority equally transcendent and eternal" (1996b: 225).

I would like to put into practice these three assumptions and, in keeping with Lincoln's Barthean penchant for using as data that which we might not initially call data – such as Marcel Duchamp's autographed, upside-down urinal (see Lincoln 1989: 142 ff.) – coupled with his profoundly self-reflexive approach, I'd like to return to my earlier, self-implicating comments on the

Congress I attended in the summer of 2000. After all, if scholarship is myth with footnotes, then scholarly meetings are myths with name badges, colorful ribbons, and one complimentary drink ticket.

Thinking back on my experience of watching television in that Durban hotel room, I cannot help but wonder if the consumption of – rather than critical reflection on – that easily swallowed nationalist myth would be an example of what some of our colleagues do when they talk about this thing called "globalization." For example, consider some of the comments I overheard after Jonathan Z. Smith delivered his plenary address to the 2000 IAHR Congress – an address that was televised live via satellite from Chicago to the hotel in Durban (and subsequently published [Smith 2001b]). At the time, it seemed ironic that a talk whose *content* focused on the need for scholars of religion to do more than merely offer decontextualized paraphrases of indigenous claims prompted some responses that focused mainly on the *form* of the lecture – a form of communication made possible, as we all know, by the military-industrial-educational complex where the rhetoric of "national interest" and "free market" drive so many technological developments. In other words, instead of applying Smith's own method of historicization or redescription to the very medium that made it possible for us to listen and watch as he spoke into a camera in Chicago, several time zones behind us (i.e. analyzing its *content*), some people saw the lecture exclusively as a wonderful example of how apparently disembodied, trans-cultural meanings and symbols are now a truly global commodity (i.e., fetishizing and celebrating its *form*). The importance of this shift from examining content to examining rhetorical form is something that Lincoln's book, *Authority*, helped bring home for me and something that occupies virtually every chapter of *Theorizing Myth*. Thus, it makes sense that while the content of Smith's talk challenged the style of scholarship practiced by much of his audience, celebrations of the form of the delivery made it possible to shift the attention away from transgressing accepted professional or indigenous norms and back to re-enforcing these very norms, thereby deauthorizing the message of this eminently authorized speaker. As a group we had thus, to paraphrase Lincoln's own words quoted earlier, allowed the people we study to set the terms in which they were to be understood, we had thus suspended our interest in the contingent and the contestable, and thereby failed to distinguish between "truths," "truth-claims," and "regimes of truth." Thus, the medium for some in attendance that evening was indeed the message, and the message was the triumph of market-driven, global technology over disparate local cultures and languages.

The world is indeed a small place, I agree, but not because of any essential similarity among its participants, such as some non-empirical Human Nature, or because of some sort of supposedly politically neutral Internet that leaps national and linguistic frontiers in a single bound. I therefore happen to agree with Wendy Doniger (but only to a point) when she writes:

the essence of prejudice has been defined as the assumption that an unknown individual has all the characteristics of the group to which he or she belongs. "People like you," or "They're all alike" is always an offensive phrase.

(1998: 31)

Now, there is an irony here for Doniger limits her analysis to racism and sexism, all the while presupposing a trans-historical sense of individualism (of the obviously liberal variety) which allows her to talk about such things as "cross-cultural human experiences" and "human truths" (3, 34). So, I would like to press her words further, for I find it equally troublesome to maintain the assumption that, due to an accident of biological and social classification, some otherwise unknown "person" necessarily "has all the characteristics of the group to which he or she belongs" – that group being "the Human Family." Simply put, Doniger's weariness of racist and sexist discourses can, indeed must, be extended to liberal humanist discourses on subjectivity as well, for they just as easily portray a part as if it were the Whole. I would argue that the global is now local not because of some necessarily shared, essential trait or truth among humans but because of the virtually unimpeded ability of one politico-economic system to classify various peoples as consumers in order to satisfy its (our!) appetite for new markets and larger profits. At this point, I cannot help but think of Macon Leary – the protagonist of Anne Tyler's wonderful novel, *The Accidental Tourist* (1985; the character was played by William Hurt in the film version). Macon, as some readers will recall, is the author of a successful series of travel books for U.S. business people who hate traveling – the logo for the series being a winged armchair. As I found out in my hotel room that night in Durban, and as was apparent after Smith's provocative plenary address, the logo for jet-setting scholars might as well be a television remote control, or perhaps even better, the image of a computer mouse: "15 minutes for 10 Rands" the English sign said in the Pretoria Internet café where I spent some time, my virtual presence making my actual absence from the U.S. irrelevant.

But perhaps this analysis of structural factors obscures my own personal culpability and, instead, I am in fact to blame for the myopia that prompted me to spend unnecessary time navel-gazing either in my hotel room or at the Internet café rather than, say, making a side trip to a game reserve, taking a tour through a township, or "going native" in some other manner. However, in transferring the analysis to the level of individual choice and preference we find another topic basic to our field, what Theodor Adorno aptly called the jargon of authenticity, which lies in the background of our field's preoccupation with, as quoted earlier, the quest for primordial origins, perfect centers, pristine faith, and free-floating meanings. We easily find this preoccupation in the work of so-called religious people – everything from Karl Barth's well-known critique of institutional religion, as opposed to the "self-manifestation" of "God Himself" in the person of Jesus Christ (see his *Church Dogmatics* vol 1, part 2), to Paul

Tillich's writings on such topics as "genuine faith" and "genuine human relations" (notably in his 1957 book, *The Dynamics of Faith*), Nicholas Lash's lament for the ways in which "religion" distorts purer, creative faith (1996), and Barry Callen's redundantly-named devotional book, *Authentic Spirituality: Moving Beyond Mere Religion* (2001). I find a similar quest to be present in the work of many who understand themselves to be non-denominational scholars of religion as well. I believe this is what Hans Penner has called the "myth of the given" (2000: 66, 69–71), what David Chidester calls "indigeneity" (2000: 433–434), and, in his critique of the movie *The Matrix*, what Slavoj Žižek had in mind when he identified the ideology implicit in utopias which posit that, "behind the incomplete/inconsistent reality we know, there is another reality with no deadlock of impossibility structuring it" (1999: 3). As might be expected, a number of my pre-travel conversation partners presupposed just such an authenticity to "South Africa," everything from the "exotic safaris" of the lady who cut my hair to the "long lost homeland" of my seat mate during the long flight from St. Louis to Johannesburg. Apparently, my travel to Africa, at least as communicated to me by some peers, might cure my unwillingness to "get my hands dirty" by simply immersing myself in the real, the authentic, the significant data so important to our work as scholars. Taming the violence that a previous generation's ethnocentrism has done to the insider's world, we are now thought to be in the privileged position to see a people's religion or their culture as they see it themselves – studying religion "on the ground" we now call it – thus building toward a truly cross-cultural common understanding of the Human Condition (for a critique of this viewpoint, see McCutcheon 2000b). This, I presume, is what earlier writers called "taking religion seriously."[2]

Such a jargon animates some brands of emancipatory criticism now popular in our field and prominent at the Durban meeting: as enlightened post-colonialists we can now apparently remove our bureaucrat's lenses to see the truly indigenous perspective in all its colorful authenticity. Take but one example: Richard King's recent book, *Orientalism and Religion* (1999).[3] In his introduction we learn that

> the study of Asian culture requires a much greater sensitivity and engagement with indigenous forms of knowledge if one is to avoid 'doing violence' to the object of one's analysis.
>
> (4)

This theme of authentic engagement recurs later in the book when we are told that

> [t]he introduction of a variety of indigenous epistemic traditions is, in my view, the single most important step that postcolonial studies can take if it is to look beyond the Eurocentric foundations of its theories and contest the epistemic violence of the colonial encounter. This challenge requires

engagement with the knowledge-forms and histories of those cultures that
have been colonized by the West.

(199)

Although such comments may indeed be motivated by what Gareth Griffiths
refers to as "a worthy liberal desire to recuperate ... Aboriginal culture," it is
also evident that, as Griffiths goes on to conclude, "it also frequently results ...
in the ... construction of the 'authentic' ... Aboriginal in opposition to the
'inauthentic' political activists" (1994: 238). Despite using language similar to
King's, Griffiths comes down on a rather different side of the issue and, agreeing
with Adorno's assessment of the jargon of authenticity, concludes that "the sign
of 'authenticity' is an act of 'liberal' discursive violence, parallel in many ways
to the inscription of the 'native' (indigene) under the sign of the savage" (238).
As evidence of this, consider how well-intentioned post-colonialists seem
unaware of the non-indigenous (and hence, by their standards, inevitably
violent?) nature of their classifications "Asia," "culture," "Eurocentrism,"
"west," not to mention the Latin-based category "religion" itself. Employing
such classifications in concert with the assumption of some unified thing known
as an "indigenous form of knowledge," suggests that their critiques have not
taken seriously one of the premises of post-colonial literature: Michel Foucault's
claim that "[w]e must conceive discourse as a violence that we do to things"
(1989). After all, in even describing, let us say, "the religions of India," we are
actively involved in the production of knowledge by means of the application of
classifications invariably foreign to the supposedly indigenous objects under
investigation – religion in India.

   Given my rather odd experience of watching parts of that Canadian movie in
my hotel room in Durban, I find myself more than ever in the position of being
rather suspicious when it comes to ambitious announcements concerning the end
of epistemic violence. After all, I fear being so bold as to think that my particular
set of curiosities, assumptions and anticipations – in a word, my "world" – overlaps, necessarily complements, or exhausts the worlds of the people I happen to
study. I tend to think that I am rather unlike them insomuch as I am a member of
a privileged, jet-setting guild whose pursuit of curiosities is made possible by large
nation-states freeing me from the kinds of routine material concerns that occupy
– indeed, dominate – the lives of some of the people I might study. Because I am
not so confident with the link between essence and manifestation, between signified and signifier, between diverse peoples and Human Nature, and, finally,
between experience and authenticity, I tend to be rather suspicious of the in-flight
travel magazine view of the world, as when the October 2000 issue of TWA's
Ambassador magazine declared that "the essence of Cairo" lies beyond the pyramids. But, if I suspend this critique for a moment, and grant that South Africa
provided access to something specific, essential, and indigenous, I might ask
which of my so-called lived experiences deserve the status of authenticity? How
far behind the pyramids must I peer? Well there were:

Colorful rayon African dresses with "Made in Taiwan" on the label; a sushi restaurant in the so-called heart of darkness where I sat beside a Swedish businessman who politely offered to help me read the English menu; an English-speaking "Zulu" warrior in full battle dress who stood on the steps outside our hotel all day on the weekends, ready, I assume, to help tourists with their luggage and maybe pose for a photo or two; open air markets where black women at each booth sold the exact same mass-produced trinkets; friends visited the Cape of Good Hope and the cell on Robben Island where Nelson Mandela was imprisoned for so long; I visited the government's Union Buildings in Pretoria, where Mandela was sworn into office; there was the massive Voortrekker Monument, with its potent myth of Afrikaaner destiny and innocence etched into its interior stone walls, acting out an ancient (con)quest right before one's eyes; I saw a slow-moving grass fire trailing a thick column of grey smoke and black, scorched earth along the side of the highway as we drove in a three car convoy – "for safety's sake," they said – from Pretoria to Durban; a braai (Afrikaans for "broil" – a "barbeque" to me) at the home of Afrikaaners teaching at the University of South Africa (Unisa); a black South African tour guide showing two of us through an anthropology museum at Unisa, a museum whose silent glass cases were filled with artifacts from what I can only assume were our guide's own collective past; after greeting a black professor at Unisa with a handshake, I was shown the more complex manner in which "real South Africans shake hands" – the manner in which I fumbled with the ritual's sequential components easily marking me as not a real South African; I met white South Africans who understood themselves to be just as real South Africans as anyone else (though I secretly wondered if they knew the secret handshake); listening between the lines, I occasionally heard a guarded nostalgia for some lost past, both historic and mythic, coming from both sides of the modern political and racial divide; on the highway back to Pretoria from Durban, I saw poor black workers speeding along in the back of a dump truck, as if it was a bus; I met a talkative Scottish vendor in an outdoor market in Pretoria who had spent considerable time working in Canada as a younger man and who therefore knew western Canada far better than I; I had several pints of good, dark British beer in an Irish pub in Durban, served by an Afrikaaner bartender; there were those young white and black children playing together at the edge of the Indian ocean, its powerful, waist-high waves crashing into them to their obvious enjoyment; talking with Unisa New Testament professors, I found that the exact same issues of turf and theory, so well known to North American scholars, also characterize the religious studies/theology divide in their setting – though the effort to build "the new South Africa" means that the links between the study of religion and jargons of justice, sin, and forgiveness are far stronger there; there were the ever-present cell phones and car alarms, both used for personal security, and the seemingly endless coils of razor wire running along the top of those omnipresent walls that encase many people's homes; guinea fowl unpolitely clucking very early, and very loudly, in the morning right outside my guest house; and there I was tossing an empty Coke can into trash bins along the Indian ocean board walk, bins bearing posters of an American Indian chief used to sell some local brand of soft drink.

If, as Adorno observes, "authenticity is determined by the arbitrariness of the subject" (1973: 126), then, predictably, this contradictory complex of sites/sights apparent to this one subject is not the idealized "South Africa" portrayed in the popular, North American imagination. Those who set off on their quest to experience the heart of Africa for themselves are thus bound to understand what James Clifford meant when he observed that "the actual experience, hedged around with contingencies, rarely lives up to the ideal" (1988: 24). Take, for example, a magazine ad for South African tourism (see pages 20–21 of the October 30, 2000 issue of *The New Yorker*). The items selected for U.S. tourist consumption thus emphasize natural or unspoiled abundance, e.g., "the majesty of Table Mountain," "the magnificent sound of elephants trumpeting," "endless savannas" and "ancient forests." But wait, the abundance does not stop there: "[w]ith the current exchange rate, we think you'll be pleasantly surprised. You'll be able to do more for less. ... Exchange a few dollars for memories of pure gold." Much as an interviewee on NPR's "Morning Edition" once earnestly described Rio's annual carnival as a time when "slaves become kings" (this is an ideological claim, since, redescribed, we could say that the *actual, permanent poor* become *symbolic, temporary kings*), so too the effectiveness of the ad relies on the reader's confusion of two otherwise distinct semantic levels: the exchange of actual labor for memories of "natural" symbols unattached from labor, the former represented by the current global unit of exchange (the U.S. dollars) whereas the latter is represented by a nostalgic unit of global exchange (gold). Just as both units of exchange possess value only insomuch as the gap between the signifier (i.e., paper or metal) and the signified (human labor) is obscured, so too, seeing only the "luxury of safari camps" and "some of the most picturesque [golf] courses in the world" is possible only if we obscure the tremendous gap between the discontinuities of the material lives of many South Africans, on the one hand, and "the magnificent sound of elephants trumpeting," on the other. Just as the ad promises, then, "[a] visit to South Africa is a journey for the senses"; the journey, however, is from a material economy to the obscurantism of a purely symbolic economy.

To those colleagues who seem so confident with their efforts to recover and re-experience "authenticity" – the cross-cultural "human experiences" and "human truths" that scholars such as Doniger believe myths to embody – I would ask what Lincoln might characterize as some destabilizing and irreverent questions, such as: Where is the authenticity in all this? Or, better put, Whose authenticity will, like cream, rise to the top? Which of these is *the* South Africa?; better put, Which of these do you *desire* to stand in for this thing we call "South Africa"? But these questions are not asked in polite society. Failing to pose just such irreverent questions, we act like guests in other people's meaning systems; wiping our feet before entering. We take for granted the presence of such worlds and thereby fail to study the mechanisms that enable people to imagine them-selves as part of coherent groups, those practices that enable someone, like me for example, to pick and choose from this wealth of what are in fact purely benign and arbitrary moments and, from them, to build an experience of, say, the authentic South Africa.

As should be clear, there is a busy economy of authenticity with political implications based upon where one is positioned within it. A little closer to home for some readers, take, for example, the case of Hilary Clinton and Rick Lazio's race for New York's senate seat. In their second televised debate on October 8, 2000, Clinton was asked about her "definition of a New Yorker" – a less threat-ening version of the "Are you an authentic New Yorker?" question that hounded this so-called carpet-bagger throughout her eventually successful senate campaign. Those U.S. readers with nothing better to do than watch CNN on a Sunday morning may recall that she began her obviously calculated answer by saying, "Well, as E. B. White defined it, a New Yorker is. ..." As with all such debates, the spin doctors started up before the echoes of the debate had quieted. George Pataki, Republican Governor of New York state, provided what was for me the most memorable post-debate spin: "I don't know who this 'Wyatt' guy is," he said in what sounded to me like a forced, New York city accent, "but he doesn't sound like a New Yorker to me ...". He went on that way in his press conference for several sentences, making for a juicy clip on Monday morning news shows, autho-rizing his own political position (and that of Lazio, the Republican candidate) by identifying with the authentic working-class people of New York, united against this interloping Democrat who quotes strangers. Ironically, though, Pataki did not realize that Clinton had just as efficiently authenticated her own status, and thereby authorized her own political position, by aligning herself with, not "some Wyatt guy," but with an intellectual, essayist, and novelist who was – it turns out – born in Mount Vernon, NY, in 1899, attended Cornell University, joined the staff of *The New Yorker* magazine in 1926, and in 1929, married Katherine Angell, the magazine's first fiction editor. Other than the children's classic, *Charlotte's Web*, and various other well-known works, White wrote a tribute to New York City itself in 1949 entitled, *Here Is New York* – which was written, interestingly enough, after White had moved to Maine.

As scholars influenced by Lincoln's study of authorizing practices, our inter-ests lie at the intersection of these competing claims to authenticity, not with adjudicating authenticity. We watch such public moments to see who does the snickering, and who among the conversants ends up with egg on their face, as when Pataki's own daughter was later reported to have teased her dad soon after his press conference for forgetting the name of the author whose books he had in fact read to her when she was young. Please, however, do not leave thinking that Pataki lost out in this little skirmish, for if you do, then we've simply repro-duced one particular standard for authenticity; in other words, you will have likely betrayed yourself as a *New Yorker* subscriber ("I read it for the cartoons," I hear some of you mumbling); surely Clinton's citation of a mid-twentieth-century New York City intellectual as an authority on her own "New Yorkishness" does not play well all across the state. The poor Governor, though, certainly lost out in the television news coverage I was watching, but that tells us more about the conditions that make mass media possible as well as its audience's view of the world than it does anything else. At least we learned that he had in fact once read to his daughter the bitter-sweet story of Wilbur the pig and Charlotte the spider – required reading for anyone hoping to portray himself as a father interested in authentic family values.

Much like the generations of myth theorists Lincoln examines throughout *Theorizing Myth*, all of us actively – if somewhat blindly – involve ourselves in the business of reproducing our stake in authenticity jargons; thus, the South Africa we all simply know to exist prior to ever setting foot there – and just where is there? – is the country re-entering "our" history by re-making itself into a culturally diverse, tolerant, free market, democracy. This is, apparently, *the* South Africa, no? At least, it is the one that seems attractive for an international clientele of largely liberal, white academics intent on publicly and elaborately confessing their guilt and feeling absolution for their own collective past. After all, despite our best efforts to exoticize it, as we all know apartheid really wasn't just "their" problem – otherwise, we would not have had years of "divestment" protests across North American university campuses. With absolution in mind, it is likely significant that during the year 2000 there were at least four international conferences on religion held in South Africa, one of which, the World Congress on Religion held in Cape Town in July, was sponsored by our own Academy and the SBL, among others (the others were the International Society for New Testament Studies, the World's Parliament of Religions, and the IAHR [see van den Heever 2001: 63]). But, in traveling to South Africa to, as I see it, celebrate the roles popular religion (hence the interest of many Congress participants in the Independent Churches in Africa) is understood to play in making "the new South Africa," we risk obscuring not only the manner in which the day-to-day lives of people living in the homelands, the shanty towns, and the squatters' camps – not to mention the corporate centers of decision-making – have changed little now that the country is once again "a member of the international community." We also risk obscuring the role that we, as supposedly enlightened global jet-setters, play in ensuring that the equality and justice of our rhetoric is not realized in practice – for if they were, then our ability to obtain research and travel grants that allow us to jet around the globe on the taxpayers' expense would surely come to an abrupt end. (See Llewellyn 2001, van den Heever 2001, and Jensen 2001 for related commentaries on the politics of the liberal inclusivism that characterized this meeting.)

Appealing to Pierre Bourdieu, we might say that the kind of essentialism necessary to celebrate the authentic popular culture of a people "offers the benefits of apparent subversion, a 'radical chic,' while at the same time leaving everything as it is, some with their actually cultured culture, capable of sustaining its own questioning, the others with their decisively and fictitiously rehabilitated culture" (1998b: 137). Much like characters in a David Lodge novel, international conference goers suffer from what Bourdieu terms "scholastic bias," entering into solidarity with the Other only by forgetting one's own immense privilege, a privilege that allows one to "see" another person's life as evidence of SOME GREAT HUMAN THEME, but without ever having to live within the practical constraints of anyone's actual lives but their own (rather like having one's cake and eating it too). Thus, as observed by Adorno in this chapter's epigraph, to confess GUILT publicly, so as to proclaim EQUALITY, the jargon on guilt and equality must obscure their own material conditions of possibility, rather like a friendly carnival huckster playing the shell game.

With the radical chic of scholarship in mind, consider Slavoj Žižek's comments in his recent book, *The Fragile Absolute*: "There is a way," he says,

> to *avoid* one's responsibility or too readily *assuming* one's guilt in an exagger-ated way, as in the case of the white male PC academic who emphasizes the guilt of racist phallogocentrism and uses this admission of guilt as a stratagem *not* to face the way he, as a 'radical' intellectual, perfectly embodies the existing power relations towards which he pretends to be thoroughly critical. ... The more the admission is candid, inclusive of openly acknowledging the inconsistencies of one's own position, the more it is false. ...

> (2000: 46)

Or, in the words of two Afrikaaner New Testament scholars commenting last year on the much publicized South African Truth and Reconciliation Commission (TRC), employing the public rhetoric of truth, guilt, forgiveness, and reconciliation serves to dichotomize and thereby personalize, simplify, and thereby obscure the structural nature of such events as, in this case, apartheid. Such personalization prevents the conditions that made this personal culpa-bility possible in the first place from ever being named and addressed. Employing the rhetoric of guilt and forgiveness is evidence that,

> [t]o the TRC, the conflict in South Africa was fairly simple and straightfor-ward – two opposing parties confronting each other. Religious discourse, inherently, allows one to operate with an objectivist worldview ... and makes it very difficult to bring diverse and pluralistic communities together. A religious rhetoric facilitates thinking in absolute and ultimate terms; it struggles to acknowledge a plurality of truths.

> (Vorster and Botha 1999: 327)

Such objectivization or dichotomization is reminiscent of Roland Barthes's sense of "inoculation," whereby one admits "the accidental evil of a class-bound institution the better to conceal its principal evil" (1973: 164). In other words, the guilt/culpability that becomes discernable and the reconciliation that then becomes possible once the evil Other is isolated and identified, as not-Self, leaves completely untouched the role that this very same rhetorical technique – what Vorster and Botha label as objectivism – played, in our case, in legitimizing apartheid policies to begin with. Thus, as elite scholars attending such international meetings, we perhaps inadvertently inoculate and thereby reproduce the very structural conditions of victimhood in seeking out and valorizing the authentic vs. the inauthentic, the true vs. the false, the innocent vs. the guilty, for we end up elevating but one part to the status of the Whole, all of which is authorized effortlessly within the confines of both our luxury hotels and our politics *du jour*. To phrase it another way, "by this retreat into preserving ['their'] ... untainted authenticity," well-intentioned elites ironically "encourage native peoples to isolate themselves from contemporary life and citizenship" by ensuring that their "distinctiveness" remain uppermost in both their and our minds (Brydon 1994: 141).

A fitting example of this preoccupation with appreciating immaterial distinctiveness (and thus reinforcing practical inequalities) occurred on the last evening of the Congress, immediately prior to the closing banquet, when a small, Shembe dance troupe entered the banquet hall, in traditional Zulu regalia, and the Congress participants were asked by the master of ceremonies to respect the sacredness of the performance we were about to witness. What little I know about this fairly recent, syncretistic Zulu/Christian group (founded in 1912 by Isaiah Shembe [d. 1935]) tells me that their dancing takes the form of day-long (or longer, I gather) events where the dancing gradually overcomes the entire gathering. I take it that the dancing is understood by participants to lead to, or to be a form of, village-wide possession. Needless to say, they danced for us for considerably less time than that. And, although the Congress participants eventually did a little dancing themselves following the banquet feast, it surely was not a result of being overcome by the spirit.

If "ritual" is the operative term for classifying the Shembe dance, then "performance" is the word I would use to classify what happened before the banquet, for we watched, for a few brief minutes, a small group who arrived and danced *for us rather than for themselves*. If the meaning of their dance is determined by the setting in which it occurs – much like the meaning of language derives from its grammar, syntax, etc. – then their dancing at the Congress meant our pleasure, or our education, or our sense of what ought to count as a cross-cultural mutual understanding – who knows which. Whichever it is, it is certain that *they* were a means to *our* end; a terribly powerful group exchanged money (for I cannot help but assume that they were paid for their services) not simply *with*, but *for*, a terribly weak group to provide an aura of nostalgia for authenticity; we thus gained an easily consumed sound bite of what is in fact a complex piece of historical, cultural information. This, I believe, is what is meant by the commodification of culture.

Now, this would not be so problematic to me if I were, say, an ethnographer observing the Shembe dancers as they worked themselves into their possession.

In that case I would be on their home turf, but intent on asking some of my own questions about this practice. There would be no presumption of a deep understanding but, instead, it would be clear that I was there to study them by means of my concepts and theories. But, at the start of a banquet in an elite resort hotel, we were requested to be respectful and watch a religious ceremony *cum* paid performance. The requested respect of that moment struck me as paternalistic to these people who were dancing for us, as if their complex group's identity could be encapsulated in a ten-minute performance (and I assume they were told how long "we" had for "them"). It was paternalistic because it goes without saying that we would never have asked, say, a Roman Catholic priest to come in and give us his best ten minutes of a Latin mass or requested a Jewish cantor to sing us a few – just a few, mind you – Hebrew prayers. Neither would we confuse a sound bite or a highlight reel of a Catholic mass for a "religious ceremony" – not that there is some essence of religiosity to each of these human performances that our prurience obscures and thus disrespects. Rather, the problem is that the usually operating aura of religion is so easily dropped when dealing with the obviously exotic Other. How was it that we could get away with asking the Shembe dancers for just a few minutes when we would never pose such a request to a rabbi or a Baptist pastor?

Assuming, once again, that they were paid for their services, the dancers had some limited material wealth to gain from making commodities of their own bodies. Judging by my quick search of the Internet, members of this group seem to have been very successful in transforming what might be called their syncretistic ritual practice into performance folk art and entertainment. Given their minority/marginalized status the price to be paid and the things to be gained from making this commodified exchange may make it well worth their while. But as the dancers left the floor that evening, I felt like I had used them and prompted them to sell something that ought not be for sale – not some sacredness, but a complex way of life that ended up being served as an appetizer on fine china. Where I was seated near the back of the banquet hall, a number of people spoke loudly throughout the dance and waiters continued to serve wine, while others watched intently, as if something magical was about to take place. Despite their efforts to see the authenticity, nothing special was happening. Instead, an international collection of travelers were about to dine and the floor show was underway. I was not in a village observing a dance or a ritual and the talkers and waiters were simply doing what it is people do at banquets. And me? I was sipping from a gin and tonic about to stand in a steam line for some roast beef in a luxury hotel.

More recently, and closer to my own "native land," a similar set of issues are involved with the AAR's initiative to spotlight scholarship that arises from within national settings outside of the U.S. Proposed by the AAR's Committee on International Connections, it commenced at the 2002 meeting, held in Toronto (the first AAR conference held outside the U.S. in many years), and understandably spotlights Canadian contributions to the study of religion. (At the 2003 meeting in Atlanta Japanese scholarship will be highlighted.) As part of this initiative the organizers of the 2002 meeting's various program units were encouraged to include Canadians on their panels or to make special reference to religion, and the study of religion, as practiced in Canada. The AAR's proposal was not met with universal support among Canadian scholars, however. I can only assume that this reaction surprised those who proposed the initiative. Although some Canadian scholars, working in Canada or the U.S., jumped at the opportunity to take their place on the national stage, a number of others felt rather alienated by this proposal, an alienation that is more than likely puzzling to well-meaning conference organizers.

From the outset, let me say that I am quite pleased that the 2002 meeting was in Toronto, the city in which I obtained my Ph.D. And I think it is potentially very interesting that those who hail from other national settings will now begin regularly to gain some formal exposure at these obviously influential meetings. But, as has become evident from some scholars' reactions, there is a real danger that the manner in which such events are organized will simply marginalize the very people conference organizers wish to include. Whether intended or not on the AAR's part, much like the Shembe troupe dancing for their dinner, such events can easily come across as paternalistic tokenism. After all, the AAR is so (understandably) dominated by U.S. scholars, and concerns mainly of relevance to U.S. scholars, that a focus on scholars/scholarship originating from other settings cannot help but be marginal, an item of mere curiosity, and thus seen by some conference goers as a largesse resulting from a paternal spirit of *noblesse oblige*. Minority focus thus reinforces the minority status. Or, as feminists pointed out some time ago, the "add women and stir" strategy is a sign of, and strategy for, continued patriarchal dominance. Ironically, then, spotlighting Canadian work can reinforce U.S. dominance of this stage for, after all, it is "their" stage since they are doing the inviting.[4]

As with much of U.S. culture, Canadians are so seamlessly integrated into the AAR that it strikes me as highly artificial to presume that there is such a thing as a Canadian perspective on comparative religion, for example. But if indeed there is some beast called a Canadian perspective, what is it? I've lived in the U.S. since 1993, am now a permanent resident, have never worked as a university professor in Canada, and am largely disconnected from the Canadian academic scene. A good friend of mine who once worked in the U.S. for a few years and holds dual U.S./Canadian citizenship, has now returned to teach in Canada. Another good friend in Canada was born and raised in South America, came to Canada as a teenager speaking no English and holds a Canadian passport. Sure, we all call ourselves Canadian, since we seem to share what Bruce Lincoln once termed sentiments of affinity, and because we share various sentiments of estrangement as well, but I am not sure how this nationalist affinity relates to our professional identity. If indeed we live fractured lives, then I'm not sure what a Canadian perspective is and simply

assuming it to exist, homogenously and unproblematically, and then seeking to
highlight "it" at a conference, strikes me as surprisingly similar to the Shembe
dancers being asked to perform. Thinking of standing inside the proverbial big
tent and hearing, "the Canadian perspective," seems terribly unproductive for
it reproduces the very notions of immaterial essences, meanings, and identities
that some of us are struggling to historicize.

If, instead of merely being added to this or that pre-existent panel, scholars
from other national settings were actively involved in helping to make key
program decisions for such conferences, if these people were playing a role at,
say, major plenary sessions, rather than merely providing the authentic insider's
viewpoint, I could imagine a different outcome for this initiative. For instance,
despite the troubles I have pointed out with the most recent IAHR Congress,
when this group meets in various national settings, the Congresses are planned
by scholars in each setting, and thus the meeting is permeated, from top to
bottom, with issues of relevance to at least some of the Mexican or South
African delegates (the two Congresses that I have attended, in 1995 and
2000). This central task of planning, of determining the structure of the
meeting's content, prevents groups from simply playing the role of colorful
exhibits.

This attitude is more than apparent in the May 2002 edition of the AAR's
periodical, *Religious Studies News*, in the article somewhat ironically entitled,
"Canada On Sale." Within the first two paragraphs one reads:

> Toronto hosts hundreds of conventions every year, many of them
> comprising predominantly United States citizens, and they do it seamlessly.
> The American Academy of Religion's meeting in Canada will operate as it
> would in any US city. And the added value of visiting Toronto should far
> out-weigh the usually negligible issues of crossing the border. One of the
> most attractive features of visiting Canada at this point in history is the US
> and Canada dollar exchange rate.
>
> (Anon. 2002a: 5)

The writer nicely identifies, unintentionally I would say, the very issue pressed
in the above paragraphs and, indeed, throughout this entire book: the techniques necessary to portray a fragmented landscape "seamlessly." Not only is the
article written to calm the nerves of its U.S.-based readers who are about to
travel to the wilds of "the great white north," but it fails to understand that,
when traveling to a professional meeting in a foreign setting, *the whole point is
that the meeting ought to be different*. However, recalling Anne Tyler's novel once
again, I found myself wondering whether Macon Leary was in fact the anonymous author of this pithy piece of travel advice. As the name of the professional
organization signals, *RSN*'s readers are admittedly mostly U.S. scholars, but
what about *RSN*'s many Canadian readers who obviously do not have U.S.
dollars to spend, or, say, its European readers, etc.; could the article not have

said, "One of the most attractive features for U.S. scholars visiting Canada …"? But to have said that would require the writer to entertain the relativity of place and identity, to understand that "Others" were also readers and members, and that there were other places where those Others feel just as at home as we do here – places not our home, but theirs.

Why ought the meeting be different? Well, because it *is* different. It is not "as if" the meeting was "in any U.S. city." It was not; it was in a foreign country – an admittedly similar national setting but a foreign country nonetheless.[5] But, as suggested above, and as indicated by this one writer, the same old seamless show just went on the road. The comparative bar graph that accompanies this article, listing U.S. and Canadian prices for a specific brand of lipstick, a bottle of Gucci's "Rush" (for those not in the know, eau de toilette), tickets for Disney's ode to Africa, *The Lion King* ("best seats" no less), Magambo Shrimp at the Rainforest Café, and a "three-button grey" Hugo Boss suit is the icing on the cake. From reading this brief article at home in Alabama I was transported back to that Durban tourist bazaar, filled with stereotypical "Africana"; it seems that the "added value of visiting Toronto" has more to do with getting a good deal on lipstick, perfume, and experiencing exported U.S. culture – no doubt to see the world as the natives of Toronto see it – than with U.S.-based scholars experiencing an intimately related yet distinctly different socio-political world just north of the 49th parallel.

After reading this article, I cannot imagine anyone *not* understanding why some people reacted the way they did to the AAR's attempt to include Canadians in an honorary role at its 2002 meeting. In making these points, however, I must stress that I fully realize that this is only an inconsequential *RSN* article and that, in this same issue of the periodical, other brief articles identify such "entertainment" sights as the Royal Ontario Museum and the Museum of Contemporary Canadian Art (where the Canadiana is more than likely behind glass and velvet ropes), not to mention the "third largest mall in Canada": the Toronto Eaton Shopping Centre (complete with the proper Canadian spelling, no less). Anticipating the need to squeeze in time for a little authentic Canadian culture somewhere along the trip, the writer wisely recommends that "[w]hen you're taking a breather from shopping, stop by the Centre Court's famous fountain or look up for renowned Canadian artist Michael Snow's sculpture of Canadian geese, 'Flight Stop'" (*RSN* May 2002: 4). After quickly inhaling some commodified Canadiana, I assume, conference goers were rested up sufficiently to plunge back into the crowds, searching for that grey Hugo Boss suit (a steal at only $586.21 U.S.).

Sarcasm aside, on one level the article I have briefly examined is obviously intended to convey important information on such topics as dollar exchange rates, U.S. Customs regulations, and how to obtain refunds on payments to the Canadian Goods and Services Tax. And, more than likely, much of this text is simply adapted, to varying degrees, from tourist information provided by various Toronto tourism authorities (and thus, the self-commodification of the text is equally interesting). But despite this, I find the article's reduction of the issue to a matter of getting a good deal on purchases – "Canada on Sale," no less – to make apparent the usually undisclosed fact that much contemporary scholarship on religion, religious experiences, and authenticities is a matter of shopping for a marketable name brand onto which one can hang a social identity. Moreover, articles such as this make apparent how easily those who inhabit dominant cultures can portray and perceive their own contingent worlds as self-evident, neutral, seamless, and thus – especially for liberal humanists – capable of embracing (a.k.a swallowing) all comers. Perhaps this also helps to explain why the U.S.'s main professional association for scholars of religion has an "International Connections" standing committee in the first place, and why the existence of such a committee would – to my ears at least – sound downright funny if it was associated with virtually any other national associations. Only dominant groups can so easily conceive of their local stage *as being anything but local*. But if the AAR leadership is indeed intent on proceeding with its internationalist aspirations, then perhaps it would benefit from some self-examination to ascertain just how inevitably provincial the organization in fact is, or at least is perceived to be by those from other equally provincial settings. In other words, its membership could first examine the Academy's self-perceived openness before assuming too quickly that it is indeed all-inclusive. Perhaps then others will not necessarily feel like they were being invited to occupy a merely honorary place in the so-called big tent. Of course there are risks to this, for in recognizing that, just as the name says, the AAR is indeed a specifically American academy means that what was once understood as the self-evident, universal standard will simply be recognized as being but one (an admittedly large and influential one, but just one nonetheless) among many standards. It would mean coming to understand that, as in the apt title of a study on the development of the nationalist concept of *Heimat* ("homeland") in nineteenth- and twentieth-century Germany, all social groups are merely comprised of "a nation of provincials" (Applegate 1990).[6] I am not sure that the Academy's leadership or the majority of its membership are willing to take this risk, however.

Rather than searching for the authenticity and absolution that lie hidden within the Shembe dance troupe, encoded within offers of honorary status to minorities, and hanging around the necks of Canadian geese sculptures high above shoppers, we as scholars could instead inquire as to whether people calling for openness, tolerance of diverse belief systems, and religious education in elementary schools could be just one more technique for reproducing a particular socio-political status quo.[7] We could thus follow Lincoln's lead and move away from discussions of culpability and innocence, assessing not the validity of the message (*content*) but examining the mode of signification (*form*) that makes various messages, meanings, culpabilities, and social worlds possible and persuasive. For, as Lincoln phrased it in the eighth thesis on method:

Those who sustain this idealized image of culture do so … by mistaking the dominant fraction … of a given group for the group or "culture" itself. At the same time, they mistake the ideological positions favored and propagated by the dominant fraction for those of the group as a whole. … Scholarly misrecognitions of this sort replicate the misrecognitions and misrepresentations of those the scholars privilege as their informants.

(1996b: 226)

Living out one such misrecognition, my Durban roommate, Willi Braun, and I took a cab one day from the Congress hotel to the tourist bureau in downtown Durban to see a much discussed African art exhibition – art, like religion, thought by many to symbolize the authentic, aesthetic sense (an analogy used by Rudolf Otto in the opening pages of *The Idea of the Holy*) and struggle of a people. But, unbeknownst to us, it happened to be National Women's Day in South Africa and the bureau was closed when we got there. Much like Gertrude Stein's comment on Cleveland (often paraphrased by the late Ninian Smart, or so I'm told), when we got there, there was no "there" there – a fitting example of what Žižek calls the illusion of traditional realism: "the belief that *behind* the directly rendered objects *is* the absolute Thing which could be possessed if only we were able to discard the obstacles or prohibitions that prevent access to it" (2000: 37). After a leisurely walk back to the hotel, past the imperial architecture of the British colonial-era Durban city hall and then through parts of town that looked nothing like the tourist district where we were staying, a friend whom we met outside our hotel asked if we had seen the art exhibit, to which I answered "No," then, pausing and pointing across the sidewalk, I added, "but I've seen that tree." In that precise moment, where our exchange flirted with the distinction between enthusiasm and sarcasm, between culture and nature, between the extraordinary and the ordinary, that's where we find the myth of the given, the illusion of traditional realism, and the jargon of authenticity exerting themselves.

Now, long after returning home from Durban, I am still not sure what to make of these contradictory experiences, though of one thing I am sure: I would be terribly remiss if I thought that they were somehow specific to South Africa or the Congress I attended.[8] I would also be remiss if I thought these experiences were, in essence, contradictory – they are contradictory only if we first assume that there *ought* to be some unitary thing, "South Africa." Without this presumption there is no contradiction since there is no disembodied standard by which to measure the supposed Africanness of this or that moment. Without this standard, we are therefore left with Foucault's heterotopia, or Didion's phantasmagoria. But the liberal ethnographer, to cite James Clifford commenting on the quest for authenticity, "who represents the essence of a culture against impure 'outside' forces encounters sooner or later a contradiction built into all such discourses that resist or try to stand outside historical invention" (1988: 88). Paraphrasing Michael Palin's character "Dennis" in Monty

Python's "The Holy Grail," as observers of such scholarship, we might shout out, "Come and see the contradictions inherent in the system!" Some readers likely recall that, while King Arthur throttled Dennis, the self-proclaimed anarcho-syndicalist, for his uncooperative attitude toward the authority bestowed upon Arthur by – as Dennis phrased it – "strange women lying in ponds distributing swords," he shouted about the "violence inherent in the system." This is a violence that coerces so as to distract from any preoccupation with the contradictions, such as Arthur's legitimacy being derived from – to quote the insightful Dennis once again – "a farcical aquatic ceremony." Although no one is currently or actually pummeling me – a luxury of the specific world that I happened to have been born into – I am nonetheless curious as to why members of our field fail to find the inevitable contradictions of their own surroundings and discourses, let alone the distant lands we often study, curious and, instead, continue what I see as an ill-conceived quest for origins, centers, purity, authenticity – in a word, the grail.

If social groups exist by making and then chasing the carrot of their own mythic narratives and ideals, then it should not surprise us that our own discipline exists by chasing after the authentic – a totem that often goes by the name of "religious experience" in our clan. As is evident from Lincoln's *Theorizing Myth*, scholars, no less than any other social actors, are busy making their groups work by internalizing and following – and thus not paying particularly close attention to – the details of rule, grammar, ritual, form. But, as in the case of a tradition in which Lincoln is one of the more notable contemporary examples, some of us will continue to find all of this ritualized tail chasing to be a curious activity. We will focus our attention on the techniques that human communities employ to sanction just this taxonomy and just that hierarchy, just this myth of authenticity and just that myth of presence, and we will try to link these narratives and practices to all of the social implications that attend these ways of dealing with the contradictions inherent in our social systems. Although not all of us will follow the lead of Michel de Certeau, becoming "anthropologists of credibility," thanks to Lincoln's work fewer of us attend professional meetings merely as representatives of competing systems of credibility. To my way of thinking, then, we come together at these meetings as scholars of mythmaking and not simply as assorted humans acting out our assorted, competing myths. As the concluding lines of *Theorizing Myth* state, "[a]s students of myth, we … turn our attention to the mythmaking of our scholarly, as well as that of other, ancestors, secure in the knowledge that our descendants will one day return the favor" (Lincoln 1999: 216).[9]

Notes

1   From the outset I must acknowledge my debt to Adorno (1973) for my title.
2   Margaret Miles's 1999 presidential address to the American Academy of Religion is but the most recent instance of this Liberal viewpoint (2000). The ease with which she "integrates the falsely polarized terms 'theological studies' and 'the study of reli-

gion'" (472, 473–474) is especially fascinating and troubling. If we assume that both discourses are historically situated and artful means by which power and privilege are negotiated (see the long quotation from Braun that closes McCutcheon 2001b), then I might agree with Miles. It is apparent, however, that this is not how she understands their similarity.

3   In Durban I chaired a review symposium on this book; the panelists were: J. E. Llewellyn (Southwest Missouri State University), Rico Settler (University of Cape Town), and Donald Wiebe (Trinity College, Toronto). The symposium, along with King's reply, appears in *Method & Theory in the Study of Religion* 14 (2002).

4   At this point I think of such recent films as the animated South Park movie (1999) or *Canadian Bacon* (1995), films that, on one level, are effective U.S. parodies of U.S. nationalism and exceptionalism. But, ironically perhaps, in order for the parody of both films to be effective, the U.S. film makers require a stereotyped Canadian Other to be compliant as the so-called comic straightman without whom there is no joke. In other words, the luxury of self-parody comes at the expense of the marginal group which functions as a means to the dominant group's end – a prop necessary for the joke to work. In working, the joke confirms the marginal group's status as a prop.

5   That the writer so easily equates an entire country, Canada, with "any U.S. city," is perhaps itself worthy of analysis.

6   I must thank Johannes Wolfart for bringing this book to my attention. Applegate's work is an attempt to document how Germans have found "the key to their national identity in the multiplicity of their provincial origins," a strategy that, she hypothesizes, has been useful in resisting "the scourge of 'Americanization'" (245).

7   See McCutcheon 2001b: ch. 10, "Our 'Special Promise' as Teachers: Scholars of Religion and the Politics of Tolerance," (155–177) for an elaboration of this thesis.

8   Portions of this essay were written while attending the annual meeting of the Society for the Scientific Study of Religion (SSSR) in Houston, October 19–22, 2000, at which a paper was presented on the increasing presence of Seventh Day Adventism in Papua New Guinea. Although at times the paper was explicitly concerned with the task of description – as in when the presenter discussed the local term "skin seven days" which, he observed, is used by some Adventist converts to classify those whom they consider only to wear their Adventism on the surface throughout the week – other parts of the paper reproduced and thereby reinforced claims to authenticity characteristic of elite Adventists. For example, commenting on the dramatic increase in Adventist converts over the past thirty years, the presenter observed that, although they had increased "in number" they had not increased in terms of "nurture." In other words, the predictable, even inevitable, presence of hybrid identities was somehow evidence to the author that authentic or true Adventism had not yet taken hold in the islands. In fact, the audience laughed at the description of a "Big Man" convert to Adventism who, nonetheless, still practiced polygamy. Hearing the muffled laughter of the audience, I recalled Lincoln's analysis of Rick Springer, the anti-nuclear activist, who strode onto a Las Vegas stage, smashed a National Association of Broadcasters award being presented to the ex-President Ronald Reagan, and began delivering his own address (1994: 128 ff.). Although the Secret Service forcefully removed Springer from the podium, Lincoln instead directs our attention to the less overt means by which the smooth operations of authority were quickly re-established by the audience's reaction to the event. Lincoln describes how, after regaining his composure, Reagan simply "quip[ped] to an appreciative crowd, 'Is he a Democrat, by chance?'" (136). Had Reagan's audience (a room full of broadcasters we must remember) instead been more interested in discerning Springer's message and rationale – for it is not often that someone is so motivated to take the stage from such an authorized speaker – such small talk would have fallen on deaf ears. Laughter was also in evidence at the 1998 SSSR meeting in

Montreal where a presenter described how Roman Catholic protestors had picketed a Hollywood film for reasons the audience found rather absurd, prompting their laughter at the Catholic picketers. In all three cases, laughter characteristic of insiders scoffing at outsiders is evidence of one's interest in expressing and reproducing a particular stake in the economy of competing authenticities. Despite perennial complaints that reductionists do not take religion seriously, I have yet to hear them laughing at the behaviors of either liberals or conservatives, in the manner that each of these groups chuckle at the obviously silly behaviors of their political foes.

9   A very small portion of this paper was thought up the night before it was originally presented as part of the closing plenary panel of the International Association for the History of Religions' XVIII Congress, Durban, South Africa, August 11, 2000. The panel, which involved eight participants, each with five minutes to reflect on the Congress, was entitled, "Visions of the Study of Religion for the New Millennium." My thanks to Willi Braun, Michel Desjardins, Darlene Juschka, Ken MacKendrick, and the students in my Rel 670 course (Fall 2000) for their constructive comments on earlier drafts of the full essay.

Part III

Reworking the residue from our imperfect past

If you knew when you began a book what you would say at the end, do you think that you would have the courage to write it?

Michel Foucault (1988b: 9)

Chapter 9

Methods, theories, and the terrors of history

Closing the Eliadean era with some dignity[1]

> What is at stake in these debates is a struggle over what the study of religion itself should be. Eliade has [simply] become a focal point for the on-going identity crisis in the field.
>
> (Murphy 1994: 383)

Since the early 1980s a number of allegations have been made regarding the personal politics of Mircea Eliade. In many regards, the "Eliade affair" is similar to other cases of notable European intellectuals of the inter-war generation whose youthful, political pasts emerged long after they had established themselves as influential figures in their respective scholarly fields. For instance, consider the following two quotations:

> the Jew, who is something of a nomad, has never yet created a cultural form of his own ... since all his instincts and talents require a more or less civilized nation to act as a host for their development.

> Since the Jew – for reasons which will at once become apparent – was never in possession of a culture of his own, the foundations of his intellectual work were always provided by others.

My guess is that you would be hard pressed to identify which statement came from Adolf Hitler's *Mein Kampf* and which came from Carl Jung's 1934 essay, "The State of Psychotherapy Today" (for those looking for the answer to this question, see Robert Ellwood's *The Politics of Myth* [1999: 63]). Although it would require a persuasive argument to establish the claim that the authors of these words shared the same politics or had the same impact on world history – claims I am not making – these quotations do provide ample (perhaps startling) evidence of the manner in which some early-twentieth-century writers all too easily reduced complex social groups to an essentially homogenous identity – a skill well known among politicians and military leaders who have sometimes put into bloody practice such rhetorics. Moreover, it provides an insight into the manner in which these essentialized groups were then ranked, insomuch as in both of these cases "the Jews" are understood as a derivative or even a para-sitic group.

In short, the politics of scholarship is hard to ignore in light of such quota-tions. The names of the literary critic Paul de Man and the philosopher Martin Heidegger come to mind as two of the best-known examples of scholars with, at the very least questionable, and at the most, extreme, political backgrounds which have only recently come to light. In the study of religion the name of Mircea Eliade sometimes joins de Man and Heidegger. But in one important regard the case of Eliade and the study of religion differs from the de Man and Heidegger affairs; whereas news of de Man's anti-Semitic wartime newspaper columns and Heidegger's explicit association with Nazism sparked considerable debates within such fields as literary criticism and philosophy,[2] the case of Eliade's life and work remains largely marginal to the work of the vast majority of scholars of religion. Although some specialized articles and book chapters have criticized aspects of Eliade's early years – most recently Steve Wasserstrom's *Religion After Religion* (1999; see also the review symposium featuring essays by Tomoko Masuzawa [2001], Hugh Urban [2001b], and Gustavo Benavides [2001a]) along with a chapter in Ellwood's book (1999) and a few of the chapters in Bryan Rennie's essay collection on Eliade (Rennie 2001a)[3] – his political writings and relationships, and, more importantly, their impact on his mature work as a scholar, have received little extended debate in the field at large.[4] Instead, while many do indeed see Eliade's work as being passé and an artifact from the recent past, they nonetheless continue to use troublesome categories and abstractions popularized in Eliade's work – e.g., "the sacred," "hierophany," "coincidentia oppositorum," and "homo religiosus" (a point made apparent in my preface).

Where we *do* see Eliade's work and politics debated, we often find the argu-ments of his critics minimalized as nothing more than what one defender dismissed as "the recurrent clamor that will probably continue over his scholarly boldness" (Beane 2001: 189), or what another scholar characterized as an ill-considered "rush to denigrate the Eliadean legacy" by means of "whispers" that "depend too much on the academic gamesmanship of those on the fast track of career advancement" (Girardot 2001: 152, 157, 160). Likening carefully researched and argued positions to mere clamor and gossip, all of which are said to be motivated by young academics who wish to cite on their c.v.s that they have slain the father figure, strikes me as a wonderful side-step around the issue at hand. After all, who would level charges against such an intellectual giant without carefully weighing not only the evidence but the implications that laying such charges might have for one's own career. Such defenses notwith-standing, precisely because of the central role played by Heidegger's, de Man's, and Eliade's writings in the recent histories of their respective fields, reassess-ments of their work are necessary. For good or ill it has become virtually impossible to cite the work of either Heidegger or de Man without taking into account, implicitly or explicitly, the Nazi past of the former and the, at least early, anti-Semitism of the latter. However, contemporary representations of Eliade as a disembodied Great Man, or, better put, Great Mind, coupled with the virtually unquestioned authority his work yet exerts in contemporary scholarship on religion, suggests the existence of a critical blind spot in the study of religion.

The problem to be addressed is not only *why Eliade's particular approach was so popular from the late 1950s onwards* (Masuzawa and Urban both raise this important question in their reviews of Wasserstrom's book[5]) but, related to this, *how and why scholars of religion in the late twentieth century have so successfully withstood the critical assessments of the politics of Eliade's life and his scholarship*.[6] That Eliade's life and writings were political should be apparent from the fact that he, like all of us, lived and acted in complex social and institutional networks where we must continually negotiate issues of power and privilege – both on a personal level and within the various institutions of relevance to our lives. That his scholarship has a politics embedded within it I have argued elsewhere (1997b: chs 1 and 2) and therefore take it for granted here. Accordingly, my concern is not with Eliade so much as with the reception and use of his work in the North American context. Given that his scholarship continues to comprise an almost paradigmatic model for the field – such ill-defined phenomenological notions as sacred space, sacred time, and the center of the world are still easily found in the work of scholars – we must not forget that we are not talking simply about an isolated critique of a marginal scholar in the otherwise rich history of the study of religion; instead, we are talking about an established scholarly discipline successfully side-stepping its engagement with its own history and the politics of its own representations – in this case, its representation of a founding figure.

From the outset, then, I must make it clear that in this chapter I am not particularly concerned with Eliade's personal political views, his actions, his supposed guilt or culpability. Although his personal politics has understandably attracted the attention of other critics (the work of Ivan Strenski [1982, 1987] and Adriana Berger [1989, 1994] being two of the best examples), whether he was or was not a card-carrying Romanian fascist is largely irrelevant to my interests. Instead, I see significant links between contemporary defenses of Eliade and his work, on the one hand, and the ways in which scholars routinely marginalize issues of context, power, and conflict in their studies of those aspects of culture they name as religion, myth, ritual, scriptures, etc., on the other. In other words, the particular way in which Eliade and his work are represented in these various defenses is simply the most recent instance of a wider, more pervasive problem in our field, a field where the dominant strategies of representation construct not only a privileged datum and methods but also the discipline's and the scholar's own privileged, apolitical context and history.

Therefore, let me repeat: in this chapter I am not concerned with Eliade's personal culpability for I see in the various defenses of his life and work much larger and more intriguing issues pertaining to the politics of this scholarly discourse (a similar point to that made by Allen 1994: 345). Quoting Tim

Murphy, we must recognize that "there are more options [in the Eliade affair] than 'for or against' Eliade" (Murphy 1994: 383). Accordingly, I see the links between the Eliade, de Man, and Heidegger affairs *not* in terms of any necessary similarity in their individual actions, beliefs, or guilt – whether such links are present is a separate debate entirely. Such individualization of these wider issues strikes me as obscurantist and thus unproductive; as in DeLillo's advice, look past the violence and the culpability and, instead, see the conditions that make both violence and peace, innocence and guilt possible. So, the links between these writers that are of interest to me are discursive links: those shared techniques their contemporary defenders use not only to protect these writers' works and continued influence in academia but also to construct and maintain a dominant and supposedly ahistorical, totalized discursive field. That cracks are showing in this totalizing armor suggests that the status of this onetime dominant approach may now be in question, leaving residue upon which we can draw in future pursuits. As I hope to demonstrate in these concluding chapters, the primary recoverable artifact upon which a new scholarly exercise can be built is the long popular sacred/profane binary (along with such pairings as private/public, religion/politics, belief/practice, faith/institution, etc.). Studied as socio-rhetorical techniques used in group building, rather than as classifications that neutrally describe some inherent quality in a thing, person, or place, such pairings become our object of study and thus might be the basis for a newly invigorated, historically committed study of social formation.

My thesis in this chapter is simply this: the very way in which some scholars of religion have responded to the debate on Eliade and politics is itself representative of the techniques that they routinely employ to construct an autonomous, irreducible, personal zone of pure subjectivity that cannot be explained or historicized but only described, interpreted, and ultimately experienced and appreciated "on its own plane of reference." I have in mind here Beane's above-quoted line concerning Eliade's "scholarly boldness." As I have consistently argued, the field constructed in this way is more akin to the practice of liberal pluralism than a scholarly study of historically entrenched human beliefs, behaviors, and institutions. Perhaps there exists no better example of how the presumed autonomy of the subject affects the reception of Eliade than the work of David Cave. He writes:

> I am largely sympathetic to Eliade's cultural and pluralistic vision and I consider informative, insightful, and valid many of his interpretations of religious experience. I have tried to read Eliade as much as possible *on his own terms* and to place him within the framework of reference he himself was trying to construct, which I contend is the new humanism.
>
> (Cave 1993: 12; emphasis added)

Agreement with the views of one's subject is not necessarily troublesome: what *is* problematic, however, is the position that maintains that Eliade and his work are somehow *sui generis*, and can sufficiently be studied *on their own terms*. Come to think of it, what precisely does this mean? Just how does one determine the intentions of an author or the "framework of reference he himself was trying to construct"? Moreover, would Cave extend the same interpretive privilege to all historical subjects we as scholars study? I am reminded here of the 1991 documentary entitled, *The Architecture of Doom*,[7] which deploys a related method in maintaining that Nazism was an aesthetic movement that simply got out of control.

In the second sentence of his book's Introduction, Cave makes it clear that his concern is to examine "the *visionary impulse behind the totality* of Eliade's prolific and manifold life work" (3; emphasis added). All connections and associations with larger issues of context, politics, and power are thereby effectively excluded from the outset – as in when Eliade himself attempted to privilege his own "creativity" and Beane celebrated his decontextualized "boldness" – for Cave is dealing with private visions, impulses, and totalities rather than with publicly available practices and institutions, such as the discourses that make talk of private visions, creativity, and boldness possible and persuasive. By means of such rhetorical techniques, Cave immediately turns our attention to abstract totalities that can only be glimpsed as they are manifested in this or that passing moment. Starting out with the textual remains of what one might as well term Eliade-the-hierophany, Cave works toward discerning the transcendental essence (i.e., the totality) to Eliade's so-called program of cultural and spiritual renewal (i.e., the new humanism). Such a method prevents his readers from ever seriously entertaining that the new humanism might instead be understood as a potent and ethnocentric political program – a point convincingly argued by Murphy (2001).

In fully accepting Eliade's own troublesome terminology and methodologies – the Eliadean jargon, if you will – and then using these as the basis for his own study of Eliade's life and work, Cave effectively precludes from the outset any form of social, political, and economic redescription; for, as the old argument goes, such reductions throw the proverbial baby out with the bath water by missing the deeper spiritual, creative, or bold impulse supposedly animating the abstract totality. However, Cave's routine talk of such things as totality, visions, essences, experiences, the sacred, the real, Being, and authentic vs. inauthentic existence arises from, and makes sense only within, an interpretive context that accords some sort of privilege to certain conceptions of reality that we as scholars of religion should analyze rather than presuppose. To borrow two terms from psychology, in reading Eliade on his own level – whatever that may turn out to be – commentators take for granted the self-evident meaning of the manifest level of analysis and forsake any analysis of latent or structural functions and implications. Such overly generous and sympathetic scholarship corresponds to the penchant in our field for phenomenological, descriptivist studies – methods extended to historical data which accords with the researcher's politics, of course.[8]

Three years after the publication of Cave's book we find another example of this general trend of privileging internal, sympathetic exegesis and commentary over analysis and critique, in Bryan Rennie's impressive, book-length study of Eliade's work on religion (1996). In the opening pages Rennie writes: "Secondary scholars have all too often criticized what on closer inspection turns out to be *their own interpretations of Eliade's thought rather than his actual thought*" (4; emphasis added). Much like Cave, who tries to assess Eliade exclusively in terms of what Eliade himself was supposedly trying to do and achieve (Cave 1993: 3), Rennie's defense and reconstruction of Eliade's thought is based on delivering the real goods (i.e., Eliade's "actual thought") unavailable to so-called secondary scholars and only available to the careful and sympathetic hermeneut pouring over primary texts. Rennie, who offers what cannot be read as anything other than an authoritative or authentic reading of Eliade's "actual thought,"[9] thus aims, much like Cave, to provide his readers with the coherent and meaningful Whole scattered throughout diverse texts. And, like Cave, Rennie achieves this essential re-reading of Eliade by using an exclusively Eliadean methodology: not the new humanism, as in the case of Cave, but the related creative hermeneutic; "My approach," he writes, "will also be an attempt to clarify *by application* Eliade's creative hermeneutics" (1996: 5; emphasis added).

By opting for the rhetorics of "actual thought" and secondary vs. primary source, which are in turn housed within a rhetoric of authentic meaning and careful hermeneutics, Rennie combats what he takes to be the widespread but misleading observation that the lack of systematization to the Eliadean *oeuvre* somehow detracts from its ability to provide contemporary scholars with a useful way to study religion. Rennie maintains that

> the radically critical, iconoclastic approach of many contemporary scholars can all too easily prevent the comprehension of the central insights of a talented thinker with a web of Lilliputian objections. ... I suggest that it is not productive to immediately apply logical criticism of the minutiae, but rather to question the coherence and consistency of the whole.
>
> (1996: 4)

Rennie's goal, then, is clear: he is not out to explain Eliade or his popularity but to present Eliade's work as a coherent, uniform Whole, thus recovering the "author" – an ironically totalizing project given the fact that Rennie also argues that Eliade is a proto-postmodernist (1996: 232–238; this view is shared by Girardot [2001: 162]).[10] This recovery effort – buttressed by a rhetoric of major vs. minor influence (i.e., criticism likened to minutiae) – is fueled by speculations concerning how Eliade himself had intended his own work to be read. Accordingly, in his efforts to understand what Eliade *really meant* by such terms as the sacred, the *coincidentia oppositorum*, and *homo religiosus*, Rennie has little choice but to parallel Cave's method of analysis whereby some posited methodology of Eliade's, which sought deep meanings, is applied to the study of Eliade's own life and work. However, given Rennie's rather obvious rhetoric (e.g., the manner in which he refers to others as "radically critical" and offering merely "Lilliputian objections"), it is not entirely clear that his overtly sympathetic reading of Eliade is any deeper, truer, or more accurate than those readings he attempts to dismiss. It is, however, rather useful for establishing one type of scholarship, and the social world in which it operates, over another. That apologists must resort to the rhetoric of deep meaning, mistaken interpretation, and the image of innocent Gulliver towering over his little, confused foes, to defend Eliade's work – rather than simply presume and assert its utility and get on with their business – makes it evident that the world in which Eliade's brand of scholarship once held an unquestioned place has by now passed away.

It comes as no surprise, then, that Rennie's book attempts to reconstruct an entirely orthodox perspective, employing a number of techniques to conserve a posited past by constraining the various possible readings of Eliade's work. Authentic subjectivity and intentionality are the last refuge of the besieged hermeneut and the liberal humanist. Simply put, since the "meaning" of a long quotation from a primary text is not obvious, but relies on a decoding, translation, paraphrase, etc., his decoding is as much a paraphrase as any other, regardless how many times one quotes so-called primary sources. To authorize this paraphrase as if it were Eliade's actual thought he uses the problematic Eliadean categories and continually cites from Eliade's long-time defender and biographer, Mac Linscott Ricketts, who understandably writes a glowing foreword to this volume. Coupled to this is Rennie's emphasis on the experiential nature of religion, which is in line with a long tradition that finds its datum in the private realm of authentic human subjectivity rather than in the empirically observable world of happenstance, material objects, and social interactions. For example, in attempting to clarify whether Eliade's notion of "the sacred" entails an external, intentional agent or, as Rennie insists, an internal component of all human experience, he firmly lands in the middle of what might be the far more important issue: whether the study of religion takes "religion" and the evidently religious nature of certain experiences for granted and then simply attempts to describe them empathetically or whether scholars ought to investigate the very construction of "religion." Whether one maintains that the sacred is an external agent or an internal experience, both positions agree that what we are studying is utterly distinct and thus unavailable for studies that employ the usual set of tools and techniques. We must keep this in mind when we read both Eliade and Rennie arguing that religious experiences are also socio-historical events. Sadly, however, they cannot have it both ways. One cannot argue for religion as a historical event *while at the same time* asserting that there is always a kernel left over once we separate it from the historical chaff, a kernel whose special nature dictates the use of special skills exercised by special hermeneuts. Ironically, many of us might have jobs in autonomous religion departments precisely because few have yet to recognize the contradiction.

For those who see no contradiction, a form of circular reasoning will be persuasive. For example, in Rennie's work we find the following: "it is unquestionably the perception of the sacred which constitutes it as it is for those who perceive it" (1996: 20); "interrelations of the elements of a mythic matrix must be accepted as they are before they can be understood for what they imply" (108). Only because the study of religion is presumed by most to require the researcher artfully to delve into deep meanings and mysteries only interpretable through intuitive insights and leaps of imagination do such claims continue to count as meaningful statements about the world around us. Immediately after offering his own rather questionable definition of religion as "the total structure of values held, traditionally transmitted through a cultural matrix ... and reinforced by mythical rather than rational means" (109), Rennie goes on to suggest that this structure is "dependent upon self-authenticating intuitions of the real ... apprehended in individual experience." In my opinion, there is really not much difference between a mystery and "self-authenticating intuitions of the real."

The study of religion as practiced by many authorizes itself by means of such a rhetoric of experiential autonomy that leads to a significant privilege for (certain) participant self-reports. Again, Rennie provides ample evidence of this approach in his claim that the "reasons why we act in a certain way are almost always grounded in ideal structures of good and bad, right and wrong, normative notions which form archetypal, exemplary structures which, in their ideality, exist quite independently of the actuality of human experience" (102). After first reading this, I was left wondering if this was simply a description of how participants perceive and then explain their actions, an explanation that sensibly appeals to the historical autonomy, and hence authority, of their own social worlds. If so, then I was eager to see Rennie's historicization of this rhetoric, as in when scholars from Durkheim to Mack (as cited in a previous chapter) argue for the thoroughly historical basis for such discourses on exemplariness and ideality. If no such theorization follows such a description, as it fails to do in this case, then readers are left simply with an account of how a group of people seem to understand their own worlds to work: normative notions and exemplary structures exist independently of human experience. The last option, that this is actually an explanation of how social life works, is not something that I am willing to entertain, for it would require me to share not only the presumption that such a thing as human experience exists (a posited point outside historical causality; there could be no trans-human experience if experiences were contextually produced), but also that norms pre-exist such experience.

I am not sure of the value of such reporting since: (i) it could have been done by the people themselves, should they wish to let others in on how they see the world to operate; (ii) it leaves their self-perceptions unexamined and untheorized; and (iii) related to this, such scholarship thereby authorizes a group's self-perceptions and the larger social world that made such self-perceptions credible. To rephrase this point, I doubt whether such scholars would simply let stand the reported self-perceptions of groups with whom they disagreed politically. The self-reports of such groups more than likely scream out for explanation. So why not so-called religious people's self-reports? Such scholarship therefore provides a terribly efficient means for preventing any social scientific analysis of this supposed ideality; in suggesting that normative notions, much like Hesiod's fully armed and outfitted Giants, simply spring forth fully developed from the earth, Rennie obscures the manner in which normative claims concerning "self-authenticating intuitions of the real" arise from and simultaneously legitimate specific social and economic interests. It is by means of this dehistoricizing emphasis on the autonomy of private experience, accessible to scholarship only through phenomenological description and careful interpretation, that the study of religion has so effectively driven a wedge between what is real (ideality or essence) and what is not (materiality or manifestation). That what is real is real *precisely because* of a complex association of pre-existent social grammars, which advantage some and not others, is a conclusion completely lost to this methodology.

Only if we come to the so-called data already equipped with such categories as sacred/secular, religion/politics, ahistory/history, and being/becoming will we come back with information on how our subjects live in this or that "mode of existence" (another vague Eliadean category which begs the very question) and how they negotiate and surmount this existentially unnerving polarity through religious symbolism. Simply put, as Ivan Strenski has so convincingly pointed out in his study of myth theorists and their work, categories such as *coincidentia oppositorum* are prescriptions disguised as descriptions. Indeed, the ultimate prescriptive or constructive category we come armed with is "religion" itself. It is this category, as well as the institutionalized manner in which we study "it" as a self-evidently autonomous aspect of interior human experience and subjectivity, that most deserves our anthropological and political analysis in the post-Eliadean era.

If one reads such categories as *coincidentia oppositorum* as a prescription based on unarticulated, implicit theories and interests, one can plainly identify the central but generally unrecognized role played by a pervasive liberal ideology throughout the modern study of religion. In other words, Eliade's work betrays not so much theological influences, as many of his critics have contended, but instead a pernicious social and political ideology which seeks to collapse unmanageable heterogeneity (e.g., diverse, worldwide beliefs and practices) into an interior zone of utter homogeneity (e.g., the experience of the sacred). In Eliade's writings of the 1960s, this process went by the name of the "new humanism" – something that Rennie somehow sees to be an anticipation of post-modernism (1996: 75). Like his thoughts on religious experiences themselves, then, Eliade's own integration of all human experience ultimately into such categories as *homo religiosus*, the implicitly sacred, the apparently desacralized West, and the sacred

East, collapses all opposition into identity and disciplines difference as utter unity. Like the liberal program in which the mosaic of the whole is said to incorporate and fulfill the particulars, "the opposition of the polarities ... is resolved [and] falls into an homogenous totality" (Rennie 1996: 38). However, it is a totality that maligns the particular, local, and historical in favor of a supposedly universal tendency, intuitive experience, and ahistorical insight.

As should now be evident, much as Eliade concocted a uniform subjectivity by maintaining that religion could only be studied on its own plane of reference, so too Cave and Rennie study Eliade on his own plane of reference and thereby reinforce the presumed seamlessness of human subjectivity. Presuming that talk of such things as the whole, totality, the real, unmediated experiences, and, one of my personal favorites, Rennie's discussion of Eliade's notion of symbols as expressing "an otherwise non-sensory modality of the real" (1996: 51), are mere descriptions, both writers demonstrate not only the ease with which the Eliadean jargon lulls like-minded readers into a non-critical stupor but also the primary means by which this entire debate on the politics of scholarship is constrained and obscured from the start.

A very useful example of the obscurantism that results from the application of this ideological posture to the Eliade affair can be found in a book published the year before Cave's: Carl Olson's, *The Theology and Philosophy of Mircea Eliade* (1992).[11] In his opening chapter, Olson writes:

> Even if Eliade was a hard-core Fascist throughout his life, for which I have not found any evidence, this political ideology did not affect his scholarship to any sinister extent, and it is unjust to taint someone and to judge them guilty by association. How can we come to grips with Eliade's prewar association with the Iron Guard? Before and after the war, it can be concluded, by reading his *Autobiography*, that he was a patriot and a Rumanian nationalist concerned with his nation's historical past, present dictatorial bondage, and uncertain future; he was also concerned with preserving its culture during its period of diaspora for its artists and intellectuals after the Second World War. Eliade's patriotic fervor is evident in his notion of 'Romanianism,' a non-political nationalism that embodied a messianic sense of the divinely-chosen nature of the Rumanian nation with a special mission to fulfil in the world.
>
> (Olson 1992: 44–45)[12]

It is gratuitous, to say the least, to assert that any scholarly work remains unaffected, or at least unaffected to any "sinister extent," by political ideologies. To make such an argument, one would have to presume that history impacts ideas or actors to varying degrees – a presumption entirely out of place in this current study but one in keeping with Eliade's and Rennie's construction of subjectivity. Just as in the case of other interpreters of Eliade's time in Romania, Olson attempts to limit any of his political involvements to early or youthful indiscretions – what Norman Girardot has called "the sins of his youth" and his "youthful transgressions" (2001: 158) – thereby protecting his later scholarly works from exposure to any sinister indictment. (Another common strategy is to limit political influence to Eliade's youthful journalism, thereby protecting his "serious" and mature scholarship.) Olson presumes a problematic notion of just what we mean by "political," as if it only refers to organized party politics as opposed to the more pervasive ways in which we routinely allocate power and authority. Even more troubling is Olson's commonly shared understanding of the relations between patriotism and nationalism; according to him, only the latter seems to be related to political motives or intentions while the former seems to be non-political or merely cultural. In terms of how dominant ethnic, social, and political groups use these concepts, "patriotism" (e.g., British or American patriotism) is understood as essentially positive, inspiring, and as affirming some sort of neutral cultural heritage, whereas "nationalism" (e.g., Québécois or Serbian nationalism) is interpreted as threatening, politically and militarily loaded, and therefore dangerous. It should be obvious, however, that there is no difference whatsoever between the two; for when someone on our side dies in an effort to maintain or destabilize certain political, social, or economic practices they are a patriot; and when someone on their side does the exact same thing, they are a nationalist zealot or a terrorist. It should be apparent that there is much at stake, both politically and socially, in maintaining the illusion of difference.

Furthermore, it is puzzling how Olson could read such profoundly political assertions as those regarding the so-called mystical and messianic mission of a divinely chosen nation as being in any way apolitical or merely patriotic. Simply put, I have no idea what "non-political nationalism" means (this category has remarkable similarity to "civil religion," a concept examined in the final chapter of this book). It virtually amounts to reading the divine right of monarchs as a merely spiritual or benignly cultural claim, as if *that* makes any sense at all. Although such a claim may make sense to those with a stake in such rhetoric – a U.S. audience comes to mind where claims regarding the country's divinely chosen mission, or Manifest Destiny, or patriotism as something apart from nationalism, all have a long, rich history – our role as redescriptive scholars is not to perpetuate such rhetorics but to contextualize, to historicize, and to explain them. Surely few modern scholars of religion would fail to recognize the highly political nature of such claims if, for example, they were made in the rhetoric of a so-called fundamentalist context. Is it too much to ask that we study our own groups with the same critical eye? Therefore, Olson's exclusion of potent political implications from critical examination is itself a highly suspicious strategy.

And last, Olson's uncritical use of disclosures found in Eliade's *Autobiography* confirms an important aspect of our field already seen in the work of Cave and Rennie: presuming religion to be an essentially personalistic, irreducible experience, actors are granted first-person interpretive authority when it comes to accounting for the details, meanings, and origins of their own experiences and lives (on the complexities of this issue, see Godlove [1994]). This is precisely what we see happening when commentators read Eliade on his own "plane of reference," as if their work was a self-legitimizing exercise in hagiography.[13] Now, this is not to say that scholars should instead routinely suspend the informant's right to interpret and explain his or her own actions and beliefs, but *that scholars must carefully devise defensible criteria to determine at what level of analysis they do or do not suspend such first-person explanatory authority.*

This is the crucial methodological point that such writers as Robert Segal and Wayne Proudfoot told us some time ago; without taking such participant reports, interpretations, and systems of thought seriously we would have no descriptive data to study, for our scholarship theorizes not simply other people's observable behaviors but also their own understandings of, and explanations for, these behaviors (i.e., theology is our object of study). Despite the fact that we as scholars might find certain sorts of physical behavior to be of interest, what we are often more attracted to is the fact that some people make sense of their behavior by appealing to such things as demonic possession or revelations. Were we to offer such people the same interpretive privilege that commentators often afford Eliade, we as scholars would have little to do but report on insider accounts. Instead, these reports are the data for our theoretically based efforts at historicization.

The way in which many commentators seem to find no good reason to read Eliade's various published journals and his two-volume autobiography as data rather than as an authoritative, transparent account of his motivations and intentions is, once again, evidence of the general suspicion of theorizing, explanation, and analysis that abounds in the regnant discourse. Indeed, Eliade's journals and the autobiography provide important points of access into this debate but surely they are not to be taken as self-evidently authoritative, read simply as Eliade's "actual thought," or as his unvarnished self-disclosures. As with all self-disclosures, they make certain subjectivities possible while excluding others. Such a prioritizing of the insider's claims at the expense of the outsider's analytic perspective is characteristic of an undefended scholarly intuition regarding what we can only term an essential experience that apparently grounds all behavior; such an intuitive basis for the field leads the way for scholars simply to become, in Bruce Lincoln's words, collectors, cheerleaders, and voyeurs, or in Burton Mack's words, caretakers for religion rather than critics of culture.

Explicitly related to Olson's obscurantism is the defense of Eliade offered in an earlier article by Rennie. In his otherwise useful response to Berger's critique of Eliade's wartime activities (Berger 1989), Rennie obscures the wartime nationalist and xenophobic activities of certain elements of the Romanian population by painting a sympathetic picture of their historical lot as an oppressed people continually striving to deal with the burden of foreign domination (see Rennie 1992 as well as 1996: 149–159). With its annexation of

Transylvania, which contributed to the doubling of Romania's size after World War I, the Romanians, according to Rennie, were finally "free from foreign domination ... [and] were determined not to cede Romanian self-determination to internal foreign influences" (1992: 376). That the rhetoric of "internal foreign influences" begs questions of the criteria used to determine ethnic and nationalist purity seems wholly lost on Rennie. As well, it is unlikely that one could find a better example of the relations between nationalism and the devaluation of others than in his comments on the Transylvanian annexation: with that annexation in mind, we can see that Rennie's comment on Romanians finally being "free from foreign domination" takes on an ironic tone. His description sounds remarkably like a rationalization for the later ethnic and religious oppression and victimization in Romania. Simply put, one can assume that the Transylvanians who awoke to find themselves part of Romania were not necessarily as pleased with the new geographic, nationalist realities as were the newly "liberated" Romanians.

Much as Olson excuses Eliade by understanding his actions as arising from "patriotic fervor" and a sense of "non-political nationalism," Rennie goes on to excuse Eliade from lending his explicit support to the cause of the Romanian fascist movement on the grounds of *ethnic purity*; that is, because, according to Rennie, the Archangel Movement was "at least *genuinely* Romanian" (emphasis added) as opposed to the new Romanian King's Italian- and German-influenced policies. According to Rennie's interpretation, then, Eliade's stand at this time is not so much political but ethnic and cultural – as if this troublesome distinction somehow assists us to understand the situation any better. However, at no time does he question just what is *genuine* about one's ethnic status and why such a status implies an apolitical privilege of some sort. Such claims are based on a spurious, essentialist understanding of social identity.

Also like Olson, Rennie explains away the eventual violent anti-Semitism of the Iron Guard to such attitudes as "blind nationalism" and "fanatical nationalism" (1992: 386, 387), both of which are akin to what he later characterizes as "virulent nationalism." These various causes are implicitly contrasted with Eliade's own motivations, termed by Rennie "essential humanism" (1992: 388) – I am reminded here of the opening of Olson's quotation where we found the implicit distinction between fascism and hard-core fascism, a distinction not that far from certain defenders of Heidegger who labeled him simply a "normal Nazi." Through speculation and arbitrary distinctions, Rennie protects Eliade from all accusations of fanaticism or nationalism and portrays his ambitions as somehow non-virulent and insightful rather than dangerous and blind. The use of the adjectives blind, fanatical, and virulent are evidence of a normative judgment that ensures that the actions of some people are held at the margins, far from the privileged cultural, spiritual, and apolitical center. Accordingly, this one representation of Eliade, and its possible uses, benefits tremendously from this implicit and unquestioned construction of a margin far removed from what we must simply accept as self-evidently and purely cultural and apolitical commitments and motives. As implied by Rennie, one appears to be held accountable for one's actions and beliefs only at the margin.

Although it is highly questionable to what extent one can determine Eliade's intentions and motivations concerning his early associations and how such associations affected his later work in religion, what is of particular interest are the ways in which Eliade's apologists have constructed their replies to such criticisms. Instead of, for example, discounting Strenski's and Berger's criticisms as being based on, say, amateur psychologizing and utter speculation – which is not to say that I would make such a critique of their work – his defenders engage in their own form of psychologizing, speculation, and obscurantism to construct elaborate interpretive edifices that function to isolate a portion of Eliade's history and/or his work, thereby ensuring that a highly abstract, essential image of Eliade *qua* intellectual remains aloof from the undisciplined terrors of historical, political existence. Implicitly, in all of these cases the phenomenological *epoché* is employed to segment, isolate, and thereby protect Eliade from his own life, work, and the academic discipline he helped to make possible.

In fact, such protection is so effective that it is the basis for Rennie's recent attempt to rehabilitate Eliade's ideological program of conceptualizing religion as an essential, universal, and total human experience capable of saving western civilization by appropriating supposedly archaic values. In his foreword to Rennie's *Reconstructing Eliade*, Mac Linscott Ricketts goes so far as to suggest that Rennie's reconstruction of Eliade's thought provides "a guide in religious studies for years to come, in an increasingly secular and postmodern twenty-first century" (Rennie 1996: ix). I do not agree: the future of the post-Eliadean field will have much more to do with a critical inquiry into the theoretical as well as the social and political interests encoded by means of the very categories and tools that scholars employ in their studies of human behavior and institutions (e.g., we will study the very distinction between the so-called sacred and secular for it has been one of the most effective rhetorical means for constructing a privileged realm of non-political human behavior). If anything, Rennie's book is not so much a programmatic guide for the future, as suggested by Ricketts, but possibly the final chapter in a closed canon, thus allowing us, in the words of Roger Corless, now to "close the Eliadean era with dignity" (1993: 377; see also 2001: 3, 9). Corless advises: "We must completely rethink what we mean by 'religion(s)' and what we think we are doing when we 'study' it/them" (2001: 4).[14] Taking his lead, I can say that, instead of uncritically deploying such ostensibly descriptive categories as the sacred, the real, Being, and experience, the post-Eliadean study of religion ought to be concerned with the ways in which power and authority are constructed and legitimated through so-called religious claims and practices *as well as* through the very scholarship on such beliefs and behaviors.

Because the three main chapters of Robert Ellwood's already mentioned *The Politics of Myth* (1999) situate Jung's, Eliade's, and Campbell's autobiographies and attempts at therapeutic social interventions within the context of their political times, Ellwood's work might be seen by some to herald the dawn of this new post-Eliadean era. After all, he clearly understands scholars to swim in these murky historical waters. Yet, typically, there are a number of subtle qualifications to his admission that these writers' politics are of relevance to their work and these qualifications are what ought to attract our attention. For example, after completing the chapter on Eliade, I was left with the distinct impression that what Ellwood and others refer to as Eliade's essentially pure, "higher" motives for a "nonpolitical nationalism" meant that he only grudgingly supported Romanian Fascist movements – holding his nose all the time, as it were. How else is one to read Ellwood's various asides (all emphases are added): "Eliade, *after some initial resistance*, was caught up in the Iron enchantment" (1999: 82); "This side of the movement [what Ellwood acknowledges as the indisputably violent, anti-Semitic side of the Iron Guard] *obviously gave pause to Eliade*" (84); "*Though perhaps with distaste*, Eliade seemed willing to accept the Legion's violence and anti-Semitism as a price that had to be paid for national resurrection" (88). Given these qualifications, when we come across Ellwood's conclusion, "Though nothing can excuse Eliade's enthusiasms," the wary reader awaits the other shoe to drop – and it does: "two factors may at least help us to understand [these enthusiasms] ..." (89).

Although understanding writers within their historic context hardly amounts to a defense of, or a support for, their viewpoint and actions, such repeated qualifications and speculations on an author's sensibilities are hard to read as anything but an attempt to downplay, in this case, Eliade's decisions, all in an effort to redeem him/his corpus, as if some essentially well-meaning, humanistic core floats over the waves of these so-called youthful indiscretions. As with others who try to defend mid-twentieth-century writers, I am left wondering just what sort of defense is mounted when the best one can do is to conclude, as does Ellwood: "In the context of his [Eliade's] times he was not the most chauvinistic of his countrymen" (84). This is hardly a ringing endorsement: "he may be bad but he wasn't the worst." Hardly persuasive also is the oft-repeated claim that Eliade couldn't have been anti-Semitic since he was friends with the Jewish novelist, Mihail Sebastin; is there any need for me to point out that the old "some of my best friends are" defense is a desperate and pretty damning rhetorical flourish?

Because of such features as the strategically useful distinctions between scholarship and journalism, youth and maturity, periphery and center, politics and spirit, the limitations placed on socio-political origins and influences, and the elevation of insider reports to the status of authoritative analysis, the representations of Eliade's defenders invite further scrutiny. Their virtual dismissal of contextualist or so-called external and secondary criticism is unwarranted insomuch as it is based on an uncritical use of Eliade's own troublesome categories and existential judgments. To paraphrase Christopher Norris commenting on similarly suspect defenses of Heidegger, the works of Cave, Olson, Rennie, and Ellwood cause us to ask why "certain intellectuals – among them thinkers of great acuity and power ... should have gone to such great lengths of ingenious argumentation" to protect Eliade's work from criticism and debate (Norris 1990: 242). For, although Cave acknowledges that indeed Eliade was "right-wing" (1993: 6), although Olson recognizes that Eliade's scholarship was indeed affected by political ideologies, although Rennie comes to agree that Eliade was "fiercely nationalistic" (1996: 143), and although Ellwood states that Eliade seemed willing to accept the Legion's violence, all four rely on ingenious ways of marginalizing and lessening the impact of these admissions. For Cave, the genius of Eliade forces us to accept the tares along with the wheat (1993: 21); Olson asserts that Eliade's non-political nationalism did not affect his scholarship to any sinister extent; Rennie maintains that Eliade's texts, when read exclusively in an Eliadean fashion, present a "deliberate statement of the author's intentions" (1996: 148); and Ellwood has us believe that Eliade held his nose while associating with many of his friends. In fact, Rennie goes on to defend Eliade by arguing that he was no more nationalist or anti-Semitic than his peers, for he "was just as opposed to Bulgarian and Hungarian usurpation of Romanian autonomy as he was of Jewish [usurpation]" (1996: 151). Defending Eliade by maintaining that he disliked "the Jews" as much as many other groups simply serves as a biting indictment of both Eliade and his defenders.

Whether or not Eliade was an anti-Semite, a nationalist, and a fascist – let alone a hardcore one! – the presence in his defenders' works of such weak arguments, unfounded assertions, the rhetoric of primacy, actuality, autonomy, and authenticity, as well as the use of such vacuous concepts as "unmediated experience," "the real," and "non-political nationalism," all suggest that there is much at stake in the Eliade affair. What is at stake is not simply the reputation of the man Eliade, as some may think, but also the ability of a group of scholars to continue to define their object of study and themselves as experts by means of assertion and intuition rather than by means of explicit theories, evidential criteria, and rational argumentation. As stated by Murphy in the epigraph to this essay, "what is at stake in these debates is a struggle over what the study of religion itself should be. Eliade has [simply] become a focal point for the ongoing identity crisis in the field" (Murphy 1994: 383). This struggle, then, is over the fate of a discipline conceived as an apolitical, autonomous, and irreducible intellectual and institutional pursuit. Accordingly, *all* scholars of religion have a stake in the Eliade affair.

The study of religion conceived as the description and appreciation of a private, *sui generis* experience exists precisely by camouflaging and obscuring not only the social, political, and economic origins and implications of so-called religious experiences but also the political interests and implications of the academic discourse on these experiences.[15] Because the very techniques by which Eliade has been defended are the same techniques by which scholars established and continue to maintain the autonomous study of religion in North America, addressing claims of extreme politics in the field in any systematic manner will entail a far greater and more sustained effort than we have so far seen. What's more, the difficulty of tackling these structural issues is further compounded by the fact that they are the same techniques whereby other, larger social groups have established and reproduced themselves – groups such as the nation-state (a point to be explored in coming chapters). Consider the case of several autobiographical asides in Ellwood's book, asides that provide interesting clues as to the appeal writers like Eliade and Campbell held for students in the 1960s, the generation that re-established our field in the U.S. The "Eliade effect" – which, if my current students are any measure, continues unabated to this day – is evident at the outset of the book:

> One day [in 1962 while Ellwood was a U.S. Marine chaplain stationed in Okinawa], I came across a review of one of Eliade's books. Something about the account led me to believe it might help. I ordered the slim volume, read it, and suddenly the significance of a wholly new way of looking at religion arose into consciousness: not theological, but in terms of its phenomeno-logical structures. ... It was one of those books that make one think, 'This was really true all the time, but I didn't realize it until now.' Soon I left the chaplaincy and enrolled as a graduate student under Mircea Eliade at the University of Chicago Divinity School.
>
> (1999: 5)

Just what Ellwood needed "help" with was dealing with what he later terms "modernity's pluralism of space and time" (111): "I could not help but believe that some indefinable spiritual presence lingered in the lovely sylvan shrines of Shinto, or that there was more than mere atmosphere in the great peace that filled temples of the Buddha" (5). Jung's, Eliade's, and Campbell's works seem to have allowed already alienated, mid-twentieth-century people to depart from a specifically local and sectarian perspective and embark on an equally salvific quest for what Ellwood calls "benign pluralism," a truly liberal quest in which the "good" of the comparative method is that it "enables one to experience vicariously the passions of other faiths as well as one's own, so leading to the enrichment of total human experience" (110–111). Simply put, the attraction of the field for those disillusioned with denominationalism was its ability to shift the ground from inevitably conflicting claims to *Truth* to infinitely variable *meanings*, "and by meaning is denominated that which comes from a universal source but is congruous with one's own dreams and deepest significant fantasies" (177). Armed with what ends up being all things to all people, how could the History of Religions fail to win converts? The attraction to studying myth, then, is obvious for, expressing the core assumption of this tradition, Ellwood writes: "Myth, like all great literature, can become universal, transcending particular cultural settings" (177). It is to his credit, however, that Ellwood immediately cautions his readers: "the mythologists ... did not always take into account that myth, like everything human, can be of quite varied moral worth. ... [A]bstractions are not the solutions to problems."

The "Eliade effect" and the role it played in moving one's gaze from sectarian contests over Truth to liberal preoccupations with homogenizing, intuited meaning is confirmed by Norman Girardot's own personal reflections (2001). Recalling how his young Jesuit professor at Holy Cross added Eliade's *The Sacred and the Profane* to the reading list for his honors class in theology, Girardot describes the manner in which first Eliade's work and then, as a graduate student at Chicago in the late-1960s, Eliade's personal influence assisted him in dealing with what he remembers as "the quaintly absurd folklore" and the "magical-mystery spookiness" (145) of the "ridiculously arcane theological and sacramental matters" (146) that characterized his Roman Catholic upbringing in the 1950s. Much like Ellwood, Girardot recalls that "there was a delicious thrill in reading something that seemed both to explain and challenge everything I had learned about religion" (147). As with Ellwood, then, Eliade's totalizing work assisted Girardot in displacing his previously taken-for-granted and all consuming socio-semantic world as being merely "delightfully wacky" and thus "parochial" and "provincial" (146).

"It's hard to say now what exactly it was about Eliade that affected me," he writes,

> I am sure that it generally had something to do with his openness to bizarre new worlds of meaning, an embracing of forms of strangeness that even went beyond the strangeness of my own tradition. ... Whatever it was, it was exhilarating for a wide-eyed and increasingly disloyal Catholic boy. ... In January of 1966 therefore (a time when the concerted bombing of North Vietnam was just beginning), I left the wooded hills of Hanover, New Hampshire, to drive to the gray Midwestern city of Chicago where I would begin my exploration of the promise and possibility of strange religions first suggested by *The Sacred and the Profane*.
>
> (147, 148)

This liberal refashioning of dogmatic Truth into elusive yet transpersonal meanings – a refashioning to which writers such as Clifford Geertz equally contributed at this time – brings us back to the issue of a writer's innocence or guilt or a story's supposedly enduring "moral worth"; for only if we presume human beings to have some sort of trans-historical, meaningful, moral center – variously called Soul, a Morality, Experience, Human Nature, or the Human Spirit – is it necessary to absolve or indict our intellectual predecessors or the tales groups tell. If we disagree with Ellwood in thinking that "evil is, by its intrinsic nature, irrational" (58) and instead see "evil" and "good" as all too understandable rhetorical tools social groups deploy in order to authorize and reproduce essentially contestable values and worlds, then we will have a rather different understanding of the politics of scholarship on myth or religion, let alone the politics of myth and religion themselves. We may then continue reading scholars like Jung, Eliade, and Campbell, not as exemplars but instead as relics – in the sense of artifact rather than venerable object. Only such a shift will enable us to come upon such writers not with the intention either to praise or chastise them – specifically, I have in mind here what one reviewer has characterized as Wasserstrom's "moral outrage" and "righteous indignation" in critiquing Eliade among others (Benavides 2001a: 449, 450) – but merely to treat them as the complex actors they – and we – undoubtedly are.

Ironically, however, the very techniques of exclusion, isolation, and protection that in the Eliade affair most deserve critique are the same strategies that provide what, along with Norris (1990: 257), we can term the discourse's conditions of possibility and its unthought axiomatics; the theoretical and methodological means by which "religion" is conceptualized and inductively studied as a seemingly autonomous, self-evident essence are therefore the strategies that also allow scholars to construct a discourse that evades the terrors of their own unruly history. These techniques simultaneously comprise a way of conceptualizing people and their interactions as well as providing the necessary blind spot that prevents those who use them from ever recognizing or addressing questions of extreme politics. This suggests that it may in fact be utterly impossible for many members of the discourse on *sui generis* religion to address the issues raised in this chapter, for it will require them to think the unthinkable, insulated as they and their datum are from the pressures of historical, political existence. As the final chapter will argue, this is an ironic insulation since the very notion of "religious experience" may well help to make possible political institutions as we know them today.

If it is only by addressing these theoretical, methodological, and ideological strategies that we can close the Eliadean era in the study of religion with any dignity at all, and thereby make room for a newly invigorated field of study, then it means that we must retool the field from top to bottom – from our curricula, to our public presence, the structures of our scholarly meetings, and our research agendas and publications. In the process, we will be redescribing how we define, classify, compare, and explain human behaviors and institutions in the public university – something addressed throughout the chapters in this book. Murphy was therefore correct in pointing out that the critique of Eliade's politics and the reception of his work in North America is much more than a mere case of being either for or against Eliade – a portrait of this debate that constitutes one way to trivialize and dismiss it. Instead, it is a critique of the way the dominant tradition carries out its work in the academy. What's more, the fact of Murphy's critical insight, along with the artful but, nonetheless, unsuccessful apologetics of some of our peers, makes it clear that this onetime dominant approach has now entered a residual phase, where its assertions regarding the special status of religion are no longer as convincing. Although one would be naive to disagree cavalierly with Beane when he opines that "the method, thought, and insights of Mircea Eliade on the nature and study of religion are simply not going to be interred so easily" (2001: 165), this one apologist's choice of imagery – the tomb – is significant, for it suggests that even

Eliade's defenders recognize – though they have, perhaps, not yet accepted – that an era has past.

Notes

1   An earlier form of this chapter was presented to the History of the Study of Religion Group of the American Academy of Religion, New Orleans, November 24, 1996. Portions of that conference paper relied on work eventually published in greater detail in McCutcheon 1997b. A slightly revised version of the AAR paper eventually appeared as a chapter in Bryan Rennie's edited volume, *Changing Religious Worlds: The Meaning and End of Mircea Eliade* (2001a). The following is a revised version of that chapter, and includes evidence from more recent works that also minimizes or argues away the politics of the study of religion. I am flattered that Rennie, as the person who invited my original AAR paper for inclusion in his edited volume, found it necessary to write a concluding chapter (2001a: 263–281) in which he replies in detail to a number of the points I make in this chapter, going so far as to inform his readers that my critique is "hopeless" (2001a: 278). Although I do not respond to his comments in the body of this chapter, I do so in several endnotes.

2   Specifically I have in mind the degree to which the most prominent deconstructive critic, Jacques Derrida, has been explicitly involved in both debates. See what Christopher Norris has termed Derrida's compassionate essay, "Like the Sound of the Sea Deep within a Shell" (Derrida 1988) on de Man and his wartime articles, as well as Derrida's response to the critical reception of this very article (Derrida 1989). See also the other essays published in the same issue of *Critical Inquiry* (15/4) that respond to Derrida's essay on de Man. On the de Man affair see also Werner Hamacher *et al.* 1988 and 1989. Concerning the case of Heidegger, see the essays by, among others, Hans-Georg Gadamer, Jürgen Habermas, and Derrida, in *Critical Inquiry* (15/2 [1989]). On the controversy surrounding Derrida's wishes to remove one of his own essays from Richard Wolin's collection on Heidegger (as documented in Wolin 1993: ix–xx), see Thomas Sheehan's (1993) *New York Review of Books* review of Wolin (1993) and the many spirited subsequent letters to the editor written by those involved in this controversy, published in the early months of 1993.

3   Apart from an earlier version of this chapter, those chapters in Rennie's edited volume that are openly critical are by Corless (2001) and Murphy (2001).

4   For example, consider the fact that, apart from Rennie's own spirited rebuttal to those critics who have tackled Eliade's politics (see his editor's conclusion [Rennie 2001a]), both the personal politics of Eliade and the politics of the field as practiced in an Eliadean manner are largely irrelevant to many of the contributors to his edited collection on Eliade. The concerns of one of his contributors, David Cave, are so far from these issues that he is preoccupied with how Eliade's "understanding of sacred space can help us advance human excellence" (Cave 2001: 248). Such an irrelevancy can be found as well in various contributions to other recent essay collections concerned with the shape of the modern field (e.g., Idinopulos and Yonan 1994, 1996; Idinopulos and Wilson 1998).

5   As phrased by Masuzawa, "Why did they [Gershom Scholem, Henri Corbin, and Mircea Eliade, the three scholars examined by Wasserstrom] become so influential despite their eccentric orientation? How did those in the religious and scholarly communities come to embrace those seemingly unorthodox, idiosyncratic representations of the tradition? What was their appeal?" (2001: 436); as phrased by Urban, "*Why did Eliade's school of the history of religions become the predominant model in the American study of religions during the period from 1956 to 1986?*" (2001b: 442; emphasis in the original). Urban goes on to conjecture on an answer with his

following sentence: "What were the *specific links* between this model of the history of religions and real U.S. Cold War policy?" (On this question see the important recent conference volume, Doležalová *et al.* 2001.) The final chapter will make an effort to further the argument that a particular rhetoric of "religion" plays a central role in all acts of social formation.

6   My thanks to Charles Lock, of the University of Toronto's English Department, who first put the matter in precisely this way during the defense of my doctoral dissertation in January 1995.

7   Directed by Peter Cohen and available through First Run Features Home Video.

8   Likely, this goes without saying. However, to make the point clear, it is not hard to imagine a host of human behaviors where these very scholars would have no trouble dropping their phenomenological neutrality and, instead, would rush to condemn the object under study. A general methodological point becomes apparent here: if the methods we use to study religion cannot be extended to the study of *any and all* human behaviors, then what business have we studying religion, or the self-disclosures of so-called religious people, in such a sympathetic manner?

9   Subsequent to first making this critique, Rennie has replied that his analysis "will never be anything other than my own interpretation. And by secondary scholars I intend only scholars who study other, particularly recent, scholars, rather than studying religious phenomena. As such, I emphatically do include myself in the category of secondary scholars" (2001a: 265). I am not sure this clarifies anything since the authority of his interpretation – and his claims concerning others' "fundamental misapprehensions" (1996: 4) of Eliade's meaning – now appears merely to be one among many. I therefore cannot understand how his interpretive framework is any more useful, right, accurate, or persuasive an apprehension of Eliade's "actual thought." Moreover, his distinction between secondary interpretations and any author's "actual thought" is a rather different distinction than the one cited above in his reply to my criticism of his earlier use of this purely rhetorical distinction (insomuch as we have no access to a stable, uniform "author's intention," then it is interpretation all the way down!). For example, in 1996 he wrote:

> I will attempt to mitigate against the possible ill-effects of this fact [i.e., that his book is inevitably his own interpretation of Eliade's work] by referring as often as an acceptable style will allow to the primary sources. Of course, even the primary sources suffer somewhat from the difficulties of translation and the influences of institutional context. Even so, it is better to read and attempt to analyze what has actually been written than to rely on derived statements of one's own construction. If this has led me to use overly long quotations, it is due to my desire for accuracy and my efforts to avoid the dangers of paraphraseology.
>
> (1996: 5)

It is obvious that, in his 1996 book, the primary/secondary distinction refers to Eliade's own writings vs. mere interpretations of them. I therefore stand by my earlier critique; however, even if "primary" referred to religious things themselves, which the above quote obviously does not (since Rennie is referring to his extensive use of long quotations of Eliade's writings, not long quotations of, say, Vedic texts), he nonetheless continues to presume some authenticity of a stable origin, whether that origin is an author's intentions or a pre-interpretive and thus pure religious phenomenon. This example of the manner in which Rennie's reply further obscures the issue in debate should cause readers to read his various rejoinders rather critically.

10 Such claims were challenged, in detail and at length, by Carl Olson (2000); see also Rennie's reply [2001b]). Portraying Eliade as a great fore-thinker (literally, a Promethian scholar not locked within his own time) is another common technique employed to resuscitate his work.

11 For a related critique of Olson's depoliticizing strategies, see the closing pages of Tim Murphy's review essay (Murphy 1994: 386–389).

12 Olson notes that Ricketts (1988: 903, 912) covers these same issues.

13 In his reply to an earlier version of this chapter, Rennie has written: "To study Eliade in his own terms might be deemed valuable and illuminating without any insistence that this is the only way to read him, wholly adequate, or that he is thus somehow *sui generis*" (2001a: 265). If indeed such readings are just one among many, then how is it that those who read Eliade "in his own terms" make repeated reference to other commentators' "fundamental misapprehensions"? Rennie appears disingenuous here, since his work is not presented as one reading among others but as the reading most faithful to Eliade's own intentions. That these intentions are somehow judged to be worth recovering and using should make it obvious that Eliade is held by such writers to be a special case, since there are a number of human actors whose intentions – if ever recoverable – would never be used in the study of their texts or actions. Once again, Rennie's reply proves inadequate.

14 Corless (2001: 3) cites Ninian Smart's review of Eliade's *The Encyclopedia of Religion*: "Maybe we are at the end of the Eliadean era, and, grateful for his great contributions, are also turning to new questions and themes" (1988: 197). Although the "new questions and themes" I work toward are not necessarily those of either Corless or Smart (e.g., the latter advised that we extend the category "religion" by seeing religious aspects in political movements), I am nonetheless indebted to both writers.

15 The explicit colonial history of comparative religion, at least in southern Africa, has been critically examined by David Chidester (1996a, 1996b).

Chapter 10

The perfect past and the irony of narrative

Bruce Lincoln's *Theorizing Myth*

> [I]f our knowledge is fragmentary, uncertain, or nonexistent, our history must take such ignorance into account. ... Origins belong to the intellectual and literary worlds, not to the world of events, either political or social.
>
> (Thompson 1999: 7, 31)

While my own autobiographical disclosures from chapter 8 are still fresh in our minds – comments pertaining to the hindsight construction of national identity so apparent to me while attending the 2000 IAHR Congress in Durban, South Africa – I would like to turn to a more detailed meditation on the role played by self-disclosures and narrative in acts of social formation. As previously mentioned, the work of Bruce Lincoln has been essential in assisting me to develop this understanding; therefore, I would like to examine in greater detail the role played by self-disclosure in his own recent book, *Theorizing Myth* (1999).

Those who tend to think that religion – or, more specifically, religious experiences and symbols – is somehow a special case, will surely wonder exactly what some of Lincoln's work has to do with the study of religion. However, those of us who find in so-called religious practices nothing that is different from the other practices that together constitute human cultures will understand what is to be gained by reading and applying methodologies from outside the rather narrow confines of hermeneutics and phenomenology. As I previously concluded, Lincoln is therefore among the few scholars of religion I would rename as anthropologists of credibility, for his work explores the displacements of, and contests over, such things as authenticity, legitimacy, meaning, and validity. His questions are therefore not, "What does it mean?" (where this "it" can stand in for text, ritual, symbol, etc.), but the more provocative, "How, why, and for whom does something come to mean in the first place?" and "What are the practical consequences of meaning?" To answer the first question means one needs to reproduce and thereby legitimize an indigenous socio-semantic system – after all, as demonstrated in the first chapter, "What does it mean" signals, "What does it mean for a specific group at a specific time?". Lincoln, however, is interested in accounting for how meaning works. For, as he phrases it in his thirteenth thesis on method:

When one permits those whom one studies to define the terms in which they will be understood, suspends one's interest in the temporal and contingent, or fails to distinguish between "truths", "truth-claims", and "regimes of truth", one has ceased to function as historian or scholar. In that moment, a variety of roles are available: some perfectly respectable (amanuensis, collector, friend and advocate), and some less appealing (cheerleader, voyeur, retailer of import goods). None, however, should be confused with scholarship.

(1996b: 13)

As already observed, it was precisely due to his work, then, that I found myself resisting the tempting nostalgia for "my home and native land"; instead, I became my own datum that warm summer evening in Durban.

Turning to *Theorizing Myth*, in the chapter on the English Orientalist William Jones (1746 – 1794) – one of the eighteenth-century fathers of the theory that a common source lies behind those languages others would name as Aryan or Indo-European (Lincoln 1999: 54) – Lincoln restates what I take to be the basic premise that enables us to resist the allure of nostalgia:

as objects of experience and of 'scientific' knowledge, primordial origins and perfect centers remain notoriously elusive. They are constituted as objects of discourse, not knowledge, by bricoleurs who collect shards of information and prior narratives, from which they confect the fictions that satisfy their otherwise unattainable desires while doing their ideological work. When students of myth ... succumb to this temptation and engage in a discourse of origins and centers, the results are particularly ironic.

(1999: 95)

Here we see Lincoln's commitment to a theory of social formation as tactical, hindsight adhocery – a theory that, he argues, applies to our work as scholars, and not just to the practices of the people we study. This quotation continues by observing that scholars of myth who "succumb to this temptation"

enter a recursive spiral, spinning their own myths while they sincerely believe themselves to be interpreting myths of others, others who may even be the product of their imagination and discourse.

There may be no simpler way to rephrase this than to quote the line from his book that will likely be cited in many of its reviews, a line quoted in my previous chapter: "If myth is ideology in narrative form," Lincoln writes in the epilogue, "then scholarship is myth with footnotes" (1999: 209; see also xii, 123, 147). *Theorizing Myth*, then, is an attempt to spin an oppositional tale, one that counters the old, old story concerning fanciful, epic *mythos* versus rational, Platonic *logos*. In his opening chapters Lincoln makes clear that what is ultimately at stake in Plato's – and our – distinction of *mythos* from *logos* is a rhetorical and thus political contest for the right to define what will count as the proper constitution of the state, the right to define the proper constitution of "the good," "the true" and "the just." Plato's *mythos* was not so much an innocent classificatory term as a tool effectively used to censure views he did not like in the arena of public discourse and persuasion.

With each subsequent chapter Lincoln presses his argument that the *mythos/logos* distinction has, most recently, been strategically allied to the creation of a European (and now North American) identity through expansionism, an interest for which people characterized as primitive, uncivilized, gullible, and thus provincial came in handy as needy beneficiaries of "civilization." If we throw in the once common view of European writers of the early modern era concerning the dawn of a slow but steady victory of science (*logos*) over mere superstition and religion (*mythos*), a dawn that must not only enlighten Europe but all the nations of the globe, we see once again that the classification "myth" is far from an innocuous academic label. It is, instead, a master signifier that authorizes and reproduces a specific world – whether that world accords with the triumph of science and modernity or with the romanticized recovering of some supposedly purer, more primitive, noble, or trans-human value upon which to base social identity and action. *Theorizing Myth*, then, is a book concerned with the socio-political work accomplished throughout the history of scholarship on myth.

There is a profoundly self-reflexive character to Lincoln's recent work, but it is a self-reflexivity that does not revel in finding one's deepest meanings lurking in the "other people's myths" (to refer to the work on myth done by his Chicago colleague, Wendy Doniger [e.g., 1986]); instead, Lincoln's reflexivity problematizes – or better, historicizes – all meaning-making industries, whether they are domestic or overseas imports. It was the impact of precisely this aspect of his work that prevented me from simply enjoying the homey nostalgia afforded by that movie in Durban, seeing it, instead, as something other than a neutral moment of innocent, globalized culture. As argued throughout *Theorizing Myth*, this sort of nostalgia for pristine origins and seamless identities is purchased at a misleadingly high price. As I have argued elsewhere, "it takes tremendous material and rhetorical effort to create ... romantic, mythic image[s]" (2001b: 95). Although not all discourses pay the same price, are characterized by the same rhetorical features, and contribute to the same social identities, Lincoln persuades his readers that they all have political, economic, and, simply put, ideological effects.

In keeping with Lincoln's commitment to self-reflexivity, I'd like to return to my earlier, self-implicating comments on my own fragmented national identity – return, that is, to the genre of self-disclosure and its relationship to social formation by way of the preface to *Theorizing Myth*. For, as I first read and then re-read the brief narrative disclosures Lincoln offers in his book's preface – especially in light of the book's overall and rigorous historicization of *all* discourses of identity, unity, and homogeneity – I found much the same irony and incongruity that I experienced in Durban. Now, I would be either naive or downright foolish to think that I've caught something in the text's opening pages of which Lincoln was not aware when he decided to start the book with a profoundly personal narrative of his family's history; thus, I have no interest whatsoever in pulling the rug out from under either him or his book by means of some game of "Gotcha."[1] Instead, I'd simply like to place on the table what I read as the book's apparently incongruous prefatory comments which seem to assume homogenous social identity and juxtapose them with Lincoln's own warning concerning what happens "[w]hen students of myth … succumb to this temptation and engage in a discourse of origins and centers." To anticipate where I'm going, let me simply ask whether calling mythmaking a "temptation" to which one sometimes "succumbs" in order to satisfy otherwise "unattainable desires" means that it could somehow be otherwise. Is it the case that, despite his best critical efforts throughout the main body of the text, Lincoln too has succumbed to these temptations when his guard dropped in his self-revelatory preface? Such a discourse on temptation and desire prompts me, in other words, to wonder whether we can somehow avoid plucking the alluring apple of myth, and, if so, do we see the shadow of traditional realism lurking in the background of Lincoln's otherwise critical method.

These questions are worth our attention because of the way in which self-disclosure can be used in scholarship. Disclosures of personal narrative, such as offered in the opening to this very book and sprinkled throughout some of its chapters, can be read as some sort of special pleading or as suggesting that all perspectives, all stories, are equally grounded and thus equally legitimate. Because former U.S. President Bill Clinton's onetime famous line, "I feel your pain," seems to be the only appropriate response to such disclosures, issues of evidence, fact, argumentation, and persuasion are thus feared by some to give way to sheer exclamation, assertion, and pronouncement. For example, take the way one reviewer commented on Lincoln's book. Instead of the book's coherence being determined by its relationship to the objective data under study, David White concludes that "[i]t is the person of Lincoln who holds these chapters together" (2001: 688). This description is both a criticism and a lament because White finds that Lincoln's focus upon the history and politics of a specific classificatory tool, "myth," and its relationship to another classificatory tool, "reason," prevents him from examining the plain old myths of this or that group and how these groups use them. It is this latter sort of scholarship that White finds more productive and more interesting. "Enclosed in his textualist cocoon of ancient mythic texts," writes White, "he [Lincoln] fails to see the active manipulation, now as then, of Hindu mythology by an array of Indian social actors, as a means of crushing religious practice that does not conform to their own limited version of Rama Rajya, their utopia" (689).

Elaborating, White concludes his review as follows:

> Hindu nationalist ideologues are today engaged in a project of systematic distortion of Indian religion, promulgating selected myth as history and

backing their propaganda campaigns with the force of violence against other Hindus, not to speak of Muslims and Christians. … When we shy away from offering "variant readings" of other people's myths in favor of criticism, that is, in favor of talking about ourselves talking about ourselves, we silence ourselves as interpreters of cultures, leaving the way open to modern-day demagogues, dilettantes, and journalists to define the discourse and appropriate or invent myths as history to their own ends. When outstanding scholars such as Lincoln abandon their fields of expertise to postmodern arguments that have been made repeatedly for a generation, they retreat from the battlefields of the culture wars, both domestic and foreign, that define our global landscape.

(690)

What is puzzling is the manner in which White himself relies upon a viewpoint that "has been made repeatedly for generations" in order to dismiss Lincoln's attempt to historicize a concept and its users. Instead, White simply employs the concept as if it referred seamlessly to the world. White's rhetoric is thus suitably modernist insomuch as those "ideologues" and "propagandists" are busy "distorting" this thing "Indian religion" to suit "their own ends." I gather that we, on the other hand, are professionals with specific "expertise" that somehow allows us to do something other than journalism and something not motivated by our own interests. Instead of troubling just what is and is not a myth or a religion, White wishes to get on with the business of determining how things we all know to be myths and religions ought and ought not to be used and interpreted. In doing this he fails to take seriously the sort of social theory that drives much of Lincoln's work. If indeed we are all social actors, none of whom has privileged access to the world by means of a god's eye viewpoint, then we are all employing related techniques for making this or that social world possible, thinkable, and actable – techniques marked by specific rhetorics with persuasive, coercive, and at times, outrightly bloody consequences. Taking this social theory seriously means that White, and not Lincoln, has shied away from the task of scholarship; in his eagerness to charge into the culture wars bearing the liberal banner, White's most useful weapon is the presumption that one discourse on human action is authoritative because it is disinterested and engaged with real cultural material, a disingenuous move for those persuaded that all actors are enmeshed in discursive efforts to recreate the conditions of their own material existence.

As should be obvious, I find White's rhetoric to be particularly revealing. For example, given his concern to critique the work of scholars such as Lincoln, I find it odd for him to announce that "the self-indulgent pursuit … of talking about ourselves talking about other people is one whose time has passed" (2001: 49). With a wave of the hand he seems to have dismissed all work in method and theory since such scholars are not talking about the myths "on their own terms," I gather. However, such a bold claim is inevitably self-defeating, given that it comes in an essay concerned with critiquing other scholars' work on other people. This irony notwithstanding, the boldness of White's pronouncement is matched only by the circularity of his reasoning:

> We may legitimately compare other people's myths not only because this is what we ought to be doing as scholars of religion, but also because when we do so we know that we are comparing relations and aspects rather than things.
>
> (53)

It seems that we compare because it is ethically proper to compare (i.e., we ought to compare, hence we compare) and, second, when we compare we are not reifying things but studying dynamic relations. The first part of this sentence comprises an example of what an Aristotelian might term an enthymeme, a highly successful rhetorical device in which those already in agreement with some unargued premise or ethical command easily draw the proper conclusion because of their unstated consensus on some matter. Technically speaking, enthymemes are not persuasive since only those already persuaded nod their heads approvingly. As Roland Barthes describes it:

> The enthymeme has the pleasure of a progress, of a journey: one sets out from a point which has no need to be proved and from there one proceeds toward another point which does need to be proved; one has the agreeable feeling (even if under duress) of discovering something new by a kind of natural contagion, of capillarity which extends the known (the opinable) toward the unknown. However, to produce all its pleasure, this progress must be supervised. ... [T]he enthymeme is not a syllogism truncated by defect or corruption, but because the listener must be granted the pleasure of contributing to the construction of the argument; it is something like the pleasure of completing a given pattern or grid.
>
> (1988: 60)

Quoting the *Port-Royal Grammaire Générale et Raisonnée*, which dates to 1660, Barthes concludes, "Such a suppression [of a part of the syllogism] flatters the vanity of those to whom one is speaking. ..." Enthymemes are thus social devices for building and expressing group cohesion.[2]

It is therefore ironic that White relies on the enthymeme in his critique of Lincoln's self-disclosures; for in attacking Lincoln as self-indulgent he quite effectively relies on a specific rhetoric to build a very specific group identity in opposition to Lincoln's. As White's above quotation went on to say, we are studying changeable relations exterior to self, not stable essences or things; however, this corrective to past historians of religions is hardly sufficient if we yet persist in believing that these relations are exterior to us, as if the observer watches passively as a world of activity passes by, each activity arriving on the scene with a specific label attached to it (e.g., "myth," "ritual," "magic," "superstition," etc.). Taking seriously that scholarship – the activity of classifying, describing, comparing – is a human activity, driven by specific, historical interests, and thus just as much part of this changeable, contestable world, means dropping the pretense of being above the fray and it means no longer portraying self-disclosure as self-indulgent. In fact, pretending that it could be otherwise, is the height of self-indulgence, for it coddles one particular sense of self/group, and leaves it standing as if it were alone and thus transcendent. These relations we study therefore do not exist somewhere out there but are relationships between groups of people in discourse and contest with each other, relationships established by people in the very act of naming and comparing. As Smith said, "[c]omparison provides the means by which *we* 're-vision' phenomena as *our* data in order to solve *our* theoretical problems" (1990b: 52) – I take his "we" to be significant, for it prevents Smith's readers from too easily reading his often quoted comments on "imagining religion" as the idle activity of the lone intelligence. Instead, I read him as telling us that comparison is, through and through, a social – and thus political – activity that comprises one of the necessary fictions of group membership; after all, much like meaning-making, such imaginative activity is a group activity that draws on pre-established conventions, scripts, techniques, grammars, interests, etc.

Therefore, if we take seriously Montaigne's observation that "we do nothing but write glosses on one another" (Essays, Bk. III, ch. XIII; 1936: 269), then group cohesion is made possible not only by such devices as texts and such techniques as comparison but also shared, public rhetorical conventions like White's enthymeme. Furthermore, if we investigate the conditions under which such things as, say, Lincoln's sense of self make possible such things as the text we are examining in this chapter, then contrary to White's lament, it is not "the person of Lincoln who holds these chapters together"; instead, a wider and publicly scrutinizable structural and rhetorical context accomplishes this act. After all, as argued by Anthony Elliott in a book aimed for the entry level undergraduate student,

> self-constitution is not only something that happens through our own actions. It is also something that happens to us, through the design of other people, the impact of cultural conventions and social practices, and the force of social processes and political institutions. Society disciplines and regulates the self, so that feelings about ourselves and beliefs about our identities are shaped to their roots by broader social forces and cultural sensibilities. ... [Moreover,] the self is not simply "influenced" by the external world, since the self cannot be set apart from the social, cultural, political, and historical contexts in which it is embedded. Social processes in part constitute, and so in a sense are internal to, the self.
>
> (2001: 2, 6)

Like the rhetorical convention of the enthymeme, self-disclosure too is evidence of a public, contestable context, and these contexts are open to study.

Although it would be inaccurate to suggest that White's scholarship on Hinduism is similar to, say, that of Eliade,[3] in reading his review of *Theorizing Myth* I could not help but be struck by the similarity of their tone. Although authorizing a rather different sense of what the study of religion ought to be (more on this below), they both wield the label of "dilettante," a favorite of Eliade's when referring to those who were not serious scholars, those who were provincials who merely dabbled, and those who blew in the breeze of what he termed cultural fashions (an instance of which would be postmodernism for White?). Although I admit to having been struck by the way in which autobiographical self-disclosures framed Lincoln's book, I fear something in his text – and something in the way social theory in our field can be used – is lost if we too quickly dismiss it by means of such labels. In the remainder of this chapter, then, I aim to re-read Lincoln's self-disclosures not merely as idle or self-indulgent navel-gazing (a reading made possible by White's realist and individualist understanding of the self), or the ongoing effort to wash away the sins of the fathers, but as an extended effort to problematize and thus historicize the manner in which such a sense of identity is continually made and remade. If indeed it is the person of Lincoln who holds this text together, then I suggest that the text makes it possible for readers to theorize just how it is that either his or their own sense of personhood can come about and can seem to endure.

To begin, then, let us turn to the actual preface. As was evident from an earlier chapter, prefaces are, in my estimation, the best parts of books – with epilogues coming in a close second (*Theorizing Myth* offers us both).[4] This is not just because that's where you find out who the writer's friends are and where you obtain enough descriptive information to write your book note for *Religious Studies Review*. Instead, it is because that is where the authorial voice speaks in a different cadence, often letting slip the guise of authority taken for granted throughout the rest of the text. When it comes to Lincoln's preface, after briefly describing the chapter-by-chapter plan of the book (ix–xii), we find a brief empty space, a silence provided by two hard returns, marking a break with the descriptivist's cool-headed detachment, and signaling, in its place, the beginning of the self-involved, autobiographical "I." The movement between these voices is made possible by Lincoln's understanding of scholarship as ideology in narrative form, an understanding that, he writes, "is a painful but important one for me, as I continue my struggle to extricate myself from a discipline, a paradigm, and a discourse that I adopted early in my academic career with insufficient critical reflection." "To a certain extent," he concludes, "writing this book has been an attempt to undo my earlier lack of awareness and make amends for it" (xii).

If *Theorizing Myth* could be seen as a confession, a coming-of-age tell-all (written, as all confessions and autobiographies are, by means of hindsight), then what follows the silence of the preface's abrupt empty space constitutes Lincoln's own origins tale; the opening paragraph reads as follows:

Although it is possible to view naïveté as a natural or innate condition, I have come to think mine was actively produced by specific choices, agents, forces, and circumstances. Reflecting on my past, I am drawn to a moment around 1955, when I was seven years old and my father was my hero. I knew he had been in the army and done service in North Africa and Italy, from the battle of Kesserine Pass through V-E Day. He never talked much about his experiences, however, which caused me some frustration. One day, I tried to learn more. "You're brave," I began, "You fought the Germans, and they were tough." He paused for a moment, then shocked me with his answer. "Not really," he said, "They were just like us: a bunch of scared kids." It was clear that he didn't want to discuss it further, and I don't think we ever returned to the subject. Still, I could draw a few lessons. We were no different from Germans. Fear was a mark of immaturity. Heroism was hard to find.

(xii)

One thing that I take away from this intimate passage – something suggested by its opening comment on the conditions that make naïveté possible – is the role played by silences in establishing limits, limits that distinguish allowable from disallowable, memorable from forgetful, who we are from who we wish to be, and therefore, us from them. Over the course of the next few pages these silences, as well as the coercive act of silencing, revisit Lincoln's narrative, as in when he observes that

[o]nly in my teens did I learn that my father had been blacklisted during the McCarthy period. Only later did I begin to hear about my relatives' involvement with radical causes. Religion was also little mentioned. Although nominally Jewish, my parents and grandparents were thoroughly secular, and we were all committed to the project of cultural assimilation. Occasionally I heard stories from my maternal great-grandmother about the pogroms she had known before leaving Russia in the 1890s. Such conversations were rare, however, and I was usually scooted out of the room when talk turned in that direction.

Although he notes that "the ethos of our household stipulated that one could talk about anything and that even the youngest had full conversational rights" (xiii), Lincoln recovers the hush that lies hidden in the cacophony of voices by understanding the silences to have originated in the desire to protect both him and his sister

from anything that might dispose us to fear. The Second World War was thus problematic, as were those pieces of family history that threatened to estrange us from the American mainstream and make us (feel) vulnerable to it. Many of my ancestors had been leftists: some Anarchists, some

Communists, some fellow travelers of various sorts. All had been Jews. Historically, other sorts of people – those who, in the recent past, had called themselves Aryan – had made it dangerous for people like us. In 1948, when I was born, all that was over, or so my parents hoped. Their determination to raise a fearless son has served me well for the most part, and I'm grateful to them, but their principled silences also left me shamefully naive.

(xiii)

Quoting these lines lends an air of illicit voyeurism, a quality that I hope to overcome; for, by opening chapter 9 with my own tale of incongruity and self-implication, I hope to have purchased the right to tackle the inevitable contradictions entailed by all acts of narrativization and social formation, whether this entails making scholars, making nations, or simply making families. So I broach the topic of Lincoln's narrative disclosures with the words of his epilogue echoing in my mind: "Students of myth seem particularly given to producing myths ... perhaps because the stories they tell about storytelling reflect back on them as storytellers. Their object of study also has crucial ambiguities at its core" (1999: 209).

I raise this point concerning "crucial ambiguities" at the core of our particular object of study, *Theorizing Myth*, because when first reading the personal disclosures quoted above, like White I too had to stop for a moment; on the one hand, I had read the quoted words of his father: " 'They [the German soldiers] were just like us,' " and, on the other hand, I had also read Lincoln's genealogical comment, "All had been Jews," he writes. The two statements struck me as being at odds with each other; it appears that, although *they* are like *us*, *we* are not like *them* whatsoever. Whereas *they* merely "called themselves Aryan" (the activity of naming connotes choice, contingency, in a word, Culture), it appears that something more than an act of self-classification may link Lincoln to his ancestors (suggesting the essentialist authority of Nature).

I had trouble reconciling the latter claim of familial homogeneity, continuity, and identity not only with the former comment about all of the soldiers simply being one large, undifferentiated group of "scared kids," but also with Lincoln's own admission that his family was a diverse group, some of whom, like his parents, were only "nominally Jewish" and were, instead, deeply committed to the process of cultural assimilation. This suggests to me that social identity exists on a sliding scale, a far cry from the sort of homogeneity shared by the adjective "all," an identity intimated by that admittedly brief sentence of Lincoln's that happened to catch my eye. Ironically, perhaps, I preferred the *heterogeneous* reading of social formation because it *harmonized* with other things I have learned from the work of Lincoln, not to mention a number of other social theorists.[5] Although there is certainly no rule that we must be entirely consistent in all we write or say – as Foucault recommended, "leave it to our bureaucrats and our police to see that our papers are in order" – I recalled one of

Lincoln's own comments in an essay on Barry Levinson's loosely autobiographical film, *Avalon*, where Lincoln observed: "this 'everyone' is a good deal more problematic than Eva [the matriarch of the film] indicates, since the people encompassed by this term participate within the social entity so designated only in imperfect and uneven fashion" (1996a: 165). Given the unevenness of social identity, an unevenness presupposed throughout the rest of *Theorizing Myth*, I was left wondering what "All had been Jews" was doing there, in the preface. Could it simply be an instance of unevenness in authorial voice and intent?

So I was left with the problem of irony, the issue of homogeneity versus heterogeneity, left wondering what to make of the, at least heuristically, useful distinction between scholarship on myth and myth itself, and left wondering where to place a particular author in all this. In that same essay on *Avalon*, Lincoln told his readers that "[t]hose who tell such stories ... tend also to be those who stand at the head of the group, who believe most deeply in the group, and in its myths (although sometimes it is a group's most manipulative and cynical members who become its narrators and leaders)" (1996a: 166). So I was left wondering whether Lincoln is the believer in the myth or the cynic – or, insomuch as he, like all of us, has an uneven identity insomuch as he is both scholar and family member, perhaps both believer and cynic.

Already having a sense about what Lincoln is up to in much of his scholarship, I came to *Theorizing Myth* anticipating that it would not deal with myths in some realist or formalist fashion, but, instead, would tackle head on what Adorno called the jargon authenticity (that I seem to detect in White's review), what Jonathan Z. Smith characterized as "a nostalgia for the fabled experience of the direct, non-mediated communication ... a yearning for the power to convert a 'talking-about' to a 'talking-with' through essentially non-linguistic means" (1990b: 54). It is precisely the rhetorical technique of nostalgia that lies in the background of our field's recurring preoccupation with, as cited earlier, the quest for pristine origins, perfect centers, and free-floating meanings. *Theorizing Myth*'s eleven chapters and epilogue far surpassed my expectation; chapter after chapter rigorously historicizes such jargons and nostalgias – perhaps better termed socio-rhetorics – as they were played out across several centuries of scholarship, making it difficult for any reader to put the book down and then continue re-telling either that old, old story about deceitful *mythos* versus coolly dispassionate *logos* (a distinction which is, ironically, the reverse of how the eighth-century BCE poets used the terms), or the more recent but equally comforting story about the bold Indo-Europeans nobly riding across the plains and bringing language and civilization with them – a story inflicted on everyone who has taken a world religions survey course. In place of myths of homogeneity Lincoln favors a model of fragmentation and polygenesis (to borrow a term from Willi Braun[6]), one that is prepared to "imagine a more irenic, more diverse past as a means to guard against scholarly narratives that encode racism and bellicosity" (213). For example, although there may have in fact been people who spoke a language we can today classify as Proto-Indo-European, we must be careful not to overlook historic difference by assuming too quickly that there also existed a coherent, self-aware community of Proto-Indo-Europeans. As Lincoln argues,

> the existence of a language family does not necessarily imply the existence of a protolanguage. Still less does the existence of a proto-language imply or necessitate the existence of a protopeople, protomyths, protoideology, or protohomeland.
>
> (216)[7]

Or, as echoed by Louis-Jean Calvet in his study of socio-linguistics, there is no persuasive "scientific argument in favour of a scenario portraying monogenesis." It is much more likely, he goes on to argue, "that the human being's capacity for language was slowly embodied through thousands of different proto-codes, evolving slowly under the pressure of social needs towards the first languages" (1998: 25). As demonstrated by Calvet in his comparative analysis of claims concerning what he terms the myth of the single source and the myth of linguistic superiority found in both Biblical and Qur'anic interpretive traditions, ideological interests fuel attempts to contain the inevitable social fact of linguistic diversity, creativity, and difference. "Language wars," he assumes, "have been part of the history of humanity ever since humanity transformed its first cries and gestures into signs" (16).

If, as Lincoln persuades his readers throughout the book, "a prime goal of ... narrative is to blur these [differences] together" (119), making narrativization itself a social engineering technique, then what is accomplished in the narrative of family homogeneity and continuity that is spun so successfully, and possibly unreflectively, in his preface? Does the existence of this myth of family necessarily imply the existence of a coherent group? If so, then what has happened to Lincoln's theory of polygenesis and his rigorous attention to the manner in which uniform tales of development are among the ways in which we transform just some happenstance gestures into meaningful signs? Is there a kernel of realism and authenticity amidst the ongoing construction and coincidences of identity? For, despite the observable differences among the people whose lives we eavesdrop on in the preface (some Communists, some Anarchists, some Russian, some American, some talking and some scooted out of the room), all differences are blurred together in those simple but – given the book's interest in deauthorizing the discourse on "the Aryans" – powerfully mythic words, "All had been Jews."

Unsure how Lincoln would answer my question, I would like to offer one answer of my own. For, unlike William Jones, whom Lincoln cites as writing, "I propose the questions but affirm nothing" (195), I admit to having a hunch, otherwise, I would not have raised the issue.

If, as I believe Lincoln would argue, social groups at all levels – from the family to the nation-state – are necessarily contradictory and discontinuous fictions and nostalgias – confections, he might call them – that exist by chasing the carrot of their own mythic ideals, ideals created through a constant contest of repression and expression, then perhaps there is something to his choice both of the theme of silences as well as his use of the past perfect construction, "had been," as in, "All *had been* Jews" (emphasis added). Up to the point of speaking of his "ancestors" in the preface, the simple past tense is primarily used, as in, "my father was my hero" or "The ethos of our house stipulated that ..." But with the mention of the ancestors, we see a slight, but I think crucial, change in tense: "Many of my ancestors *had been* leftists" we are told; "All *had been* Jews" (emphasis added). There is thus a sense in which supposed homogeneity, iden- tity, and authenticity are items of an elusive, silenced past, a past that cannot easily be grasped and that will never be present again. What's more, it is not only that the past contains gaps, fragments, and silences but that any discourse on such a past has no recourse but to employ its own artifice to hear something above the din of silences.

If I am right, then this particular shift in tense signals for us the recalibration of identity as "identity" – a contestable item of ongoing discourse, a contesta- tion that takes place in the improvised space made possible by the counterpoint, as in "world" vs. world. In this way, Lincoln's preface may house no contradictions or ambiguities whatsoever; instead, its autobiographical narrative may be the most significant yet subtle demonstration of the point of the entire book – suggesting we were correct in taking Lincoln's "saying before- hand" utterly seriously. As already quoted, I take that point to be that,

> as objects of experience and of 'scientific' knowledge, primordial origins and perfect centers remain notoriously elusive. They are constituted as objects of discourse, not knowledge, by bricoleurs who collect shards of information and prior narratives, from which they confect the fictions.
>
> (1999: 95)

Of course, I could be entirely wrong; perhaps I should instead read the preface as a brief glimpse into Lincoln just being a Lincoln and not a scholar of his own Lincoln-ness; given that we all wear many hats, such a reading hardly amounts to a "Gotcha." No doubt we all go to films, we all read novels, some of us buy lottery tickets and all of us have family histories and celebrations; we all routinely suspend our ability to disbelieve. But in using the past perfect tense to qualify this sense of a perfectly homogenous past, untamed *history* – with all of its silences, discontinuities, and unexpected moments – unavoidably enters the picture, preventing us from portraying *that-which-merely-happens-to- be-the-case* as if it were *that-which-goes-without-saying* (to adapt a nomenclature from the preface of Roland Barthes's *Mythologies*). For there can be no mistaking that such a speaker is talking with the benefit of hindsight about *a past, past moment* which, in its own time, had its own duration and signifi- cance, but which has long since come to an end; the past perfect thus indicates a time *before* a specified time in the historic past, an identity *before* a specified identity which is itself distant from the speaker's own, suggesting a disconti-nuity – what Thompson, in this chapter's epigraph, called an ignorance – and thus a silence lurking between the speaker's object of discourse and the speaker's own present moment. History, with all its gaps and fissures, is this silence (see Trouillot 1995).

I think here of some recent comments of the French film-maker Jean-Luc Godard. Commenting on his dislike of new digital film editing technologies, he lamented the loss of history:

> "With digital there is no past," he continued. "I'm reluctant to edit on these so-called 'virtual' machines, these digital things, because as far as I'm concerned, there's no past. In other words, if you want to see the previous shot, O.K., you do this" – he tapped the table like a button – "and you see it at once. It doesn't take any time to get there, the time to unspool in reverse, the time to go backward. You're there right away. So there's an entire time that no longer exists, that has been suppressed."
>
> (Brody 2000: 65)

If, for example, "All my ancestors *are* Canadian" is an instance of some digital present leaping seamlessly across the bottomless gaps of history – a truly ideo-logical form of speech, characteristic of discourses on Human Nature as well – then "All *had been* Jews" may be the voice of the participant-observer subtly but significantly historicizing an admittedly intimate discourse on authenticity, thereby slowly and deliberately unspooling and then switching the reel. Recalling Joan Didion's comments quoted in a previous chapter, it is the differ-ence between seeing history as a well-written script, on the one hand, and as sheer improvisation, on the other, as "flash pictures in variable sequence, images with no 'meaning' beyond their temporary arrangement, not a movie but a cutting room experience" (2001: 13). Quoting Lincoln's own second thesis on method, the past perfect may very well signal a "discourse which speaks of things temporal and terrestrial in a human and fallible voice" (as already suggested in this chapter's epigraph from Thompson), whereas the eternal, digital present tense constitutes data for critical reflection insomuch as it is a "discourse whose defining characteristic is its desire to speak of things eternal and transcendent with an authority equally transcendent and eternal" (1996b: 225).

As I read it then, opting for the past perfect at this point suggests that, much like Didion's reflections on the disillusionment associated with the politically tumultuous U.S. summer of 1968, *Theorizing Myth* is indeed a coming-of-age story. "I wanted still to believe in the narrative and in the narrative's intelligi-bility," she writes, looking back on that time in her life, "but to know that one could change the sense with every cut [i.e., the editing of film in the cutting room] was to begin to perceive the experience as rather more electrical than ethical" (Didion 2001: 13). But, much like Didion's *The White Album*, Lincoln's self-disclosures do not simply chronicle one author's ongoing struggle to create a sense of self from scraps on the cutting room floor, but to extricate his sense of self from a discourse that early on enveloped his own social identity – an identity that he, like all of us, had no choice but to adopt, long before we were given the tools that enabled us to engage in sufficient critical reflection on the groups to which we happen to belong and the selves we turn out to be. (In this vein, I take it as significant that, when later discussing Eliade's supposed anti-Semitism, Lincoln says not that he is himself Jewish, but "of Jewish descent" [146]; I see here an unwillingness simply to reproduce naively an apparently monolithic social identity.[8]) Despite the obvious differences between my experiences of discontinuity and ambiguity that night in Durban and Lincoln's autobiographical comments, I suspect that they are both the result of second-order, self-reflexive commentary and analysis, far removed from the nostalgia for authenticity that so often comes with the use of auto/biography by scholars of religion. For if, as Anthony Giddens has remarked, self-identity is "the capacity to keep a particular narrative going" (1991: 54), then Lincoln's work examines what fuels the narrative engine we all inevitably employ. With regard to the history and politics of the study of "myth" as well as the history and politics of "the family," I therefore read Lincoln as a skilled narrator who, sometimes subtly (e.g., his extremely kind but critical comments on Eliade's work [146]) and sometimes bluntly, is recalibrating a pecking order (to paraphrase comments found on 150, 207) rather than celebrating it.

In tackling a book of such tremendous historical sweep and unquestioned theoretical significance, focusing my attention on an admittedly brief autobiographical remark might lead to accusations that I have made much ado about nothing. Given the manner in which at least one reviewer has lamented Lincoln's effort to place the author, along with the datum of concern to the author, squarely on the table, I believe that it is a moment well worth taking seriously. Taking seriously that known and knower are inextricably linked, that classification schemes are human productions that entail practical, material consequences troubles those who, like White, are intent on studying human practices "on their own terms" (White 2001: 48) – an oddly Eliadean project, White's complaints against Eliade's retrograde Romanticism notwithstanding. His interest in studying cultural practices "on their own terms," which helps to explain his complaints against Lincoln, seems to presume the very sort of god's eye viewpoint found among all modernist approaches, going against his claim that "the days of metanarratives chronicled in … [the 1959 *History of Religions* edited volume] are well behind us. Our thinking has changed radically" (49). The modernist effort to recover a stable, objective world by experiencing it "on its own terms," shares much in common with Eliade's work, although putting this seeming raw material to rather different – "progressive" left rather than the "regressive" right – political work. Differing from Eliade and White, Lincoln's concern is to place his own competing interests as an ever-changing political actor on the table – not as an end in itself, as with so much use of the autobio-graphical method in our field, but as a means to draw attention to the silences, discontinuities, and the artful blurring of difference within all forms of social identity, silences undiscovered in much of our peers' work on cultural practices and identity construction. This, unlike Hegel's coy preface and White's hope for disinterested scholarship, Lincoln's opening disclosures not only announce but realize his historical project. *Theorizing Myth*, then, is held together by a theo-retical operation – not the person of Lincoln, as White suggests, as much as the wider structures that make Lincoln's various personae items of articulate reflec-tion and problematization. This makes *Theorizing Myth* something rather different from, say, Augustine's or Rousseau's *Confessions*, for in problematizing self- and group-identity, it avoids the temptation to revel in self-disclosure.

Thus, what started as my puzzlement with Lincoln's personal narrative on a seemingly perfect past has now ended with an appreciation for his ability to place readers so easily both within and outside of his, and thus their own, frag-mented social worlds, thus troubling the way in which selves usually seem to float smoothly along. Apparently, the critical questions I posed at the outset of this essay have, like arrows fired at Prince Siddhartha, all turned to flowers.[9]

Notes

1   I borrow the name of this game from Burton Mack (2001a).

2   My thanks to Willi Braun for helping to point this out.

3   After all, White does agree with many of those who critique Eliade's work; disagreeing with those (such as Rennie or Girardot, cited in a previous chapter) who have tried to rehabilitate Eliade as a postmodernist, he has written elsewhere: "it is more accurate to see Eliade's construction of Religious Man as the swan song of Romanticism, a last nostalgic *Western* imagining of archaic or primitive people that, while it opposed the Enlightenment view of these as so many benighted heathens, was fully as Western and modernist in its appropriation of other people's myths as were the Enlightenment rationalists" (2000: 48).

4   Given the way in which his opening chapters overturn the traditional privilege played by *logos* over *mythos*, there is likely an interesting meditation that could be done on Lincoln's choice to close the book with an *epi-logos*.

5   An interesting point to pursue would be the degree to which this chapter's effort to harmonize the apparent contradictions in Lincoln's book – contradictions that likely attend all social acts and artifacts, including texts and theories – qualifies this very chapter as an instance of rhetorical mythmaking.

6   In a letter circulated in 1999 among the members of the SBL's seminar on "Ancient Myths and Modern Theories of Christian Origins," Braun writes: "By way of analogy, by effect of my 'tribal' heritage I am interested in the history and historiography of Anabaptist origins in the 16th century. Recent work has shown that Anabaptisms popped up in various modes in various locales as convergent though without evident generative relationships to each other – a convergent polygenesis that can be explained without recourse to what [Daniel] Dennett calls a 'pathway of transmis-sion,' but rather by means of an argument that analogous, family-resemblance types of social emergences are generated by socio-material environmental conditions. My monogenesis vs. polygenesis terminology (using 'genesis' as 'beginning' rather than 'origin') is borrowed from James M. Stayer, Werner O. Packull, and Klaus

Deppermann, 'From Monogenesis to Polygenesis: The Historical Discussion of Anabaptist Origins,' *Mennonite Quarterly Review* 49 (1975): 83–121, an article which launched a revisionist historiography of Anabaptist beginnings" (quoted with permission of the author; see Braun 2002 for the published version of these comments). Also, on the notions of mono- versus polygenesis, see Smith 2001a and Calvet 1998: 17–25.

7   Commenting on the sort of theories that are necessary for monogenetic approaches, Lincoln writes: "theories of influence and diffusion are, most often, crude instruments for asserting the dependence of one group on another and thereby establishing the differential value, power, originality, and 'authenticity' of the peoples in question" (2001: 326).

8   Lincoln's brief comments on Eliade – "The kindness and friendship he showed me were particularly remarkable in light of the charges that have been leveled against him. ... I did not know him in the 1930s and 1940s, but my experience makes it impossible for me to believe he harbored anti-Semitic hatreds in his mature years" (146) – suggest that we can appeal to his own thoughts on the unpredictability of affinity/estrangement (e.g., 1989: 8–11) to help understand the two simultaneous acts of (conceivably contradictory) social formation evident in the text: the formation of an oppositional scholarly identity and a dominant familial identity. In other words, what is fascinating is how, on the more local level of interpersonal relationships, the portrait of Eliade-the-person almost qualifies him as "familial" (hence, the above portrait whose endearing quality is surpassed only by the preface's portraits of Lincoln's own family), whereas – when understood as Eliade-the-theorist – Lincoln's succinct treatment of Eliade's scholarly program makes it entirely clear that, as Lincoln finishes the above quotation, "This having been said, I see only a limited future for the kinds of research he pursued." Only if we understand "Eliade" in some realist fashion are we presented with a contradiction; if instead, "Eliade" is capable of signifying everything from a local personal relationship that extends and changes over time to an enduring style of scholarship with practical but obscured implications, then it is sensible that overlapping and possibly paradoxical social formations (feelings of affinity/estrangement) can be possible at this one discursive point. After all, as Lincoln himself has noted, "[b]ecause there are virtually infinite grounds on which individual and group similarity/dissimilarity may be perceived and corresponding sentiments of affinity/estrangement evoked, the borders of society are never a simple thing" (1989: 10).

9   An earlier version of this article was presented to a combined meeting of the "Critical Theory and Discourses on Religion Group" and the "Ritual Studies Group" of the American Academy of Religion, in Nashville, TN (November 20, 2000). The other panelists were Robert Segal and Jay Geller; Bruce Lincoln was the respondent.

Chapter 11

"Religion" and the citizen's unrequited desires

Chips from the religion industry's workshop

> If no one's theories can be made to look ridiculous, how are we going to tell our theories apart?
>
> (Phillips 1998: 13)[1]

In a 1998 issue of the *Journal of the American Academy of Religion* a spirited exchange took place that rivaled the scenes of academic give-and-take lampooned by the British novelist, David Lodge. Lamenting what he considered to be the disproportionate influence that Foucault's earlier works (e.g., *Discipline and Punish*) have enjoyed among some scholars of religion, Ivan Strenski (1998b) took issue with, among others, the thesis of David Chidester's *Savage Systems* (1996b) and the work of Gary Lease (1994; see also 1997). That same year, in a separate essay entitled, "On 'Religion' and its Despisers" (1998a), Strenski took aim at Lease once again, but this time along with the work of Tim Fitzgerald (1997; see also 2000b), and some of my own work. Although I escape most of his critique, Strenski outed me as part of what he called an "inbred clique," "crowd," and "gang," represented in large part by the members of the IAHR-affiliated North American Association for the Study of Religion (NAASR) and its quarterly journal, *Method & Theory in the Study of Religion* (*MTSR*).[2] This "nihilistic" and "polemical" group's work is, in his estimation, "alternatively an exercise in naivete, bad faith, or ignorant mischief, or indeed, all of the above" (1998a: 118). Having read his critique I could not help but feel that my work ended up looking a little ridiculous.

Although there is hardly a need to reply in print to every critic's comments (though I recommend Chidester's [1998] and Lease's [1998] own replies, along with Strenski's rejoinder [1998c]), over the intervening years I have come to realize that there is more than meets the eye to Strenski's ridicule and his warning that the approach to the study of religion represented by this ill-defined gang – an approach that shifts attention away from studying the history of particular religions to the history of the very classification "religion" itself – is "dangerous" and a program of study whose "implementation would be a disaster for the study of religion" (1998a: 118). I find in his critique a number of troublesome assumptions concerning the slippery notions of private/public – a taxonomy widely used throughout the precarious kinship group we call the study of religion as if it had no history, as if it was a self-evident fact of human existence. Related to this, I wish to press Strenski's claim of working toward a truly scientific discipline, for the sort of critique that he has leveled at the work of some of his peers bypasses the usual operations of prolonged and public argumentation, refutation, and revision. With all this in mind, I have decided that a direct, public reply is required. But it is not simply a reply to one scholar, for this admittedly minor and all too forgettable academic controversy is indicative of much larger, more enduring, and generally undisclosed, theoretical and political issues that lie at the very heart of our enterprise. Simply put, just as chapter 7 argued that theologians were elite mythmakers whose various rhetorics could be historicized, so too those who use "religion" in their scholarly efforts to classify the world may turn out to be mythmakers as well, just as deserving of historicization and serious study.

Curiously, Strenski's rhetorical tone – what one reviewer mildly labeled as "somewhat vituperative" (Geertz 2001: 344) – reproduces the sort of remarks found in some other dismissive and outright condescending replies to my work (i.e., Griffiths 1998a, 1998b; Anon. 1998).[3] Any comparativist worth his or her weight knows that not all similarities necessarily denote significance. However, I tend to think that something is afoot when a self-proclaimed and avowedly non-theological scientist of religion, such as Strenski, engages in the same non-substantive hyperbole as, say, a self-proclaimed and avowedly conservative Christian theologian as well as an editor for a liberal Christian periodical. Given that Strenski's past writings suggest that he, unlike Griffiths and the *Christian Century*'s editors, is committed to explaining those things we call religion as being thoroughly human activity – and given the positive and considerable influence some of Strenski's earlier work had on my own thinking at a formative stage – it is worth asking why he has vocally attacked the above loosely related group by resurrecting Schleiermacher's Romantic rhetoric.

As might be anticipated from his loud bark, for the most part Strenski's criticisms have little substantive bite to them. For example, his effort to out the members of a gang merely prompts me to reply that this activity we call scholarship is made possible by conversations among loosely knit individuals, comprising schools of thought – everyone from the Pre-Socratics to Strenski's own longtime relationship with his doctoral supervisor, the late Ninian Smart, and his continued preference for the Smartian "dimensions of religion" (Strenski 1998a: 130), demonstrate as much. (On the sociology of intellectual schools of thought, see Collins 1998.) Therefore, I see his comment on this supposed "inbred clique" as more an example of name-calling than critique. This having been said, the assumptions that inform some of his other criticisms deserve attention because they bring to light some of the basic points that a small group of writers have indeed been trying to investigate on a number of different, largely unrelated publishing fronts, all regarding just what is entailed in labeling part of the world as "religion." Despite the similarities I happen to see within this group, I can, of course, only speak for myself in this chapter.

Strenski repeats a few basic arguments in his various criticisms: the first relies on the common distinction between the production of disinterested knowledge and its on-the-ground, practical uses; as Strenski phrases it, "[m]ere knowledge and classification do not dictate the uses to which they will be put" (1998b: 362). The second criticism concerns how effectively these two apparently distinct activities can be connected. Strenski suggests that writers have over-estimated the influence comparative religionists have (had) on political decision-makers. "[T]he issue," Strenski observes, "is ... whether anyone paid attention – especially governmental agencies" (363). As he phrased it else-where: "The lords of the theory class might profitably reflect on their irrelevance to cultural creation and cultural understanding at the level of mass human existence" (1998a: 117). And the third prioritizes "ordinary" over tech-nical definitions of religion, as in: "The particular wisdom of ordinary usage [of the category religion] lies in its reflecting a deep feature of the world in which we live" (116). Somewhat reminiscent of the often-cited U.S. Supreme Court judge's comment concerning defining pornography, Strenski observes that just as everyone knows what art is when they see it, so too everyone knows what religion is when they see it.

In my reading, crucial to his criticisms is the subject/object binary (i.e., inter-ested vs. disinterested knowledge) as well as the related private/public binary (i.e., personal viewpoint vs. government agencies; the ivory tower "lords of the theory class" vs. "mass human existence"). Just these presumptions allow him to portray a relatively settled, reasonable, and dominant "us" and a uniform "culture" in opposition to the unstable, rather stupid, maverick cabal of "theory lords." For instance, he observes how the category "religion" is so basic to "*our* system of cultural *a prioris* ... [that] it is not only too late to purge 'religion' from *our* conceptual vocabularies, it is uncannily ill-timed too" (117; emphasis added). Just who constitutes this public and obvious "our"? To whose culture is he referring? Moreover, just who is trying to replace the category "religion" in indigenous classificatory schemes? Is there not a real difference between, say, scholarly redescriptions of the self-disclosures of a group of people who employ "religion" to name and divide up their world, on the one hand, and those same scholars trying to get these people to stop using "religion," on the other? I know of a number of scholars doing the former but no one doing the latter, suggesting Strenski's criticisms have pretty much missed the entire point of the people he attacks.

"[T]o make sense of the world," as Strenski describes the task of the scholar (1998a: 132), requires – I believe – that one employ a particular social artifact we call a theory to redescribe the world as it has been first described by the various groups of people whom we happen to study. For people in language families indebted to Latin, or the many cultures impacted by exported European politics and their attendant socio-classificatory systems, "religion" – to borrow some of Strenski's own words – does indeed *make up* a fundamental part of their lived-in world (116; my emphasis).[4] I couldn't agree more. But we know that not everyone the world over uses the term in their indigenous acts of classification and that those who *do* use it tend to mean a myriad of things by it. So, I feel justified to ask if this thing some of us call religion – or the particular way in which just some of us use "religion" – is so obviously a part of "the Human Condition" that we as scholars of course use it when describing other people's "lived-worlds"? Or, as I think to be the case, is "religion" part of an historically specific socio-cognitive tool box, a means by which we moderns "make sense of the world" for ourselves and our cultures? If the former, what evidence supports claims concerning universal features of the Human Condition? If the latter, then what necessary implications attend the claims that we all too easily make concerning "their religion"? After all, if indeed "religion" is part of just our vocabulary, then talk of "their religions" bears a striking resemblance to self-important English speakers assuming that if they talk loudly and slowly enough, "foreigners" will understand them.

In opting for the latter of the two options just presented, I am not suggesting some brave new world where we discard "religion" to recover some far deeper, self-evident thing (say, faith, or spirituality). That would be an ahistoric move unbecoming of a scholar. Nor am I suggesting that we discontinue using the term; so long as it is retooled and used as part of our first order, descriptive vocabulary and not as part of our second order explanatory language, "religion" is as useful as any other arbitrary descriptor (such as "culture"). I say this in hope of preempting comparisons between my position and those of a past generation of normative scholars as diverse as Cantwell Smith and Karl Barth, all of whom were deeply interested in doing away with history by questing for experiential origins. The popularity of this tactic has hardly diminished today; just watch an episode of Oprah for the way in which organized religion is distinguished from pristine, personal spirituality. ("I'm not religious, but I'm spiritual" my students will sometimes tell me.) Given that scholars are hardly above their cultural contexts, one would therefore expect this quest for experiential origins to be present among contemporary writers as well. For example, although for Jeremy Carrette (2000) religion is indeed a taxonomic tool with a questionable history – on that much we can certainly agree – in the conclusion to his study of Foucault and religion we find him discussing the "traditional Western conception of religion" (143), as if there were some other way of conceiving of religion which is more accurate, free of so-called Western bias, or, simply put, better. In other words, it seems as if Carrette presumes that, behind our historical and thus contestable *term* "religion," there lies the unadulterated true *concept* of religion.[5] Much the same presumption seems to inform the work of Richard King (1999), when, in his often insightful, postcolonial critique of "religion," he attempts to avoid the "erasure of indigenous perspectives" which comes, he says, from importing alien and imperializing values and concepts (such as "religion"). This same lament for the insider's perspective is found in

Ann Taves's work on religious experience when she writes that the categories of scholarship carry with them "presuppositions and associations that may be at odds with, and thus distort, the experience of our historical subjects (1999: 8). Such a critique of "violating the lived experience" (9) notwithstanding, both King and Taves end up talking about such things as "religions," as if the so-called indigenous perspective somehow has naturally occurring *religious* aspects.

This attempt at critique prompts us to inquire how – if we take Foucault's critique of epistemology seriously and to its logical conclusion – any effort to classify, know, understand, and act can escape such a criticism. After all, indigenous groups do not employ the concept "indigenous" and they more than likely do not conceive of themselves as being indigenous, not until an outsider from a far more powerful group classifies them in this manner, either to help them or to purchase the logging rights to their land. As Paul Johnson argues, "the indigenous is a quite modern discursive style and strategy which at least in part responds to crises of dislocation, such that the more actual transformation and mobility encountered, the more valued the ideology of unchanging permanence and territorial stability become" (Johnson: forthcoming). If so, then efforts to recover the pre-discursive, indigenous perspective and so-called lived experience may very well turn out to be yet another modernist, imperial act of construction, an act common among scholars of religion. As Johnson concludes,

> in the study of religion, indigenous religions are not typically decon-structed, both because scholars of religion often share the view that the monolithic ontology of modernity should be resisted as merely one construction of "reality," and because indigenous communities are seen to be the victims of modernity. ... [T]he analytical inconsistency between eagerness to critically interrogate ethnicity and the resistance to evaluating indigenousness with the same tools is politically motivated.
>
> (forthcoming, n. 13)

As was argued by Brian Spooner in a fascinating article on oriental rugs, quests for authenticity and indigeneity are hardly an innocent nostalgia for things as they once might have been; instead, each is a concept that "belongs to industrial (even more to 'postcolonial') society" (1986: 226).[6] If so, then such rhetorics are artifacts of a specific and rather luxurious social world where consumers can shop for a brand of purity that naturalizes their own changing tastes. Instead of setting out on such quests, we could try to account for the fact that certain transient tastes become, for a short time, fashionable, and for that time, are steeped in timelessness, all in the service of "working out and working up our individualism in our everyday lives" (Spooner 1986: 227).

It is just such a change in focus that distinguishes my interest in "religion" from writers such as Carrette, King, and Taves. Following Foucault's efforts to write a history of the subject, I believe it is more interesting to write not a history of religion – whether it be conceived in support of, or in opposition to, dominant discourses – but a history of the ability to think and enact "religion" in the first place. In this regard I have followed Lease when he commented that "there is no religion: rather such a history can only trace *how* and *why* a culture or epoch allows certain experiences to count as 'religion' while excluding others" (1994: 472; emphasis added). I have cited this passage on several previous occasions because it drives home so nicely the fact that investigating such a "how and why" requires us to lay bare the strategies that enable the conditions of social formation – a Foucaultian project if ever there was one. It is a project outlined more recently by Talal Asad, when he writes: "How, when, and by whom are the categories of religion and the secular defined? ... [W]hat conception of religion makes our secular moral and political practices possible?" (1999: 193). In such a project – what Asad calls the anthropology of the secular or what Michel de Certeau once referred to as an anthropology of credibility (1997) – it is not just that, as Carrette accurately phrases it, "[r]eligion [in the sense of an institutionalized 'faith'] is constituted as a political force which brings people under a certain system of control" (2000: 136); but, more than this, the very taxons "religion" and "faith," along with "public" and "private" and "secular" and "sacred," are themselves constituted as a political force when used as part of either a folk or scholarly discourse, a force which brings people under a certain system of classification, credibility, and thus control.

Such a project enables us to accomplish what Carrette set out, but in my opinion failed, to do in his study of Foucault and religion: to study the discursive field of religion – including scholarship on religion – as a process of governmentality (2000: 139; see Foucault 1979; I will return to this topic below). My point is that the future of the study of religion likely does not lie in searching for a more adequate or accurate definition of religion; instead, *it lies in the direction of a thoroughly self-reflexive historicization of the very existence of this socio-cognitive category, regardless its definition* (a point made by Masuzawa 2000 but one which was, at the time, under-appreciated by me). Such work asks what is entailed in presuming that any moment of human praxis somehow escapes the uncharted ebb and flow of contingent, social history. Those sites of human praxis that I have in mind – sites where social formation is enabled by means of appeals to religion and faith – include the academic clan of which I happen to claim membership.

Whether or not such a change in focus is dangerous (dangerous to whom, we should ask), Strenski is at least correct to see a growing number of writers studying just what is entailed when we as scholars "imagine religion" – to borrow J. Z. Smith's provocative yet, in my opinion, sadly misunderstood phrase. Such writers are curious about the sort of practical effect that attends the act of grouping together such an odd list of historically disparate human concoctions as those things we call Japanese Pure Land Buddhism, Therevada Buddhism, Vedanta, Judaism, various U.S. Pro-Life organizations, Islam, Scientology, Heavens Gate, Roman Catholicism, and neo-Orthodox Protestantism (I take this list from Strenski 1998a). Although there is no one party line shared by the writers Strenski names as a group, given my own interests a general position does emerge from my reading of their work: as suggested above, the very category "religion," along with the social arrangements made possible by classifying this or that as "religious" or "secular," has been one means by which large-scale social formations have been reproduced by idealizing and thus controlling both their own and various other populations.

Since these scholars understand their role to be that of studying the mechanisms by which culture works, they are interested in determining the impact and import of "religion" as opposed simply to reinforcing this classification's generally undisclosed effects by busying themselves with describing various religions' features or dimensions. Such a determination will, undoubtedly, lead us to theorize and thus rename the event under consideration; whereas the folk taxon "religion" stands in to name a set of human behaviors selected for study, "ideology" or "authorizing practices" may be what I choose to name these behaviors once they are redescribed by means of a social theory. Citing what I can only assume was a casual and thus forgettable email I sent to him in July of 1996, Strenski claims I want to "replace" the category religion with authorizing practices; sadly, he seems to miss my point entirely, wishing only to seize the opportunity to criticize my apparent terminological "barbarism of remarkable infelicity" (1998a: 124). That scholarly terminology is often cumbersome and driven by theories rather than the need to inspire delight in readers should be obvious; no one, after all, criticizes the biologist for talking about deoxyribonucleic acid. In fact, Strenski's rhetoric of "barbarism" brings to mind King's and Taves's hopes to avoid erasing or distorting the indigenous perspective, as if there were some measure by which our terminology could be compared to the so-called pristine experiences under consideration. It appears that Cantwell Smith's well-known methodological rule (1959) concerning the need for all statements to accord with the participant's own self-perception and self-description still haunts the field.

Smith's rule notwithstanding, how does this theorizing, with its attendant renaming of the behaviors under study, actually proceed for this nihilistic cabal? Well, let me cite a few pieces to this puzzle. First off, there's Malory Nye, who nicely phrases the general problem some of us are examining:

> the concept of religion is a trope, or a typology ... it is untranslatable into many of the languages that religion scholars work in ... it bears little relation to any 'emic' discourses. This notwithstanding, there remains a considerable taken-for-grantedness about it, since it seems to work well enough (most of the time) and there does not seem to be enough at stake to question use of the word or to find an alternative conceptualization.
>
> (2000: 451)

Focusing on just one of those sites where this taken-for-grantedness is now a little hard to take, we can turn to David Chidester's study of colonial era scholarship: "in southern Africa comparative religion was conducted on frontier battlefields. Comparisons were not merely intellectual exercises. They were entangled in the European conquest and subjugation of Africans" (1996b: 219; see the excerpt, 1996a). The politics of comparative religion as practiced on the frontier can also be linked to a particular ideology; as argued by Fitzgerald,

> The construction and dissemination of this myth of "religion", which has begotten both liberal ecumenical theology and the so-called science of religion, is now being achieved through the agency of special university departments and publishing lists. … It is a gentle, kind, and rather optimistic philosophy, but it hides from itself the relation between the institutions which it describes as "religious" and the exercise of power. It also tends to disguise its own relation to power, for example as an agency for mystifying the relationship between rich western countries and the postcolonial third world. And it represents itself as an objective science, the factual study of a putative human religiosity.
>
> (1997: 109)

To sum up: as Lease was quoted as saying, this group argues that there is no such thing as "a religion" or "the history of a religion," strictly speaking, because there is no religion out there or in here anywhere. Instead, all we have to study are assorted human actions that may be labeled – by specific people for specific reasons – as religion. As recommended by Lease, we can therefore tackle writing a natural history of this labeling technique and study its practical consequences. Dropping the nineteenth-century loadings of "natural history," we might instead term this an archaeology or genealogy of "religion."

Tackling this natural history we find that "religion" – as opposed to the widely found human behaviors we generally group together, calling them religious – rose to prominence in the early modern European world, just as nation-states were also arising. As Peter van der Veer and Hartmut Lehmann have argued "both 'nation' and 'religion' are conceptualized as universal categories in Western modernity and … their universality is located precisely in the history of Western expansion. … Only through historical analysis can one deconstruct the commonplace dichotomy of a supposedly secular and modern West and a religious and backward Rest" (1999: 4). Linking the concept of religion to that of nation, we can now add to this disparate list the anthropologist Talal Asad, who theorizes that the religious/secular classification is an historically concocted binary – not that there are any other sorts, by the way – that is up to some rhetorical and political work:

> Several times before the Reformation, the boundary between the religious and the secular was redrawn, but always the formal authority of the Church remained preeminent. In later centuries, with the triumphant rise of modern science, modern production, and the modern state, the churches

would also be clear about the need to distinguish the religious from the secular, shifting, as they did so, the weight of religion more and more onto the moods and motivations of the individual believer. Discipline (intellectual and social) would, in this period, gradually abandon religious space, letting "belief," "conscience," and "sensibility" take its place.

(Asad 1993: 39; see also 1999, 2001)

To round out the list, most recently the scholar of Christian origins, William Arnal, has followed up on earlier efforts to link discourses on religion to the advent of the nation-state:

> there is no such thing as religion *in the world*. Of course this may be said of any taxon, but in the case of "religion," the formulation of the category has more to do with the normative *interests* of modernity than with the intellectual or theoretical motives of students of religion. "Religion" is an artificial agglomeration of specific social behaviors, whose basis of distinction from other social behaviors is a function of the specific characteristics of modernity.

(2001: 4)

Or, as he phrased it elsewhere:

> our definitions of religion, especially insofar as they assume a privatized and cognitive character behind religion (as in religious *belief*), simply reflect (and assume as normative) the West's distinctive historical feature of the secularized state. Religion, precisely, is *not* social, *not* coercive, *is* individual, *is* belief-oriented and so on, because in our day and age there are certain apparently free-standing cultural institutions, such as the Church, which are excluded from the political state. Thus, [as] Asad notes, it is no coincidence that it is the period after the "Wars of Religion" in the seventeenth century that saw the first universalist definitions of religion; and those definitions of "Natural Religion," of course, stressed the propositional – as opposed to political or institutional – character of religion as a function of their historical context.

Arnal then concludes: "The concept of religion is a way of demarcating a certain socio-political reality that is only problematised with the advent of modernity in which the state at least claims to eschew culture *per se*" (2000: 31).

What emerges from this quick survey of writers is, to my way of thinking, an important point that, as it turns out, Strenski correctly labels as threatening and dangerous – threatening and dangerous, that is, to those interested in reproducing a very specific lived-in world: the world of nation-states. I read these writers as arguing that the development of a coordinated discourse on privatized, spiritual, and emotive dispositions called "religion" is linked to the development of a technique capable of imagining and managing large-scale, shared social identities in which practical and observable material differences among diverse and far removed group members can be idealized and internalized, and thereby domesticated, internalized, managed, and thus *not acted upon*. In other words, "religion" is, perhaps, one of the most useful technologies of, and corollaries to, the modern nation-state; it is a technique for creating *Wholes* by imaginatively creating *holes* to contain possible dissent, restricting it within the asocial and thus safe zone of personal experience and feeling. It may therefore be no coincidence that religion is understood by the U.S. Supreme Court – the final court of appeals in what is today the globe's most successfully reproducible and influential nation-state – to be strictly a matter of the "citadel of individual heart and mind" (as phrased in the majority decision in the much cited "public school prayer" case, Abington v. Schempp 1963). Such privatization is thus one of the key techniques for taking practical and potentially explosive political differences and making them into mere opinions, choices, flavors, tastes, viewpoints, worldviews, feelings, and beliefs – all of which are banished from competing in the public forum of fact, debate, reason, organization, and action. After all, "freedom of *belief*" is conveniently different from "freedom of *action*." So long as you act in a rather narrowly specified and thus "civil" manner, you can believe whatever you like in the citadel of your individual heart and mind – a rhetoric that simultaneously marginalizes and isolates difference while appearing to protect and insulate it.[7]

At this point two things must be made clear. First, I am not criticizing this "religion" effect; if I were, then Strenski would be correct to label me naive since one of its many effects may very well turn out to be the idea of the public university and so-called secular science, both of which comprise the intellectual and institutional spaces in which I earn my living. Instead, I am merely attempting to account for the success of thinking "religion" and, in turn, the rapid success and longevity of the nation-state. Somewhat like Dan Sperber's use of an epidemiological metaphor in his study of culture, in which he attempts to explain why some ideas are more contagious than others (1996), I am simply interested in trying to explain (i) how the collective idea that a private zone of personal conscience and belief so successfully reproduced itself in the early modern period in Europe, and (ii) why its effects are still being felt today. As Asad and Arnal have both suggested, one clue to answering this comes from simultaneously asking how the shared idea of the nation-state so successfully reproduced itself at this same time. So, unlike some other critics of "religion" I have no interest in discovering the real or indigenous concept behind our inevitably limited word "religion." Instead, I wish to link the idea and the word to practical, material existence, employing a theory of social formation to explain how and why specific groups of human beings have come to think and act "religion" in the first place.

Second, I realize that there are significant gaps among the scholars just cited. For instance, whereas Fitzgerald argues for scholars to discontinue their use of "religion" as a descriptor altogether, employing in its place the wider category "culture," as already stated, I argue that, when properly theorized and redescribed, "religion" is just as useful – and as arbitrary! – an analytic taxon as any other, including our other primary, Latin-based tool, "culture." The use of "religion" is therefore one's data, not part of one's explanation. But the gap that is perhaps most important to recognize is that, although I find the above named writers useful in outlining a political theory of "religion," some of them could be read as relying on modernist realism when it comes to talking of religions. For example, in his widely read critique of Clifford Geertz's attempt to define religion as a universal human activity, Asad (1993) recommended instead studying religions locally, so as to recover the nuances of difference among particular religions, differences otherwise lost to scholars such as Geertz. The danger of this position was already seen in the cases of King and Carrette: it can be read to employ "religion" as if there exists some pre-hegemonic, indigenous, and more authentic "on the ground," local activity recoverable only once we drop our so-called universalistic, Enlightenment pretensions.[8] Or, to phrase it another way, when van der Veer and Lehmann recommend that "it is essential to follow the transformation of religious notions when they are transferred from a purely religious context to the sphere of national politics" (1999: 7), they seem to fail to press their own critical insights far enough, insomuch as they may assume that, whereas "nation" and "secular" are historically recent, modernist constructs, "religion" somehow predates them. I find a similar tension in Benedict Anderson's justifiably influential work on nationalism (1991; see also 1999), where he appears to distinguish religion from nationalism instead of seeing the two as necessary correlates, what Asad most recently called "Siamese twins" (2001: 21). So, instead of consistently applying their own claims that "sacred/secular" concepts and social spaces arise simultaneously, and that a dialectic exists between "private faith" and "public practice," such writers may be read as slipping back into old modernist habits, failing to see their own descriptions of "particular religions" and pre-modern religious identities from out of which national identities developed, as being an effect of their own modernist, nationalist context. Simply put, although humans for a considerable length of historical time may very well have, say, posited the existence of invisible things we call ancestors, spirits, demons, gods, etc., grouping just these thoroughly social, historical behaviors together, calling them religion, faith, piety, etc., and then distinguishing these practices from so-called secular activities is both an effect of, and ground for, modernity. Studying these effects is, to quote Masuzawa, serious activity.

> This is no idle navel-gazing of the academy. For, as a casual glance would make amply clear, this imaginative production of "religion" has given us the "religion"-saturated world in which we live. ... [S]omething about the world – that is to say, much more about the world than academic ideas and analytic schemata – has changed in the course of the manufacture of "religion."
>
> (2000: 129)

But where to start if this is what we wish to study? Well, the specific social impact of this rhetoric can be demonstrated in a number of cases. Although some historic examples will be examined in the final chapter, for the time being consider a recent example from the U.S.: the case of John Ashcroft, President-elect George W. Bush's nominee for the post of U.S. Attorney General (the head of the federal legal system). During his eventually successful U.S. Senate confirmation hearings in January of 2001, this vocal member of the Assemblies of God denomination (a U.S. branch of Pentecostalism), with a long record of active and public support for a variety causes that are generally portrayed by the U.S. media as outside the civil and ordered mainstream (e.g., such as working against legal abortion), calmed the nerves of his former Senate colleagues by saying that, (i) although he did indeed have deeply held beliefs, (ii) he would *not* act on them and if confirmed as Attorney General would, instead, uphold the "law of the land." Within this discursive setting, the sincerity or depth of one's convictions is apparently determined by one's ability *not* to act on them! That no one saw this rhetoric as either hypocritical, bizarre, or downright laughable – but, instead, applauding it as the mark of great integrity – attests to the tremendous utility of the private/public rhetoric and its ability to police and internalize dissenting positions while simultaneously providing them with an apparently safe haven.[9] This, I take it, is precisely what Foucault meant by governmentality – the means by which techniques of self-policing and the marginalization of dissent make possible coherent, large-scale, seemingly "civil" social identities.

Religion, conceived as a distinct, private experience of meaning, is thus the ultimate "Other," useful in all acts of social formation, insomuch as it "is substantively empty – or infinitely fillable with aeolian qualities" (Braun 2000: 8). The seemingly unassailable zone of private experience (i.e., the inviolable citadel of the human heart) is thus the refuge and the end of dissent, for there discord finds a safe haven *but only insomuch as it is not acted upon*. Indeed, the posited split between belief and practice, text and context – in the words of postcolonial critic Partha Chatterjee – enables anticolonialism to create "its own domain of sovereignty within colonial societies well before it begins its political battle with the imperial power" (1993: 8). Such marginal groups, for whose members this concept religion "is an aspect of their culture, a valuable support in a hostile environment" (Sarup 1996: 3), thus obviously benefit from the ability to divide

> the world of social institutions and practices into two domains – the mate-
> rial and the spiritual. The material is the domain of the "outside," of the
> economy and of statecraft, of science and technology, a domain where the
> West had proved its superiority and the East had succumbed. ... The spiri-
> tual, on the other hand, is an "inner" domain bearing the "essential" marks
> of cultural identity. The greater one's success in imitating Western skills in

the material domain, therefore, the greater the need to preserve the distinctness of one's spiritual culture.

(Chatterjee 1993: 8; quoted in van der Veer 2001: 69)

A striking, and surprisingly explicit, example of this technique for the revision and survival of marginal groups was contained in a *New York Times* op-ed piece written by the noted British novelist, Salman Rushdie, not long after the September 11, 2001, attacks on the U.S. After detailing how "radical politics" had co-opted "a faith" – what he terms "the obscurantist hijacking of their religion [i.e., Islam]" by so-called "Islamists" – he concludes his article by writing:

Many of them [those Muslims who currently advocate the need for what Rushdie significantly terms a "Reformation in the Muslim world"] speak of another Islam, their personal, private faith.

The restoration of religion to the sphere of the personal, its depoliticization, is the nettle that all Muslim societies must grasp in order to become modern. ... If terrorism is to be defeated, the world of Islam must take on board the secularist-humanist principles on which the modern is based, and without which Muslim countries' freedom will remain a distant dream.

(2001: A25)[10]

Whether or not Rushdie is correct in his portrait of Islam or his apparent understanding of modernity and freedom as seemingly abstract and stable Platonic types, he astutely understands the price of admission into a modernity in part made possible by such previous internalizations as Martin Luther's *sola scriptura* and John Wesley's "strange warming of the heart": the distinction between private and public that makes possible both internalization of dissent and the conformity of practice. However, insomuch as this artful technique is successfully employed in making a space for marginal groups within alien and potentially hostile environments, it should be more than obvious that such success is ironically evidence that these groups have necessarily succumbed to a larger hegemony insomuch as they have had to rethink and retool their own group identity and sense of self, in the process privatizing and internalizing that which previously had been public and taken for granted. It is not a restoration, as Rushdie portrays it, but a revision. For, insomuch as "Hinduism" comes eventually to be successfully portrayed as a "religion," entitled to the rights and obligations once reserved only for Christians, "it" – like Christianity before it – now falls under the governance of the State, ensuring that while private Hindu belief is indeed acceptable, the practice of, say, *sati* (so-called widow burning) is outlawed (as it was by the British in 1829) and the *caste* system ridiculed, as it most recently was in the liberal media during the boycotted, 2001 international human rights conference held in Durban, South Africa. "Religion" thus houses a disparate and desperate citizenry's necessarily unrequited desires.[11]

If we adopt this approach to the problem of "religion" then we have a new way of understanding the manner in which modern religious pluralist movements arose directly from Europe's previous, double-barreled missions/colonial activity. Having gained political, economic, and military control over large expanses and diverse populations, a non-coercive, economically productive technique for having people submit to a civil rule was required and, in the hands of liberal humanists, aeolian "religion" stepped up to play the role. Much like Margaret of Parma, King Philip II of Spain's regent in the Low Countries (and Charles V's illegitimate daughter), who in 1566 set aside one church in towns where Calvinists could meet (Tracy 1999: 113), the concept religion, and the social space it designates, is the manufactured safe haven of already contained dissent. That Philip soon sent ten thousand Spanish troops north from Italy to squash Calvinist dissent, actions that led to the establishment of the council of troubles (Netherlanders, however, called it the council of blood) which issued 12,203 death sentences between 1567 and 1573 (Tracy 1999: 113; see 318, n. 64 for the source of this estimate) makes it obvious that large scale governance cannot solely rely on coercive violence.

Making this move to studying the political impact of "religion" also provides a way of understanding the preoccupation with dialogue and conversation seen among many contemporary British and U.S. scholars of religion. As a direct result of their own expansionist practices, such onetime and current global powers are now comprised of peoples so diverse, with such potentially conflicting interests, and ways of organizing, as to necessitate the deployment of effective social management techniques. A case in point is Diana Eck's "Pluralism Project" and her latest book, *A New Religious America* (2001), in which she is explicitly concerned with the flood of different people who entered the U.S. after the 1965 Immigration and Naturalization Act (which altered some U.S. immigration priorities from European to Asian groups). The book is a fascinating mix of nationalist rhetoric of U.S. exceptionalism ("The United States has become the most religiously diverse nation on earth" [4]) coupled with the rhetoric of postmodern diversity ("Who do we mean when we say 'we' [as in, We the people ...]" [5]). Given the approach to "religion" outlined in this chapter, it is not difficult to see Eck's project as being a nationalist response to the contemporary global corporatization of formerly national life – an effort to strengthen the now potentially irrelevant notion of the nation-state by reinvigorating the role played by private conscience in the post-1965 world of increased U.S. diversity. In this "new America," where the "covenants of citizenship to which we adhere place us on common ground" (24), the rhetoric of religion as a form of conscience and faith (a common way in which Eck and other pluralists define religion) is more important than ever in reproducing a civil society. It thus turns out that Eck is more accurate than she likely intended when she wrote that "our society becomes stronger as each group's religious freedom is exercised, as people like Sikhs articulate principles like equality and freedom in their own voice and in their own key" (7). "Our" society is indeed strengthened insomuch as "they" too internalize unmanageable difference, live the rhetoric of faith, accept what "civil" ought to mean, circumscribe competing practical interests within the far from benign "covenant of citizen-ship," and not bring "their" *kirpan*'s to "our" schools.[12]

Despite his ardent criticisms, we can now quote Strenski himself to sum up this survey of contemporary theorists and the sort of scholarship on religion that they help to make possible: these writers generally agree that "'religion' is that social entity which comes into being when diverse of dispersed cultural forms are brought under the command and control of an over-arching system" (1998a: 129–130). More than this, however – and, despite his scare quotes around the word religion, I believe this is a step Strenski is unwilling to take or incapable of taking – they argue that not just the apparently obvious behaviors termed "reli-gious" but the very classification of them *as* "religion," the very selection and conceptualization of just these behaviors, is itself a technique whereby over-arching and totalized social systems can come into being. To press forward and question "religion" in this manner therefore means interrogating the mecha-nisms of one's own social – or, better put, national – world and one's role as an individual – or, better put, a citizen – within it. I believe that Strenski cannot do this because of the tremendous effort he has invested in policing how we ought to use "religion" and because of his use of these very privatization tech-niques. For example, somewhat reminiscent of Cantwell Smith, he finds this cabal's theorizing of the category "religion" to be outrightly "offensive to the dignity of the spiritual and religious lives of literally billions of fellow human beings" (116). The ease with which he here employs the private/public, spiri-tual/political rhetoric, much less the assumption that scholarship is meant not to "insult" the people under study, coupled with his explanatorily empty comment on the "sacredness" being a result of the "spiritual imagination" (130), all suggest, at most, that Strenski's recent work ought to be considered as data for the above listed group of scholars. His fear over the loss of "religion" thus seems to have more to do with his interests in reproducing a very particular socio-political world than it does with any "purely theoretical" or so-called "scientific" considerations. In the least, then, we can cite Wiebe's review of the book in which Strenski's essay appears, and say that

> [t]he vehemence of his attack ... and his concern that reductionistic expla-nations by NAASR scholars might offend the dignity of billions of people seem to put the lie to Strenski's self-definition as a scientific student of reli-gion.
>
> (Wiebe 2000: 438)

And this is precisely where Strenski's curious and impassioned attack of those who thoroughly historicize our field's primary taxon re-enters the discussion. As I recall, his own provocative book, *Four Theories of Myth in Twentieth-Century History* (1987), concludes with a chapter that similarly attempts to protect contemporary scholars from the sins that he deftly identifies in the works of four of our most influential scholarly fathers. "Perhaps because we may live in less catastrophic times," Strenski concludes,

> we may not see such theorists again. If the social stability of the industrialized West translates into stability within the professional academic realm, then we may expect the professions to be able to maintain boundaries and even (with the help of demographics) to reinforce them. Such stability would mitigate against the appearance of theorists such as ours, who at crucial points in their lives found themselves unable – doubtless against their wills – to act as professionals. In all four cases, we are dealing with *disrupted* academic careers, with men who, for significant periods, were forced to deviate from the normal course of career development.
>
> (1987: 198)

We see here once again the dual binaries of private/public and subjective/objective (i.e., changeable personal viewpoints vs. the stable standards of professionalism), not to mention abnormal/normal, all working in the interest of reproducing not only "the profession" but also the "stability of the industrialized West." Maintaining the realm of privacy – so as to reproduce a very particular and profitable (i.e., "stable") public – is therefore a crucial rhetorical move for writers such as Strenski who are intent on manufacturing an external realm of normal, objective, professional, and verifiable scientific truth, a realm which brings with it their self-identity and social authority. I believe that it is no accident that professionalism is here linked with the notion of industry – in both senses of the word (i.e., diligence and commerce).

Accordingly, historicizing not only "religion" but also the political import of presuming that an internal realm of private belief, experience, and feeling somehow eludes the social world of political contestation, is indeed a very dangerous business – literally *business* – in the opinions of scholars such as Strenski. Although I had yet to connect up the dots between the discourse on belief, the category "religion," and the advent of the nation-state, in 1997 I phrased it as follows:

> in the case of Strenski, the terrors of history, or one's social, cultural, economic, and political context, can be escaped and, if not escaped, then possibly ignored and minimized [through one's participation in "the profession"]. It is for this reason that Strenski's own method is properly described as conservative. Like the attempts to dismiss Eliade's nationalistic or xenophobic journalistic writings as somehow unique or separate from his mature and scholarly writings, Strenski's appeal to different categories of scholars (the normal and the abnormal) utilizes strategies of exclusion and containment to privilege and isolate one group over another. And it is precisely at this point that Strenski's attempt to construct a defensible,

privileged position is most open to critique. Strenski's discourse on abnormal writers exists solely at the expense of an arbitrarily created and denigrated category of historically disenfranchised grand theorists.

(1997b: 98)

Given my many agreements with his early work on "myth," I found it rather difficult, but necessary, writing those words; after all, his influential 1987 book opens with a paragraph that I had approvingly used as an epigraph in *Manufacturing Religion*, a paragraph that I still find to be provocative of thought:

> Myth is everything and nothing at the same time. It is *the* true story or a false one, revelation or deception, sacred or vulgar, real or fictional, symbol or tool, archetype or stereotype. ... Thus, instead of there being a real thing, myth, there is a thriving *industry*, manufacturing and marketing what is called "myth." "Myth" is an illusion – an appearance conjured or "construct" created by artists and intellectuals toiling away in the work-shops of the myth industry.
>
> (1987: 1–2)

Strenski's current critique is ironic, then, because, if one were to replace the word "myth" with "religion"[13] and then re-read the paragraph, it would qualify the author for honorary status among the so-called dangerous, inbred clique! In hindsight, then, Strenski circa 1987 – the "first" Strenski who was determined to undermine those disciplinary patriarchs with whom he disagreed on questions of politics and theory – turns out to have been a member of the very disenfranchised and disruptive cabal whom the "final" and fully professionalized Strenski now so vehemently berates. Today, long after the opening words in *Four Theories of Myth* were first penned, the terrain apparently looks entirely different to him. Because the reasons for this shift are likely numerous and complex, they will not detain us at this point. But amidst the change, one thing remains constant: a potent rhetoric of crisis and danger – it's just that it is now directed at a new adversary.

When one juxtaposes the work of those who historicize "religion" to Strenski's own studies, we thus find examples of two very different approaches to writing disciplinary history. Whereas Strenski focuses on issues of individual culpability when examining moral agents making decisions that do or do not conform to some abstract professional standard, Arnal, Asad, Chidester, Fitzgerald, Lease, Masuzawa, Nye, van der Veer, and others, all shift the ground and examine the wider structural (i.e., political, economic, nationalist, etc.) constraints that determine what gets to count as a professional, or a moral agent, in the first place. The height of Strenski's rhetoric – a rhetoric that treads on the usual sense of professionalism he supported just over a decade ago – suggests that there is a very real threat to all modernist, liberal ideologies, whether they are politically liberal and humanistic or politically conservative and theological, when one radically historicizes the kind of claims to individual autonomy that come pre-packaged in the rhetoric of experience and in presumptions of religion's socio-political autonomy – not to mention radically historicizing the very taxon by which we as a group of intellectuals demarcate a part of the social world in preparation for our inquiry.[14]

In formulating an answer to Strenski's critique of the despisers of "religion," then, we can say that it is not a matter of over-estimating the influence individual scholars of religion have in determining such things as a government's foreign policy; after all, these are the very people who provide the information and expert testimony used by governments in their dealings with citizens. Here I specifically have in mind the American Academy of Religion's current cooperation with U.S. law enforcement (e.g., the FBI), a relationship that came out of the government's handling of the 1993 Branch Davidian stand-off in Waco, Texas (see Herrick 2001; for commentaries on this relationship, see Baum 2001: 19; Gallagher 2001: 44). As phrased by the political theorist John Ransom,

> practitioners of the human sciences such as psychiatrists, social workers, and demographers, provide the wielders of power with both crucial information about the objects of its exercise and knowledge about how to shape and transform human material.
>
> (1997: 22)

But, far more than this, we must not fail to recognize that the choices and interests of people *qua* scholars are shaped by and conform to pre-existing structures of power and privilege – exercises that are part of the very process of professionalization. Focusing as he does on issues of historical agency – what Strenski has characterized as work that focuses on "consequential" cultural workers (1995) – rather than examining structural circumstances in which agency and consequence are established and contested, allows us to continue to convince ourselves that the seemingly inconsequential State-sponsored profession of defining, describing, sorting, and interpreting human beliefs somehow floats free of its ever-present socio-political pre-conditions, much as timeless authorial intentions were once thought by some to reside within a text. Our object of study in such a neutered, hermeneutical art reinforces a number of Liberal assumptions concerning the autonomy and accountability of the individual, the free-floating status of positive science, the self-evident existence of unimpeded choice, the evils of impersonal structure, all wrapped up in the universal nature of the Human Condition. Only in such an idealist setting could we focus on the people of great consequence, as if they somehow rose above the din of the faceless masses. However, so long as we play our assigned roles as experts arguing over the precise meaning of this or that esoteric symbol or colorful yet toothless custom, there may be little need of governmental agencies in Liberal democracies to pay much attention to our work, since we are already the priestly spinners of the fictions necessary for such governments to exist.

In the end, then, what most troubles Strenski is what we, as scholars of religion, will end up *doing* should we risk breaking our silence concerning how our own social worlds are made possible. What will happen if, like David Lodge's young upstart in the conference audience near the close of his novel, *Small World*, we stand at the microphone and ask a few skeptical and thus unsettling questions, thus marking in public a fracture point in our apparent discursive unity?

> Persse got to his feet again and padded back to the microphone in a huge, expectant silence. "What I mean is," he said, "What do you *do* if everybody agrees with you?"
>
> "Ah." Arthur Kingfisher flashed a sudden smile that was like sunshine breaking through cloud. … "That is a very good question. A very in-ter-est-ing question. I do not remember that question being asked before." He nodded to himself. "You imply, of course, that what matters in the field of critical practice is not truth but difference. If everybody were convinced by your arguments, they would have to do the same as you and then there would be no satisfaction in doing it. To win is to lose the game."
>
> (Lodge 1995: 319)

Apparently motivated by the quest for truth and the goal of winning the game, Strenski fears what scholars will *do* should this dangerous cabal win the day. As the panelist in the above novel replied, to see it as an issue of winning is already to have lost the game, for the game – the discourse enacted on the field of critical practice – exists only insomuch as disciplinary rules are (i) portrayed as universal and (ii) exposed as ad hoc historical products wearing a thin veneer of rhetoric. And round it goes. In other words, the discursive game is played only because there are disagreements. Cease the disagreements and, like ending karma, samsara comes to an end. Or, as cited in an earlier chapter, Don DeLillo's nun dryly comments: "You are sure that you are right but you don't want everyone to think as you do." How could you be right if everyone agreed? Then there would be no sense to "being right" and one would win a hollow victory.

Strenski's fear, then, is misplaced for – as Louis Menard has recently observed – "skepticism is the ally of inquiry," since "[t]he greater our awareness of the fallibility of our understanding and the provisional nature of our concepts, the more techniques we devise for perfecting our data" (2001: 80). Strenski once rather boldly stood up within the academy and proposed some skeptical questions of his own and, in the process, took as his data "myth" and not myths; today, that field is stronger than ever, giving us such provocative works on "myth" as those of Bruce Lincoln (e.g., 1999). The disagreements made the discourse possible. Sadly, Strenski seems to fear that our field will, in some apocalyptic fashion, shrivel up and blow away if we follow his lead and make "religion" our data, subjecting it to the same scrutiny to which he once subjected "myth."

I, for one, am not convinced by his dire predictions; who knows, those who follow our historicization of "religion" might look upon our debates over the status of the category religion, reductionism, the problem of meaning, and those tired accusations of "throwing babies out with the bath water" as nothing more than merely quaint anecdotes from yesterday's news. To me, that's precisely the sort of future that a truly "scientific" attitude would be willing to entertain and, in fact, hope for: that, someday soon, one's present certainties will hardly remain certain at all. It strikes me that this is the only sort of progress for which we can hope. All too often, however, members of social groups portray the world as they happen to have found it as the only world possible, ensuring that changes be seen as declines or corruptions. Appealing to Joe Queenan's delight-fully caustic critique of the self-sure Baby Boomer generation, Queenan writes: "mistaking the heroes of one's youth for the heroes of everyone's youth ... we try to gain access to history through the back door. Baby Boomers have never come to terms with the fact that the past is not stagnant, that it keeps expanding to include younger people's pasts" (Queenan 2001: 147).

Entering through the front door and coming to terms with the ad hoc nature of history – including the history of an academic discipline and its categorial tool box – means coming to terms with the fact that the deluge will not follow us and that our impassioned arguments will someday be grist for someone else's mill. Using rhetoric such as Strenski's to make and mark difference is simply how discourses work and I am flattered that my work can serve him so effec-tively in his effort to set his own work apart and champion a particular sort of study of religion. But, as I understand it at least, the hope of a scientific discourse is not to win and thus end the game; instead, it is a hope for a day to arrive when, in hindsight, the certainties of the past will no longer be certain at all and the rhetorics no longer persuasive. The only progress for which we can hope is that we will someday be out of fashion. If so, then in closing, I can do no better than quote the writer who informs so many of the exchanges cited throughout this book:

> let us leave off our polemics ... they hardly survive in areas now deserted by serious workers; this particular controversy, which might have been so fruitful, is now acted only by mimes and tumblers.
>
> (Foucault 1989: 201)[15]

Notes

1 My thanks to my friend, Pedja Klasnja, for this wonderful quotation.
2 In the interest of full disclosure, from 1990 until 2002 I served as an editor of this journal and Strenski has served on its editorial advisory board since the journal's inception in 1989. Over the years, his work has been published and reviewed in *MTSR* – including a 1989 review symposium on his *Four Theories of Myth* (see *MTSR*1/1 and 1/2) and Karen Field's – who translated the most recent edition of

Durkheim's *Elementary Forms of Religious Life* – more recent review of his 1997 book, *Durkheim and the Jews of France* (see 11/2).

3 Regarding such criticisms, see also Griffith's paternalistic review essay (2000) on Wiebe's *The Politics of Religious Studies* (1999) and Tim Fitzgerald's *The Ideology of Religious Studies* (2000b), along with Wiebe's review essay (2001) on Griffith's latest book, *Religious Reading* (1999). As well, see Tite's article (2001) on the manner in which critics such as Griffith miss the mark.

4 Note how this comment seems to disagree with his assertion that the term religion "reflects a deep feature of the world in which we live," insomuch as this latter statement seems to employ a referential theory of meaning.

5 I detect a similar assumption in a critique of my work generated by Benavides (2000), in which he recommends that I shift attention from studying scholars of religion and "religion" to studying the richer soil provided by the religions themselves. However, without the modernist rubric "religion," I'm not sure how one can simply get on with studying religion in the field, as it were.

6 My thanks to Kurtis Schaeffer for bringing this article to my attention.

7 I am reminded of an old joke my dad recently told me concerning a certain fellow who was sued for slander after he publicly called someone a son-of-a-bitch. After losing the case in court he confirmed with the judge that freedom of belief was indeed a fundamental tenet of their society, to which he then replied, "Well, then, I still think he's a son-of-a-bitch."

8 Asad's recommendation does not necessarily have to be read in this fashion. For instance, more recently Asad has written: "My problem with universal definitions of religion is that by insisting on an essential singularity, they divert us from asking questions about what the definition includes and what it excludes – how, by whom, for what purposes, and so on. And in what historical context a particular definition of religion makes good sense" (2001: 20). I find these comments to resonate with Lease's proposed project for studying how and why certain series of behaviors and institutions come to count as religion in any given setting.

9 However, William Wineke, in his editorial for the *Wisconsin State Journal*, wrote: "We're in this weird situation where Ashcroft's opponents fear he is lying and his supporters fear he is telling the truth" (January 27, 2001), E1.

10 I am indebted to Johnson (2002) for bringing Rushdie's article to my attention.

11 I am indebted to Arnal (2001) for this particular way of phrasing the problematic and, thus, for my chapter's title.

12 I recall a charged debate in Canada in the 1980s not only over whether young Sikh males should be allowed to bring their *kirpan* (ceremonial dagger) to school with them, but also whether Sikh adult males should be allowed to wear their turban instead of other forms of ceremonial headwear, as in the case of Baljit Dhillon who sued for his right to be an officer in the Royal Canadian Mounted Police (RCMP) while retaining his turban. Although he eventually won his case in the 1990s, in building its case against him, and in favor of "tradition," the RCMP had collected an approximately 200,000 signature petition. The Canadian Amateur Boxing Association once attempted to bar a Sikh boxer from competing, for fear that his beard would harm his opponents, and even the Royal Canadian Legion, an organization of war veterans, has tried to bar Sikhs from entering its legion halls due to the fact that Sikhs refuse to remove their "hats" upon entering. Given the much celebrated tolerance and multiculturalism of post-1960s Canada (federally mandated bilingual and biculturalism policies, recognizing both French and English languages/cultures, were adopted in 1969, a federal government Minister for Multiculturalism was appointed for the first time in 1972, and by the mid- to late-1980s federal laws recognized multiculturalism), the passions roused by various forms

of head coverings provides sufficient evidence that even seemingly non-threatening forms of marginal practice are deeply threatening to the status quo.

13 As an aside, I should say that it would seem ludicrous to imagine that, for Strenski, the object to which "religion" refers is somehow more real than in the case of "myth" – unless, of course, one places stock in his various casual asides concerning such things as, say, Martin Luther's "religious genius" or the fact that Eliade was a "gentle, refined and deeply religious ... person" (1995: 285, 286). In fact, the problem for Strenski with the apparent antisemitism of the latter seems to be that it conflicts with Eliade's supposed "religiousness," suggesting that Strenski assumes religion has something to do with being good and well mannered. In a word, religion, for him, seems to have something to do with being human(e). If, as I have proposed in this chapter, one instead assumes that the social formations we name as religions are mechanisms whereby groups concoct seemingly coherent identities and behavioral standards, then there is nothing – to borrow Strenski's word – any more "disquieting" about some so-called religious people being Antisemitic than anyone else being Antisemitic.

14 A useful example of this rhetoric of pure and originary experience is found in Eck's thoughts on her grandmother's immigration from Sweden to the U.S. Reflecting on her own experience of visiting the exhibits at Ellis Island, Eck writes: "I wound up in the exhibit halls, viewing a perspective on America's immigration saga that Grandma would not have had, so immediate and personal was her own experience" (26). Although I would agree that her grandmother did indeed have experiences, they certainly were not part of the saga to which Eck has access while visiting Ellis Island. Moreover, her grandmother's experiences were not purer or closer to some posited real but, more than likely, entirely different from the complex, narrative script that people, in hindsight, today tell themselves about "coming to America." Likely, her grandmother had nostalgias of her own. That we can see the gap between ill-defined experience and hindsight narrative when viewing, for example, other people's triumphalist narratives of past and arrival (as in the Afrikaner Voortrekker Monument that I had the good fortune to visit in Pretoria, South Africa, while attending the 2000 meeting of the IAHR) but not our own is, perhaps, all too understandable yet no less lamentable.

15 See my essay "Religion, Ire, and Dangerous Things," in the *Journal of the American Academy of Religion* (scheduled for publication in the spring of 2004) for a related attempt to respond to Strenski's criticisms.

Chapter 12

"Religion" and the governable self

> [Socrates's] mission is useful for the city – more useful than the Athenians'
> military victory at Olympia – because in teaching people to occupy them-
> selves with themselves, he teaches them to occupy themselves with the city.
> … I think that the main characteristic of our political rationality is the fact
> that this integration of the individuals in a community or in a totality results
> from a constant correlation between an increasing individualization and the
> reinforcement of this totality.
>
> (Foucault 1988b: 20, 161–162)

Although critique can be an end in itself, after calling for an end to the
Eliadean era and suggesting that the sacred/profane rhetoric may provide, to
some degree, a form of recoverable residue upon which we can rebuild a scholarly pursuit, some might find me remiss not to close by saying something about
how we might proceed from where we happen to find ourselves, thus venturing
a speculative guess about just what a thorough historicization of the rhetoric of
"religion" might look like. With broad brush strokes this final chapter offers one
possible answer to the question of what might arise from the residue that
remains after a disenchanted, post-Cold War generation – raised on the deconstructive suspicion spawned by the student uprisings of the late 1960s and
sobered by the alienating, post-1970s academic job market – has decided that
the once obvious autonomy of religious experiences is not only a theoretically
bankrupt concept but a politically suspect device. Having ceased to be
persuaded by the notion of religion as something autonomous and extraordinary
– whether it is considered good or bad, productive or destructive – what we
have left to explain, then, is why so many individuals have found this very idea
particularly contagious, appealing or, better put, useful.

In this move toward problematizing our ability to think and enact "religion,"
a number of scholars have started out by looking to the term's etymology.[1] As
many have pointed out before, any modern language whose development has
been affected by Latin-influenced cultures likely possesses something equivalent
to the English term "religion." This means that, *for language families unaffected
by Latin, there is no equivalent term to "religion"* – unless, of course, we pompously
assert that our local word captures something essential to the entire human

species, thereby distinguishing local *word* from universal *concept* (i.e., although they do not call "it" religion, they still have *It*; "a rose by any other name would smell as sweet"). This bold assertion is made all the easier by the long history of European influence on other cultures/languages by means of trade and conquest. For example, although "religion" is hardly a traditional concept in the sub-continent that we today know as India, the long history of contact with Europe has ensured that modern, English-speaking Indians have no difficulty conceiving of what we call Hinduism as being their "religion" – although, tech-nically speaking, to a person we might call a Hindu, "Hinduism" is not a religion but is, rather, *sanatana dharma* (Sanskrit for the eternal system of duty/obligation and, thus, the cosmic order that results). As might be expected, despite its authoritative status in the history of textual studies, the Christian New Testament is not much help in settling these issues, for its language of composition, koine ("common") Greek, naturally lacked the historically later Latin root word/concept *religio*. Thus, English translations will routinely use "religion" to stand in for such terms as *eusebia* (e.g., 1 Timothy 3:16; 2 Timothy 3:5) and *threskeia* (e.g., James 1: 27), terms that are in fact closer to the Sanskrit *dharma* (duty, obligation), the Chinese *li* (rules of propriety determining social rank), or even the Latin *pietas* (the quality that comes of successfully main-taining one's proper social position, such as in the notion of filial piety) than our term "religion."

Etymological quests for the original meaning are thus not much help in sorting out this problem in taxonomy, for even in Latin our modern term "reli-gion" has no equivalent – if, by "religion," you align yourself with contemporary popular wisdom and mean by it a coordinated and obviously set apart system of believing in such invisible beings as gods and demons, working toward an after-life of some sort, telling tales of origins and endtimes, enacting rule-governed behaviors (i.e., rituals), or just being plain old good. As others have pointed out before me, the furthest back our etymological quest gets us is to the root of *religio*, "-*leig*," meaning simply "to bind" (Smith 1998: 269). From here we get to a series of etymologically related terms which, in their original contexts, simply meant such things as "the act of binding something tightly together" or "the act of paying close or careful attention to something." But this is hardly what we seem to mean by religion today.

So, where does this leave us? Well, it leaves us with a lot of questions in need of investigation: If a group of people do not have the concept, how can we study "their religion," let alone such other things as "their culture," "their economy," "their gender," or "their race"? This may sound silly, but for those no doubt well-meaning liberal scholars who endeavor not to "erase the indigenous perspective," someone must remind them that all of these concepts are our inevitably alien importations; they are the devices we in our culture use to map the world so as to make it knowable, and thereby establish specifically lived-worlds within it. (If such commentators took their own position seriously it would mean that they would simply remain silent when it comes to talking *about* the Other since it is inevitably and necessarily a talking *in place of* the Other.) Other related questions in need of attention would be: Is cross-cultural, comparative analysis of all such localized human meaning even possible? Is "religion," like "literature," "life," or "culture," simply an arbitrary taxon some of us in the guild use to organize and talk about aspects of the observable world that strike us as curious? Why is it that a term which, long ago, referred to actions (like binding or taking monastic vows) came to be so tightly associated with the world of inner emotions, values, disembodied beliefs, and belief systems that refer to insubstantial, invisible beings and lives beyond death? Moreover, why did such discourses on "religion" arise in the European world when and where they did? Why was it such a contagious notion, spreading the world over, and why do we continue to imagine it to be part of "the Human Experience"? Taking these questions seriously means that, in this newly emergent field, where we are further "perfecting our data" – to borrow a phrase once again from Louis Menard – "our object of interest would then be 'religion' as the general name of a generic anthropological category, a nominal, intellectual construction, surely not to be taken as a 'reality'" (Smith 2001b: 142).

But if our object of study is "religion," those who use it, and its socio-political effects, then we must be on our guard when proceeding with our studies of cross-cultural, cross-historical human behaviors and institutions, for this local or domestic classification, "religion," is so basic to our own way of knowing and reproducing our own social world that the temptation to deploy it in a matter-of-fact, descriptive manner when talking about others may sneak up on us in surprising ways, with unanticipated implications. This point is made very nicely by Susan Reynolds with regard to historical studies that employ the concept "nation." In her study of social organization in medieval Western Europe she notes:

> Most medieval historians would deny that they are nationalists, but that is because, like many historians of the phenomenon of nationalism, they see it as something aggressive, xenophobic, and deplorable, but do not look hard at the ideas which underlie it. Nationalist ideas, however, are more widespread than the unpleasant manifestation of nationalist emotions. ...
> The fundamental premise of nationalist ideas is that nations are objective realities, existing through history. Some such premise, however unarticulated, seems to be implied in much writing about the history of Europe, including medieval Europe, with its teleological emphasis on the development of modern states – the predestined "nation-states." It seems normally to be taken for granted that the nation-states of today are the true nations of history and that only they can ever have inspired loyalties which deserve to be called nationalist. ... [A]ny past unit of government which no one claims to be a nation now is *ipso facto* seen as having been less naturally cohesive in the past. It evidently did not enjoy the manifest destiny to solidarity and survival which is the essential attribute of the true nation. ...

[B]elief in the objective reality of nations inevitably diverts attention from itself: since the nation exists, belief in it is seen not as a political theory but as a mere recognition of fact. The history of nationalism becomes less a part of the history of political thought than of historical geography.

(1984: 251–253)

A practical example of this that has direct bearing on our field is found in Keith Whitelam's study of, as he phrases it, the invention of ancient Israel (2001; see also Silberman 1990 and Thompson 1999). He argues that "the dominant model for the presentation of Israelite history has been, and continues to be, that of a unified national entity in search of national territory struggling to maintain its national identity and land through the crises of history. It is a concept of the past which mirrors the presentation of the present" (21). By means of this hindsight gaze, Whitelam demonstrates how the contemporary nationalist imagination "has been projected back into the past to provide the legitimation and justification of the present" (22). Or, as he phrases it a little later in his book,

The foundation of the modern state has dominated scholarship to such an extent that the retrojection of the nation state into antiquity has provided the vital continuity which helps to justify and legitimize both.

(58)

Or, as the Canadian essayist and political commentator, Michael Ignatieff, puts it, one of the essential components of nationalism is the presumption "that the people of the world [past and present, we might add] naturally divide into nations" (2000: 87).

Just as the concepts nation or nation-state – let alone individual or citizen – are today so utterly basic, even vital, to many of our self-understandings and ability to self-organize that we routinely cast them backward in chronological time and outward in geographic space, so too, it is difficult not to understand, say, ancient Romans or Egyptians as having a "religion." After all, common sense tells us that religion is a human universal. But, as Reynolds points out quite nicely, there is something at stake in so easily projecting, in this case, backward in history or outward in culture our local classification, for along with its ability to organize certain sorts of human behaviors comes attendant socio-political implications. By means of such projection we may be doing something more than neutrally or passively classifying the world around us; instead, by means of such classifications we may very well be actively presenting back to ourselves the taxonomies that help to establish our own contingent and inevitably provincial social world as if their components were self-evident, natural, universal, and necessary. Scholarship on religion, then, "is not about some disinterested construction," as Whitelam argues in the case of modern histories of ancient Israel, "but an important question of contemporary identity and power" (73).

Before proceeding, an important point stressed in parts of this book must be repeated. Unlike some other writers who have recently tackled the problem of "religion," this book has not assumed that, once we have swept away what we take to be some outdated or troublesome definition for "religion" then some more accurate concept of religion or faith or spirituality will, like a phoenix, arise from the ashes of our current historical situation. This was the late Cantwell Smith's hope when he replaced "religion" with "personal faith in transcendence," something he took to be a universal aspect of Human Nature. However, as Foucault persuaded some of us, discourse is an inevitable violence that we do to things, suggesting that no one discourse will ever be any closer to "the way things are." Although he was writing of the discourse on sexuality/sex, I think Foucault's comments are just as applicable to religion: "One must not suppose," he cautioned,

> that there exists a certain sphere of sexuality that would be the legitimate concern of a free and disinterested scientific inquiry were it not the object of mechanisms of prohibition brought to bear by the economic or ideological requirements of power.
>
> (1990: 98)

Or, as he phrased it in the opening pages to the second volume, *The Use of Pleasure*, his series of studies

> was intended to be neither a history of sexual behaviors nor a history of representations, but a history of "sexuality" – the quotation marks have a certain importance. ... I wanted first to dwell on that quite recent and banal notion of "sexuality": to stand detached from it, bracketing its familiarity, in order to analyze the theoretical and practical context with which it has been associated. ... To speak of sexuality in this way, I had to break with a conception that was rather common.
>
> (1985: 3, 4)

Foucault strikes me as not attempting to discover some pristine or prepolitical sense of sex, freed from our sadly oppressive or petty morality, but, instead, as trying to determine "the modes according to which individuals are given to recognize themselves as sexual subjects" (1985: 5). Applying Foucault's attempt to historicize various techniques and experiences of subjectivity – or the means by which "the everyday individuality of everybody," as he phrased it in *Discipline and Punish* (1977a: 191), was brought to consciousness, making it an item of discourse – means that we too must break with a conception that is rather common. We can make a break with it by entertaining that the thing we routinely call religious experience or faith is the result of a complex discourse on religion (which is merely my rephrasing of J. Z. Smith's well-known point). In making this break we must remind ourselves that behind or before this discourse there lurks no purer, more real cross-cultural thing (i.e., faith, the sublime, spirituality, the holy, etc.). Taking the social and historical scale of analysis as our only available reference point, we come to see that there exists only assorted human behaviors, none any more or less significant, meaningful, or valuable than any other.[2]

If, then, discourses are by definition a "violence we do to things" – and if the generic, indistinguishable stuff of the world gets to count as isolatable "things" (i.e., items of discourse) only in light of competing, institutionalized systems of value, classification, and rank – then what criteria do we have to adjudicate these many violences we do? Which meanings will rise to the top and liberate us from what we portray to be our oppressive structures? However, if – as the old saying goes – there's no accounting for taste, then perhaps we can dispel with the myth of the given that fuels this quest for indigeneity and, instead, *try to account for why certain local and transient tastes and meanings become, for a time, fashionable or persuasive*. In this vein, I have adapted for the title of this final chapter a phrase of Foucault's, "the government of individualization" (1982: 781), to help make explicit the socio-political role our field's primary classification plays in human affairs.

A step toward just such a project appears to have been made by Peter Harrison in his impressive book, *"Religion" and the Religions in the English Enlightenment* (1990; see also Wiebe 1994). On the opening page he writes:

> The concepts "religion" and "the religions," as we presently understand them, emerged quite late in Western thought, during the Enlightenment. Between them, these two notions provided a new framework for classifying particular aspects of human life.
>
> (1)

Harrison's book is thus an exercise in studying the practical impact of these socio-cognitive categories during a specific period of European history. Despite his misgivings concerning Cantwell Smith's preference for "faith" over "religion" (misgivings clearly spelled out in Harrison's epilogue [174–175]), he nonetheless employs this traditional distinction, thus undermining what strikes me as the most promising and provocative part of his study. For example, soon after we find the above-quoted thesis statement, Harrison elaborates by employing the very interior/exterior, private/public scheme he appears to historicize: "In the present work I shall be examining in more detail this process of *the objectification of religious faith*" (2; emphasis added). Rather than seeing the concept and institution of "religion" or "faith" as one technique whereby an interior, seemingly apolitical zone is fabricated and named, Harrison – like Carrette, King, and Taves – seems to presume the existence of an inner, purely subjective disposition or attitude that somehow predates (both chronologically and logically) its setting, thus being objectified, externalized, expressed, manifested, controlled, or reified by means of the word "religion." Like many other critics of "religion," then, a traditional realism creeps back in, despite the appearance of a social constructionist critique. What such critics take away with one hand, they swiftly give back with the other.

A similar technique is found in an even more recent essay on the "strengths and weaknesses" of Durkheim's contributions to the study of religion. After acknowledging that "the word religion is our word," Thomas Idinopulos elaborates:

> The word, religion, is our modern word for the very good reason that the sheer differentiation of functions and roles in modern life forces us to distinguish between politics, labor, commerce, leisure, art, religion, etc. The word, religion, acquired its own distinct meaning when the forces of secularization became so dominant in western culture that religious belief and practice became distinctly human acts. For once secularity became fully evident in society it was possible to speak by contrast of the religious way of life.
>
> (2002: 9–10)

Instead of seeing the practical use of "religion" in opposition to "secularity" to have been one of the techniques that enabled the so-called process of modernist differentiation, Idinopulos argues that the brute fact of socio-political differentiation "forces us to distinguish" within what previously seems to have been a homogeneously sacred realm. Or, as Idinopulos phrases it, due to the unholy "forces of secularization ... religious belief and practice *became* distinctly human acts" (emphasis added). Prior to secularization, and prior to religious beliefs and practices *becoming* human acts, I presume they were simply religious acts. Drawing on the proverbial example of the ancient person as one who lives in a thoroughly romantic world of uniform meaning, he goes on to say, "this interweaving of religion with everything else in life was true of archaic people" (10). But if "religion" is indeed *our* word, then how can it be used so easily to discuss just what archaic people did or did not weave together? Taking his own position seriously means it is impossible to talk about religion prior to so-called secularization, and thus ancient people – who no doubt used classification systems of their own in an elaborate manner – must therefore have inhabited a world which was neither religious nor secular, neither sacred nor profane. Apart from pitching what he admits to be a local word backward in time as if it refers to some necessary feature of human experience (as identified above, this is a technique commonly found in nationalist studies of nationalism), the trouble with his evidently Cantwell Smithian analysis is that in attempting to historicize the word "religion," Idinopulos romanticizes ancient life by presupposing that sacred and secular refer to historically distinct things (or, better put, "forces"), with one arising after the other.[3] As stated above, whereas the word "religion" has a history, the concept (i.e., religious practices) seems to be eternal and universal. Presuming these two discursive moments to be substantively different, and that one (i.e., religion as concept, or religion-as-matter-of-fact) historically precedes the other (i.e., the forces of secularization that invented the word "religion") – rather than seeing word/concept and religious/secular as part of the same socio-rhetorical moment, as devices for concocting meaningful worlds by means of the varying degree of tension in which they can be held – signifies that Idinopulos's work reproduces the strategy that this chapter is seeking to historicize. In his essay we read the old, old story of a homogenous, meaningful past fractured and thus desacralized by the impersonal forces of modernity. It is a story that has not changed much and still holds much allure for scholars.

Although my own conclusion to the preceding eleven chapters could profitably cite the words from Harrison's own concluding chapter – "I hope that this study has highlighted the need to revise some cherished assumptions about the constructs 'religion' and 'the religions'" (175) – the future of the study of "religion" (and, as Foucault said above, "the quotation marks have a certain importance") does not lie in the direction of searching for a more adequate or accurate definition of religion that accords with, protects, or recovers the interior and prior zone called faith. Neither does he share the presumption that a homogeneously sacred sphere or zone of faith lies in the historical background of the sadly limited, modernist, and disillusioned sacred/secular dichotomy. Instead, *it lies in the direction of thoroughly historicizing the private/public, belief/practice, Church/State, and sacred/secular binaries*, scrutinizing their historical development, their rhetorical deployment, questioning the narrative widely accepted by historians that the engine of secularization drives European history, and asking what is entailed in presuming that *any* moment of human praxis – including the praxis of discourses on privacy, intuition, feeling, piety, and faith – somehow escapes the uncharted ebb and flow of contingent and thus contestable social history. It lies in the direction of taking seriously Jonathan Smith's position that "[r]eligion is not a native category. It is not a first person term of self-categorization. It is a category imposed from the outside on some aspect of native culture" (1998: 269). The historical fact of these widely circulating classifications – and not their supposed one-to-one fit to social reality – thus comprises the residue that we inherit from a previous generation of scholars, the raw material with which we have to work. So, unlike some recent scholars who, in the midst of their critique of, say, Eliade's dehistoricization of religious symbols, nonetheless recommend that we "return to the realm of social, political, and material context in the study of *religious* symbols and experiences" (as this position is described by Urban [2001b: 438; emphasis added]; Urban is here citing Wasserstrom [1999: 243–244] on the origins of this call for historicizing religious symbols), my question regards the presumed necessity of the qualifier "religious." What is accomplished by segregating some obviously historical, political, etc., symbol systems and actions by classifying them as religious? Why not simply call them political?[4]

Take, for example, the following claim which, at first glance, seems to accord with the project of this present book: "the rhetorical power of the doctrinal, ritual, and symbolic forms that constitute religion is such that those who study these forms tend to succumb to their charms" (Benavides 2001a: 455). It is crucial that the project being recommended here be distinguished from this, insomuch as Benavides is interested in the rhetorical power of what we usually see to be a religion's sub-components (i.e., its ritual or symbolic forms, much like Ninian Smart's "dimensions") rather than the rhetorical power of the very presumption that just these human practices ought to have a special designation (e.g., ritual rather than habit) and, further, are naturally to be collected together and called religion's dimensions, i.e., that there is such a distinguishable thing as religion, let alone its assorted sub-components. Anticipating the conclusion of this chapter, I would venture to say that scholars such as Benavides have understandably succumbed to the charms of a socio-cognitive device that makes their social worlds possible – "religion."

To repeat Foucault's words, in this final chapter my aim is for readers simply "to stand detached from it [in our case, 'religion'], bracketing its familiarity, in order to analyze the theoretical and practical context with which it has been associated." For our object of study is the normally operating assumptions about how we classify, rank, and value our worlds, and which worlds are made possible by which classifications. As already stated in the book's opening, then, this chapter presses readers "to learn to what extent the effort to think one's own history can free thought from what it silently thinks, and so enable it to think differently" (Foucault 1985: 9). A thorough historicization of "self" and "religion," and thus of "State" and "secular," would therefore take as its data these very classifications and inquire what goes into, and what comes of, presuming the world is somehow naturally divided between sacred and secular, private and public, self and group. In Tomoko Masuzawa's words, this involves scholars being "dispatched to inspect the exact date of [their] manufacture, to investigate the history, the process, the mechanism, the circumstances of manufacture" (2000: 129). Most recently, the Dutch scholar of nationalism, Peter van der Veer, has returned from the archives with valuable information concerning the circumstances surrounding the manufacture of the related category "spirituality." In his study of the simultaneous impact of colonialism in both the British center as well as the colonized Indian periphery, he demonstrates persuasively that "a master concept like 'spirituality' is not epiphenomenal to 'real history' but rather productive of historical change" (2001: 69). When it comes to the master rhetorical trope "religion," this is precisely the position argued in this chapter.

With the dusty archives in mind, the example of the eighteenth-century German writer, Friedrich Schleiermacher, is often used when talking about the rise of the modern concept of "religion" as a deeply personal feeling characteristic of the self in its purest, most noble, or basic form. Despite having often drawn on the example of Schleiermacher myself when critiquing the rhetorical uses of "religious experience" and "piety" (McCutcheon 2001b: 4), I now see that, because his is an example that generally functions to lodge the issue of the category "religion" within what is seen as a distinctly unique human pursuit, theology, drawing on his work as an example can serve to reinforce the modern concept rather than redescribing and historicizing it. In other words, one cannot employ the theologian/non-theologian classification (e.g., "According to the theologian Schleiermacher ..."; "As an atheist, Marx argued ...") while attempting to historicize the very concept by means of which such distinctions are held to be meaningful – that is, the concept religion. Instead, I would like to close this book with a meditation on the manner in which the presumption that an inner, spiritual life exists functions to discipline potentially unruly human material characterized by differing interests, creating of them a collective Whole, a nation of "civil" citizens comprised of governable selves. The following is therefore not meant as a definitive study but a sketch of one direction for a future research program.

In doing so I assume that the future of the study of religion lies in the direction of exploring just what Foucault may have meant by his term governmentality (1979), a term he used for the "contact between technologies of domination of others and those of the self" (Foucault 1988b: 19). To venture a rather speculative claim, the groundwork for which was laid in an earlier essay (McCutcheon 2001b: ch. 10), *large-scale socio-political organizations such as the liberal nation-state may not have been possible without the modern disciplining concept religion and the so-called civil, social institutions made possible by the infectious presupposition of a set apart private zone of belief, meaning, and value.* My contention, then, is that future scholarship in our field will investigate *how it is that this particular socio-rhetoric makes selves (a.k.a., citizens) appropriate to the needs of those whose material interests dominate the modern, liberal-democratic nation-state.* I therefore believe that Marx and Engels were indeed correct when they speculated that all critique was premised on a critique of religion – not, as they surely meant, those obviously distinct institutions such as Christianity and what they took to be their seemingly oppressive hold on the working class, but rather the very fact that we continue to exist as members of groups by presuming to exist an interior, private life of the mind/spirit/faith. Although not wanting to overstate my case, I would hazard to say that all critique may well turn out to be premised on a critique of "religion." If so, then – and this is the truly ironic part – any use of this category, whether as part of one's criticism or praise for this or that religion, may equally well help to reproduce the larger social group.

Due to the recent history of immigration that has made much of North America a supposed cultural mosaic, we can easily see the practical utility of this discourse on religion, along with the reason for the contemporary concern among some intellectuals with using the study of religion *qua* deeply personal, private beliefs as a tool for resolving the apparent problem of observable cultural difference (the many) by essentializing and dehistoricizing it within the heart of unseen yet universal religious identity (the esoteric One). As previously noted, Diana Eck's most recent work on the topic of religious pluralism in the U.S.

comprises but the most obvious example (2001). It may therefore not be a coincidence (though demonstrating a causal link must await another day) that the triumphant rebirth of this personalized discourse on religion in the U.S. roughly coincided with the Immigration Act of 1965, which, in the words of the literary critic Stanley Fish, "shifted [U.S.] immigration priorities from those Nordic European peoples who had furnished America with its original stock to Asian and African peoples from Third World countries" (1994: 83). Thus, the presence of a new and alien "them" required innovative socio-rhetorical tools to re-make what had previously seemed to be a seamless "us," helping to explain why the U.S. denominational system in the early twentieth century (long prior to these changing immigration trends) was so successful in exerting its control over higher education and thus fighting off the early advances of the young humanistic discipline of Comparative Religion – but not so a few short decades later. That the U.S. Supreme Court was so preoccupied with issues of religion and the public sphere throughout the late 1950s and 1960s (including, but not limited to, the much cited 1963 Abingdon v. Schempp public school prayer decision) is also evidence of this; the Court's invocation of the notion of religion as a zone of unverifiable yet important private opinion juxtaposable to some stable and self-evident zone of public practice (signified by the often used trope, "rule of law") has served the nation-state well when it came time to adjudicate between familiar, normal, and civil behavior, on the one hand, and alien, abnormal, and illegal activities, on the other – all the while making and remaking a specific idea of the nation in the process.

But the prominent rhetoric of private experience we find in modern nation-states is hardly new; after all, conflicts in the midst of the so-called social mosaic have been around for a very long time. In some historic periods, in some contemporary regions of the world, and at specifically stressed moments in our own world, physical coercion (e.g., torture, warfare, incarceration, etc.) ensures the smooth operation of a social world. However, it is the shift from organizing social life by controlling the behavior of bodies to controlling the thinking of minds and the perception of selves that most attracts my interest. Examples that bear a direct relevance for private/public and Church/State rhetorics as they have developed in the contemporary U.S., for example, can be found far earlier than Schleiermacher, in the political writings of such influential early European nation-builders and political theorists as Thomas Hobbes, John Locke, and Jean Jacques Rousseau. Despite some obvious and significant disagreements between the writings of these three, they all employ a highly individualist sociology – "MAN is born free; and everywhere he is in chains," as Rousseau famously phrased it – which makes it possible for them to imagine a pure, individual zone of preference and opinion which is free from the realm of fact and public intervention and thus no threat to public order. Whether this rhetorical space is used by such writers to ensure the safety of their own dissenting group, under siege from a dominant group, or used by them to limit the scope of influence exercised by dissenters, the outcome is the same: a status quo is effectively reproduced by individualizing and marginalizing opposition. It is precisely this technique of governing that is accomplished by means of "religion" insomuch as it connotes a supposedly asocial zone, long thought to be the residence of the Human Spirit – what Robert Solomon has characterized as a "transcendental pretense" (1988: 3). Because of the impact this pretense has had in political philosophy, I wish to spend some time on a few historic examples that predate our current rhetoric of private experience. However, a future cross-cultural project might involve studying the manner in which what I am calling the rhetoric of privacy, or what Hugh Urban names as the syndrome of the secret (2001b, see also 1998), contributes to all acts of social formation.

Before proceeding, it should be noted that such a historical, cross-cultural study was indeed begun with the impressive, multi-volume *A History of Private Life*. However, as provocative as these volumes are, at times they cannot help but pitch backward in time our contemporary classification system, thereby reproducing its (and our social world's) legitimacy rather than historicizing it (as observed by Reynolds in her study of modern nationalism and medieval Europe). For instance, although his work has influenced my own thinking significantly, in his chapter on private life in the Roman Empire entitled, "Tranquilizers," Paul Veyne (1987: 207–233) discusses private and public religion in the Roman empire, apparently without considering the implications of assuming that a portion of human practice – that part having to do with beliefs in gods and after life – is obviously set apart *as* religious (whether practiced privately or publicly). Describing private vs. public religion fails to theorize how the artifice of privacy, belief, and experience are created in the first place by means of this and other such powerful classifications and discourses. Much like taking hallways for granted in the study of private domestic space, his default distinction of religious vs. non-religious assumes, rather than problematizes, the existence of a distinct zone of belief and faith. Instead, I am hypothesizing that a technique for constructing large-scale social identities may well be a socio-rhetoric of privacy (along with the politico-legal fictions it helps to establish) contained in the discourse on religion, whereby zones of possible public discontent are individualized and spiritualized, and thus contained within safe zones of non-substantial and ethereal "experience," "faith," and "belief."

To support this hypothesis, I turn to the work of several of the better-known early-modern political theorists of the nation-state. I do so knowing full well that the following, brief survey of their work, along with the various contemporary examples upon which I will draw, serves only as a broad outline of what must no doubt be a larger, more detailed, and likely collaborative future project. So, to borrow the opening words from Whitelam's study of the politics of writing the history of ancient Israel, anyone portraying the following as anything but the general framework for such a future project "runs the risk of being misunderstood as arrogant because it appears to imply the ability to control a vast range of material which is beyond the competence of most individuals and certainly beyond my abilities" (2001: 1).

With this important qualification in mind, take the example of Thomas Hobbes's study of (in fact, prescription for) the workings of a "civil" society, *Leviathan* (1651). We read:

> Fear of power invisible, feigned by the mind, or imagined from tales *publicly allowed*, religion; *not allowed*, superstition. And when the power imagined is truly such as we imagine, true religion.
> (Part 1, ch. 6 [1962: 51]; emphasis added)[5]

Although these words were written well over 300 years ago, we see in them an elaborate taxonomy which accomplishes practical, political work. For Hobbes, religion is to be distinguished from mere superstition (what many today would rename as "cult"), not so much because one is true (though Hobbes predictably goes on to distinguish religion from true religion, which, of course, he associates with Christianity), but because one is "publicly allowed" – that is to say, allowed to exist by the sovereign. Hobbes rightly understood that classification is a political act; in this case, the right to name something as religion was possessed only by those in power (as it still is). More than this, the thing so identified as a religion was understood purely to be matter of personal preference:

> by reason of different fancies, judgments, and passions of several men, hath grown up into ceremonies so different, that those which are used by one man, are for the most part ridiculous to another.
> (Part 1, ch. 12 [90])

So religion – which, for Hobbes, had its origins in the belief in ghosts, our ignorance of the actual causes of things, our devotion toward that which we do not understand and thus fear, and our desire to know the future – is a matter of private emotion, tastes, and personal judgments concerning an invisible world. Moreover, a particular subset of these dispositions were sanctioned by the sovereign and could, therefore, be expressed or manifested in public.

Only if we presume that religion and secularity are substantively distinct – one holy and the other unholy, one the zone of the Church and one the sphere of the State, one the realm of belief and faith and the other the province of action and politics – will we see writers such as Hobbes to be an early representative of the inexorable "forces of secularization." If we make a shift in our thinking then we no longer will see two conflicting impersonal systems, historical epochs, or modes of thought. Instead, we will see politically engaged actors artfully using tools to negotiate power and place within ever-changing and uncontrollable structural settings. For example, we will see Hobbes's writings on civility and "religion" in light of his own context. We will learn of his longtime relationship with the pro-royalist Devonshires (in 1608 he began working as a tutor for the young William Cavendish, the son of William Cavendish Sr., the first earl of Devonshire; eventually Hobbes took on the role of being an advisor to the family) and his role in the political turmoil that predated the English Civil War. Not just his political writings but his use of the classification "religion" will be placed within the context of his defenses of Charles I which forced Hobbes to flee to France due to the English Parliament's public conflicts with the King (Hobbes was in France from 1640 until 1651).

An especially useful model for how to make such a shift in our thinking can be found in the opening chapters to Bruce Lincoln's *Theorizing Myth* (1999), where he examines the role of *mythos* and *logos* in ancient Greek literature. Swimming against the stream of yet another old, old story – the one that pits irresistible, cool-headed rationality against impassioned storytelling – Lincoln understands these two types of speech not as substantively different and not as representing two different modes of thought, but as rhetorical techniques useful for authorizing and contesting specific social arrangements. It is precisely this shift, from content to form, that is necessary if we are to see writers such as Hobbes (let alone Plato) as thoroughly historical actors working within larger political settings to concoct meaningfully inhabitable worlds by means of negotiation, classification, and rhetoric. This is the shift that allows us to rewrite a history of, for example, such events as the Reformation; instead of the old story of warring religious beliefs and creeds, all of which are somehow separate from (and sadly appropriated by) the politics of feuding lords, we can understand the manner in which concrete, practical contests and political realignments were waged all across European society by means of various rhetorics.[6] "Church" and "State" thus function like "*mythos*" and "*logos*," as two poles of the same contest. Instead of presuming an inner world of faith already to exist – and thus something that political writers either attempt to recover or malign – this shift allows us to see how the rhetorical fabrication of such a zone makes certain social worlds possible, more attractive, or less legitimate.

With this shift from content to form in mind, consider the case of John Locke who, by the winter of 1685–6, had drafted the Latin text for his first "*Epistle de tolerantia*"[7] while hiding for two years in Holland from the Stuart royalists. In such a circumstance the distinction between private sentiment and public order was understandably quite useful. Having spent three and a half years in France, he returned to England in May of 1679; the previous August there was the fabricated revelation of the "Popish Plot" in which a conspiracy to assassinate Charles II aimed at replacing him with his Catholic brother James. As a result, the Parliament had been dissolved by Charles (on the details of Locke's context see Milton 1994). Locke's letter thus communicates his concern over the effects of dissent, effects that occurred at the intersection of what he understood as private, personal conscience and the collective interests represented by the sovereign, public authority. Because the thing called religion was identified by its claims concerning an unseen world and the origins and destiny of history – "the establishment of opinions, which for the most part are about nice and intricate matters that exceed the capacity of ordinary understandings" (Locke 1955: 7) –

Locke advised that, while freedom of conscience ought to prevail, the government's authority would have to be exercised to ensure the smooth public interactions of its citizens. (As he phrased it in *The Second Treatise of Government*, individuals unite in a society "for the mutual preservation of their lives, liberties, and estates, which I call by the general name 'property.'") Although one is free to hold and propose beliefs of all sorts, one is *not* free to impose them or put them into practice, insomuch as such beliefs – what he terms "the diversity of opinions" – are all too fallible and unverifiable.

"All the life and power of true religion," he was then able to conclude, "consists in the inward and full persuasion of the mind; and faith is not faith without believing. ... [T]rue and saving religion consists in the inward persuasion of the mind" (18). Once established, this private zone of belief makes civil society possible:

> I esteem it above all things necessary to distinguish exactly the business of civil government from that of religion, and to settle the just bounds that lie between the one and the other. If this be not done, there can be no end put to the controversies that will be always arising between those that have, or at least pretend to have, on the one side, a concernment for the interests of men's souls, and, on the other side, a care of the commonwealth.
>
> (17)

That Locke's sense of "civility" and "commonwealth" are hardly common – after all, he has no trouble *not* tolerating those who undermine the State by means of their intolerance, their atheism, or their treasonous service to foreign powers (15) – should be more than obvious to us at this historic juncture. Come to think of it, he's not all that different from contemporary writers on this score. Commenting on his experiences at the 2000 International Association for the History of Religions (IAHR) Congress in South Africa, where the highly praised values of civility and religious tolerance were much praised, my former colleague, Jack Llewellyn, has observed: "Now, I believe in tolerance as much as the next person, that is to say, only up to a point." Although lacking the obvious irony of Llewellyn's Voltaire-like comment, Rousseau made much the same point: "It is impossible to live in peace with people one believes to be damned," he wrote; for "to love them would be to hate the God who punishes them; *it is an absolute duty either to redeem or to torture them*" (Book IV, ch. 8; 1982: 186–187; emphasis added). As is apparent from the blunt manner in which Rousseau phrases the point, toleration

> is often [always, I would add] actually not a transcendent value, but one that operates within a framework that defines its boundaries. In all the cases that I have mentioned so far, in the U.K., Israel, Nigeria, Scandinavia, and South Africa, I think that the overarching project might

be identified as *nation building* or *nation managing*. Classes about religion [or so the standard argument goes] should promote tolerance because that will serve to reduce civil strife (which is in the interests of the state even as it serves to further marginalize those who aren't part of the elite). ... It would be good for business if there was less civil strife and religious education should engender tolerance towards that end.

(Llewellyn 2001: 62; emphasis added)

Llewellyn is certainly onto something here. But before proceeding, it should be pointed out that, given a social theory that starts with the premise that all social formations are the products of techniques that portray one particular set of local interests and values as if they were self-evidently corporate and thus transcendent – to the exclusion of a host of historically prior and currently competing local interests and institutions – it is hardly an indictment to recover the specific interests served by rhetorics of tolerance, civility, and the commonwealth. To phrase it another way, Locke's "Mahometans" are quite easily and naturally excluded from his State, for it would be "ridiculous for anyone to profess himself" to be one while also being "faithful to a Christian magistrate" (15). What should attract our attention, then, is not that such discourses on toleration are hypocritical (for such a judgment is propelled by the assumption that it could somehow be otherwise) or that all discourses on tolerance contain an inevitable element of intolerance, but, instead how easily boundary policing and maintenance are glossed over when like-minded – or, better phrased, like-interested and like-organized – people converse on the so-called common good and supposedly civil society.

With the complexity of tolerance discourses in Locke's era in mind, Christopher Hill's recent essay (2000) on toleration in seventeenth-century England should be mentioned. Although several of the essays in this book, *The Politics of Toleration in Modern Life*, endeavor to promote a specific brand of contemporary tolerance (and hence a specific idea of the group – in this case the U.K.), Hill nicely historicizes tolerance discourses from that period, revealing the politics of inclusion.[8] Recovering the practical setting of these rhetorical techniques – "English men and women were being burnt alive for their religious beliefs as late as 1612," Hill writes, "and the Archbishop Neile of York ... said in 1639 that he thought it would be a good thing to revive the practice. Burning heretics had done the church a great deal of good, he said nostalgically" (2000: 27) – Hill convincingly demonstrates that "the evolution of toleration was not a smooth intellectual process, proceeding from argument to argument until all were convinced" (27). In other words, by historicizing discourses on toleration Hill dispels the generally held presumptions that (i) toleration is a universal, politically neutral, and thus self-evident transcendent value that, (ii) once proposed, proceeds by its own inner momentum, catching on like wildfire since everyone involved cannot help but see how sensible it is to "live and let live" on what is sometimes called a level playing field. Instead of seeing tolerance as a disengaged, universal theory, Hill persuades his readers that such discourses are political techniques whereby social agents work, in the midst of conflicts between a variety of oppositional and dominant discourses, to make a specific sort of political space, as in the already mentioned case of Hobbes who, in Hill's opinion, "was right in thinking that some bishops [who returned with Charles II] would have liked to burn him" (28). That was 1660; as late as the 1690s, Hill observes, Englishmen were still being hanged for blasphemy.

Although Hill seems at first to employ the categories of "religious" and "political" in the traditional manner – assuming the latter to refer to such things as party politics or active forms of participation in the political process, Hill suggests that, for example, John Bunyan (1628–1688) was motivated by religious beliefs to preach in 1659 against the wealthy (32) – it soon becomes clear that we can read this as a form of descriptive analysis whereby we take seriously the participant perspective of historic actors such as Bunyan. For instance, Hill notes that, "when, Bunyan faced the Bedfordshire justices in 1661, *he thought* he was refusing to give up his God-given vocation of preaching" (31; emphasis added); however, since the gentry's perception was that "he was a dangerous agitator who was stirring up class hostility in the very delicate situation of post-restoration England" (31), our goal as scholars is not to adjudicate between these two sets of participant perceptions but, rather, to study the conflict between the two, as they meet in a specific, historical and material setting. It is the conflict between these two sets of interests, each of which is encoded within a different rhetorical style, that comprises the setting of discourses on tolerance and intolerance. Taking materialist analysis seriously, then, Hill accurately understands just why the gentry of Bunyan's day refused simply to see him as "a godly non-conformist preacher" (30) and, instead, found his pro-"hedge-creeper and highwayman" rhetoric to be dangerous to their practical interests. They jailed him for twelve years (Bunyan would not silence himself by agreeing not to preach) because his public talk (a form of political praxis) had crossed a line.

If we collapse the supposed distinction between those aspects of the public spheres we label "religion" and "politics," we will press beyond Hill's already insightful analysis, disagreeing when he seems to conclude that, "though Bunyan was certainly not a political figure, he had politics forced upon him by the policies of post-restoration governments" (31). Speaking out in public against the gentry, regardless of the rhetorical/institutional setting of such speech or the manner in which it is authorized (i.e., appeals to Scripture, the Will of God, self-evident Truths, universal features of Human Nature, etc.), is fundamentally a political act; it is not that it becomes political only once external structures are "forced upon" us (as if our subjectivity were a content that miraculously predates its various contexts), but that it is political from the outset, since it is speech that originates from within a specific structural (i.e., economic, social, etc.) context. Being careful not to project backward in history our own modern technique for managing dissent, we will therefore agree with

Hill when he concludes that "in the seventeenth century, when state and church were one – perhaps in other societies where party and state are one – toleration is a *political* issue, inseparable from politico-social questions which historians of toleration sometimes overlook" (36). Such historians of toleration, much like Reynolds's depiction of scholars of nationalism and, I would add, like many scholars of religion, overlook this precisely because of their own contemporary and terribly successful device for constraining opposition: their use of the politically expedient categories of religion, faith, inspiration, motivation, intention, agency, experience, etc.

One example of a failure to avoid projecting our modern techniques backward in history will have to suffice: in his, at times, provocative recent work, *Terror in the Mind of God: The Global Rise of Religious Violence*, Mark Juergensmeyer (2000) endeavors to recover the participant viewpoint in understanding why religious people engage in violent action. Taking these people seriously, however, means elevating to the level of analysis their own participant disclosures concerning such things as their "religious motivation." In other words, instead of reading their claims concerning, say, "the Word of God" or "the Will of Allah" as potent rhetorical devices or cues of relevance to members of their specific group and thus effective for organizing and authorizing their group's strategic, oppositional behaviors, Juergensmeyer reads their claims at face value and is left with the problem of how such deeply religious people could commit such abhorrent acts.[9] Such liberal writers thus attempt "to have their cake and eat it too": (i) they wish to respect the participant's (perhaps even their own) self-understanding, thus representing religion as something deeply important and transcendent, no matter which or whose religion; yet, as members of obviously dominant social groups which are, at least in part, dependent on the scholar's work to re-create the conditions of the group's dominance (ii) such writers have little choice but to try to distinguish "their" violent actions from "our" peaceful, civil, normal, and purpose-giving religion – religion "at its best," as Juergensmeyer prescribes it (240).

To accomplish this disengagement, Juergensmeyer develops a two-fold typology of violence: "exaggerated violence" (120), or "performative violence" (122 ff.), which is symbolic, dramatic, and theatrical, is distinguished from practical or "strategic violence," which is real and effective. Whereas the former is merely an expression of faith that, once manifested in public, "forces those who witness it directly or indirectly into that 'consciousness'" (125), the latter is "focused ... on an immediate political acquisition" (124). Or, to rephrase the point: "Such explosive scenarios are not *tactics* directed toward an immediate, earthly, or strategic goal, but *dramatic* events intended to impress for their symbolic significance. As such, they can be analyzed as one would any other symbol, ritual, or sacred drama" (123). Readers must be clear on one point: it is not that all historic acts can be studied both in terms of their symbolic and practical consequences (more on the troublesome nature of this distinction below), but that these two spheres are rather sharply distinguished from each other. For example, the harsh manner in which he distinguishes the symbolic from the real is evident in the following: "The very act, however, *is sometimes more than symbolic*: by demonstrating the vulnerability of governmental power, to some degree it weakens that power. Because power is largely a matter of perception, symbolic statements *can lead to* [which means that they sometimes do not lead to] real results" (132; emphasis added). A little earlier Juergensmeyer had commented, "I can imagine a line with 'strategic' on the one side and 'symbolic' on the other, with various acts of terrorism located in between" (123). Although some might dispute my critique by reading him to be saying that all violent acts have both components, with one or the other emphasized, I would counter by noting that, regardless the participants' intentions, *all human acts are thoroughly practical, strategic, earthly, and thus political* (meaning something other than "party politics" or the sort of action that leads to a change in a specific government policy, which I assume Juergensmeyer to have in mind when he uses the term "political"). Moreover, it is highly problematic to distinguish symbolic from real in the first place, for I cannot conceive of any real historical human action which is not symbolic, from wearing clothes, to setting a breakfast table and writing a book – even using the symbolic/real typology itself is both symbolic *and* political! They are both, and can never be more one than the other – not, unless, as participants, observers, and analysts we seek to lessen this or that real impact by deploying a symbol system that serves to segregate the action to the realm of mere theatrical expression, as if an inner, creative impulse can or cannot be manifested in social life. It is as if such things as "art" could be either political or aesthetic, or more one than the other, instead of seeing discourses on aesthetics (or discourses on symbols, i.e., semiotics) as being historical and thus political through and through.

This is why I find Juergensmeyer's typology, and the sort of study of violence it makes possible, to be but an instance of conflict management and status quo maintenance. Studying certain sorts of violence – for instance, the Aum Shinrikyo nerve gas attack in the Tokyo subway in 1995 (Juergensmeyer's ch. 6; see also 123–124) – as more symbolic and religious than practical, as ritual rather than politics, segregates a particular zone of human action within the realm of inner meaning, thereby reserving the public realm of action for those actions some "we" find less troublesome and less perplexing. Deploying these conflict management techniques (i.e., the thoroughly modernist binaries of private/public, faith/action, symbolic/real, in which the former is consistently privileged over the latter), Juergensmeyer is able to look back in history and, just as Reynolds, Whitelam, Ignatieff, and Hill observed, remake the past in a manner conducive to the contemporary need for a specific type of public civility. For instance, unlike the historian Hill who commented, "in the seventeenth century, when state and church were one," Juergensmeyer writes:

> From the time that modern secular nationalism emerged in the eighteenth
> century as a product of the European Enlightenment's political values, it

has assumed a distinctly anti-religious, or at least anticlerical, posture. ...
[The work of Locke and Rousseau] had the effect of taking religion – at
least Church religion – out of public life. ... Modernity signaled not only
the demise of the Church's institutional authority and clerical control, but
also the loosening of religion's ideological and intellectual grip on society.

(224–225)

The important point is that Hill understands that religion/politics,
sacred/secular, and Church/State are co-existing binaries that co-developed and
are necessarily used in concert with one another (a point to which I return
below), not two substantively and historically separate zones, one of which
happens to predate the other (as suggested previously by Harrison and
Idinopulos). If the position being argued throughout the preceding chapters is
understood as supporting the latter reading – such that the European
Enlightenment is thought to have oppressively privatized faith – then a subtle
but significant difference between my position and those of writers such as
Juergensmeyer has been lost or overlooked. Whether, for example, pre-seven-
teenth-century Europeans, or people from contemporary cultures other than our
own, believe(d) in gods or a life after death, or whatever we today happen to
define religion to be, I would argue that they were not religious. Instead, taking
seriously the historic or cultural specificity of these people means entertaining
that they were simply going about their particular social life, appealing to and
employing local classification schemes that were useful in reproducing their
specific worlds that satisfied specific biological and social needs they happened
to have. Failing to take seriously that, in a previous European era, people organizing themselves and mapping their worlds by means of effective rhetorical
techniques somewhat different but directly related to our own, many commentators have little choice but to envision a homogenous zone of the sacred that
historically preceded, and was oppressively constrained by, the Enlightenment.
(At this point I can hear the echo of Joseph Campbell's analysis of the supposedly pure authenticity of Native American spirituality or ancient tribal life, for
example.) For in the midst of this sacred/secular antagonism (which is significantly different from understanding it, as I do, as a binary working in concert to
make a specifically meaningful social space legitimate and another illegitimate),
we recover once again the notion of a private faith distinguishable from its
embodiment in ritual and institution (i.e., references to "Church religion" and
the "anti-clerical" critique of the Enlightenment). This very distinction, the
one that fuels studies such as Juergensmeyer's, is the modernist technique that
ought to comprise the data of analysis.

With Juergensmeyer's above quotation in mind, then, we return to the eighteenth century, moving forward from the work of Hobbes and Locke to that of
Rousseau, the third theorist whose writings form the backdrop of our own preoccupation with private variance and public civility, with inner faith and outer
expression. Rousseau deserves our attention because he is the European political

theorist best known for the manner in which he "reveals and celebrates the atomistic, autonomous self" (Gutman 1988: 100), an approach that is evident in his view that the "essential worship is that of the heart" (Rousseau 1979: 308). That his own life – like that of Hobbes and Locke – was characterized by overt political controversy (e.g., *Emile* [1762] was ordered burned by the French government and his own arrest was ordered; he escaped to Prussia; the government of Berne eventually ordered him out of its territory, etc.) likely has much to do with the manner in which the privacy of "religion" is used in his writings to create room within dominant groups for dissent. As might be expected, then, in writing *The Social Contract* (1762) he drew quite naturally on the same rhetorical techniques already found in other early-modern political theorists. For instance, Jesus, he observes,

> came to establish a spiritual kingdom on earth; this kingdom, by separating the theological system from the political, meant that the state ceased to be a unity, and it caused those intestine divisions which have never ceased to disturb Christian peoples. Now as the new idea of a kingdom of another world could never have entered the minds of pagans, they always regarded Christians as true rebels who, under the cloak of hypocritical submission, only awaited the moment to make themselves independent and supreme, and cunningly to usurp that authority which they made a show of respecting while they were weak. Such was the cause of their persecutions.
>
> What the pagans feared did indeed happen; then everything altered its countenance; the humble Christians changed their tune and soon the so-called kingdom of the other world was seen to become, under a visible ruler, the most violent despotism of this world.
>
> However, since princes and civil laws have always existed, the consequence of this dual power has been an endless conflict of jurisdiction, which has made any kind of good polity impossible in Christian states, where men have never known whether they ought to obey the civil ruler or the priest.
>
> (Book IV, ch. 8; 1982: 178–179)

Without sanctioning Rousseau's understanding of history or his theory of the rise of Christianity, we can still find merit in his observation concerning the practical work done by the Church/State split: without the internalization of conscience, an unending conflict will exist within populations comprised of subgroups with complex and competing interests. Yet marginal or emergent social formations have little choice but to utilize this distinction so as to carve out a zone in which to exist – making Matthew 22:21, "Then he said to them, 'Render therefore to Caesar the things that are Caesar's, and to God the things that are God's," a fascinating study in tactical, emergent social engineering.

Rousseau's understanding of "the spiritual kingdom" makes evident that the internalization of dissenting voices by means of spiritualization is well under way in his day as well.[10] "Of all Christian authors," he insightfully observes, "the philosopher Hobbes is the only one who saw clearly both the evil and the remedy, and who dared to propose reuniting the two heads of the eagle and fully restoring the political unity without which neither the state nor the government will ever be well constituted" (180). This remedy, as already demonstrated, was made possible by a romanticized sense of early Christianity wedded to a thoroughly individualist sociology where group membership was premised on unaccountable personal choice, taste, and preference – as in Locke's view of a church as "a voluntary society of men, joining themselves together of their own accord" (20) – a presumption we today find among U.S. rational choice theorists of religion. Or, as Rousseau phrased it,

> the religion of the private person, or Christianity, not the Christianity of today, but that of the Gospel, which is altogether different. Under this holy, sublime and true religion, men, as children of the same God, look on all others as brothers, and the society which unites them is not even dissolved in death.
> But this religion, having no specific connexion [sic] with the body politic, leaves the law with only the force the law itself possesses, adding nothing to it.
>
> (182)

This "religion of the private person" or what he also names "true religion" in distinction to the religion of the citizen and the religion of the priests, "has neither temples, nor altars, nor rites, and is confined to the purely internal cult of the supreme God and the eternal obligations of morality, is the religion of the Gospel pure and simple, the true theism, what may be called natural divine right or law." Making the private/public and spiritual/political binaries explicit, he concludes,

> Christianity is a wholly spiritual religion, concerned solely with the things of heaven; the Christian's homeland is not of this world. The Christian does his duty, it is true, but he does it with profound indifference towards the good or ill success of his deeds. Provided that he has nothing to reproach himself for, it does not matter to him whether all goes well or badly here on earth. If the state prospers, he hardly dares to enjoy the public happiness; he fears lest he become proud of his country's glory; if the state perishes, he blesses the hand of God that weighs heavily on His people.
> For such a society to be peaceful and for harmony to prevail, every citizen without exception would have to be an equally good Christian.
>
> (183)

His argument? Public peace depends upon the privatization, spiritualization, and thus the containment of existing dissent – a position eerily similar to

Salman Rushdie's previously quoted comments in *The New York Times* regarding the need for a Protestant-styled Reformation of Islam (Rushdie 2001).

Despite their political differences, like Rushdie today, Hobbes, Locke, and Rousseau were political actors who effectively utilized the same rhetorical technique in their pursuit of a "civil" society wherein one group's interests are writ large in public and all others develop techniques of interiorization; all of these writers employ the private/public binary, or the religious/political binary, to ensure some sort of power sharing (imbalanced though it may be); although it is hardly an innocent technique, it does avoid, to some extent, the sort of physical coercion often employed when competing groups' practical and material interests collide. As Hill observes in his study of post-restoration England: "All dissenters came ultimately to accept partial freedom, *religious rather than political*. [I would add that, by means of precisely this distinction, and the countless practical implications felt throughout any society classified in this manner, the] ... English nation ceased to be coterminous with the Church of England" (emphasis added). He then goes on to conclude:

> After 1689 it was discovered that the existence of the two nations [i.e., the English Church and the English State] did not mean anarchy, or loss of government control. Once dissenters had accepted their position as a subordinate part of the nation, with freedom of religious worship at the expense of exclusion from central and local government and from the universities, a *modus vivendi* could be worked out. ... Dissenters, or most of them, now asked only to be left alone.
>
> (40)

Hill's conclusion deserves emphasis: "*Tolerance [e.g., the English Toleration Act of 1689] proved a more effective way of controlling dissent than persecution. ... [T]he breakdown of one type of authoritarianism tends to lead to the temporary victory of another authoritarianism*" (42).[11]

With all this in mind, we finally return from Europe to North America when, shortly after Rousseau penned *The Social Contract*, a bill was introduced, into the General Assembly of the Commonwealth of Virginia, entitled a "Bill Establishing a Provision for Teachers of the Christian Religion" (in 1784). Proposing tax support of such teachers, the bill was contested in the following session of the Assembly by James Madison who had written and distributed his "Memorial and Remonstrance Against Religious Assessments." In his opening lines we find familiar words:

> The Religion then of every man must be left to the conviction and conscience of every man; and it is the right of every man to exercise it as these may dictate. This right is in its nature an unalienable right. It is unalienable; because the opinions of men, depending only on the evidence contemplated by their own minds, cannot follow the dictates of other men.

... Before any man can be considered as a subject of Civil Society, he must be considered as a subject of the Governor of the Universe. ... We maintain therefore that in matters of Religion, no man's right is abridged by the institution of Civil Society and that Religion is wholly exempt from its cognizance.

(Alley 1988: 18–19)

Prior to concluding that a spirit of extreme libertarianism was sweeping through Virginia, one must keep in mind that by "religion" Madison meant matters of private "conviction and conscience." This old distinction was again effective; the tax levy in support of Christian teachers was defeated, and the following year Thomas Jefferson introduced yet a new bill in the Assembly, "for establishing religious freedom." Predictably, it was passed. In that bill's preamble the rhetoric of opinion and principles appears once again:

That to suffer the civil magistrate to intrude his powers into the field of opinion, and to restrain the profession or propagation of principles on supposition of their ill tendency, is a dangerous fallacy which at once destroys all liberty.

However, so-called civil society requires that this "liberty" not get out of hand – or, better put, not get out of mind and not call into question a specific form of constrained practice and organization. Therefore, Jefferson proceeds:

that it is time enough for the rightful purposes of civil government for its officers to interfere *when principles break out into overt acts against peace and good order*.

(1988: 352; emphasis added)

Or, as the U.S. Supreme Court has argued, "even when the action is in accord with one's religious convictions [it] is not totally free from legislative restrictions" (Alley 1988: 416). Apparently, what belongs to the Church is an idealistic phantom devoid of all behavioral content (apart from politically neutral "ritual" and "worship") and what belongs to the State are all matters material and empirical, e.g., matters social, economic, and political.

Although one could cite recent U.S. examples of Appalachian Pentecostals denied the right to handle snakes or Rastafarians punished for using ganja, one of the earliest examples of this rhetoric in use in a U.S. legal setting comes from a 1879 Supreme Court case, Reynolds v. United States, 98 (U.S.) 145. This case, brought against a member of the Church of Jesus Christ of Latter Day Saints (i.e., a Mormon) and assistant to Brigham Young, involved a charge of polygamy (Alley 1988: 349–356). Despite demonstrating that "the members of the Church believed that the practice of polygamy was directly enjoined upon the male members by the Almighty God, in a revelation to Joseph Smith, the founder and prophet of said Church," George Reynolds's conviction by the lower court was upheld by the higher court. "The only defense," read the higher court's majority opinion, "of the accused in this case is his belief that the law ought not to have been enacted [due to his action being prompted by his religious convictions]. *It matters not that his belief was a part of his professed religion: it was still belief and belief only*" (Alley 1988: 355; emphasis added).

Having contextualized the work of Hobbes, Locke, and Rousseau, and having historicized more recent discourses on tolerance and rhetorics of interiority, quickly tracing them from their appearance in early-modern European political theory to their continued use in contemporary legal and scholarly work, we come to William Arnal's analysis, which has informed much of the preceding:

> one of the current political *effects* of this separation [of belief from practice and Church from State] – one of the political ends served currently by it – is the evisceration of substance, i.e., collective aims, from the state. That is to say, the simple positing of religion is a covert justification for the modern tendency of the state to frame itself in increasingly negative terms: the secular state is the institutional apparatus by which the social body *prevents* the incursion by others into the personal and various other goals of individuals, rather than being the means of achievement for common projects and the collective good.

Arnal goes on to conclude that "[t]his very definition of the modern democratic state in fact creates religion as its alter-ego: religion, as such, is the space in which and by which any substantive collective goals (salvation, righteousness, etc.) are individualized and made into a question of personal commitment or morality" (2000: 32). A practical example of the legacy of this powerful technique is found in a recent book on religious minorities in the U.S. in which the author, Eric Mazur, writes in the opening lines of the Preface:

> the fundamental victory that had been won for religious freedom in the debate over the Virginia Declaration of Rights, Article 16, written by George Mason to grant all "the fullest toleration in the exercise of religion," was amended by James Mason (with the help of Patrick Henry) to make all "equally entitled to the full and free exercise of religion."
>
> (1999: ix)

Contrary to Mazur, I would say than "the fundamental victory" was won for the State; by means of the rhetoric of tolerance it has successfully forged sociopolitical conformity (i.e., civility) since the seventeenth century. For by the time of the late twentieth century we now seem to take for granted that "religious freedom" and "the free exercise of religion," is a substantial, tangible thing that somehow trumps other sorts of freedoms. In seeing the distinction between the two phrasings he quotes as being between "granting someone permission *to do* something while reserving the right to later deny that permission," on the one hand, and "recognizing a person's inherent right *to do* something whether you like it or not" (ix; emphasis added), Mazur seems to have accepted a tightly constrained and circumscribed zone of "human doing" (i.e., the freedom to adopt certain rituals and forms of worship) that was offered to the seventeenth-century's English dissenters – those who, to recall Hill on this point, accepted "partial freedom" to meet privately to practice rituals at the expense of their ability to participate openly in other forms of public life.

To rephrase: I have no doubt that Mazur understands that the freedom "to do" that he is celebrating has obvious practical limits to it that are highly policed. After all, as he acknowledges, "we must remember that the task of American constitutional order is to provide religious freedom while preserving itself [i.e., American constitutional order]. ... There are limits on religious freedom, limits of which we are constantly reminded by constitutional order itself" (142). That some small, and tightly controlled, degree of freedom "to do" does exist is, of course, nothing to sneeze at, especially if you are a citizen of a liberal nation-state and also a member of such sub-communities as those called the Mormon Church, the Church of Scientology, Jehovah's Witnesses, Santeria, Neo-Paganism, a member of the Communist party, an anarchist, or a practitioner of vodoun, a Native American attempting to use peyote, and a Rastafarian attempting to use ganja. So of course I would agree with authors such as Helena Kennedy, when she writes: "Tolerance has a pivotal role in helping to define and realise [sic] so many freedoms within our society" (2000: 117); my fear is that in rushing to celebrate, enjoy, and extend these so-called realized freedoms, we too easily overlook the manner in which these so-called freedoms have been defined, to whose benefit their definition contributes, and the manner in which they are almost invisibly policed. For, by joining liberal commentators and focusing only on how to extend these freedoms to yet new groups we miss the contributions to be made to critical analysis by those who reconstruct the histories of, and the roles played by, these freedoms. In other words, discourses on protecting, extending, or limiting, religious freedoms are part of the policing activity of nation formation, whether carried out in a liberal or conservative fashion. For to focus on these – just these and only these – types of actions and ways of organizing, as if "worship" exhausted the sorts of behaviors that can conceivably fall under "the inherent right to do" that is *allowed* by the Constitution, means that one leaves unidentified the practical, historical constraints on forms of doing and ways of organizing necessary for any nation-state to reproduce itself smoothly and successfully.

In a world of such massive practical difference, I find it productive to understand the current preoccupation in social democracies with religious freedoms and tolerance to be an instance of what Michael Ignatieff, following Sigmund Freud's lead, has characterized as "the narcissism of minor difference" (Ignatieff 2000: 100). As Freud wrote in a paper delivered to the Vienna Psycho-Analytic Society in December of 1917, and first published the following year:

it is precisely the minor differences in people who are otherwise alike that form the basis of feelings of strangeness and hostility between them. It would be tempting to pursue this idea and to derive from this 'narcissism of minor differences' the hostility which in every human relation we see fighting against feelings of fellowship and overpowering the commandment that all men should love one another.

(1964: 199)[12]

The status of the commandment notwithstanding, this technique is handy for distracting attention away from observable similarity and need and reproducing various competing sub-group identities by limiting debates to discourses on essentialized, interiorized, and minor variance. As Ignatieff comments with regard to debates on race – that "relatively minor difference" between humans based on observable skin color – "[e]conomic differences within groups of identical skin colour [*sic*] can be much more decisive in determining the life chances of individuals than differences between racial groups" (100). To make his point he draws on the example of Marxist organizers in the U.S. south who, between the 1930s and the 1960s, attempted to shift the debate from separate racial identity to shared class interests. Such a shift, they reasoned, would assist southern working-class whites *and* blacks, who shared far more than what seemed to distinguish them, to organize and thus change the material conditions of their collective lives. Such a shift did not take place, however, and despite obviously important and groundbreaking changes taking place in race relations in the U.S. over the past forty years, dramatic economic disparities have increased between lower classes of all races and regions, on the one hand, and a relatively small number of U.S. cultural, political, and economic elites, still largely comprised of white males, on the other.

If one can argue that the preoccupation with racial identity – a presumed inner, even biologically based experience manifested externally by means of differing skin colors, cuisines, styles of dress, ways of speaking and acting, etc. – helps to reproduce a practical status quo, then how much more effective is the preoccupation with differences and similarities between various groups' speculations on the existence of invisible beings and their speculations on the meaning of the universe? For, by celebrating, extending, and drawing attention to the freedom of religious belief and practices, one effectively shifts attention from the countless other sites where conformity of behavior and organization, not to mention the maintenance of dramatic material disparities, are crucial for reproducing the material conditions that make the idea of the State possible and persuasive. Simply put, celebrating the freedom of ritual practice (a celebration we find prominent within the industrialized, social democracies, systems where much depends on the smooth reproduction of disparity) is a sleight of hand whereby groups focus on a small, virtually ineffectual part as if it were the productive Whole, failing to understand "freedom" not to be an absolute, ahistoric value but part of a discourse shaped by a larger grammar of conformity and control.

This is why I find discourses on religion, the freedom of religion, and tolerance to be so interesting for, in agreement with Hill, such techniques "proved a
more effective way of controlling dissent than persecution."[13] Today, as the
inheritors of this rhetoric, and the social world it has made possible, we perceive
ourselves to be fulfilled, individual members of some of the most successfully
and widely reproducible social formations the world has yet seen, celebrating
our "God-given freedom" to believe whatever we like. Yet we exist within
powerful infrastructures that prompt us to maintain a startling conformity of
behavior and social expectation – everything from our unprompted ability to
stand patiently in orderly, straight lines outside movie theaters, to our unquestioned willingness to work all our lives to pay mortgages in order to own private
property.

So, when discussing the politics of "religion" we implicitly are discussing
pairs of concepts, such as sacred/secular, that in themselves are meaningless but
which, when held in varying degrees of tension, make worlds possible insomuch
as they provide spaces in which contestability can (and cannot) take place.
That the distance between these so-called metaphysical concepts is slippery and
that the spaces they make possible are inherently negotiable means that specific
rhetorical instances of these pairings are artifacts of specific political moments,
recoverable by means of a genealogy (I think here of Alles [2001] study of "the
holy" in the work of Otto). As Tim Fitzgerald has most recently phrased it, with
regard to the modern sacred/secular pairing:

> This conceptual separation was a product of the struggle of new classes
> against the restrictions imposed by the church [understood, here, not as a
> religious institution but simply as one more institution vying for control],
> its unaccountability, and its control of thought and action. Only by
> defining in a new way the realm of the "religious" and the realm of the
> "secular" could the separation of church and state be achieved and a bour-
> geois civil society be developed. ... It amounts, in effect, to the
> replacement of one ideological system by another.
>
> (2001: 111)

As Fitzgerald goes on to conclude, "the religion-secular distinction is the new
ideological system in which the principles expressed by 'no taxation without
representation' are central and definitive. ... [W]e cannot research 'religion' as
though it were something distinct from, or independent of, the central democratic capitalist principles" (111).

But conceiving of piety and private religion as "something distinct from"
certain forms of public political practice is crucial for this unifying rhetoric's
effective displacement of dissent. One of the more useful, recent examples of
how this is achieved is Rousseau's often cited notion of civil religion (see *The
Social Contract*, Book IV, ch. 8; Rousseau 1982: 176–187), especially as it was re-
popularized in the late 1960s by the U.S. sociologist, Robert Bellah (1967).

Reminiscent of some of Eliade's defenders, who coin such suspect neologisms as "non-political nationalism" or "messianic nationalism" in their attempts to minimalize his obvious political rhetorics and involvements, Bellah took what many historians would simply understand as a routine form of nationalist rhetoric (e.g., references to God in U.S. Presidential inaugural speeches) and retooled it as the much more palatable "civil religion" – the expression of a general, inner conviction shared among members of a nation, manifested in state pomp and circumstance, and the means whereby civil society and public virtue are instilled and ensured. Predictably, I cannot see historians of nationalism finding this category to provide them with anything new to study – unless, of course, they turned their attention to study civil religion theorists as nationalist propagandists – making oddly appropriate Bellah's own observation that the notion of civil religion "turned out to be far more tendentious and provocative than I at first realized" (1978: 16). It is tendentious indeed, in the direction of promoting, by means of aestheticization, a particular brand of U.S. nationalism. It is provocative to the degree that no one seems to have caught on that this so-called descriptive term is fueled by a specific political rhetoric. For, insofar as this category has now been applied in the analysis of cultures worldwide, we could go so far as to identify a particular brand of "global religious republicanism that he [Bellah] identifies with the destiny of American religion itself" (Kelly 1984: 225).

I therefore assume that political theorists and scholars of nationalism would find this term to be an instance of obscurantism – insomuch as it spiritualizes what are all too obviously political concerns – thus finding its use as but one more site of nationalist rhetoric deserving of study. For example, in attempting to distinguish civil religion from the sort of political chauvinism he associates with outright nationalism (i.e., national self-worship, as he might have phrased it), Bellah asserts – for how would one persuasively argue the following thesis? – that civil religion *at its best* comprises

> a genuine apprehension of universal and transcendent religious reality as seen in or, one could almost say, as revealed through the experience of the American people. Like all religions, it has suffered deformations and demonic distortions. At its best, it has neither been so general that it has lacked incisive relevance to the American scene nor so particular that it has placed American society above universal human values.
>
> (1990: 179–180)

Or, as phrased by Michael Novak, not long after Bellah first penned these words in 1970, civil religion is

> a public perception of our national experience, in the light of universal and transcendent claims upon human beings, but especially Americans; a set of

values, symbols, and rituals institutionalized as the cohesive force and center of meaning uniting our many peoples.

(1974: 127)

In asserting that civil religion, "at its best," is a chosen people's genuine apprehension of a religious reality, an experience of national cohesiveness in step with universal human values, Bellah's and Novack's circular logic and normative claims beg the very questions that other scholars seek to answer. In other words, whereas such writers are captivated with answering questions concerning the role of religion in U.S. society (e.g., Bellah 1987), we could instead problematize this brand of scholarship and ask what is the practical role played by this rhetoric of religion as something "universal" and "transcendent," and thus distinct from (and at times deformed and distorted by) the messy world of history and politics?

Just as "patriotism" is the way in which we consume our own domestic nationalism,[14] so too "civil religion" – or even what Benjamin Franklin, in 1749, had called "Publik Religion" (1961: vol. 3, 433) and, one hundred and ten years later, what Martin Marty had called "religion-in-general" (1959: 32, 86) – is an effective tool not only for "joining the unchurched to the religiously subscribed in a lexicon of meanings" (as described by Kelly 1984: 223), but, in doing so, for domesticating one form of active and public political talk and action, lending it an air of inevitability, piety, sanctity, and placing it above so-called petty, partisan politics and thus beyond any form of effective critique or commentary. It is therefore a technique useful for authorizing and deauthorizing alike. Take, for example, the uncredited entry on "civil religion" in the *HarperCollins Dictionary of Religion*: while acknowledging that it refers to "the set of religious or quasi-religious beliefs, myths, symbols, and ceremonies that unite a political community and that mobilize its members in the pursuit of common goals" (Smith, Green 1995: 274), the article ensures that readers understand this obvious nation-building technique to be clearly distinguished from the messy world of power politics. By briefly canvassing scholarly opinion on the *morality* of the thing this category supposedly allows us to study – "Scholars remain divided on the religious and moral significance of civil religions" – the writer unwittingly demonstrates the political utility of this way of classifying what, in virtually any other context, we would have no difficulty understanding as overt political action.[15] It thus enables its users to organize all the more effectively, for while recognizing that they are actively engaged in "unit[ing] a political community and ... mobiliz[ing] its members in the pursuit of common goals" they are able to segregate these overt political practices within the realm of emotion, morality, piety, and belief. This wonderfully effective depoliticization of politics is all the more apparent in the closing lines of the dictionary entry: "Although subject to abuse," the writer comments, "they [civil religions] can inspire positive national accomplishments, contain sources of moral judgment, and serve to correct nationalistic pretension." Once again, a certain form of political action is made possible by distinguishing public from private, contestable from incontestable, allowing us exclusively to understand and value certain forms of public action and organization by means of interiorist rhetorics (e.g., morality). Immersed in this binary rhetoric it never dawns on those who employ this category that classifying overtly political practice as merely a civil religion is itself the height of "nationalistic pretension." Thus, the very classification "civil religion," much like "religion" itself, is what Eric Hobsbawm might have called a "powerful assimilating mechanism" (1992: 280).

Be clear, however, on the following point: in making this critique of "civil religion" I am not aligning myself with such critics as George Kelly who lament the role liberal scholars such as Bellah have played in watering down the impact of religion (by watering down religion itself) in recent U.S. politics. Instead, I press such critics even further; for when Kelly writes that "the genius of our civilization is in holding the two [i.e., the realms of religion and politics] distinct," (1984: 242), I fear he assumes some substantive or ontological distinction between these two spheres of human experience and action. Instead, echoing the epigraph from Foucault that opened this chapter, I would contend that the genius of our particular form of civilization is in its (our) ability to persuade its members (ourselves and our peers) that there are in fact two distinct zones, one of experience and insight and the other of action and organization. Socrates's mission is indeed useful for the city.

Whether intended or not, such different figures as Rousseau and the U.S. President Dwight Eisenhower both seem to have understood the political utility that resulted from this dichotomous system. The former went on at great length concerning the political utility of a vague set of private beliefs in non-empirical matters. "Now, it is very important," he observed,

> to the state that each citizen should have a religion which makes him love his duty, but the dogmas of that religion are of interest neither to the state nor its members, except in so far as those dogmas concern morals and the duties which everyone who professes that religion is bound to perform towards others. Moreover, everyone may hold whatever opinions he pleases, without the sovereign having any business to take cognizance of them. For the sovereign has no competence in the other world; whatever may be the fate of the subjects in the life to come, it is nothing to do with the sovereign, *so long as they are good citizens in this life.*
>
> (Book IV, ch. 8; 1982: 185–186)

"The dogmas of civil religion," Rousseau concludes,

> must be simple and few in number, expressed precisely and without explanations or commentaries. The existence of an omnipotent, intelligent, benevolent divinity that foresees and provides; the life to come; the happiness of the just; the punishment of sinners; the sanctity of the social

contract and the law – these are the positive dogmas. As for the negative dogmas, I would limit them to a single one: no intolerance. Intolerance is something which belongs to the religions we have rejected. ... [A]ll religions which themselves tolerate others must be tolerated, provided only that their dogmas contain nothing contrary to the duties of the citizen.

(186–187)

Or, as Eisenhower far more succinctly observed: "Our government makes no sense unless it is founded in a deeply felt religious faith – and I don't care what it is" (cited in Herberg 1955: 97). This is an astute judgment, not because civil government requires the sort of intrinsically ethical basis provided by deeply felt religious values (as I am sure Eisenhower meant) but, given the critique of this chapter, it is an astute observation because uniform behavioral and organizational systems (i.e., form) are possible only when the inevitable contradictions, competing interests, and outright dissent (i.e., varying contents) that exist in any social group have a place to go – a very deep, emotive and *non*-performative place. That place we have come to call "religion," "faith," "spirituality," "conscience," and even "Human Nature." A similar argument could likely be made for all aspects of modern identity politics (i.e., discourses that presume an essential, inner, shared identity based on gender, ethnicity, culture, sexuality, etc.).

So, to answer Alan Wolfe's rhetorical question, "Are we better off when religion is as broad, but also as thin, as the kinds of faith one finds on American college campuses today?" (2002: B10), one can answer that *it all depends who his faithful "we" signifies.* If it signifies an as yet undomesticated minority group, then they certainly can use this technique to their practical advantage, to domesticate themselves while bringing along with them certain social markers of relative distinctiveness, ensuring a small but nonetheless important degree of autonomy by means of appeals to their specifically "religious" or "cultural" or "ethnic" heritage, embodied in a small but, to the group, significant number of cuisines, dietary regulations, styles of dress, greeting rituals, private ceremonials, dialects, hair styles, etc. (A case in point is the late 1980s and early 1990s trials over the practice of Santeria in Hialeah, Florida, in which the sacrifice of chickens was unsuccessfully contested by the city council [see Mazur 1999: 1–4].) If this "we" refers to an integrated yet nonetheless marginalized group whose members seek to organize to effect practical change so as to integrate themselves further into the status quo, then (just as with dominant groups which also employ this rhetoric) "religion" can be a powerful organizing technique to authorize and universalize some set of specific, local interests. Thus, contests over such admittedly important yet nonetheless local issues as higher wages or the right to participate fully in the institutions of a representative democracy (thus, ironically perhaps, further reinforcing the institutions of the nation-state, rather than contesting them or exempting oneself from them entirely) take on the significance of epic battles in which the local stakes, gains, and losses are writ large on the canvas of the universe itself. "Sin," "suffering," "punishment," "liberation," and "redemption" then become some of the rhetorical markers that help such groups to organize and sustain their movements.

The opposite case would be some posited, oppositional "we" that seeks not integration but outright contestation with dominant principles and practices. In this case, the interiorized space made possible by the discourse on faith can be just as important a technique for organizing and authorizing practical action. For example, consider the writings of the onetime Egyptian public schools inspector, Sayyid Qutb (b. 1906), who published his little book *Milestones* (also entitled in English *Signposts along the Road*) in 1964, after having lived in the U.S. from 1948 to 1950 (on an Egyptian Education Ministry grant).[16] Having seen firsthand the "bankruptcy of the West," his opening line makes his premise clear: "Mankind today is on the brink of a precipice ... because humanity is devoid of those vital values for its healthy development and real progress." With this starting point, he goes on to outline a political program of action based on (i) restoring Islam to its "original" form (since it is now "buried under the debris of the man-made traditions of several generations" [Qutb 1993: 7]) and, then, (ii) saving civilization ("Islam is the only system that possesses these values and this way of life [i.e., ideals and values "previously unknown in the West, that can restore harmony to human nature"]" [6]). Of specific interest is the third chapter, where we read that, although this program for "restoring harmony to human nature" is rooted in a faith (8) and a belief (138), it must be realized in an explicitly political program (i.e., "a way of life"):

> The Muslim society cannot come into existence ... simply as a creed in the hearts of individual Muslims, however numerous they may be, unless they become an active, harmonious, and cooperative group, distinct by itself, whose different elements, like the limbs of a human body, work together for the support, and expansion, and for the defense against all those elements that attack its system.
>
> (40)

There is a deep irony here, for as I understand the Protestant Reformation, this was what in fact was accomplished there: a coordinated rhetoric of pristine social origins, textual meanings, and interior faith was successfully used to organize overt political action that made it possible for disconnected authorities at different governmental levels, all across Europe, to oppose the centuries of accumulated "debris of man-made traditions" (in this case Roman Catholic) and exert new forms of control over reorganized lands, wealth, and people.

As Sheldon Wolin describes it, in the case of John Calvin's Protestantism, "it was nothing less than a comprehensive statement covering the major elements of a political theory" (1960: 179). However, unable to look past the different, even apparently contradictory content (i.e., Christian vs. Muslim doctrines), commentators seem incapable of seeing how political rhetorics such as, for example, Calvin's and Qutb's employ the very same techniques of contestation and organization (for different but equally political ends, of course). As phrased by Roxanne Euben,

> the rationalist categories that dominate current social scientific scholarship on Islamic fundamentalism are particularly problematic because the more our stories about politics – about authority and what constitutes legitimate political action – are wedded to a rationalist epistemology [that distinguishes rationality/irrationality, belief/practice, private/public, etc.], the more difficulty we may have in compassing the significance of practices and ideas guided by and defined in terms of belief in divine truths unknowable by purely human means.
>
> (1999: 51)

Subscribing to just such an epistemology, Rushdie's advocacy for a Protestant-styled Reformation in Islam, is certainly not recommending Qutb's plan. Instead, such overt action is no doubt an example for liberal commentators of how "a faith" is co-opted by radicals who are conceited enough to think that they too know how the world ought to be organized. That the complex and often violent events we have come to know as the Protestant Reformation can now be so widely understood simply to have been an interiorized doctrinal dispute between the faithful – begun, or so the old story tells us, by a lone free-thinker nailing his bold theses to the church door – indicates just how successful some of these political techniques are for realigning power and privilege. Only the naive would fail to see them still in use today.

Of course, advocating oppositional organization and overt political action that takes place well outside of people's private "hearts and minds" (as outlined more concretely in the "call to arms" contained in the last four chapters of *Milestones*) is a dangerous form of speech for it runs counter to a depoliticized Islam-of-the-heart. Little wonder, then, that soon after its publication, *Milestones* was banned and "was considered grounds to indict its author for conspiring against the ruling ideology and system of government" (as phrased in Ahmad Hammad's foreword to the English edition of Qutb's text that I am using). That Qutb was arrested and then executed by Nasser's government in the summer of 1966 – ironically, perhaps, a government he had once supported – is thus hardly surprising (regardless whether one agrees or disagrees with his views). Given this, that he is today seen by many to be "perhaps the most influential thinker for the religio-political insurgency of the Egyptian Muslim Brotherhood, and for Sunni Islamic fundamentalism more broadly" (Euben 1999: 53–55), should then also come as no surprise.

To return to answering Wolfe's question, if his "we" signifies the members of a thoroughly integrated, dominant group, then although the use of the suitably vague and interiorist rhetoric of religion necessitates that members of this group not physically coerce others and force their local practices on their equally provincial peers, the efficiency by means of which privatization declaws actual dissent does pave the way toward the successful reproduction of an uncontested hegemonic status. It thus ensures that their one local picture of the world easily stands in for a "matter of fact" in opposition to the many competing, "mere opinions" that comprise the necessary background noise and color of dominant social life. As many others have noted before me, I have in mind the accepted but necessarily marginal status of colorful "ethnic" styles of dress and spicy "ethnic" foods that greatly help to naturalize and normalize the dominant and apparently non-ethnic (i.e., default) culture. After all, "white" or Anglo-Saxon (or whatever one calls it), food is hardly considered "ethnic" and whereas the U.S. "South" has widely recognized and much heralded southern food (with significant regional [e.g., Cajun] and racial [e.g., soul food] differences in various types of southern cuisines), I cannot for the life of me think what "northern food" would signify in the U.S.

The disciplinary rhetoric of religion, then, is ideological in Kenneth Burke's sense, for, like all discourses, it comprises "an aggregate of beliefs sufficiently at odds with one another to justify [and thus contain] opposite kinds of conduct" (1968: 163).[17] For example, as demonstrated by Eddie Glaude Jr., the Biblical narrative has historically been used very differently by U.S. whites and U.S. African-Americans; whereas members of the former drew heavily on the notion of the U.S. as the New Israel, members of the latter group found far more useful the imagery of the Egyptian captivity. "Here we have an example," he writes, recalling Burke's notion of ideology, "of how battles are waged within ideologies, drawing on the same language [and rhetorical techniques, we might add] for quite different ends" (forthcoming; see also Glaude 2000). And this internal "divide and conquer" contestation is very useful to one idea of the State and those whose specific interests are writ large across it, for, in the words of the politically liberal Pew Charitable Trusts, which in 2001 awarded twelve grants totaling over twenty million dollars under the aegis of its religion program, "we believe that civil society is strengthened and democracy bolstered when citizens develop an appreciation of the various religious traditions that hold deep meaning for so many Americans."[18] I agree; specific "we"s do benefit from rhetorics of deep meanings, but they all benefit in rather different ways and to significantly different degrees.

"Religion" – whether it is seen as a private feeling to be experienced, and then expressed by the subject, an inner faith that informs and propels ethical action, or the unseen source from which supposedly moral or authentic public action and organization originates – may very well be among the most important modern technologies of manageable selves/groups. Rephrasing Mazur's book title, what is fascinating is thus not so much the Americanization of religious minorities, but instead, that the socio-political process he refers to as "Americanization" might better refer to the successful technique of containing competing minority differences and potential dissent within the self-policed and inviolable sphere of "religion." This is simply the most recent phase of what, from the sixteenth-century on, has been the practice of making specifically *religious* minorities, groups defined and controlled by means of an inner preoccupation with the life of the spirit. In return for the right to exist on the margins of power these groups' members have little choice but to manufacture a toothless public persona in their struggle to reproduce a non-threatening version of themselves in an alien environment. Although he theorized on the social and psychological role played by those social institutions he presumed were obviously religions – suggesting there is considerable distance between his theory and that which is being offered here – I believe Freud was onto something, but only if we use his work instead to discuss the role played by the concept religion itself. "The outcome of the struggle," he wrote in 1928, with regard to a revelatory dream told to him in a letter written by a U.S. academic, "was displayed once again in the sphere of religion" (1952: 246). The recent trend in the U.S. to reporting that one is "spiritual" and not "religious" (a distinction comparable to Martin Luther's rhetoric of *sola scriptura* vs. the institutions and hierarchy of the Church) may very well indicate that an even more privatized sphere of display has been developing, a development in step with the public triumphs of late capitalism, poised on the brink of globalization. The outcome of the practical struggles and contests that are already taking place across a shrinking globe will likely be displayed and displaced in the sphere created by "religion" as much as "spirituality."

Harkening back to the epigraph from Foucault that opened this final chapter, this modernist discourse on religion, faith, and spirit is but another way of "teaching people to occupy themselves with themselves," which in turn "teaches them to occupy themselves with the city." Or, as Chomsky was quoted in one of the two epigraphs that opened this book: "[t]he beauty of our society is: it isolates everybody." This suggests, then, that the scholars and ideological managers who casually wield and apply such classifications play an essential role as caretakers for both the governable self and the city insomuch as the very use of these classifications disciplines what is all too public and thus contestable, ensuring that portions of it become private and isolated within a politico-legal fiction: the impenetrable citadel of the heart and mind. Perhaps this means that our scholarship on religion – as opposed to our thoroughly historically grounded scholarship on the discourse of religion – is more an exercise in conflict management and self-help than it is a bold analytic activity.

My hope is that there is more to do than just care for a particular idea of the city, an idea that requires us to mis-perceive one province as if it were the metropolis. The critique that has slowly built throughout the preceding chapters holds out a model for a rather different sort of intellectual, those who happen to use "religion" in their studies of social formations. For, following Foucault, I maintain that "[t]he role of an intellectual is not to tell others what they have to do. By what right would he do so?" As he goes on to conclude, and, borrowing his words, as I now conclude as well:

The work of an intellectual is not to shape others' political will; it is, through the analyses that he carries out in his own field, to question over and over again what is postulated as self-evident, to disturb people's mental habits, the way they do and think things, to dissipate what is familiar and accepted, to reexamine rules and institutions and on the basis of this re-problematization (in which he carries out his specific task as an intellectual) to participate in the formation of a political will (in which he has his role as citizen to play).

(Foucault 1988a: 265)

Notes

1 The early work of Wilfred Cantwell Smith (1963) cannot go unnoticed when discussing the history of the category "religion."

2 It is understandable that some can read Foucault otherwise. A few pages later, speculating on the reasons that prompted the institutionalization of sex by means of the discourse on sexuality, he writes: "What was at issue in these strategies? A struggle against sexuality? Or were they part of an effort to gain control of it? An attempt to regulate it more effectively and mask its more indiscreet, conspicuous, and intractable aspects?" (1990: 105). His repeated use of the pronoun "it" in the preceding suggests that behind the discourse on sexuality there lurks some more real thing: sex. Applying this to religion, it is conceivable that liberal theologians and humanists alike can use Foucault to recover what they maintain to be a deeper, essential nature to religion that eludes reductionists, whom they equate with those who seek to control the essentially creative and free force of religion *cum* spirituality. Reading Foucault in this manner, however, is a convenient sidestep around the issue, since apart from various discourses on sex, and the various institutions from which they arise and to which they contribute, there is only human beings behaving. Likewise, apart from various discourses on religion and their institutions, there is simply human beings behaving.

3 I identify his work as influenced by Cantwell Smith because Smith's nearly 40-year-old book, *The Meaning and End of Religion*, is the only work on "religion" that Idinopulos cites (see 9, n. 18). This is not to say that newer works are somehow more valuable; however, I cannot see how anyone can discuss the historicity of "religion" without taking into account Jonathan Z. Smith's many contributions to this topic, contributions consistently made over the past twenty years.

4 For example, during a recent lecture at the University of Alabama on integrating web technologies into classroom teaching, Natalie Gummer of Beloit College showed her audience a site devoted to a series of web links, developed by her students, for sites devoted to the religions of the world. In the brief abstract describing a site devoted to the Vatican, the student had written that the Vatican was the "worldwide headquarters" of the Roman Catholic church. Whether intended by the student or not, classifying the Vatican as "headquarters" immediately took it out of its usually religious and apolitical realm and dropped it squarely in the middle of the world of international politics, business, and military activity. The question to be asked is why it sounds odd to classify the Vatican as the headquarters? What set of values, and what social world, is being challenged by using this term? And what set of values and social world are reproduced when labeling it in some other way?

5 My thanks to Pam Sailors, of the Department of Philosophy at Southwest Missouri State University, for helpful comments on Hobbes.

6 Such a shift allows us to see analyses based solely on doctrine as simply the descriptive level in need of historicization. For example, Tracy (1999) has three separate sections to his study of Europe from 1450 to 1650: doctrine, politics, and society and community. Reading such a work by means of the shift I am advocating breaks down this division of intellectual labor, so that doctrine is but one means whereby political contests are waged.

7 "A letter concerning toleration," published in 1689; eventually three rejoinders were to appear, the last of which was published after Locke's death.

8 The chapters in this edited volume, originally published by Edinburgh University Press in 1999, are a collection of addresses (delivered publicly between 1988 and 1998) from the University of York's Morrell Trust annual lectureship on toleration as a philosophical concept.

9 For instance, he has little choice but to discuss such things as "overtly religious conflicts such as the Crusades, the Muslim conquests, and the Wars of Religion" (156) as if the rhetoric of destiny and divinity that propelled such early geo-political conflicts was the substantial issue over which groups were fighting, rather than the widely accessible technique whereby practical interests were encoded, communicated, and normalized.

10 Despite asserting the existence of a spiritual kingdom, in footnote 44 in this same chapter Rousseau shows ample evidence that he was able to generate a social theory of seemingly religious offices – at least those offices with which he disagreed.

> It should be noted that the clergy find their bond of union not so much in formal assemblies, as in the communion of Churches. Communion and excommunication are the social compact of the clergy, a compact which will always make them masters of peoples and kings. All priests who communicate together are fellow-citizens, even if they come from opposite ends of the earth. This invention is a masterpiece of statesmanship: there is nothing like it among pagan priests; who have therefore never formed a clerical corporate body.

Although employing the private/public distinction for his own ends, Rousseau has much in common with contemporary scholars intent on historicizing so-called spiritual claims. In the above quotation he makes it clear that he can discuss communion and excommunication divorced from the theological manner in which devotees themselves discuss these rituals.

11 As was evident in my earlier use of Hill's work, to a degree he seems to vacillate on whether religion is in fact distinct from politics (or, as argued throughout the preceding chapters of this book, simply a specific form of political rhetoric) and whether discourses on toleration are purely political (or, as many liberal scholars of religion seem to maintain, have a morally superior aspect to them). For example, in the sentence that follows the one just quoted, and which ends his essay, he writes, "Only when both sides have exhausted themselves can the possibility of *neither* winning outright be grasped, and the small voice of reason make itself heard" (42). Given his essay's attempt to problematize what others take to be the apparent common sense and inner momentum to discourses on tolerance, this line's emphasis on "the small voice of reason" undermines his thesis that discourses on tolerance are at their heart political techniques.

12 As noted by the *Standard Edition*'s editor, Freud takes up this theme once again in his 1921 essay, "Group Psychology and the Analysis of the Ego" and in the fifth chapter of *Civilization and its Discontents*.

13 To be fair, Mazur correctly identifies the limits of tolerance, as in when he concludes that there are indeed problems in store for "those communities whose worldviews cannot accommodate the ultimate authority of an increasingly non-religiously iden-

tified federal government. Those religious communities whose ideologies conform to – or do not threaten – the temporal and spatial ideology of the constitutional order will find the means to avoid continued conflict with it" (143). However, seeing the federal government as increasingly non-religious suggests his insight as to the practical limits of tolerance is different from the one argued in this chapter.

14 I have yet to find a persuasive means to distinguish these two, since the very distinction seems a nationalist technique. For example, despite the usefulness of some of his work on the politics of tolerance, Ignatieff attempts to distinguish patriotism from nationalism insomuch as the former is the tolerant form whereas the latter is intolerant. However, if discourses on tolerance are, by definition, necessarily intolerant at key though usually undisclosed points (thus collapsing the normally understood distinction between these two), then any further distinctions premised on the substantive difference between tolerance and intolerance are also doomed to collapse. This is apparent when Ignatieff then goes on to write: "The intense love of country one meets with in the United States, or occasionally in Britain *in time of war*, is more properly called patriotism than nationalism. As an uncontested emotion, patriotism can be, though it is not always, *free of intolerant aggression towards other nations or peoples*" (86; emphasis added). If going to war is not an example of "intolerant aggression towards other nations or people," then I'm not sure what is; therefore, despite Ignatieff's best efforts, patriotism ends up being indistinguishable from nationalism.

15 I recall Amy Dockser Marcus, former Middle East correspondent for *The Wall Street Journal* writing in the "International News" section of the Toronto *Globe & Mail* on October 4, 1996, a survey of the conflict over the city of Hebron, or al Khalil as it is known to its mostly Palestinian inhabitants (see also Marcus 2000). After detailing the conflicting Palestinian and Israeli claims concerning their legitimacy to control the city – claims which in both cases were propelled by religious rhetorics steeped in references to the ancient Canaanites and Abraham – she quotes an Arab archeologist who says flatly, "This is about nation-building." As I recall, when I first read this I laughed because in 1992 the supporters of the then U.S. Presidential candidate, Bill Clinton, had used the phrase, "It's the economy, stupid," as their slogan. Unlike many scholars of religion who persist in studying the so-called sacred or transcendent themes of this or that event, I thought to myself, "It's nation-building, stupid," was something that this archeologist astutely understood.

16 My thanks to Bruce Lincoln for sharing with me an early version of the first chapter to his *Holy Terrors: Thinking about Religion after September 11* (2002b), for bringing Qutb's work to my attention, and suggesting other sources.

17 I am indebted to an unpublished article of Eddie Glaude's for bringing Burke's understanding of ideology to my attention (see Glaude forthcoming).

18 See http://www.pewtrusts.com/grants/grants_item.cfm?image=img3&program_area_id=7.

Afterword

Il faut cultiver notre jardin.
Voltaire, *Candide*

This morning, April 26, 2002, on National Public Radio's "Morning Edition," reporter Jeff Young broadcast an item on "free speech zones" at West Virginia University. These zones, which have been instituted on a number of U.S. university campuses, are specifically designated, public areas set aside by university administrations where such things as protests or the distribution of materials not officially sanctioned by or necessarily connected to the day-to-day business of the university are allowed to take place. As reported in January 2001, in the weekly newspaper that covers issues of relevance to U.S. colleges and universities, *Chronicle of Higher Education*:

> At the University of Mississippi, protesters are limited to demonstrating in front of Fulton Chapel, designated in 1997 as the university's free-speech zone. [Within two years two other zones were also created on this campus.] Officials say a specified protest area is needed to prevent demonstrators from disrupting the business of the campus. Last August [2000], Arthur Baker, a student and cofounder of a conservative campus group, was arrested for failing to obey a police officer who ordered him to move his protest against the student newspaper to the area. ... At New Mexico State, students can protest freely in three designated areas of the campus, but they must get permission from the university to demonstrate elsewhere. In September [2000], Mr. Rudolph, a graduate student, was arrested for distributing a flier outside the zone without first getting permission from the university's student-affairs office. The flier was an advertisement for Mr. Rudolph's underground newspaper, which criticized the university's speech policy.[1]

Such zones are not unique to university campuses; they were also used to manage protestors at the August, 2000, Republican Party's National Convention in Philadelphia and, long before the September 11, 2001 attacks in the U.S. such zones were already planned to be part of the 2002 Salt Lake City Winter Olympics.[2] Predictably, the existence of such sites has been contested successfully in some cases, prompting some university administrations to forgo the idea. One case in point is Iowa State University. On October 19, 2001, the student newspaper, the *Iowa State Daily*, reported that the university President "announced a proposal to allow broader use of university grounds and facilities by students, staff, faculty and the general public."[3]

Although free expression is generally celebrated to be a non-negotiable, absolute value in social democracies – and thus the means by which a diverse citizenry can obtain the much needed information on which its informed participation in the affairs of the State is based – the fact that such physically set-apart and policed zones exist is sufficient evidence that there are obvious limits that come with any social grouping. After all, even idealists appealing for their right to say and their right to believe understand that these rights do not extend to their right to do and their right to organize. Because dissenting beliefs and speech can only exist within such specific zones as the disembodied mind of the individual or in front of certain buildings on a campus, "freedom" is rather more structured and controlled than you would think if you only listened to politicians rallying the troops to fight for freedom and love of country.

In the background of all of the chapters in this book was the concern to investigate the generally undisclosed ground rules that stipulate the nature and extent of such things as common sense, freedom, and civility. Beginning with an examination of the rhetoric employed within one specific, emerging academic discipline, the chapters slowly tried to persuade readers that the techniques used to create theoretical and institutional turf – the same techniques that marginalize academic dissent – are also operative far outside the university's ivy-covered towers. Like academic disciplines, our wider social worlds are highly diverse and thus characterized by competition over scarce resources. In academic disciplines, not everything gets to count as a theory, as a persuasive conclusion, or as legitimate data; in the wider social world not everyone gets to speak, let alone freely enter, the public square. Some of us must obtain parade permits and be off the streets by night fall.

If I have been able to persuade some readers that the ways in which we classify and rank the world, making parts of it knowable and useful, have something to do with the ways in which we create and manage such things as free speech and civil society, then I will have succeeded. Making these linkages seems to require quite a leap, I realize, but taking human beings seriously as thoroughly embedded in a historical world means seeing the consequences of their – I should say, our – intellectual productions as being just as practical as the consequences of our material and institutional productions. For, like the appearance of control that is created when public zones are roped off and monitored by campus police, the very concept "religion" enables us to fabricate and then manage a place deep within the human heart and conscience. To repeat Bill Arnal's words, it is a "space in which and by which any substantive collective goals … are individualized and made into a question of personal commitment or morality." It is a space created by what Plato has Socrates tell his listeners was chiseled into the front porch wall of Apollo's temple at Delphi: *gnôthi sauton*, "know thyself." It results in Voltaire's small, private garden tended by the lone farmer. It is the ironic "beauty" of our society, according to Chomsky: it isolates everybody.

This conclusion turns Durkheim's well-known theory of religion into a theory of "religion," for the coordinated use of such designations as "sacred," "faith," "spiritual," "authentic," "experience," etc. – all of which are the residue from a previous generation's intellectual labors – can now be understood to be the means by which some aspect of the contestable, historical world ends up being set apart, sometimes privileged, and generally forbidden. It is by means of this act of setting apart – driven by a variety of practical and competing interests and accomplished at a host of rhetorical sites – that mere parts get to stand in for the Whole and one of the provinces gets to rule as if it were the metropolis.

Notes

1   This article, which appeared on January 12, 2001, was entitled, "Promoting Order or Squelching Campus Dissent." The web archived version appears at http://chronicle.com/free/v47/i18/18a03701.htm. See also the *New York Times* article, "Student Life: Boxing in Free Speech," archived at http://www.uh.edu/admin/media/topstories/nytimes040901speech.htm.

2   See the February 13, 2001, article in the magazine, *Sports Illustrated*, archived at http://sportsillustrated.cnn.com/more/news/2001/02/13/aclu_complaint_ap/.   One such zone was planned for Park City, Utah, one of the competition sites for the Games. See the *Park Record*'s article on this topic, archived at http://www.parkrecord.com/Stories/0,1002,8138%257E237707%257E122%257E,00.html).

3   This article is archived at http://www.iowastatedaily.com/vnews/display.v/ART/2001/10/19/3bcfc9648bb89.

References

Adams, Charles J. (ed.) (1965). *A Reader's Guide to the Great Religions*. New York: Free Press.

Adorno, Theodor W. (1973) [1964]. *The Jargon of Authenticity*. Knut Tarnowski and Frederic Will (trans.). Evanston: Northwestern University Press.

—— (1981) [1952]. *In Search of Wagner*. Rodney Livingstone (trans.). London: Verso.

Allen, Charlotte (1996). "Is Nothing Sacred? Casting Out the Gods from Religious Studies," *Lingua Franca* 6/7: 30–40.

—— (1998). "Response to *Bulletin* 26/4," *Bulletin of the Council of Societies for the Study of Religion* 27/2: 45–46.

Allen, Douglas (1992). "Review of M. L. Ricketts, *Mircea Eliade: The Romanian Roots*," *Journal of the American Academy of Religion* 60: 174–177.

—— (1994). "Recent Defenders of Eliade: A Critical Evaluation," *Religion* 24: 333–351.

Alles, Gregory D. (1989). "Wach, Eliade, and the Critique from Totality," *Numen* 35: 108–138.

—— (2001). "Toward a Genealogy of the Holy: Rudolf Otto and the Apologetics of Religion," *Journal of the American Academy of Religion* 69/2: 323–341.

Alley, R. S. (ed.) (1988). *The Supreme Court on Church and State*. New York: Oxford University Press.

Anderson, Benedict (1991). *Imagined Communities: Reflections on the Origin and Spread of Nationalism*. 2nd edn. London: Verso.

—— (1999). "The Goodness of Nations." In Peter van der Veer and Hartmut Lehmann (eds.), *Nation and Religion: Perspectives on Europe and Asia*, 197–203. Princeton: Princeton University Press.

Andresen, Jensine (ed.) (2001) *Religion in Mind: Cognitive Perspectives on Religious Belief, Ritual, and Experience*. Cambridge: Cambridge University Press.

Anonymous (1998). "Review of Russell McCutcheon, *Manufacturing Religion*," *Christian Century* 115/5: 187.

—— (2002a). "Canada on Sale," *Religious Studies News* 17/3: 5.

—— (2002b). "Religion Class Taken Hostage," *Religious Studies News* 17/3: 12, 20.

Applegate, Celia (1990). *A Nation of Provincials: The German Idea of Heimat*. Berkeley: University of California Press.

Arnal, William E. (2000). "Definition." In Willi Braun and Russell T. McCutcheon (eds.), *Guide to the Study of Religion*, 21–34. London, U.K.: Continuum.

—— (2001). "The Segregation of Social Desire: 'Religion' and Disney World," *Journal of the American Academy of Religion* 69/1: 1–19.

Arnal, William E. and Michel Desjardins (eds.) (1997). *Whose Historical Jesus?* Studies in Christianity and Judaism No. 7. Waterloo, ON: Wilfrid Laurier University Press.

Asad, Talal (1993). *Genealogies of Religion: Discipline and Reasons of Power in Christianity and Islam.* Baltimore: Johns Hopkins University Press.

—— (1999). "Religion, Nation-State, Secularism." In Peter van der Veer and Hartmut Lehmann (eds.), *Nation and Religion: Perspectives on Europe and Asia,* 178–196. Princeton: Princeton University Press.

—— (2001). "Reading a Modern Classic: W. C. Smith's *The Meaning and End of Religion,*" *History of Religions* 40/3: 205–222.

Baird, Robert D. (1971). *Category Formation and the History of Religion.* The Hague: Mouton.

Barrows, John Henry (ed.) (1893). *The World's Parliament of Religions: An Illustrated and Popular Story of the World's First Parliament of Religions, Held in Chicago in Connection with the Columbian Exposition of 1893.* 2 vols. Chicago: Parliament Publishing Co.

Barthes, Roland (1973) [1957]. *Mythologies.* Annette Lavers (trans.). Hammersmith, London: Paladin.

—— (1988) [1985]. *The Semiotic Challenge.* Richard Howard (trans.). New York: Hill and Wang.

Baum, Robert (2001). "The Ethics of Religious Studies Research in the Context of the Religious Intolerance of the State: An Africanist Perspective," *Method & Theory in the Study of Religion* 13/1: 12–27.

Beane, Wendell C. (2001). "Methodological, Pedagogical, and Philosophical Reflections on Mircea Eliade as Historian of Religions." In Bryan S. Rennie (ed.), *Changing Religious Worlds: The Meaning and End of Mircea Eliade,* 165–189. Albany, NY: State University of New York Press.

Bellah, Robert N. (1967). "Civil Religion in America," *Daedalus* 96/1: 1–21.

—— (1978). "Religion and Legitimation in the American Republic," *Society* 15/4: 16–23.

—— (1987). "Conclusion: Competing Visions of the Role of Religion in American Society." In Robert N. Bellah and Frederick E. Greenspahn (eds.), *Uncivil Religion: Interreligious Hostility in America,* 219–232. New York: Crossroad Publishing Co.

—— (1990) [1970]. *Beyond Belief: Essays on Religion in a Post-traditional World.* New York: Harper and Row.

—— (1992) [1975]. *The Broken Covenant: American Civil Religion in Time of Trial.* 2nd edn. Chicago: University of Chicago Press.

Benavides, Gustavo (2000). "What Raw Materials Are Used in the Manufacture of Religion?" *Culture and Religion* 1/1: 113–122.

—— (2001a). "*Afterreligion* after Religion," *Journal of the American Academy of Religion* 69/2: 449–457.

—— (2001b). "Religious Studies Between Science and Ideology," *Religious Studies Review* 27/2: 105–108.

Berger, Adriana (1989). "Fascism and Religion in Romania," *Annals of Scholarship* 6: 455–465.

—— (1994). "Mircea Eliade: Romanian Fascism and the History of Religions in the United States." In Nancy A. Harrowitz (ed.), *Tainted Greatness: Anti-Semitism and Cultural Heroes,* 51–74. Philadelphia: Temple University Press.

Bérubé, Michael (1995). "Standard Deviation: Skyrocketing Job Requirements Inflame Political Tensions," *Academe* 81/6: 26–29.

—— (1996). "The Blessed of the Earth," *Social Text* 14/4 (1996): 75–95.

Bourdieu, Pierre (1998a) [1996]. *On Television*. Priscilla Parkhurst Ferguson (trans.). New York: The New Press.

—— (1998b) [1994]. *Practical Reason: On the Theory of Action*. Stanford: University of California Press.

Brauer, Jerald C. (1985). "Mircea Eliade and the Divinity School," *Criterion* 24/3: 25.

Braun, Willi (1997). "Socio-Rhetorical Interests: Context." In William E. Arnal and Michel Desjardins (eds.), *Whose Historical Jesus?* 92–97. Studies in Christianity and Judaism No. 7. Waterloo, ON: Wilfrid Laurier University Press.

—— (1999). "Amnesia in the Production of (Christian) History," *Bulletin of the Council of Societies for the Study of Religion* 28/1: 3–8.

—— (2000). "Religion." In Willi Braun and Russell T. McCutcheon (eds.), *Guide to the Study of Religion*, 3–18. London, U.K.: Continuum.

—— (2001a). "The Blessed Curse of Thought: Theorizing Religion in the Classroom," ARC (Journal of the Faculty of Religious Studies, McGill University, Montreal) 29: 161–177.

—— (2001b). "The Past as Simulacrum in the Canonical Narratives of Christian Origins," *Religion & Theology* 8/3–4: 213–228.

—— (2002). "Smoke Signals from the North: A Reply to Burton Mack's 'Backbay Jazz and Blues'." In Ron Cameron and Merrill Miller (eds.), *Redescribing Christian Origins*. Society for Biblical Literature Symposium Series. Atlanta: Society of Biblical Literature.

Braun, Willi and Russell T. McCutcheon (eds.) (2000). *Guide to the Study of Religion*. London, U.K.: Continuum.

Braun, Willi and Russell T. McCutcheon (2002). "Beyond the Annual Meeting: An Interview with the Authors," *Religious Studies News* 17/3: 15.

Brody, Richard (2000). "An Exile in Paradise: How Jean-Luc Godard Disappeared from the Headlines and into the Movies," *The New Yorker* (November 20): 62–76.

Brown, Delwin (1997). "Academic Theology and Religious Studies," *Bulletin of the Council for the Study of Religion* 26/3: 64–66.

Brown, Peter (1992). *Power and Persuasion in Late Antiquity: Towards a Christian Empire*. Madison: University of Wisconsin Press.

—— (1997). *Authority and the Sacred: Aspects of the Christianisation of the Roman World*. Cambridge: Cambridge University Press.

Brydon, Diana (1994). "The White Inuit Speaks: Contamination as Literary Strategy." In Bill Ashcroft, Gareth Griffiths, and Helen Tiffin (eds.), *The Post-Colonial Studies Reader*, 136–142. London and New York: Routledge.

Burke, Kenneth (1968). *Counter-Statement*. Berkeley: University of California Press.

Burris, John P. (2001). *Exhibiting Religion: Colonialism and Spectacle at International Expositions, 1851–1893*. Charlottesville: University Press of Virginia.

Callen, Barry L. (2001). *Authentic Spirituality: Moving Beyond Mere Religion*. Grand Rapids: Baker Book House.

Calvet, Louis-Jean (1998). *Language Wars and Linguistic Politics*. Michel Petheram (trans.). New York: Oxford University Press.

Carrasco, David (2000). "Member-at Large Interview," *Religious Studies News* 15: 3/4: 16, 18.

Carrette, Jeremy (2000). *Foucault and Religion: Spiritual Corporality and Political Spirituality*. London and New York: Routledge.

Cave, David (1993). *Mircea Eliade's Vision for a New Humanism*. New York: Oxford University Press.

—— (2001). "Eliade's Interpretation of Sacred Space and its Role Toward the Cultivation of Virtue." In Bryan S. Rennie (ed.), *Changing Religious Worlds: The Meaning and End of Mircea Eliade*, 235–248. Albany, NY: State University of New York Press.

Certeau, Michel de (1997) [1974]. *Culture in the Plural*. Luce Giard (ed.). Minneapolis: University of Minnesota Press.

Chatterjee, Partha (1993). *The Nation and its Fragments*. Princeton, NJ: Princeton University Press.

Cherry, Conrad (1995). *Hurrying Toward Zion: Universities, Divinity Schools, and American Protestantism*. Bloomington: University of Indiana Press.

Chidester, David (1996a). "Anchoring Religion in the World: A Southern African History of Comparative Religion," *Religion* 26: 141–160.

—— (1996b). *Savage Systems: Colonialism and Comparative Religion in Southern Africa*. Charlottesville: University Press of Virginia.

—— (1998). "No First or Final Solutions: Strategies, Techniques, and Ivan Strenski's Garden in the Study of Religion," *Journal of the American Academy of Religion* 66/2: 369–376.

—— (2000). "Colonialism." In Willi Braun and Russell T. McCutcheon (eds.), *Guide to the Study of Religion*, 423–437. London U.K.: Continuum.

Chomsky, Noam (1991). *Necessary Illusions: Thought Control in Democratic Societies*. Concord, Ontario: Anansi Press.

—— (1994). *Manufacturing Consent: Noam Chomsky and the Media. The Companion Book to the Award-Winning Film by Peter Wintonick and Mark Achbar*. Mark Achbar (ed.). Montreal: Black Rose Books.

Clifford, James (1988). *The Predicament of Culture: Twentieth-Century Ethnography, Literature, and Art*. Cambridge: Harvard University Press.

—— (1997). *Routes: Travel and Translation in the Late Twentieth Century*. Harvard: Harvard University Press.

Collins, Randall (1998). *The Sociology of Philosophies: A Global Theory of Intellectual Change*. Cambridge, MA: Harvard University Press.

Corless, Roger (1993). "After Eliade, What?" *Religion* 23: 373–377.

—— (2001). "Building on Eliade's Magnificent Failure." In Bryan S. Rennie (ed.), *Changing Religious Worlds: The Meaning and End of Mircea Eliade*, 3–9. Albany, NY: State University of New York Press.

Cox, Harvey (2000). "Letter to the Editor," *The New Yorker* (October 30): 12.

DeLillo, Don (1986) [1984]. *White Noise*. New York: Penguin Books.

Derrida, Jacques (1976). *Of Grammatology*. Gayatri C. Spivak (trans. and intro.). Baltimore: The Johns Hopkins Press.

—— (1988). "Like the Sound of the Sea Deep within a Shell: Paul de Man's War," *Critical Inquiry* 14: 590–652.

—— (1989). "Biodegradables: Seven Diary Fragments," *Critical Inquiry* 15: 812–873.

Devi, Maitreyi (1995) [1976]. *It Does Not Die*. Chicago: University of Chicago Press.

Didion, Joan (2001) [1979]. *The White Album*. New York: Farrar, Straus, and Giroux.

Doležalová, Iva, Luther H. Martin, and Dalibor Papoušek (eds.) (2001). *The Academic Study of Religion During the Cold War: East and West*. New York: Peter Lang.

Doniger, Wendy (1986). "The Uses and Misuses of Other People's Myths," *Journal of the American Academy of Religion* 54: 219–239.

—— (1998). *The Implied Spider: Politics and Theology in Myth*. New York: Columbia University Press.

Downing, Christine (1993). "A Somewhat Mitigated Disaster: The Status of the Religious Studies Department at San Diego State University as of February 1993," *Bulletin of the Council of Societies for the Study of Religion* 22/2: 39–43.

Dreyfus, Hubert L. and Paul Rabinow (1983). "On the Genealogy of Ethics: An Overview of Work in Progress," 229–252. *Michel Foucault: Beyond Structuralism and Hermeneutics*. 2nd edn. Chicago: University of Chicago Press.

Duby, Georges, Dominique Barthélemy, and Charles de la Roncière (1988) [1985]. "Portraits." In Georges Duby (ed.), *A History of Private Life: II. Revelations of the Medieval World*, 33–309. Philippe Ariès and Georges Duby (gen. eds.), Arthur Goldhammer (trans.). Cambridge: Harvard University Press.

Dugdale, Antony (1997). "Why Unionize?" *Religious Studies News* 12/4 (November): 13.

Dunning, Stephen N. (1997). "Saving Religious Studies: The Situation at Penn Four Years Later," *Bulletin of the Council of Societies for the Study of Religion* 27/3: 67–68.

Durkheim, Emile (1995) [1912]. *The Elementary Forms of Religious Life*. Karen Fields (trans.). New York: The Free Press.

Dyson, Freeman J. (2002). "Science & Religion: No Ends in Sight," *The New York Review of Books* 49/5 (March 28): 4–6.

Eagleton, Terry (1992). *The Significance of Theory*. Oxford, U.K.: Blackwell.

Earhart, Byron (1967). "Toward a Unified Interpretation of Japanese Religion." In Joseph Kitagawa (ed.), *History of Religions: Essays on the Problem of Understanding*, 195–225. Chicago: University of Chicago Press.

Eck, Diana (2001). *A New Religious America: How a "Christian Country" Has Now Become the World's Most Religiously Diverse Nation*. San Francisco: Harper San Francisco.

Eliade, Mircea (1958). *Patterns in Comparative Religion*. Rosemary Sheed (trans.). New York: Sheed & Ward.

—— (1973). *Australian Religions: An Introduction*. Ithaca, NY: Cornell University Press.

—— (1974) [1949]. *Myth of the Eternal Return*. Willard R. Trask (trans.). Princeton: Princeton University Press.

—— (ed.). (1987). *The Encyclopedia of Religion*, 16 vols. New York: Macmillan.

—— (1988). *Autobiography Vol. II, 1937–1960, Exile's Return*. Mac Linscott Ricketts (trans.). Chicago: University of Chicago Press.

—— (1989a). *Journal II: 1957–1969*. Fred H. Johnson (trans.). Chicago: University of Chicago Press.

—— (1989b). *Journal III: 1970–1978*. Teresa Lavender Fagan (trans.). Chicago: University of Chicago Press.

—— (1990a) [1981]. *Autobiography Vol. I, 1907–1937, Journey East, Journey West*. Mac Linscott Ricketts (trans.). Chicago: University of Chicago Press.

—— (1990b). *Journal I: 1945–1955*. Mac Linscott Ricketts (trans.). Chicago: University of Chicago Press.

—— (1990c). *Journal IV: 1979–1985*. Mac Linscott Ricketts (trans.). Chicago: University of Chicago Press.

—— (1995) [1950]. *Bengal Nights*. Chicago: University of Chicago Press.

Eliade, Mircea and Joseph M. Kitagawa (eds.) (1959). *The History of Religions: Essays in Methodology*. Chicago: University of Chicago Press.

Elliott, Anthony (2001). *Concepts of the Self*. Cambridge: Polity Press.

Ellwood, Robert (1999). *The Politics of Myth: A Study of C. G. Jung, Mircea Eliade, and Joseph Campbell*. Albany, NY: State University of New York Press.

Euben, Roxanne L. (1999). *Enemy in the Mirror: Islamic Fundamentalism and the Limits of Modern Rationalism*. Princeton: Princeton University Press.

Faure, Bernard (1993). *Chan Insights and Oversights: An Epistemological Critique of the Chan Tradition*. Princeton: Princeton University Press.

Fish, Stanley (1994). *There's No Such Thing As Free Speech: And It's a Good Thing Too*. New York: Oxford University Press.

—— (1999). *The Trouble with Principle*. Cambridge, MA: Harvard University Press.

Fitzgerald, Tim (1997). "A Critique of the Concept of Religion," *Method & Theory in the Study of Religion* 9/2: 91–110.

—— (2000a). "Experience." In Willi Braun and Russell T. McCutcheon (eds.), *Guide to the Study of Religion*, 125–139. London U.K.: Continuum.

—— (2000b). *The Ideology of Religious Studies*. New York: Oxford University Press.

—— (2001). "A Response to Saler, Benavides, and Korom," *Religious Studies Review* 27/2: 110–115.

Flower, Ruth (1997). "The Higher Cost of Higher Education – In Perspective," *Academe* 83/5: 95.

Foucault, Michel (1973) [1970]. *The Order of Things: An Archaeology of the Human Sciences*. New York: Vintage.

—— (1977a) [1975]. *Discipline and Punish*. Alan M. Sheridan (trans.). New York: Pantheon.

—— (1977b). "Nietzsche, Genealogy, History." In Donald F. Bouchard (ed. and intro.), *Language, Counter-Memory, Practice: Selected Essays and Interviews*, 139–164. Donald F. Bouchard and Sherry Simon (trans.). Ithaca, NY: Cornell University Press.

—— (1979) [1978]. "Governmentality," *Ideology and Consciousness* 6: 5–21.

—— (1980). *Power/Knowledge: Selected Interviews and Other Writings, 1972–1977*. Colin Gordon (ed.). New York: Pantheon.

—— (1982). "The Subject and Power," *Critical Inquiry* 8: 777–795.

—— (1985) [1984]. *The Use of Pleasure, Vol. 2 of the History of Sexuality*. Robert Hurley (trans.). New York: Random House.

—— (1988a). *Politics, Philosophy, Culture: Interviews and Other Writings, 1977–1984*. Lawrence D. Kritzman (ed.), Alan Sheridan and others (trans.). New York: Routledge.

—— (1988b). *Technologies of the Self: A Seminar with Michel Foucault*. Luther H. Martin, Huck Gutman, and Patrick H. Hutton (eds.). Amherst: University of Massachusetts Press.

—— (1989) [1969]. *The Archeology of Knowledge*. Alan M. Sheridan Smith (trans.). London: Routledge.

—— (1990) [1976]. *The History of Sexuality, Vol. 1: An Introduction*. Robert Hurley (trans.). New York: Vintage Books.

—— (1996) [1978]. "What is Critique?" In James Schmidt (ed.), *What is Enlightenment? Eighteenth-Century Answers and Twentieth-Century Questions*, 382–398. Kevin Paul Geiman (trans.). Berkeley: University of California Press.

—— (1999). *Religion and Culture*. Jeremy Carrette (ed.). New York: Routledge.

Franklin, Benjamin (1961). "Proposals Relating to the Education of Youth in Pennsylvania." In Leonard W. Labaree (ed.), *The Papers of Benjamin Franklin*, 21 vols. New Haven: Yale University Press.

Freud, Sigmund (1952) [1928]. "A Religious Experience." In James Strachey (ed.), *Collected Papers*, vol. 5, 243–246. The International Psycho-Analytic Library, No. 37. London: Hogarth Press.

—— (1964) [1917]. "The Taboo of Virginity (Contributions to the Psychology of Love III)." In James Strachey (ed.), *The Standard Edition of the Complete Psychological Works of Sigmund Freud*, vol. 11, 191–208. London: Hogarth Press.

Frisina, Warren (1997). "Religious Studies: Strategies for Survival in the 90s," *Bulletin of the Council of Societies for the Study of Religion* 26/2: 29–34.

Fuller, Robert C. (2001). *Spiritual, But Not Religious: Understanding Unchurched America*. New York: Oxford University Press.

Gallagher, Eugene (2001). "Teaching Outside the Classroom," *Bulletin of the Council of Societies for the Study of Religion* 30: 42–45.

Gamwell, Franklin I. (1988). "Welcome to Mr. and Mrs. Laurence Rockefeller," *Criterion: A Publication of The Divinity School of The University of Chicago* 27/1 (Winter): 7–8.

Gawande, Atul (1999). "A Queasy Feeling: Why Can't We Cure Nausea?" *The New Yorker* 75/17 (5 July): 34–41.

Gay, Peter (2001). "Witness to Fascism," *New York Review of Books* 48/14 (October 4): 44–47.

Geertz, Armin (2001). "Review of T. Idinopulos and B. Wilson (eds.), *What is Religion?*," *Journal of Religion* 81: 343–346.

Geertz, Armin W., and Jeppe Sinding Jensen (1991). "Tradition and Renewal in the Histories of Religions: Some Observations and Reflections." In Armin W. Geertz and Jeppe Sinding Jensen (eds.), *Religion, Tradition, and Renewal*, 11–27. Aarhus, Denmark: Aarhus University Press.

Geertz, Clifford (1993) [1973]. "Thick Description: Toward an Interpretive Theory of Culture." In *The Interpretation of Cultures: Selected Essays*. New York: Basic Books.

Gellner, Ernest (1992). *Postmodernism, Reason, and Religion*. London: Routledge.

Giddens, Anthony (1991). *Modernity and Self-Identity: Self and Society in the Late Modern Age*. Stanford: Stanford University Press.

Gilbert, Sandra (1996). "The (Academic) Job System and the Economy, Stupid; or, Should a Friend Let a Friend Get a Ph.D.?" *Academe* 82/5: 12–15.

Gill, Sam (1998). *Storytracking: Texts, Stories, and the Histories in Central Australia*. New York: Oxford University Press.

Girardot, Norman J. (2001). "Smiles and Whispers: Nostalgic Reflections on Mircea Eliade's Significance for the Study of Religion." In Bryan Rennie (ed.), *Changing Religious Worlds: The Meaning and End of Mircea Eliade*, 143–163. Albany, NY: State University of New York Press.

Glaude, Eddie Jr. (2000). *Exodus! Religion, Race, and Nation in Early Nineteenth-Century Black America*. Chicago: University of Chicago Press.

—— (forthcoming). "Myth and African American Self-Identity." In Craig Prentiss (ed.), *Religion, Myth, and the Creation of Race and Ethnicity: An Introduction*. New York: New York University Press.

Godlove, Terry (1994). "Religious Discourse and First Person Authority," *Method & Theory in the Study of Religion* 6: 147–161.

Green, Ronald M. (1987). "Theodicy." In Mircea Eliade (general ed.), *Encyclopedia of Religion*, vol. 14, 430–441. New York: Macmillan Press.

Griaule, Marcel (1965). *Conversations with Ogotemmêli*. Oxford: Oxford University Press.

Griffiths, Gareth (1994). "The Myth of Authenticity." In Bill Ashcroft, Gareth Griffiths, and Helen Tiffin (eds.), *The Post-Colonial Studies Reader*, 237–245. London and New York: Routledge.

Griffiths, Paul J. (1998a). "Review of Russell McCutcheon, *Manufacturing Religion*," *First Things: A Monthly Journal of Religion and Public Life* 81 (March): 44–48.

—— (1998b). "Some Confusions About Critical Intelligence: A Response to Russell T. McCutcheon," *Journal of the American Academy of Religion* 66/4: 893–895.

—— (1999). *Religious Reading: The Place of Reading in the Practice of Religion*. New York: Oxford University Press.

—— (2000). "The Very Idea of Religion," *First Things: A Monthly Journal of Religion and Public Life* 101 (May): 30–35.

Grottanelli, Cristiano and Bruce Lincoln (1985). "A Brief Note on (Future) Research in the History of Religions," *Centre for Humanistic Studies Occasional Papers* (University of Minnesota), 4. Reprinted in *Method & Theory in the Study of Religion* 10/3 (1998): 311–325.

Gutman, Huck (1988). "Rousseau's *Confessions*: A Technology of the Self." In Luther H. Martin *et al.* (eds.), *Technologies of the Self: A Seminar with Michel Foucault*, 99–119. Amherst: University of Massachusetts Press.

Gyatso, Janet (1999). "Healing Burns with Fire: The Facilitations of Experience in Tibetan Buddhism," *Journal of the American Academy of Religion* 67/1: 113–147.

Hamacher, Werner, Neil Hertz, and Thomas Keenan (eds.) (1988). *Wartime Journalism, 1939–1943*. Lincoln, NB: University of Nebraska Press.

—— (1989). *Responses: On Paul de Man's Wartime Journalism*. Lincoln, NB: University of Nebraska Press.

Harrison, Peter (1990). *"Religion" and the Religions in the English Enlightenment*. Cambridge: Cambridge University Press.

Hart, Darryl G. (1999). *The University Gets Religion: Religious Studies in American Higher Education*. Baltimore: Johns Hopkins University Press.

Hastings, James (ed.) (1908). *The Encyclopaedia of Religion and Ethics*, 13 vols. New York: C. Scribner's Sons.

Heathorn, Stephen (1994). "Review of Benedict Anderson, *Imagined Communities*," *Method & Theory in the Study of Religion* 6/1: 105–109.

Hedrick, Charles (1976). "One Man's Opinion: A Reply to Norman E. Wagner," *Bulletin of the Council on the Study of Religion* 7/4: 3–5.

Herberg, Will (1955). *Protestant, Catholic, Jew*. Garden City, NY: Doubleday & Co.

Herrick, Susan (2001). "New Religious Movement Scholars Watch FBI Simulate Crisis," *Religious Studies News* 16/1: 5.

Hill, Christopher (2000). "Toleration in Seventeenth-Century England: Theory and Practice." In Susan Mendus (ed.), *The Politics of Toleration in Modern Life*, 27–43. Durham, NC: Duke University Press.

Hitchens, Christopher (2002). "The Medals of His Defeats," *The Atlantic Monthly* 289/4 (April): 118–137.

Hobbes, T. (1962) [1651]. *Leviathan, or the Matter, Forme and Power of a Commonwealth Ecclesiastical and Civil*. M. Oakeshott (ed.), R. S. Peters (intro.). New York: Collier Books.

Hobsbawm, Eric (1992) [1983]. "Mass-Producing Traditions: Europe, 1870–1914." In Eric Hobsbawm and Terrence Ranger (eds.), *The Invention of Tradition*, 263–307. Cambridge: Cambridge University Press.

Hobsbawm, Eric and Terrence Ranger (eds.) (1992) [1983]. *The Invention of Tradition*. Cambridge: Cambridge University Press.

Hoffmann, Bill and Cathy Burke (1997). *Heaven's Gate: Cult Suicide in San Diego*. New York: Harper Paperbacks.

Horyna, Břetislav (2001). "Czech Religious Studies: Past, Present, Future," *Method & Theory in the Study of Religion* 13/3: 254–268.

Humphries, Michael L. (1999). *Christian Origins and the Language of the Kingdom of God*. Burton L. Mack (foreword). Carbondale: Southern Illinois University Press.

Hussain, Amir (2002). "Death is a Master from …," *Religious Studies News* 17/2: 11.

Idinopulos, Thomas A. (2002). "The Strengths and Weaknesses of Durkheim's Methodology for the Study and Teaching of Religion." In Thomas A. Idinopulos and Brian C. Wilson (eds.), *Reappraising Durkheim for the Study and Teaching of Religion*, 1–14. Leiden: E. J. Brill.

Idinopulos, Thomas A. and Brian C. Wilson (eds.) (1998). *What is Religion? Origins, Definitions, and Explanations*. Leiden: E. J. Brill.

—— (2002). *Reappraising Durkheim for the Study and Teaching of Religion*. Leiden: E. J. Brill.

Idinopulos, Thomas A. and Edward Yonan (eds.) (1994). *Religion and Reductionism: Essays on Eliade, Segal, and the Challenge of the Social Sciences for the Study of Religion*. Leiden: E. J. Brill.

—— (1996). *The Sacred and its Scholars. Comparative Methodologies for the Study of Primary Religious Data*. Leiden: E. J. Brill.

Ignatieff, Michael (2000). "Nationalism and Tolerance." In Susan Mendus (ed.), *The Politics of Toleration in Modern Life*, 77–106. Durham, NC: Duke University Press.

Jensen, Tim (2001). "Reflections on the IAHR Congress, Durban, South Africa (August 2000)," *Bulletin of the Council of Societies for the Study of Religion* 30/3: 64–65.

Johnson, Paul C. (2002). "Death and Memory at Ground Zero: A Historian of Religion's Report," *Bulletin of the Council of Societies for the Study of Religion* 31/1: 3–7.

—— (forthcoming). "Migrating Bodies, Circulating Signs: Brazilian Candomblé, the Garifuna of the Caribbean, and the Category of Indigenous Religions," *History of Religions*.

Juergensmeyer, Mark (2001) [2000]. *Terror in the Mind of God: The Global Rise of Religious Violence*. Berkeley: University of California Press.

Jung, Carl G. (1990) [1957]. *The Undiscovered Self, with Symbols and The Interpretation of Dreams*. R. F. C. Hull (trans.), William McGuire (intro.). Princeton, NJ: Princeton University Press.

Keller, Mary (2001). "Review of Jeremy Carrette, *Foucault and Religion* and Michel Foucault, *Religion and Culture*, Jeremy Carrette (ed.)," *Journal of the American Academy of Religion* 69/4: 920–924.

Kelly, George A. (1984). *Politics and Religious Consciousness in America*. New Brunswick: Transaction Books.

Kennedy, Helena (2000). "The Politics of Intolerance." In Susan Mendus (ed.), *The Politics of Toleration in Modern Life*, 107–118. Durham, NC: Duke University Press.

King, Richard (1999). *Orientalism and Religion: Postcolonial Theory, India, and "The Mystic East"*. London and New York: Routledge.

Kirn, Walter (2001). *Up in the Air*. New York: Doubleday.

Kitagawa, Joseph (ed.) (1967). *The History of Religions: Essays on the Problem of Understanding*. Chicago: University of Chicago Press.

—— (ed.) (1985). *The History of Religions: Retrospect and Prospect.* New York: Macmillan Publishing Company.

—— (1987a). "The History of Religions at Chicago," *The History of Religions: Understanding Human Experience,* 133–144. Atlanta: Scholars Press.

—— (1987b). *On Understanding Japanese Religion.* Princeton: Princeton University Press.

Kuklick, Bruce (1989). "John Dewey, American Theology, and Scientific Politics." In Michael J. Lacey (ed.), *Religion and Twentieth-Century American Intellectual Life,* 78–93. Cambridge: Cambridge University Press.

Kuper, Adam (1988). *The Invention of Primitive Society: Transformations of an Illusion.* New York: Routledge.

Lacan, Jacques (1982). "The Mirror-stage as Formative of the Function of the I." In *Écrits: A Selection,* 1–7. Alan Sheridan (trans.). New York: W. W. Norton and Co.

Lapel, Christian and Russell T. McCutcheon (2001). "Canadian Scholars Working in the U.S.: An Unofficial Primer on the INS." Posted at the Canadian Society for Studies in Religion web site: http://www.ccsr.ca/cssr/requests.html#ins.

Lash, Nicholas (1996). *The Beginning and the End of "Religion".* Cambridge: Cambridge University Press.

Lease, Gary (1994). "The History of 'Religious' Consciousness and the Diffusion of Culture: Strategies for Surviving Dissolution," *Historical Reflections/Reflexions Historiques* 20/3: 453–479.

—— (1997). "Rationality and Evidence: The Study of Religion as a Taxonomy of Human Natural History." In Jeppe Sinding Jensen and Luther H. Martin (eds.), *Rationality and the Study of Religion,* 136–144. Aarhus, Denmark: Aarhus University Press.

—— (1998). "Public Redemption: Strenski's Mission for Religious Studies," *Journal of the American Academy of Religion* 66/2: 377–380.

Lincoln, Bruce (1986). *Myth, Cosmos, and Society: Indo-European Themes of Creation and Destruction.* Cambridge, Mass.: Harvard University Press.

—— (1989). *Discourse and the Construction of Society: Comparative Studies of Myth, Ritual, and Classification.* New York: Oxford University Press.

—— (1991). *Death, War, and Sacrifice: Studies in Ideology and Practice.* Chicago: University of Chicago Press.

—— (1994). *Authority: Construction and Corrosion.* Chicago: University of Chicago Press.

—— (1996a). "Mythic Narrative and Cultural Diversity in American society." In Laurie L. Patton and Wendy Doniger (eds.), *Myth & Method,* 163–176. Charlottesville: University Press of Virginia.

—— (1996b). "Theses on Method." *Method & Theory in the Study of Religion* 8/3: 225–227.

—— (1999). *Theorizing Myth: Narrative, Ideology, and Scholarship.* Chicago: University of Chicago Press.

—— (2001). "The Center of the World and the Origins of Life," *History of Religions* 40/4: 311–326.

—— (2002a). *Holy Terrors: Thinking about Religion after September 11.* Chicago: University of Chicago Press.

—— (2002b). "The Other War: The One of Words," *Bulletin of the Council of Societies for the Study of Religion* 31/1: 9–10.

Llewellyn, J. E. (2001). "Reflections on the IAHR Congress, Durban, South Africa (August 2000)," *Bulletin of the Council of Societies for the Study of Religion* 30/3: 62.

Loader, J. A. (1987). "Liberation Theology and Theological Argument," *Journal of Theology for Southern Africa* 59: 3–18.

Locke, John (1955) [1689]. *A Letter Concerning Toleration* 2nd edn. W. Popple (trans.), P. Romanell (intro.). New York: Liberal Arts Press.

Lodge, David (1992) [1975]. *Changing Places.* New York: Penguin Books.

—— (1995) [1984]. *Small World.* New York: Penguin Books.

Ludwig, Theodore (1998). "Review of Russell McCutcheon, *Manufacturing Religion*," *The Cresset Trinity* 34–36.

Luhrmann, Tanya M. (1991). *Persuasions of the Witch's Craft: Ritual Magic in Contemporary England.* New Haven: Harvard University Press.

—— (1997). "Witches, Magic, Ordinary Folks," *U.S. News & World Report* (April 7): 35.

Mack, Burton L. (1991) [1988]. *A Myth of Innocence: Mark and Christian Origins.* Philadelphia: Fortress Press.

—— (1995). *Who Wrote the New Testament? The Making of the Christian Myth.* New York: HarperCollins.

—— (1996). "On Redescribing Christian Origins," *Method & Theory in the Study of Religion* 8/3: 247–269.

—— (2000). "Social Formation." In Willi Braun and Russell T. McCutcheon (eds.), *Guide to the Study of Religion,* 283–296. London U.K.: Continuum.

—— (2001a). "Caretakers and Critics: On the Social Role of Scholars Who Study Religion," *Bulletin of the Council of Societies for the Study of Religion* 30: 8–14.

—— (2001b). *Christian Myth: Origins, Logic, and Legacy.* London U.K.: Continuum.

Malley, Brian (1995). "Explaining Order in Religious Systems," *Method & Theory in the Study of Religion* 7/1: 5–22.

Manganaro, Marc (1992). *Myth, Rhetoric, and the Voice of Authority: A Critique of Frazer, Eliot, Frye, and Campbell.* New Haven: Yale University Press.

Marcus, Amy Dockser (2000). *The View from Nebo: How Archeology is Rewriting the Bible and Reshaping the Middle East.* Boston: Little Brown.

Marsden, George (1994). *The Soul of the American University: From Protestant Establishment to Established Nonbelief.* New York: Oxford University Press.

Marty, Martin E. (1959). *The New Shape of American Religion.* New York: Harper.

—— (1985). "What is Modern About the Modern Study of Religion," *The University Lecture in Religion at Arizona State University, February 21, 1985.* Department of Religious Studies: Arizona State University.

—— (1997). *The One and the Many: America's Struggle for the Common Good.* Cambridge, MA: Harvard University Press.

Marx, Karl and Friedrich Engels (1988) [1846]. *The German Ideology.* C. J. Arthur (trans.). New York: International Publishers.

Masuzawa, Tomoko (2000). "The Production of 'Religion' and the Task of the Scholar," *Culture and Religion* 1: 123–130 .

—— (2001). "Reflections on the Charmed Circle," *Journal of the American Academy of Religion* 69/2: 429–436.

Mazur, Eric Michael (1999). *The Americanization of Religious Minorities: Confronting the Constitutional Order.* Baltimore: Johns Hopkins University Press.

McCutcheon, Russell T. (1991). "Ideology and the Problem of Naming," *Method & Theory in the Study of Religion* 3/2: 245–256.

—— (1997a). "A Default of Critical Intelligence? The Scholar of Religion as Public Intellectual," *Journal of the American Academy of Religion* 65/2: 443–468.

—— (1997b). *Manufacturing Religion: The Discourse on Sui Generis Religion and the Politics of Nostalgia.* New York: Oxford University Press.

—— (1998). "Redescribing 'Religion' as Social Formation: Toward a Social Theory of Religion." In Thomas A. Idinopulos and Brian C. Wilson (eds.), *What is Religion? Origins, Definitions, and Explanations,* 51–71. Leiden: E. J. Brill. Reprinted in McCutcheon 2001b: ch. 2.

—— (1999). "Of Strawmen and Humanists: A Reply to Bryan Rennie," *Religion* 29/1: 91–92.

—— (2000a). "Myth." In Willi Braun and Russell T. McCutcheon (eds.), *Guide to the Study of Religion,* 190–208. London, U.K: Continuum.

—— (2000b). "Taming Ethnocentrism and Trans-cultural Understandings." In Armin W. Geertz and Russell T. McCutcheon (eds.), *Perspectives on Method and Theory in the Study of Religion Adjunct Proceedings of the XVIIth Congress of the International Association of the History of Religions, Mexico City, 1995,* 298–306. Netherlands: Brill Academic Publishers. Reprinted in McCutcheon 2001b: ch. 5.

—— (2001a). "Bruce Lincoln's *Theorizing Myth*: The Perfect Past and the Jargon of Authenticity," *Studies in Religion/Sciences Religieuses* 30/1: 1–11.

—— (2001b). *Critics Not Caretakers: Redescribing the Public Study of Religion.* Albany, NY: State University of New York Press.

—— forthcoming. "Critical Trends in the Study of Religion in the U.S." In P. Antes, A. W. Geertz and R. Warne (eds.), *New Approaches to the Study of Religion.* Religion and Reason Series. Berlin and New York: Verlag de Gruyter.

McNulty, Cris (n.d.). "Reagan and the Record Business," http://users.drew.edu/~cmcnulty/.

Menard, Louis (2001). "False Fronts," *The New Yorker* (July 23): 78–82.

Messer-Davidow, Ellen (2002). *Disciplining Feminism: From Social Activism to Academic Discourse.* Durham, NC: Duke University Press.

Miles, Margaret (2000). "Becoming Answerable for What We See," *Journal of the American Academy of Religion* 68/3: 471–485.

Milton, J. R. (1994). "Locke's Life and Times." In Vere Chappell (ed.), *The Cambridge Companion to Locke,* 5–25. New York: Cambridge University Press.

Montaigne, Michel de (1936) [1580–8]. *The Essays of Michel de Montaigne,* vol. 3. Jacob Zeitlin (ed. and trans.). New York: Alfred Knopf, Inc.

Muesse, Mark W. (1997). "Religious Studies and 'Heaven's Gate': Making the Strange Familiar and the Familiar Strange," *The Chronicle of Higher Education* 43/33 (April 25): B6–B7. Reprinted in Russell T. McCutcheon (ed.), *The Insider/Outsider Problem in the Study of Religion: A Reader,* 390–394. London: Continuum.

Murphy, Tim (1994). "Review of Carl Olson, *The Theology and Philosophy of Eliade,*" *Method & Theory in the Study of Religion* 6: 382–389.

—— (2001). "Eliade, Subjectivity, and Hermeneutics." In Bryan S. Rennie (ed.), *Changing Religious Worlds: The Meaning and End of Mircea Eliade,* 35–47. Albany, NY: State University of New York Press.

—— (Forthcoming). "*In hoc signo vinces*: Elements of a Semiotic Theory of Religion," *Method & Theory in the Study of Religion.*

Nelson, Cary (1995a). "Lessons from the Job Wars: Late Capitalism Arrives on Campus," *Social Text* 13/3: 119–134.

—— (1995b). "Lessons from the Job Wars: What is to be Done?" *Academe* 81/6: 18–25.

—— (1996). "Introduction: How Not to Handle a Labor Dispute," *Social Text* 14/4: 5–11.

—— (1997a). *Manifesto of a Tenured Radical.* New York: New York University Press.

—— (1997b). "Superstars," *Academe* 83/1: 38–43, 54.

—— (ed.) (1997c). *Will Teach for Food: Academic Labour in Crisis.* Minneapolis: University of Minnesota Press.

Newman, Kathy M. (1996). "Poor, Hungry, and Desperate? Or Privileged, Histrionic, and Demanding? In Search of the True Meaning of 'Ph.D.'," *Social Text* 14/4: 97–131.

Nietzsche, Friedrich (1969) [1887]. *On the Genealogy of Morals.* Walter Kaufmann (trans.). New York: Random House.

Nord, Warren (1995). *Religion and American Education: Rethinking a National Dilemma.* Chapel Hill: University of North Carolina Press.

Norris, Christopher (1988). *Paul De Man: Deconstruction and the Critique of Aesthetic Ideology.* London: Routledge.

—— (1990). *What's Wrong With Postmodernism: Critical Theory and the Ends of Philosophy.* Baltimore: The Johns Hopkins University Press.

Novak, Michael (1974). *Choosing Our King: Powerful Symbols in Presidential Politics.* New York: Macmillan.

Nye, Malory (2000). "Religion, Post-Religionism, and Religioning: Religious Studies and Contemporary Cultural Debates," *Method & Theory in the Study of Religion* 12: 447–476.

Olson, Carl (1992). *The Theology and Philosophy of Mircea Eliade: A Search for the Centre.* London: Macmillan.

—— (2000). "Mircea Eliade, Postmodernism, and the Problematic Nature of Representational Thinking," *Method & Theory in the Study of Religion* 11/4: 357–385.

Otto, Rudolf (1950) [1923]. *The Idea of the Holy.* 2nd edn. J. W. Harvey (trans.). London: Oxford University Press.

Paden, William (2000). "World." In Willi Braun and Russell T. McCutcheon (eds.), *Guide to the Study of Religion,* 334–347. London U.K.: Continuum.

Penner, Hans (2000). "Interpretation." In Willi Braun and Russell T. McCutcheon (eds.), *Guide to the Study of Religion,* 57–71. London U.K.: Continuum.

Perkins, Judith (1995). *The Suffering Self: Pain and Narrative Representation in the Early Christian Era.* New York: Routledge.

Phillips, Adam (1998). *The Beast in the Nursery: On Curiosity and Other Appetites.* New York: Pantheon Books.

Pope, Alexander (1950) [1733–1734]. *Essay on Man.* Maynard Mack (ed.). London: Methuen & Co.

Power, Samantha (2001). "Bystanders to Genocide: Why the United States Let the Rwandan Tragedy Happen," *Atlantic Monthly* (September): 84–108.

Prentiss, Craig (ed.) (2001). "Reflections on the IAHR Congress, Durban, South Africa (August 2000)," *Bulletin of the Council of Societies for the Study of Religion* 30/3: 61–65.

—— (2002). "Editorial," *Bulletin of the Council of Societies for the Study of Religion* 31/1: 2–3.

Preus, J. Samuel (1987). *Explaining Religion: Criticism and Theory from Bodin to Freud.* New Haven: Yale University Press.

Queenan, Joe (2001). *Balsamic Dreams: A Short but Self-Important History of the Baby Boomer Generation.* New York: Henry Holt and Co.

Qutb, Sayyid (1993) [1964]. *Milestones.* [Ma'alim fil-Tariq] Ahmad Zaki Hammad (foreword). Indianapolis: American Trust Publications.

Ransom, John S. (1997). *Foucault's Discipline: The Politics of Subjectivity*. Durham, NC and London: Duke University Press.

Reichel-Dolmatoff, Gerardo (1971). *Amazonian Cosmos*. Chicago: University of Chicago Press.

Rennie, Bryan S. (1992). "The Diplomatic Career of Mircea Eliade: A Response to Adriana Berger," *Religion* 22: 375–392.

—— (1996). *Reconstructing Eliade: Making Sense of Religion*. Albany, NY: State University of New York Press.

—— (ed.) (2001a). *Changing Religious Worlds: The Meaning and End of Mircea Eliade*. Albany, NY: State University of New York Press.

—— (2001b). "A Response to Carl Olson's 'Mircea Eliade, Postmodernism, and the Problematic Nature of Representational Thinking,'" *Method & Theory in the Study of Religion* 12/3: 416–421.

—— (forthcoming). "Review of M. Sebastian, *Journal, 1935–1944*," *Religion*.

Reynolds, Susan (1984). *Kingdoms and Communities in Western Europe, 900–1300*. New York: Oxford University Press.

Ricketts, Mac Linscott (1988). *Mircea Eliade: The Romanian Roots, 1907–1945*. 2 vols. Boulder, CO: East European Monographs.

Rimer, Sara (1999). "Columbine Students Seek Answers in Their Faith," *New York Times* (Sunday, June 6) Section 1: 22, cols. 1–4.

Roeper, Richard (2000). "Springsteen on Diallo: Try Actually Listening." *Chicago Sun-Times* (June 14).

Ross, Andrew (1996). "The Labor Behind the Cult of Work," *Social Text* 14/4: 25–29.

Ross, James R. (2000). *Fragile Branches: Travels Through the Jewish Diaspora*. New York: Riverhead Books.

Rousseau, Jean-Jacques (1979) [1762]. *Emile, or, On Education*. Allan Bloom (intro., and trans.). New York: Basic Books.

—— (1982) [1762]. *The Social Contract*. Maurice Cranston (trans.). New York: Penguin Book.

Rudolph, Kurt (1985). *Historical Fundamentals and the Study of Religions*. Joseph M. Kitagawa (intro.). New York: Macmillan Company.

Rushdie, Salman (2001). "Yes, This is About Islam: How Radical Politics Co-opts a Faith," *The New York Times* (Friday, November 2): A25, cols. 1–4.

Russo, Richard (1997). *Straight Man*. New York: Vintage Books.

Rybczynski, Witold (1988). *Home: A Short History of an Idea*. London: Heinemann.

—— (1990). *The Most Beautiful House in the World*. New York: Penguin Books.

Saler, Benson (2001). "On What We May Believe about Beliefs." In Jensine Andresen (ed.), *Religion in Mind*, 47–69. Cambridge: Cambridge University Press.

Sandys-Wunsch, John (1996). "Editorial," *Studies in Religion* 25/2: 139–140.

Sarup, Madan (1996). *Identity, Culture, and the Postmodern World*. Athens, GA: University of Georgia Press.

Schneider, Carol Geary (2001). "President's Message: When 'Understanding' is not Enough," *Liberal Education* (a publication of the Association of American Colleges and Universities) 87/4 (Fall): 2–3.

Schwartz, Arthur (2001). "Growing Spiritually During the College Years," *Liberal Education* (a publication of the Association of American Colleges and Universities) 87/4 (Fall): 30–35.

Scott, Joan Wallach (1989a). "History in Crisis? The Other's Side in the Story," *American Historical Review* 94/3: 680–692.

—— (1989b). "Review of Gertrude Himmelfarb, *The New History and the Old: Critical Essays and Reappraisals*," *American Historical Review* 94/3: 699–700.

—— (1991). "The Evidence of Experience," *Critical Inquiry* 17: 773–797.

Sebastian, Mihail (2000a). "Diary: Friends and Fascists," *The New Yorker* (October 2): 106–113.

—— (2000b). *Journal, 1935–1944*. Patrick Camiller (trans.), Radu Ioanid (intro.). Chicago: Ivan R. Dee.

Sharf, Robert H. (1998). "Experience." In Mark C. Taylor (ed.), *Critical Terms in Religious Studies* 94–115. Chicago: University of Chicago Press.

Sharpe, Eric J. (1986). *Comparative Religion: A History*. LaSalle, Illinois: Open Court.

Sheehan, Thomas (1993). "Heidegger: The Normal Nazi," *New York Review of Books* 14 January: 30–35.

Shepard, Robert (1991). *God's People in the Ivory Tower: Religion in the Early American University*. New York: Carlson Publishing Co.

Silberman, Neil Asher (1990). *Digging for God and Country: Exploration, Archeology, and the Secret Struggle for the Holy Land, 1799–1917*. New York: Doubleday.

Smart, Ninian (1988). "Review of Mircea Eliade (ed.), *The Encyclopedia of Religion*," *Religious Studies Review* 14/3: 193–199.

Smith, Jonathan Z. (1982). *Imagining Religion: From Babylon to Jonestown*. Chicago: University of Chicago Press.

—— (1990a). "Connections," *Journal of the American Academy of Religion* 58/1: 1–15.

—— (1990b). *Drudgery Divine: On the Comparison of Early Christianities and the Religions of Late Antiquity*. Chicago: University of Chicago Press.

—— (1991). "The Introductory Course: Less is Better." In Mark Juergensmeyer (ed.), *Teaching the Introductory Course in Religious Studies: A Sourcebook*, 185–192. Atlanta: Scholars Press.

—— (1995). "Religious Studies: Whither (Wither) and Why?" *Method & Theory in the Study of Religion* 7/4: 407–413.

—— (1997). "Are Theological and Religious Studies Compatible?" *Bulletin of the Council of Societies for the Study of Religion* 26/3: 60–61.

—— (1998). "Religion, Religions, Religious." In Mark C. Taylor (ed.), *Critical Terms for Religious Studies* 269–284. Chicago: University of Chicago Press.

—— (2000a). "Acknowledgments: Morphology and History in Mircea Eliade's *Patterns in Comparative Religion* (1949–1999) Part 1: The Work and its Contexts," *History of Religions* 39/4: 315–321.

—— (2000b). "Acknowledgments: Morphology and History in Mircea Eliade's *Patterns in Comparative Religion* (1949–1999) Part 2: The Texture of the Work," *History of Religions* 39/4: 322–351.

—— (2001a). "Close Encounters of Diverse Kinds." In Susan L. Mizruchi (ed.), *Religion and Cultural Studies*, 3–21. Princeton: Princeton University Press.

—— (2001b). "A Twice-Told Tale: The History of the History of Religions' History," *Numen* 48/2: 131–146.

—— (2002). "What Does the Census Data Say about the Study of Religion," *Religious Studies News* 17/2: 7, 23.

—— n.d. "The Necessary Lie: Duplicity in the Disciplines," <http://teaching.uchicago.edu/handbook/tac12.html>.

Smith, Jonathan Z. (general ed.), William Scott Green (associate ed.) (1995). *The HarperCollins Dictionary of Religions*. New York: HarperCollins.

Smith, Wilfred Cantwell (1959). "The Comparative Study of Religion: Whither – and Why?" In Mircea Eliade and Joseph Kitagawa (eds.), *The History of Religions: Essays in Methodology*, 31–58. Chicago: University of Chicago Press.

—— (1991) [1963]. *The Meaning and End of Religion*. Minneapolis: Fortress Press.

Snyman, Gerrie F. (1999). "'Will it Happen Again?' Reflections on Reconciliation and Structural Contraception," *Religion & Theology* 6/3: 379–410.

Solomon, Robert C. (1988). *Continental Philosophy since 1750: The Rise and Fall of the Self*. New York: Oxford University Press.

Sperber, Dan (1996). *Explaining Culture: A Naturalistic Approach*. Oxford: Blackwell.

Spiegler, Marc (1997). "Big Brains No Gains," *American Demographics* (January): 42–45.

Spivak, Gayatri Chakravorty (1976) [1967]. Translator's preface. In Jacques Derrida, *Of Grammatology*, lx–lxxxvii. Gayatri Chakravorty Spivak (trans.). Baltimore: Johns Hopkins University Press.

Spooner, Brian (1986). "Weavers and Dealers: The Authenticity of an Oriental Carpet." In Arjun Appadurai (ed.), *The Social Life of Things: Commodities in Cultural Perspective*, 195–235. Cambridge: Cambridge University Press.

Staal, Frits (1989). *Rules Without Meaning: Ritual, Mantras, and the Human Sciences*. New York: Peter Lang.

Stanner, W. E. H. (1963). *On Aboriginal Religion*. Sydney: University of Sydney.

Strenski, Ivan (1982). "Love and Anarchy in Romania: Review of Mircea Eliade, *Autobiography*," *Religion* 12: 391–403.

—— (1987). *Four Theories of Myth in Twentieth-Century History*. Iowa City: University of Iowa Press.

—— (1995). "Review of Nancy A. Harrowitz (ed.), *Tainted Greatness: Antisemitism and Cultural Heroes*," *Religion* 25: 285–294.

—— (1998a). "On 'Religion' and its Despisers." In Thomas A. Idinopulos and Brian C. Wilson (eds.), *What is Religion? Origins, Definitions, and Explanations*, 113–132. Leiden: E. J. Brill.

—— (1998b). "Religion, Power, and Final Foucault," *Journal of the American Academy of Religion* 66/2: 345–367.

—— (1998c). "Respecting Power, Worshiping Power, and Knowing the Difference: Rejoinder to David Chidester and Gary Lease," *Journal of the American Academy of Religion* 66/2: 381–383.

Sullivan, Lawrence (1987). "An Encyclopedia for a New Generation," *Parabola* 12/2: 84–8.

Taves, Ann (1999). *Fits, Trances, and Visions: Experiencing Religion and Explaining Experience from Wesley to James*. Princeton: Princeton University Press.

Taylor, Mark C. (ed.) (1998). *Critical Terms for Religious Studies*. Chicago: University of Chicago Press.

Thompson, Thomas L. (1999). *The Mythic Past: Biblical Archaeology and the Myth of Israel*. New York: Basic Books.

Thoreau, Henry David n.d. [1854] *Walden*. New York: Peebles Press International.

Tite, Philip L. (2001). "Categorical Designations and Methodological Reductionism: Gnosticism as Case Study," *Method & Theory in the Study of Religion* 13/3: 269–292.

—— (2002). "Reinforcing Ivory Towers Through Marginalization," *Bulletin of the Council of Societies for the Study of Religion* 31/1: 14–17.

Tracy, James D. (1999). *Europe's Reformations, 1450–1650*. New York: Rowman & Little-field Publishers, Inc.

Trouillot, Michel-Rolph (1995). *Silencing the Past: Power and the Production of History*. Boston: Beacon Press.

Tyler, Anne (1985). *The Accidental Tourist*. New York: Viking Press.

Urban, Hugh B. (1998). "The Torment of Secrecy: Ethical and Epistemological Problems in the Study of Esoteric Traditions," *History of Religions* 37/3: 209–248.

—— (2001a). "Scholartracking: The Ethics and Politics of Studying 'Others' in the Work of Sam D. Gill," *Method & Theory in the Study of Religion* 13/1: 110–136.

—— (2001b). "Syndrome of the Secret: 'Esotericism' and the Work of Steven M. Wasserstrom," *Journal of the American Academy of Religion* 69/2: 437–447.

van den Heever, Gerhard (2001). "Reflections on the IAHR Congress, Durban, South Africa (August 2000)," *Bulletin of the Council of Societies for the Study of Religion* 30/3: 63–64.

van der Veer, Peter (2001). *Imperial Encounters: Religion and Modernity in India and Britain*. Princeton, NJ: Princeton University Press.

van der Veer, Peter and Hartmut Lehmann (1999). "Introduction." In Peter van der Veer and Hartmut Lehmann (eds.), *Nation and Religion: Perspectives on Europe and Asia*, 3–14. Princeton: Princeton University Press.

Veyne, Paul (1987) [1985]. "The Roman Empire." In Paul Veyne (ed.), *A History of Private Life: 1. From Pagan Rome to Byzantium*, 207–233. Philippe Ariès and Georges Duby (gen. eds.), Arthur Goldhammer (trans.). Cambridge: Harvard University Press.

Voltaire [François Marie Arouet] (1966) [1759]. *Candide, or Optimism*. Robert M. Adams (ed. and trans.). New York: W. W. Norton & Co.

—— (1972) [1764]. *Philosophical Dictionary*. Theodore Besterman (ed. and trans.). London and New York: Penguin Books.

Vorster, Johannes N. and Pieter J. J. Botha (1999). "Religious *Topoi* and South Africa's Truth and Reconciliation Commission," *Religion & Theology* 6/3: 325–349.

Wach, Joachim (1958). *The Comparative Study of Religions*. Joseph Kitagawa (ed.). New York: Columbia University Press.

—— (1988). *Introduction to the History of Religions*. Joseph Kitagawa and Gregory Alles (eds.). New York: Macmillan Publishing Co.

Wallace, Dewey D. (1988). "Comparative Encyclopedias Compared," *Religious Studies Review* 14: 119–206.

Wasserstrom, Steven M. (1999). *Religion After Religion: Gershom Scholem, Mircea Eliade, and Henry Corbin at Eranos*. Princeton: Princeton University Press.

Watt, Stephen (1995). "The Human Costs of Graduate Education; Or, The Need to Get Practical," *Academe* 81/6: 30–35.

Weber, Max (1993) [1922]. "Theodicy, Salvation, Rebirth." In Talcott Parsons (intro.) and Ephraim Fischoff (trans.), *The Sociology of Religion*, 138–150. Boston: Beacon Press.

Welch, Claude (1971). *Graduate Education in Religion: A Critical Appraisal*. Missoula: University of Montana Press.

Wessinger, Catherine (2000). *How the Millennium Comes Violently: From Jonestown to Heaven's Gate*. New York: Seven Bridges Press.

White, David Gordon (2000). "The Scholar as Mythographer: Comparative Indo-European Myth and Postmodern Concerns." In Kimberly C. Patton and Benjamin C. Ray (eds.), *A Magic Still Dwells: Comparative Religion in the Postmodern Age*. Berkeley: University of California Press.

—— (2001). "Review of Bruce Lincoln, *Theorizing Myth*," *Journal of Religion* 81/4: 688–690.

Whitelam, Keith W. (2001) [1996]. *The Invention of Ancient Israel: The Silencing of Palestinian History*. London: Routledge.

Wiebe, Donald (1978). "Is a Science of Religion Possible?" *Studies in Religion* 7/1: 5–17.

—— (1984). "The Failure of Nerve in the Academic Study of Religion." *Studies in Religion* 13: 401–422.

—— (1994). "Review of Peter Byrne, *Natural Religion and the Nature of Religion* and Peter Harrison, *"Religion" and the Religions in the English Enlightenment*," *Method & Theory in the Study of Religion* 6/1: 92–104.

—— (1999). *The Politics of Religious Studies*. New York: St. Martin's Press.

—— (2000). "Review of A. L. Molendijk and P. Pels (eds.), *Religion in the Making: The Emergence of the Sciences of Religion* and T. Idinopulos and B. Wilson (eds.), *What is Religion? Origins, Definitions, and Explanations*," *Method & Theory in the Study of Religion* 12/3: 433–440.

—— (2001). "On Religious Studies and the Rhetoric of *Religious Reading*," *Method & Theory in the Study of Religion* 13/3: 334–351.

Williams, Raymond (1990) [1977]. *Marxism and Literature*. New York: Oxford.

Wolfe, Alan (2002). "Faith and Diversity in American Religion," *The Chronicle of Higher Education* (February 8): B7–B10.

Wolin, Richard (1993). *The Heidegger Controversy: A Critical Reader*. Cambridge, MA: MIT Press.

Wolin, Sheldon (1960). *Politics and Vision: Continuity and Innovation in Western Political Thought*. Boston: Little, Brown and Co.

Zaleski, Carol (2002). "A Letter to William James," *The Christian Century* 119/2 (January 16–23): 32.

Žižek, Slavoj (1999). "The Matrix, or, The Two Sides of Perversion." Paper presented at the International Symposium at the Center for Art and Media, Karlsruhe, October 28. Available at http://on1.zkm.de/netCondition/matrix/zizek.html.

—— (2000). *The Fragile Absolute or, Why is the Christian Legacy Worth Fighting For?* London: Verso.

Index